About This Book

Why is e-Learning and the Science of Instruction important?

This is a book about what works in e-learning. Increasingly, organizations are turning to e-learning to save travel costs and instructional time. In fact e-learning in both synchronous and asynchronous formats is on the rise, accounting for nearly one-third of all training delivery of workforce learning. However, dollars saved are only an illusion if the quality of the training suffers.

There are many books on the market that offer useful advice for design and development of e-learning. But unlike what's in these books, the answers we present are not based on opinion; they are based on empirical research. Much of this new research is inaccessible to those producing or evaluating online learning because it has been distributed primarily within the academic research community. This book bridges the gap by summarizing research-based answers to questions that practitioners involved with multimedia learning ask about effective e-learning.

What's new in the second edition?

The popularity of the first edition was testimony to consumer interest in our evidence-based guidelines about how to best use visuals, text, audio, practice exercises, and examples in e-learning. In our second edition, we have updated the previous chapters by adding new research, guidelines, and examples. You will also find two new chapters on simulations/games and on segmenting and sequencing of e-learning content. In all of our chapters, we have expanded our coverage to show how our guidelines apply to virtual classroom forms of e-learning. Finally, to illustrate our guidelines, we include a CD with a multimedia lesson example and counterexample.

What can you achieve with this book?

If you are a designer, developer, or consumer of e-learning, you can use the guidelines in this book to ensure that your courseware meets human psychological learning requirements. In particular you can learn the best ways to:

- Communicate your content with words and visuals

- Use audio to describe visuals

- Avoid overloading learners with extraneous media effects

- Design examples and practice exercises that build new skills

- Use networked collaborative facilities effectively for learning

- Evaluate simulations and games for relevance to your instructional goals

How is this book organized?

Chapters 1 and 2 lay the foundation for the book by defining e-learning and describing how the methods used in e-learning can promote or defeat learning processes.

Chapters 3 through 9 summarize the multimedia principles developed by over twenty-five years of research by Richard Mayer at the University of California. In these chapters, you will read the guidelines, the evidence, and examples of how to best use visuals, text, and audio, as well as content segmenting and sequencing in e-learning.

Chapters 10 through 14 focus on guidelines related to important instructional methods and approaches in e-learning, including use of examples, practice and feedback, collaboration facilities, navigation tools, and techniques to build critical thinking skills.

Chapter 15 is new to this edition and introduces the research and issues to consider in use of games and simulations in e-learning.

Chapter 16 integrates all of the book's guidelines into a comprehensive checklist and illustrates how they apply in concert to asynchronous and synchronous e-learning examples.

See the Introduction for a summary of what is covered in each chapter.

About Pfeiffer

Pfeiffer serves the professional development and hands-on resource needs of training and human resource practitioners and gives them products to do their jobs better. We deliver proven ideas and solutions from experts in HR development and HR management, and we offer effective and customizable tools to improve workplace performance. From novice to seasoned professional, Pfeiffer is the source you can trust to make yourself and your organization more successful.

Essential Knowledge   Pfeiffer produces insightful, practical, and comprehensive materials on topics that matter the most to training and HR professionals. Our Essential Knowledge resources translate the expertise of seasoned professionals into practical, how-to guidance on critical workplace issues and problems. These resources are supported by case studies, worksheets, and job aids and are frequently supplemented with CD-ROMs, websites, and other means of making the content easier to read, understand, and use.

Essential Tools   Pfeiffer's Essential Tools resources save time and expense by offering proven, ready-to-use materials—including exercises, activities, games, instruments, and assessments—for use during a training or team-learning event. These resources are frequently offered in looseleaf or CD-ROM format to facilitate copying and customization of the material.

Pfeiffer also recognizes the remarkable power of new technologies in expanding the reach and effectiveness of training. While e-hype has often created whizbang solutions in search of a problem, we are dedicated to bringing convenience and enhancements to proven training solutions. All our e-tools comply with rigorous functionality standards. The most appropriate technology wrapped around essential content yields the perfect solution for today's on-the-go trainers and human resource professionals.

Essential resources for training and HR professionals

e-Learning

and the Science of Instruction

Proven Guidelines for Consumers and
Designers of Multimedia Learning
Second Edition

Ruth Colvin Clark • Richard E. Mayer

Published by Pfeiffer
An Imprint of Wiley
989 Market Street, San Francisco, CA 94103-1741 www.pfeiffer.com

For additional copies/bulk purchases of this book in the U.S. please contact 800-274-4434.

Pfeiffer books and products are available through most bookstores. To contact Pfeiffer directly call our Customer Care Department within the U.S. at 800-274-4434, outside the U.S. at 317-572-3985, fax 317-572-4002, or visit www.pfeiffer.com.

Pfeiffer also publishes its books in a variety of electronic formats. Some content that appears in print may not be available in electronic books.

ISBN-13: 978-0-7879-8683-4

Library of Congress Cataloging-in-Publication Data

Clark, Ruth Colvin.
    e-learning and the science of instruction : proven guidelines for consumers and designers of multimedia learning/Ruth Colvin Clark, Richard E. Mayer. —2nd ed.
        p. cm.
    Includes bibliographical references and index.
    ISBN 978–0–7879–8683–4 (cloth)
1. Business education—Computer-assisted instruction.   I.   Mayer, Richard E., 1947–II. Title.
    HF1106.C55 2008
    658.3'12402854678—dc22

                                                                                          2007013434

Acquiring Editor: Matthew Davis
Director of Development: Kathleen Dolan Davies
Developmental Editor: Susan Rachmeler
Production Editor: Dawn Kilgore
Editor: Rebecca Taff
Manufacturing Supervisor: Becky Morgan

Printed in the United States of America
SECOND EDITION
Printing   10 9 8 7 6 5 4 3 2

CONTENTS

ACKNOWLEDGMENTS

IN THIS NEW EDITION, we have added sample lessons on a CD to illustrate the application and violation of our principles. We benefited from the instructional design, programming, and audio expertise of Alan Koenig of Arizona State University, who created these multimedia samples.

We also thank the following researchers or practitioners who reviewed our work and/or gave us access to their examples and research for inclusion in this second edition:

Robert Atkinson, Arizona State University

Education Networks of Australia

Susanne Lajoie, McGill University

Herve Potelle, University of Poitres

Lloyd Rieber, University of Georgia

Dan Suthers, University of Hawaii

Ruta Valaitis, McMaster University

Richard Van Eck, University of North Dakota

Finally, we are grateful to support from the Pfeiffer team and especially to Matt Davis and Leslie Stephen for editorial support.

GETTING THE MOST FROM THIS RESOURCE

Purpose

The training field is undergoing an evolution from a craft based on fads and folk wisdom to a profession that integrates evidence into the design and development of its products. Part of the training revolution has been driven by the use of digital technology to manage and deliver instructional solutions. This book provides you with evidence-based guidelines for both self-study (asynchronous) and virtual classroom (synchronous) forms of e-learning. Here you will read the guidelines, the evidence, and examples to shape your decisions about the design, development, and evaluation of e-learning.

Audience

If you are a designer, developer, or consumer of e-learning, you can use the guidelines in this book to ensure that your courseware meets human psychological learning requirements. Although most of our examples focus on workforce learning, we believe instructional professionals in the educational and academic arenas can equally benefit from our guidelines.

Package Components

Because many of our guidelines pertain to use of media elements such as audio and animation that are difficult to illustrate in a book format, we have included two examples on the accompanying CD. The CD includes the following items:

- How to Design a Relational Database: Multimedia Example Lesson
- How to Design a Relational Database: Multimedia Counter-Example Lesson

The counter-example lesson can be run in two ways. First, you can play the lesson in regular mode. In addition, if you click on the commentary button, you can hear a summary of the violations.

Our guidelines checklist, found in Chapter 16, is also placed on the CD, allowing you to print it out and refer to it in a more convenient format.

Package Components

Table I.1 summarizes the content of the book's chapters. In this second edition, two new chapters have been added. Chapter 9 provides evidence on the best ways to segment and sequence e-learning content. Chapter 15 introduces the research and issues surrounding games and simulations in e-learning. In addition, we have expanded the first edition with virtual classroom examples that show how to adapt our guidelines to a synchronous e-learning environment.

Table I.1. A Preview of Chapters.

Chapter	Includes
1. e-Learning: Promise and Pitfalls	• Our definition of e-learning • e-Learning development process summary • Research on e-learning effectiveness • Potential pitfalls in e-learning • Three architectures for e-learning design

Table I.1. (Continued).

Chapter	Includes
2. How People Learn from e-Courses	• An overview of human learning processes and how instructional methods can support or disrupt them • A brief explanation of what makes a good research study and what the statistics mean
3. Applying the Multimedia Principle: Use Words and Graphics Rather Than Words Alone	• Evidence for whether learning is improved in e-lessons that include visuals • Types of visuals that best promote learning • Who benefits most from visuals? • Static illustrations versus animations
4. Applying the Contiguity Principle: Align Words to Corresponding Graphics	• Evidence for the best placement of text and graphics on the screen • Evidence for sequencing of text or audio in conjunction with visuals • Effective and ineffective applications of the contiguity principle, as well as the psychological basis for the results
5. Applying the Modality Principle: Present Words as Audio Narration Rather Than On-Screen Text	• Evidence for presenting words that describe graphics in audio rather than in text • When the modality principle does and does not apply • Effective and ineffective applications of the modality principle, as well as the psychological basis for the results
6. Applying the Redundancy Principle: Explain Visuals with Words in Audio OR Text: Not Both	• Evidence for use of audio to explain graphics rather than text and audio • Situations in which adding on-screen text to narration is a good idea

(Continued)

Table I.1. (Continued).

Chapter	Includes
7. Applying the Coherence Principle: Adding Interesting Material Can Hurt Learning	• Evidence for omitting distracting graphics and stories, sounds and background music, and detailed textual explanations • Evidence for omitting extraneous words added for interest, to expand on key ideas or for technical depth
8. Applying the Personalization Principle: Use Conversational Style and Virtual Coaches	• Evidence for conversational style, voice quality, and polite speech to improve learning • Evidence for best use of computer agents to present instructional support • Evidence for making the author visible to the learner through the script
9. Applying the Segmenting and Pretraining Principles: Managing Complexity by Breaking a Lesson into Parts	• Evidence for breaking a continuous lesson into bite-sized segments and allowing learners to access each segment at their own rate • Evidence for sequencing key concepts in a lesson prior to the main procedure or process of that lesson
10. Leveraging Examples in e-Learning	• Evidence and guidelines to transition from examples to practice assignments through fading • Ways to ensure examples are processed by adding questions • How to design examples that support learning of procedural and strategic skills
11. Does Practice Make Perfect?	• How to design practice that supports job skills • Evidence and guidelines for design of effective practice feedback • Determining the amount and placement of practice in your lessons

Table I.1. (Continued).

Chapter	Includes
12. Learning Together Virtually	• Descriptions of types of computer-supported collaborative learning • Factors that lead to learning in use of online collaborative facilities
13. Who's in Control? Guidelines for e-Learning Navigation	• Distinction between learner and program control • Evidence for the accuracy of student decisions over their learning • Guidelines for ways to implement learner control
14. e-Learning to Build Thinking Skills	• Evidence about the effectiveness of thinking-skills training programs • Guidelines for design of e-learning to promote thinking skills, including use of job-specific cases, making thinking processes explicit, and defining job-specific thinking skills
15. Simulations and Games in e-Learning	• What are simulations and games? • Evidence for effectiveness of simulations and games • Techniques to balance motivation and learning, including matching game types to learning goals, making learning essential to game progress, building in guidance, and managing complexity
16. Applying the Guidelines	• A checklist and summary of the guidelines in the book • Four short discussions of how the guidelines apply to e-learning samples

Glossary

The Glossary provides definitions of the technical terms used throughout the book.

CHAPTER OUTLINE

The e-Learning Bandwagon

What Is e-Learning?

Self-Study Versus Virtual Classroom e-Learning

e-Learning Development Process
    Performance Analysis
    Defining e-Learning Content
    Defining the Instructional Methods and Media Elements
    How Delivery Platforms and Software Shape Instruction

Two Types of e-Learning Goals: Inform and Perform
    Near Versus Far Transfer Perform Goals

Is e-Learning Better? Media Comparison Research

What Makes e-Learning Unique?
    Practice with Feedback
    Social Software and Collaboration
    Tailored Instruction
    Simulations and Games

e-Learning: The Pitfalls
    Pitfall One: Losing Sight of the Job
    Pitfall Two: Media Abuse

What Is Good e-Courseware?
    Training Goals
    Learner Differences
    Environment
    e-Learning Architectures
    Interactivity in e-Learning

Learning in e-Learning

1

e-Learning

PROMISE AND PITFALLS

IN THIS CHAPTER we define e-learning as training delivered on a computer (including CD-ROM, Internet, or intranet) that is designed to support individual learning or organizational performance goals. We include e-courses developed primarily to provide information (inform courses), as well as those designed to build specific job-related skills (perform courses).

Since our first edition, synchronous forms of e-learning, also called virtual classrooms, have assumed a large and growing share of online training courseware. Therefore we expanded this edition to illustrate how our guidelines apply to virtual classrooms.

Instructional methods that support rather than defeat human learning processes are an essential ingredient of all good e-learning courseware. The best methods will depend on the goals of the training (for example, to inform or to perform); the learners' related skills; and various environmental factors, including technological, cultural, and pragmatic constraints. We distinguish among three design architectures for e-learning: receptive, directive, and guided discovery.

The e-Learning Bandwagon

In our first edition, we asked whether the proliferating cyber courses of the late 20th Century were harbingers of a new age in learning or just another overstatement of the expectations that had surrounded nearly everything associated with the dot com bubble. The trends in delivery media for workforce learning in the last six years, shown in Figure 1.1, are pretty convincing. e-Learning is here to stay! In our first edition, we reported that in the year 2001, approximately 11 percent of all training was delivered via computer (including the Internet, intranets, and CD-ROM). As we write the second edition at the end of 2006, we see that figure has risen to 29 percent (Industry Report, 2006). That means close to one-third of all workforce learning is delivered electronically!

Part of the increase in e-learning reflects the emergence of a whole new form of electronic delivery practically unheard of when we wrote the first

---

Figure 1.1. Percentage Training Hours Delivered by Classroom and Technology.

Based on data from Sugrue and Rivera, 2005.

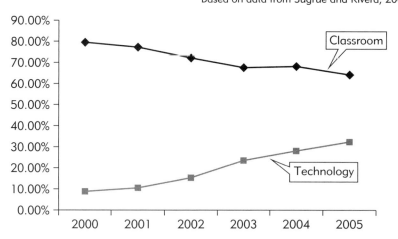

edition: the virtual classroom. In 2003, the first data on use of virtual class-rooms reported 3 percent of all training hours were delivered via synchronous e-learning (Sugrue & Rivera, 2005). In just a few short years, that number has grown to 15 percent! The lure of travel savings and rapid deployment of training has made the virtual classroom a popular alternative to asynchronous e-learning. However, it remains to be seen how the mix of synchronous and asynchronous forms of e-learning will balance out. For example, in 2006, self-study asynchronous forms of e-learning rose from 7 percent in 2005 to 15 percent of all delivery hours (Industry Report, 2006). What is certain is that e-learning of all types is growing as a dominant delivery medium for workforce learning.

e-Learning is used across the board to support diverse organizational training goals. The training requirements that make heaviest use of e-learning include profession or industry-specific training at 74 percent, compliance training at 68 percent, and desktop application training at 66 percent (Industry Report, 2006). Some training areas relying less on online learning include sales, customer service, executive development, and interpersonal skills training. These training goals have interpersonal skills as a common element that is perceived to benefit most from face-to-face classroom instruction.

Annual investments in training are high and growing. As you can see in Figure 1.2, over the past four years between fifty and sixty billion dollars

Figure 1.2. Dollars Invested in U.S. Workforce Learning.

Based on Industry Report, 2006.

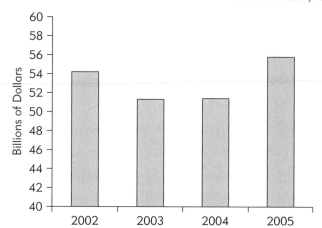

were spent on training workers in corporate and governmental organizations in the United States (Industry Report, 2006). And these figures don't include the most expensive element of training, the salary time and lost opportunity costs of those taking training. Organizations are turning to e-learning to save training time and travel costs associated with traditional face-to-face learning. However, cost savings are only an illusion when e-learning does not effectively build knowledge and skills linked to desired job outcomes. Does e-learning offer a potential opportunity to cost-effectively build the skills required for the knowledge-based economy of this century? Part of the answer will depend on the quality of the instruction embedded in the e-learning products you are designing, building, or selecting today.

What Is e-Learning?

We define e-learning as instruction delivered on a computer by way of CD-ROM, Internet, or intranet with the following features:

- Includes content relevant to the learning objective
- Uses instructional methods such as examples and practice to help learning
- Uses media elements such as words and pictures to deliver the content and methods
- May be instructor-led (synchronous e-learning) or designed for self-paced individual study (asynchronous e-learning)
- Builds new knowledge and skills linked to individual learning goals or to improved organizational performance

As you can see, this definition has several elements concerning the what, how, and why of e-learning.

What. e-Learning courses include both content (that is, information) and instructional methods (that is, techniques) that help people learn the content.

How. e-Learning courses are delivered via computer using words in the form of spoken or printed text and pictures, such as illustrations, photos, animation, or video. Some forms of e-learning (asynchronous) are designed for individual self-study. New e-learning formats called virtual classrooms or synchronous e-learning are designed for real-time instructor-led training. Both formats may support asynchronous collaboration with others through tools such as wikis, discussion boards, and email.

Why. e-Learning courses are intended to help learners reach personal learning objectives or perform their jobs in ways that improve the bottom-line goals of the organization.

In short, the "e" in e-learning refers to the "how": the course is digitized so it can be stored in electronic form. The "learning" in e-learning refers to the "what": the course includes content and ways to help people learn it; and the "why" refers to the purpose: to help individuals achieve educational goals or to help organizations build skills related to improved job performance.

Our definition indicates that the goal of e-learning is to build job-transferable knowledge and skills linked to organizational performance or to help individuals achieve personal learning goals. Although the guidelines we present throughout the book do apply to lessons designed for educational or general interest learning goals, our emphasis is on instructional programs that are built or purchased for workforce learning.

Self-Study Versus Virtual Classroom e-Learning

Our first edition focused exclusively on self-study forms of e-learning, also called asynchronous e-learning. Figure 1.3 shows a screen shot from an asynchronous course on How to Construct Formulas in Excel. Asynchronous courses are designed to be taken by individuals at their own time and pace. In contrast, Figure 1.4 shows a screen shot from a virtual classroom course on How to Construct Formulas in Excel.

Take a close look at Figure 1.4 if you are new to the virtual classroom. From WebEx to Live Meetings, most virtual classroom tools incorporate similar functions, although the screen interfaces may differ. Figure 1.4 shows a screen capture from Elluminate virtual classroom software. The largest

Figure 1.3. A Screen Capture from an Asynchronous Excel Lesson.

From Clark, Nguyen, and Sweller, 2006.

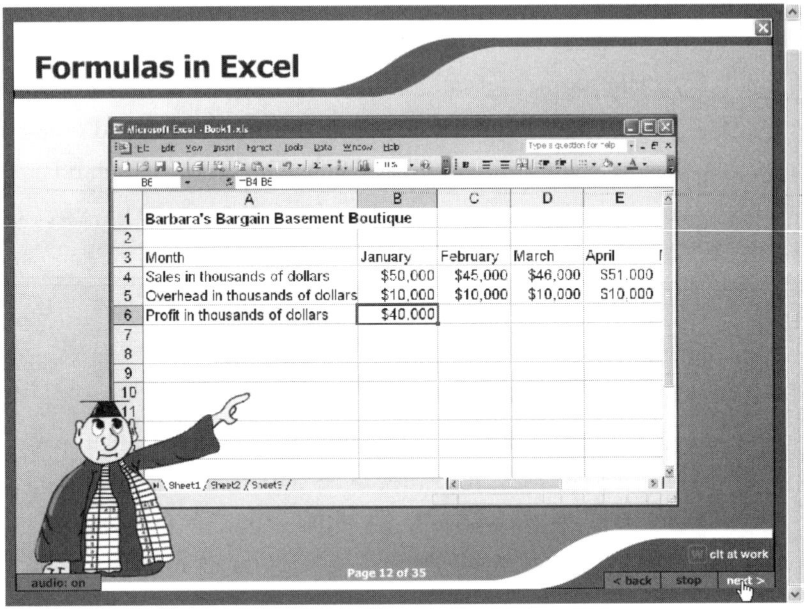

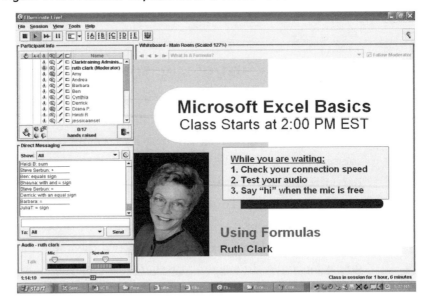

Figure 1.4. A Screen Capture from a Virtual Classroom Excel Lesson.

portion of the screen is devoted to the whiteboard on which the instructor can project slides. To the upper left of the whiteboard is the participant window showing the names of everyone attending the session. Below the participant window is a chat box in which everyone can type text messages. At the bottom left is an audio control box used by instructors or participants when they want to speak. The instructor and class participants wear headsets with microphones, allowing them to speak and to hear what others are saying.

Clark and Kwinn (2007) characterize virtual classroom technology as a hybrid tool, one that incorporates some features of both asynchronous e-learning and instructor-led face-to-face classrooms. Like asynchronous e-learning, the virtual classroom relies on screen real estate to communicate content and instructional methods. Also like asynchronous e-learning, virtual classrooms benefit from frequent learner interactions to sustain attention and promote learning. Like face-to-face classrooms, virtual classrooms are instructor-led. Therefore, presentation rates are not controlled by learners as in most asynchronous e-learning. In addition, opportunities for social presence are higher in the virtual classroom than in asynchronous e-learning, since virtual classrooms are typically designed for group learning, while asynchronous e-learning is typically designed for individual self-study.

e-Learning Development Process

We saw in Figure 1.2 that training investments in business and industry are nearing $60 billion! To get a return on investment, all training initiatives, including e-learning, must improve job performances that lead to achievement of organizational operational goals. Operational goals are bottom-line indicators of organizational success, such as increase in market share, decrease in product flaws or errors, increase in customer satisfaction, or fewer accidents, to name but a few. Unless some analysis and planning accompanies any e-learning project, any return on investment is likely to be by chance alone. In Figure 1.5 we summarize a systematic process for e-learning projects. Since there are many good books on e-learning development, we provide only a brief overview here.

Figure 1.5. Alignment of e-Learning with Operational Outcomes.

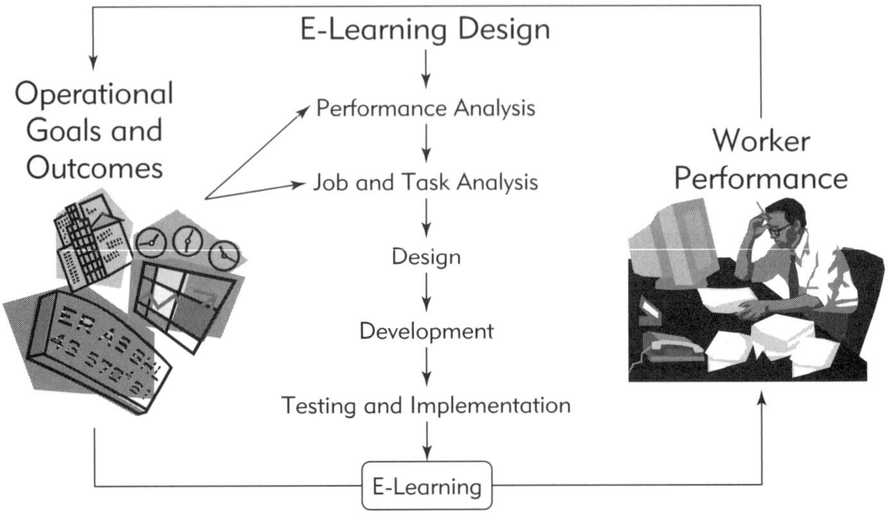

Performance Analysis

All e-learning projects should begin with a performance analysis to determine that (a) training will help realize important organizational goals by filling a gap in worker knowledge and skills related to operational outcomes and (b) e-learning is the best delivery solution. Often training is requested to solve organizational problems that are not caused by a lack of knowledge and skills. In these cases, the root cause(s) of the problems should be defined and an expensive solution like training should be avoided (Clark & Nguyen, 2007). If training is needed, the analysis should consider the tradeoffs among various delivery alternatives such as classroom instruction, job coaching, working aids, asynchronous and synchronous e-learning, or a blend of several of these.

Defining e-Learning Content

Following the performance analysis, a team begins by defining the content needed to perform the job or achieve the educational objective. In order for training to pay off with improved job performance, an e-learning development effort must start by defining the job tasks associated with operational goals and the knowledge needed to perform these tasks. The e-learning development team observes and interviews people who are expert at a job to define the job skills and knowledge. For courseware developed for broader educational purposes, rather than a job analysis, the development team conducts a content analysis to define the major topics and related subtopics to be included.

Based on either the job or content analysis, the team categorizes the content of an e-lesson into facts, concepts, processes, procedures, and strategic guidelines. Table 1.1 defines these content types, which have been described in detail by Ruth Clark (2007). For example, the screen in Figure 1.3 from asynchronous e-learning is designed to teach use of formulas with Excel. The content being illustrated is a procedure: how to enter a formula into the spreadsheet. In this segment of the lesson, a learning agent shown in the lower left is describing in audio an animated demonstration of the steps to construct and enter a formula to calculate January profit in the spreadsheet.

At the completion of the job or content analysis, the design team will create a course blueprint that includes lesson outlines and learning objectives. The blueprint will serve as a model for the course development effort to follow.

Table 1.1. Five Types of Content in e-Learning.

Content Type	Definition	Example
Fact	Specific and unique data or instance	Operator symbols for Excel formulas
Concept	A category that includes multiple examples	Excel formulas
Process	A flow of events or activities	How spreadsheets work
Procedure	Task performed with step-by-step actions	How to enter a formula into the spreadsheet
Strategic Principles	Task performed by adapting guidelines	How to do a financial projection with a spreadsheet

Defining the Instructional Methods and Media Elements

Instructional methods support the learning of the content. Instructional methods include techniques such as examples, practice exercises, and feedback. In our example screen shown in Figure 1.3, the main instructional method is a demonstration. We define media elements as the audio and visual techniques used to present words and illustrations. Media elements include text, narration, music, still graphics, photographs, and animation. In the Excel course, audio narration presents the words of the learning agent and an animated graphic illustrates the steps of the demonstration. One of our fundamental tenets is that, to be effective, instructional methods and the media elements that deliver them must guide learners to effectively process and assimilate new knowledge and skills.

How Delivery Platforms and Software Shape Instruction

e-Learning, as we use the term, includes training delivered via CD-ROM, intranets, and the Internet. In our first edition, we reported that approximately 40 percent of computer-delivered training used CD-ROM, while 22 percent used the Internet and 30 percent used intranets (Galvin, 2001). In the intervening five years, upgrades in organizations' networks in combination with the advantages of networked delivery make Inter- and intranet solutions the predominant distribution choice at close to 90 percent of all e-learning (Sugrue & Rivera, 2005).

Your choice of delivery platform and software can influence which instructional methods and media elements can be included in the courseware. For example, limitations in bandwidth, no sound cards, or lack of headsets may limit the use of some media elements such as audio and video. Most of the major virtual classroom tools support audio and brief video clips. As we will see in later chapters, lack of audio is a constraint that will negatively impact the instructional quality of your e-learning courseware. In contrast, simple graphics are often as useful or better for learning than more complex visuals such as animations and video.

Two Types of e-Learning Goals: Inform and Perform

As summarized in Table 1.2, the guidelines in this book apply to e-learning that is designed to inform as well as e-learning that is designed to improve specific job performance. We classify lessons that are designed primarily to build awareness or provide information as *inform programs,* also known as briefings. A new employee orientation that reviews the company history and describes the company organization or a product knowledge update are examples of topics that are often presented as inform programs. The information presented is job relevant, but there are no specific expectations of new skills to be acquired. The primary goal of these programs is to transmit information. In contrast, we classify programs designed to build specific skills as *perform programs.* Some typical examples of perform e-learning are lessons on software use, designing a database, or evaluating a bank loan applicant. Many e-courses contain both inform and perform learning objectives, while some are designed for inform only or perform only.

Table 1.2. Inform and Perform e-Learning Goals.

Goal	Definition	Example
Inform	Lessons that communicate information	• Company history • New product features
Perform Procedure	Lessons that build procedural skills (also called near transfer)	• How to log on • How to complete an expense report
Perform Principle	Lessons that build strategic skills (also called far transfer)	• How to close a sale • How to analyze a loan

Near Versus Far Transfer Perform Goals

We distinguish between two types of perform goals: (1) procedural, also known as near transfer, and (2) principle-based or strategic, also known as far transfer. Procedural lessons such as the Excel examples in Figures 1.3 and 1.4

are designed to teach step-by-step tasks, which are performed more or less the same way each time. Most computer-skills training falls into this category. This type of training is called near transfer because the steps learned in the training are identical or very similar to the steps required in the job environment. Thus the transfer from training to application is near.

Principle-based lessons, also called far transfer, are designed to teach task strategies that do not have one correct approach or outcome. Thus the situations presented in the training may not be exactly the same as the situations that occur on the job. These tasks require the worker to adapt strategies to various job situations. Typically, some element of problem solving is involved. The worker always has to use judgment in performing these tasks, since there is no one right approach for all situations. Far-transfer lessons include just about all soft-skill training, supervision and management courses, and sales skills. Figure 1.6 illustrates a screen from a principle-based course on analyzing a commercial loan. The lesson begins with an assignment to research and recommend a new bank client who has applied for a commercial loan.

Figure 1.6. Far-Transfer Course on Loan Analysis.
With permission from Moody's Investment Service.

The learner has access to data from the various office resources shown in the interface, including the computer, fax machine, telephone, and books. Since the worker will always have to use judgment in applying training guidelines to the job, we say that the transfer from training to job is far.

Is e-Learning Better? Media Comparison Research

Contrary to the impression left by recent reports on the use and benefits of e-learning, much of what we are seeing under the e-learning label is not new. Training delivered on a computer, known as computer-based training or CBT, has been around for more than thirty years. Early examples delivered over mainframe computers were primarily text on a screen with interspersed questions—electronic versions of behaviorist psychologist B.F. Skinner's teaching machine. The computer program evaluated answers to the multiple-choice questions, and prewritten feedback was matched to the learner responses. The main application of these early e-lessons was training in the use of mainframe computer systems. As technology has evolved, acquiring greater capability to deliver true multimedia, the courseware has become more elaborate in terms of realistic graphics, audio, color, animation, and complex simulations. But as you will see, greater complexity of media does not necessarily ensure more learning.

Each new wave of instructional delivery technology (starting with film in the 1920s) spawned optimistic predictions of massive improvements in learning. For example, in 1947 the U.S. Army conducted one of the first media comparisons with the hypothesis that film teaches better than classroom instructors (see box for details). Yet after fifty years of research attempting to demonstrate that the latest media are better, the outcomes have not supported the media superiority view.

THE FIRST MEDIA COMPARISON STUDY

In 1947 the U.S. Army conducted research to demonstrate that instruction delivered by film resulted in better learning outcomes than traditional classroom or paper-based versions. Three versions of a lesson on how to read a micrometer were developed.

The film version included a narrated demonstration of how to read the micrometer. A second version was taught in a classroom. The instructor used the same script and included a demonstration using actual equipment, along with still slide pictures. A third version was a self-study paper lesson in which the text used the same words as the film, along with pictures with arrows to indicate movement. Learners were randomly assigned to a version and after the training session they were tested to see whether they could read the micrometer. Which group learned more? There were no differences in learning among the three groups (Hall & Cushing, 1947).

With few exceptions, the hundreds of media comparison studies have shown no differences in learning (Clark, 1994; Dillon & Gabbard, 1998). Since our first edition, there have been two new major reports synthesizing research on the effectiveness of online learning. A report by Bernard et al. (2004) integrating research studies that compared outcomes from electronic distance education to outcomes from traditional classroom instruction yielded the achievement effect sizes shown in Figure 1.7. (See Chapter 2 for information on effect sizes.) As you can see, the majority of effect sizes are close to zero, indicating no practical differences in learning between face-to-face and electronic distance learning. However, the bars at either end of the histogram show that some distance learning courses were much more effective than classroom courses and vice versa. A review of online learning by Tallent-Runnels et al. (2006) concurs. The research team concludes that:

> "Overwhelming evidence has shown that learning in an online environment can be as effective as that in traditional classrooms. Second, students' learning in the online environment is affected by the quality of online instruction. Not surprisingly, students in well-designed and well-implemented online courses learned significantly more, and more effectively, than those in online courses where teaching and learning activities were not carefully planned and where the delivery and accessibility were impeded by technology problems." (p. 116)

Figure 1.7. Electronic Distance Learning vs. Face-to-Face Instruction: Histogram of Effects.

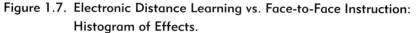

Adapted from Bernard et al., 2004.

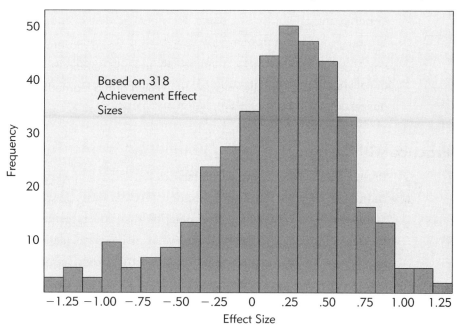

From all the media comparison research, we have learned that it's not the delivery medium, but rather the instructional methods that cause learning. When the instructional methods remain essentially the same, so does the learning, no matter how the instruction is delivered. When a course uses effective instructional methods, learning will be better, no matter what delivery medium is used.

Nevertheless, as we will discuss in the following sections, each medium offers unique opportunities to deliver instructional methods that other media cannot. It's a common error to design each new medium to mirror older ones. For example, some e-lessons appear to be books transferred to a screen. To exploit each medium fully, the unique capabilities of the technology should be used in ways that effectively support human learning.

What Makes e-Learning Unique?

Can we conclude from the media comparison research that all media are equivalent? Not quite. Not all media can deliver all instructional methods. For example, the capability of a paper document to deliver audio or animation is quite limited. Four potentially valuable instructional methods unique to e-learning are (1) practice with automated tailored feedback, (2) integration of collaboration with self-study, (3) dynamic adjustment of instruction based on learning, and (4) use of simulation and games.

Practice with Feedback

In the Excel courses illustrated in Figures 1.3 and 1.4, the learner has opportunities to practice the steps to input a formula into the spreadsheet. The asynchronous course includes a simulation that directs learners to construct and enter the correct formula to achieve an assigned calculation. If an incorrect formula is used, the program gives automated feedback telling the learner his or her answer is wrong, providing a hint and asking the learner to try again. Prior to this hands-on practice, the learners have seen an animated, narrated demonstration of the steps required to input a formula. Similar instructional methods are used in the virtual classroom version. Here, the instructor provides a demonstration by sharing an Excel spreadsheet from the desktop. Following the demonstration, the instructor assigns learners calculations using the shared application. What is unique in asynchronous e-learning is that the learner's actions taken in the simulation are evaluated by a program that responds with hints or feedback supporting immediate correction of errors. In synchronous e-learning, the instructor reviews student answers and gives feedback, as in a traditional face-to-face classroom. Chapter 11 in this book describes what to look for in effectively designed practice in e-learning.

Social Software and Collaboration

The first CBT lessons were for solo learning. There was little or no interaction with others. But the power of the Internet erases that limitation. In the virtual classroom participants communicate in real time through text chat or audio. In both virtual classrooms and asynchronous e-learning, learners can collaborate at independent times by email and discussion boards. With the emergence of synchronous e-learning as well as social software such as wikis and blogs, we anticipate a growing trend in leveraging collaborative tools for learning.

We do have evidence that, under the right conditions, learning and working together can result in better outcomes than learning and working by oneself. Unfortunately, we do not yet have sufficient research to specify all of the conditions required to optimize collaborative learning facilities. Chapter 13 reviews the research we do have and provides limited guidelines for ways to harness the collaborative facilities of the Internet for learning purposes.

Tailored Instruction

e-Learning is the only technology-based delivery vehicle that can make ongoing dynamic adjustments to the instructional path based on learners' responses. For example, if the learner makes errors on a practice problem of intermediate complexity, the program can offer either an easier problem or a similar problem accompanied by increased instructional help. This tailoring of instruction based on learning progress is called *adaptive instruction*. Adaptive instruction can be implemented in asynchronous e-learning and is most beneficial when training time and costs can be saved by tailoring lessons to individual requirements.

Simulations and Games

In Figure 1.6 we introduce a course that is based on a simulated case study for learning an effective process to analyze and recommend funding for a commercial loan applicant. After receiving a new commercial loan to evaluate, the learners can access the various objects in the office such as the fax, computer, or telephone. They can also visit the loan applicant to conduct an interview. Once the learners have collected sufficient data, they indicate whether the loan is approved or denied. Thus, a new loan agent can experience in a short time a number of real-world loan situations in the safety of a controlled environment. The bank loan course illustrates the power of simulation in which realistic job problems are compressed into a short time-frame. The motivational appeal of online games has prompted great interest in constructing learning games based on software simulations. However, not all games are equally effective. In Chapter 15, we summarize evidence and guidelines for use of simulations and games in e-learning.

e-Learning: The Pitfalls

Despite these impressive capabilities of computer-delivered instruction, we see two common barriers to the realization of the potential of online learning. These are: (1) losing sight of the job, leading to transfer failure, and (2) media abuse, leading to over or under use of technology in ways that defeat learning.

Pitfall One: Losing Sight of the Job

To design powerful learning environments whose lessons both transfer to the workplace and improve the performance of the organization is not easy, no matter whether planned for classroom or multimedia delivery. To teach higher-order problem-solving skills like the ones illustrated in the bank loan program (Figure 1.6), the designer must first define what those skills are. Research on expertise shows that these skills are job-specific. In other words, the knowledge base underlying a physician is different from one that makes a programmer. There is no one set of skills that support expertise across the diverse contemporary workforce.

Whether planning for near- or far-transfer learning, a detailed job and task analysis is a prerequisite and a labor-intensive process. e-Lessons that bypass the job analysis process run the risk of presenting knowledge and techniques out of context. As you will see in Chapters 10 and 11, lack of job context risks transfer failure. In the end, teaching knowledge and skills that do not result in job performance changes will not yield a return on investment.

Pitfall Two: Media Abuse

Sometimes "technophiles" use all of the technology features available to them and in so doing overload learners' processing capabilities. For example, they may decide to include audio in the form of music and narration, on-screen text, and animated visuals in an online simulation. As you will read in Chapter 2, humans have limited capacity to absorb information and over-enthusiastic use of software features can depress learning. In contrast, "technostics" tend to ignore media capabilities. For example, books may be transferred to screens, resulting in page turner e-learning. Alternatively, face-to-face classrooms may be converted to virtual classrooms with no modifications to take advantages of the features of the technology. Unlike face-to-face events, however, in e-learning classes, the learner can easily minimize the application or exit the session to engage in more productive or motivating activities. In this book we advocate a balance between the technophile and technostic approaches in which you apply research evidence on how to use technology features in ways that promote learning.

What Is Good e-Courseware?

A central question for our book is, "What does good courseware look like?" Throughout the book we recommend specific features to look for or to design into your e-learning. However, you will need to adapt our recommendations based on four main considerations—the goal of your training, the prior knowledge of your learners, the environment in which you will deploy your training, and the instructional architectures you use in your e-learning lessons.

Training Goals

The goals or intended outcomes of your e-learning will influence which guidelines are most appropriate for you to consider. Earlier in this chapter we made distinctions among three types of training designed to inform the student, to perform procedures, and to perform strategic tasks. For inform e-lessons, apply the guidelines in Chapters 3 through 9 regarding the best use of media elements, including visuals, narration, and text to present information. To train for procedural skills, apply these guidelines and add to them relevant suggestions regarding the design of examples and practice sessions in Chapters 10 and 11. If, however, your goal is to develop strategic or far-transfer skills, you will want to apply the guidelines from all the chapters, including Chapter 14 on teaching problem-solving skills and Chapter 15 on games and simulations.

Learner Differences

In addition to selecting or designing courseware specific to the type of outcome desired, lessons should include instructional methods appropriate to the learner's characteristics. While various individual differences such as learning styles have received the attention of the training community, research has proven that the learner's prior knowledge of the course content exerts the most influence on learning. Learners with little prior knowledge will benefit from different instructional methods than will learners who are relatively experienced.

For the most part, the guidelines we provide in this book are based on research conducted with adult learners who were new to the course content. If your target audience has greater background knowledge in the course content, some of these guidelines may be less applicable. For example, Chapter 5 suggests that if you explain graphics with audio narration rather than text, you reduce the mental workload required of the learner and thereby increase learning. However, if your learners are experienced regarding the skills you are teaching, overload is not as likely and they will probably learn effectively from text or audio.

Environment

A third factor that affects e-learning is the environment—including such issues as technical constraints of the delivery platform, network, and software, cultural factors in institutions such as the acceptance of and routine familiarity with technology, and pragmatic constraints related to budget, time, and management expectations. In this book we focus on what works best from a psychological perspective, but we recognize that you will have to adapt our guidelines to your own unique set of environmental factors.

e-Learning Architectures

Although all e-learning is delivered on a computer, different courses reflect different assumptions of learning, which we introduce here and describe in detail in Chapter 2. During the past one hundred years, three views of learning have evolved, and you will see each view is reflected in courses available today. The three views are reflected in the design architecture you select for your training (Clark, 2003). The three architectures and the learning assumptions on which they are based, summarized in Table 1.3, are *receptive* based on an *information acquisition* view, *directive* based on a *response strengthening* view, and *guided discovery* based on a *knowledge construction* view.

Table 1.3. **Three e-Learning Architectures.**

Architecture	View	Inter-Activity	Used for
Receptive	Information acquisition	Low	Inform training goals such as new hire orientation
Directive	Response strengthening	Medium	Perform procedure training goals such as software skills
Guided Discovery	Knowledge construction	High	Perform strategic training goals such as problem solving

Interactivity in e-Learning

The interactivity of the lessons (from low to high) is one important feature that distinguishes lessons built using the various architectures. Receptive types of e-learning fall at the lower end of the interactivity scale, as they incorporate little or no opportunity for explicit learner responses. Receptive lessons are used most frequently for inform training goals. For learning to occur, it is up to the viewers of a receptive lesson to initiate mental processing of the information themselves, since no external processing opportunities are included. In the mid-range of interactivity are directive e-learning programs. Directive lessons follow a sequence of "explanation-example-question-feedback." These architectures, commonly designed for perform procedure training goals, incorporate highly structured practice opportunities designed to guide learning in a step-by-step manner. The Excel lessons shown in

Figures 1.3 and 1.4 apply the directive architecture. Guided discovery forms of e-learning, including simulations and games, fall in the high interactivity range of the continuum. For example, Figure 1.6 shows the interface for a guided discovery course in which the learner is constantly engaged by clicking on various on-screen objects that provide data or activities related to commercial bank loan analysis.

Learning is possible from any of these three architectures if learners engage in active knowledge construction. In receptive courses, it will be up to the learner to actively process the content provided. In directive and guided discovery architectures, knowledge construction is overtly promoted by the interactions built into the lessons. In the next chapter we describe more about the psychological processes needed for learning and how instructional methods in these architectures can support or defeat those processes.

Learning in e-Learning

The challenge in e-learning, as in any learning program, is to build lessons in ways that are compatible with human learning processes. To be effective, instructional methods must support these processes. That is, they must foster the psychological events necessary for learning. While the computer technology for delivery of e-learning is upgraded weekly, the human side of the equation—the neurological infrastructure underlying the learning process—is very old and designed for change only over evolutionary time spans. In fact, technology can easily deliver more sensory data than the human nervous system can process. To the extent that audio and visual elements in a lesson interfere with human cognition, learning will be depressed.

We know a lot about how learning occurs. Over the past twenty years, hundreds of research studies on cognitive learning processes and methods that support them have been published. Much of this new knowledge remains inaccessible to those who are producing or evaluating online learning because it has been distributed primarily within the research community. This book fills the gap by summarizing research-based answers to questions that multimedia producers and consumers ask about what to look for in effective e-learning.

COMING NEXT

Since instructional methods must support the psychological processes of learning, the next chapter summarizes those processes. We include an overview of our current understanding of the human learning system and the processes involved in building knowledge and skills in learners. We provide several examples of how instructional methods used in e-lessons support cognitive processes. In addition, we present some guidelines to help you understand and evaluate research evidence presented throughout the book.

Suggested Readings

Clark, R.C. (2000). Four architectures of learning. *Performance Improvement, 39*(10), 31–37.

Clark, R.C., & Kwinn, A. (2007). *The new virtual classroom: Evidence-based guidelines for synchronous e-learning.* San Francisco, CA: Pfeiffer.

Mayer, R.E. (Ed.). (2005). *The Cambridge handbook of multimedia learning.* New York: Cambridge University Press.

CHAPTER OUTLINE

How Do People Learn?

How Do e-Lessons Affect Human Learning?

What Is Good Research?

How Can You Identify Relevant Research?

How Do You Interpret Research Statistics?

What We Don't Know About Learning

2

How Do People Learn from e-Courses?

FROM LAS VEGAS-STYLE MEDIA with games and glitz at one extreme to page turners consisting of text on screens at the other, many e-learning courses ignore human cognitive processes and as a result do not optimize learning. In writing this book, we were guided by two fundamental assumptions: the design of e-learning courses should be based on a cognitive theory of how people learn and on scientifically valid research studies. In other words, e-learning courses should be constructed in light of how the mind learns and experimental evidence concerning e-learning features that promote best learning. In this chapter we describe the memory systems and processes involved in learning. We have added new information on recent advances in human learning. We also summarize important features of experimental studies to help you interpret the relevance and applicability of research to your work. We have added new material concerning the value of experimental research evidence in education.

DESIGN DILEMMA: YOU DECIDE

Suppose you are in charge of the training department at Thrifty Savings and Loan. Your boss, the HR director, asks you to develop a series of e-learning courses to be delivered via the corporate intranet: "With the recent merger, we need more cost-effective ways to deliver training to the local branches. We need to create both self-study lessons as well as virtual classroom sessions. By using technology we can save money and also make learning fun. My kids really enjoy playing games online and surfing the web! Let's showcase our training to upper management by using the cutting edge of learning technology."

Your director of human resources is espousing what can be called a technology-centered approach to e-learning. For her, e-learning courses should take advantage of powerful, cutting-edge technologies, such as video, games, blogs, or animations available on the web. In taking a technology-centered approach, she is basing her decisions about how to design e-learning courses on the capabilities afforded by new technologies.

Your intuition is that something is wrong with the technology-centered approach. You remember reading about the disappointing history of educational technology (Cuban, 1986). In every era, strong claims have been made for the educational value of hot new technologies, but the reality somehow has never lived up to expectations. You wonder why there have been so many failures in the field of educational technology. Perhaps expectations have been unrealistic? Today, many of the same old claims about revolutionizing learning can be heard again, this time applied to online games, simulations, or to the Web-2. You decide it's time to take a learner-centered approach, in which technology is adjusted to fit in with the way that people learn. But you wonder if there is a learning theory with sufficient detail to guide practical decisions in e-learning design. And even if there is a useful theory, is there any evidence to guide decisions that may stem from a theory?

Based on your own experience or intuition, which of the following options would you select?

A. Online applications such as games, simulations, and blogs are engaging and should be a central feature of all new e-learning initiatives.

B. Online applications such as games, simulations, and blogs may interfere with human learning processes and should be avoided.

C. We don't know enough about human learning to make specific recommendations about how to use new technology features.

D. Not sure which options are correct.

How Do People Learn?

Let's begin our review of what works in e-learning with a summary of how learning happens in any instructional setting.

Three Metaphors for Learning

Place a check mark next to your favorite description of how learning works:

☐ Learning involves strengthening correct responses and weakening incorrect responses.

☐ Learning involves adding new information to your memory.

☐ Learning involves making sense of the presented material by attending to relevant information, mentally reorganizing it, and connecting it with what you already know.

Each of these answers reflects one of the three major metaphors of learning that learning psychologists have developed during the past one hundred years, as summarized in Table 2.1 (Mayer, in press). Your personal view of how learning works can affect your decisions about how to design instructional programs.

If you checked the first answer, you opted for what can be called the response-strengthening view of learning. The learner is a passive recipient of rewards or punishments, and the teacher is a dispenser of rewards (which serve to strengthen a response) and punishments (which serve to weaken a response). In Chapter 1 we referred to training based on a response-strengthening view as a directive instructional architecture. A typical instructional method is to

Table 2.1. Three Metaphors of Learning.

Metaphor of Learning	Learning Is:	Learner Is:	Instructor Is:
Response Strengthening	Strengthening or weakening of associations	Passive recipient of rewards and punishments	Dispenser of rewards and punishments
Information Acquisition	Adding information to memory	Passive recipient of information	Dispenser of information
Knowledge Construction	Building a mental representation	Active sense maker	Cognitive guide

present simple questions to learners, and when they respond tell them whether they are right or wrong. This was the approach taken with programmed instruction in the 1960s and is prevalent in many e-learning lessons today. Our main criticism of the response-strengthening metaphor is not that it is incorrect, but rather that it is incomplete—it tells only part of the story because it does not explain meaningful learning.

If you checked the second answer, you opted for what can be called the information-acquisition view of learning, in which the learner's job is to receive information and the instructor's job is to present it. A typical instructional method is a textbook or PowerPoint presentation, in which the instructor conveys information to the learner. In Chapter 1 we refer to the information-acquisition view as the basis for a receptive instructional architecture. This approach is sometimes called the empty vessel or sponge view of learning because the learner's mind is an empty vessel into which the instructor pours information. Our main criticism of this view—which is probably the most commonly held view—is that it conflicts with much of what we know about how people learn.

If you opted for the third alternative, you picked a metaphor that can be called knowledge construction. According to the knowledge-construction view, people are not passive recipients of information, but rather are active sense makers. They engage in active cognitive processing during learning, including attending to relevant information, mentally organizing it into a coherent structure, and integrating it with what they already know. Although we find some merit in each of the metaphors of learning, we focus most strongly on this one. In short, the goal of effective instruction is not only to present information but also to encourage the learner to engage in appropriate cognitive processing during learning.

Principles and Processes of Learning

Figure 2.1 presents a model of how people learn from multimedia lessons. In the left column, a lesson may contain graphics and words (in printed or spoken form). In the second column, the graphics and printed words enter the learner's cognitive processing system through the eyes, and spoken words enter through the ears. If the learner pays attention, some of the material is selected for further processing in the learner's working memory—where you can hold and manipulate just a few pieces of information at one time in each channel. In working memory, the learner can mentally organize some of the selected images into a pictorial model and some of the selected words into a verbal model. Finally, as indicated by the "integrating arrow," the learner can connect the incoming material with existing knowledge from long-term memory—the learner's storehouse of knowledge.

As you can see, there are three important cognitive processes indicated by the arrows in the figure:

1. *Selecting words and images*—the first step is to pay attention to relevant words and images in the presented material;

Figure 2.1. Cognitive Theory of Multimedia Learning.

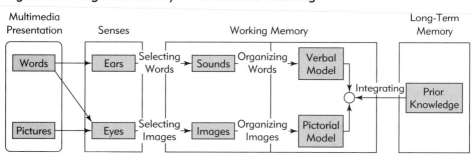

2. *Organizing words and images*—the second step is to mentally organize the selected material in coherent verbal and pictorial representations; and

3. *Integrating*—the final step is to integrate incoming verbal and
   pictorial representations with each other and with existing
   knowledge.

Meaningful learning occurs when the learner appropriately engages in all of
these processes.

   This learning model reflects four principles from research in cognitive
science:

1. *Dual channels*—people have separate channels for processing visual/
   pictorial material and auditory/verbal material;

2. *Limited capacity*—people can actively process only a few pieces of
   information in each channel at one time;

3. *Active processing*—learning occurs when people engage in appropriate cognitive processing during learning, such as attending to
   relevant material, organizing the material into a coherent structure,
   and integrating it with what they already know; and

4. *Transfer*—new knowledge and skills must be retrieved from long-
   term memory during performance.

Managing Limited Cognitive Resources During Learning

The challenge for the learner is to carry out these processes within the constraints of severe limits on how much processing can occur in each channel
at one time. You may recall the expression: "Seven plus or minus two." This
refers to the capacity limits of working memory. Let's explore three kinds of
demands on cognitive processing capacity:

1. *Extraneous processing*—is cognitive processing that does not support
   the instructional objective and is created by poor instructional layout;

2. *Essential processing*—is cognitive processing aimed at mentally
   representing the core material (consisting mainly of selecting the

relevant material) and is created by the inherent complexity of the material; and

3. *Generative processing*—is cognitive processing aimed at deeper understanding of the core material (consisting mainly of organizing and integrating) and is created by the motivation of the learner to make sense of the material.

The challenge for instructional designers is to create learning environments that minimize extraneous cognitive processing, manage essential processing, and foster generative processing.

How Do e-Lessons Affect Human Learning?

If you are involved in designing or selecting instructional materials, your decisions should be guided by an accurate understanding of how learning works. Throughout the book, you will see many references to cognitive learning theory, as described in the previous section. Cognitive learning theory explains how mental processes transform information received by the eyes and ears into knowledge and skills in human memory.

Instructional methods in e-lessons must guide the learner's transformation of words and pictures in the lesson through working memory so that they are incorporated into the existing knowledge in long-term memory. These events rely on the following processes:

1. Selection of the important information in the lesson;

2. Management of the limited capacity in working memory to allow the rehearsal needed for learning;

3. Integration of auditory and visual sensory information in working memory with existing knowledge in long-term memory by way of rehearsal in working memory; and

4. Retrieval of new knowledge and skills from long-term memory into working memory when needed later.

In the following sections, we elaborate on these processes and provide examples of how instructional methods in e-learning can support or inhibit them.

Methods for Directing Selection of Important Information

Our cognitive systems have limited capacity. Since there are too many sources of information competing for this limited capacity, the learner must select those that best match his or her goals. We know this selection process can be guided by instructional methods that direct the learner's attention. For example, multimedia designers may use an arrow or color to draw the eye to important text or visual information, as shown in Figure 2.2.

Figure 2.2. Visual Cues Help Learners Attend to Important Elements of the Lesson.

The e-Learning and the Science of Instruction CD.

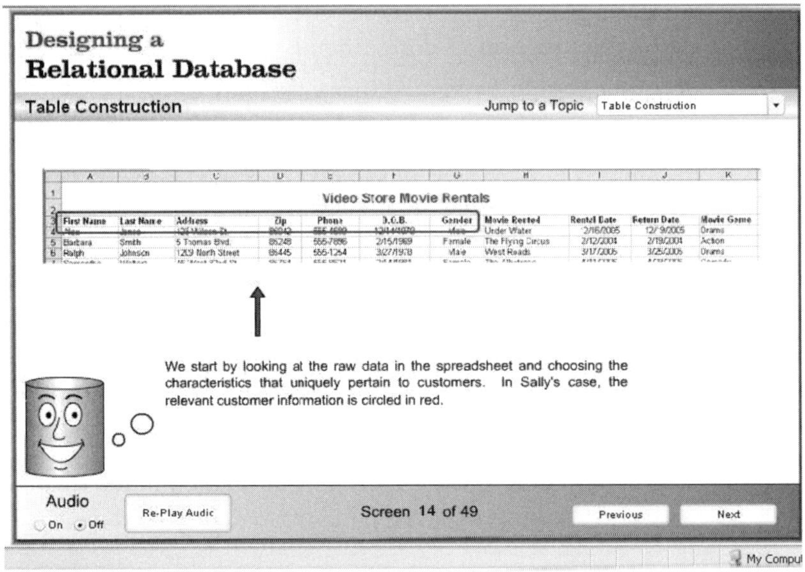

Methods for Managing Limited Capacity in Working Memory

Working memory must be free to rehearse the new information provided in the lesson. When the limited capacity of working memory becomes filled, processing becomes inefficient. Learning slows and frustration grows. For example, most of us find multiplying numbers like 968 by 89 in our heads to be a challenging task. This is because we need to hold the intermediate products of our calculations in working memory storage and continue to multiply the next set of numbers in the working memory processor. It is very difficult for working memory to hold even limited amounts of information and process effectively at the same time.

Therefore, instructional methods that overload working memory make learning more difficult. The burden imposed on working memory in the form of information that must be held plus information that must be processed is referred to as *cognitive load*. Methods that reduce cognitive load foster learning by freeing working memory capacity for learning. In the past ten years, we've learned a lot about ways to reduce cognitive load in instructional materials. Many of the guidelines we present in Chapters 4 through 12 are effective because they reduce or manage load. For example, the coherence principle described in Chapter 7 states that better learning results when e-lessons minimize irrelevant visuals, omit background music and environmental sounds, and use succinct text. In other words, less is more. This is because, by using a minimalist approach that avoids overloading working memory, greater capacity can be devoted to rehearsal processes, leading to learning.

Methods for Integration

Working memory integrates the words and pictures in a lesson into a unified structure and further integrates these ideas with existing knowledge in long-term memory. The integration of words and pictures is made easier by lessons that present the verbal and visual information together rather than separated. For example, Figure 2.3 illustrates two screens from two versions of a lesson on lightning formation in which the text is placed next to the graphic (Version A) or is placed at the bottom of the screen (Version B). Version A, the integrated version, resulted in better learning than Version B. Chapter 4 summarizes the contiguity principle of instruction that recommends presenting pictures and words close together on the screen.

Once the words and pictures are consolidated into a coherent structure in working memory, they must be further integrated into existing knowledge structures in long-term memory. This requires active processing in working memory. e-Lessons that include practice exercises and worked examples stimulate the integration of new knowledge into prior knowledge. For example, a practice assignment asks sales representatives to review new product

Figure 2.3. Screens from Lightning Lesson with Integrated Text and Graphics (A) and Separated Text and Graphics (B).
Adapted from Mayer, 2001a, 2005b. © Cambridge University Press 2005.
Reprinted with the permission of Cambridge University Press.

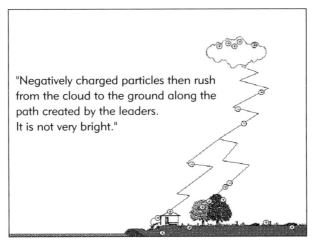

(A)

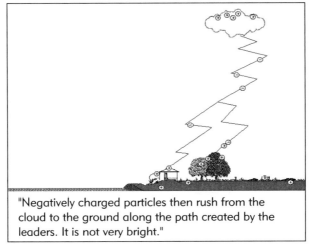

(B)

features and describe ways that their current clients might best take advantage of a product upgrade. This assignment requires active processing of the new product feature information in a way that links it with prior knowledge about their clients.

Methods for Retrieval and Transfer

It is not sufficient to simply add new knowledge to long-term memory. For success in training, those new knowledge structures must be encoded into long-term memory in a way that allows them to be easily retrieved when needed on the job. Retrieval of new skills is essential for transfer of training. Without retrieval, all the other psychological processes are meaningless, since it does us little good to have knowledge stored in long-term memory that cannot be applied later.

For successful transfer, e-lessons must incorporate the context of the job in the examples and practice exercises so the new knowledge stored in long-term memory contains good retrieval hooks. For example, one multimedia exercise asks technicians to play a Jeopardy™ game in which they recall facts about a new software system. A better alternative exercise gives an equipment failure scenario and asks technicians to select a troubleshooting action based on facts about a new software system. The Jeopardy™ game exercise might be perceived as fun, but it risks storing facts in memory without a job context. These facts, lacking the contextual hooks needed for retrieval, often fail to transfer. In contrast, the troubleshooting exercise asks technicians to apply the new facts to a job-realistic situation. Chapters 10 and 11 on examples and practice in e-learning provide a number of guidelines with samples of ways multimedia lessons can build transferable knowledge in long-term memory.

Summary of Learning Processes

In summary, learning from e-lessons relies on four key processes:

- First, the learner must focus on key graphics and words in the lesson to select what will be processed.

- Second, the learner must rehearse this information in working memory to organize and integrate it with existing knowledge in long-term memory.

- Third, in order to do the integration work, limited working memory capacity must not be overloaded. Lessons should apply cognitive load reduction techniques, especially when learners are novices to the new knowledge and skills.

- Fourth, new knowledge stored in long-term memory must be retrieved back on the job. We call this process transfer of learning. To support transfer, e-lessons must provide a job context during learning that will create new memories containing job-relevant retrieval hooks.

All of these processes require an active learner—one who selects and processes new information effectively to achieve the learning goals. The design of the e-lesson can support active processing or it can inhibit it, depending on what kinds of instructional methods are used. For example, a lesson that follows a Las Vegas approach to learning by including heavy doses of glitz may overload learners, making it difficult to process information in working memory. At the opposite extreme, lessons that use only text fail to exploit the use of relevant graphics, which are proven to increase learning (see Chapter 3).

All of our recommendations are based on high-quality research. But what constitutes "good" research? We address this question in the next section.

What Is Good Research?

We recommend that e-learning courses incorporate methods that are based on high-quality research. We favor *evidence-based practice*—the idea that instructional techniques should be based on research findings and research-based theory. Shavelson and Towne (2002, p. 1) eloquently summarize the argument for evidence-based practice in education: "One cannot expect reform efforts in education to have significant effects without research-based knowledge to guide them."

Certainly, it is easier to base courses on the design recommendations of experts, but it's always worthwhile to ask, "Yes, but does it work?" Until fairly recently, there was not much of a research base concerning the design of e-learning environments. However, as we sit down to write the second edition of this book, we are finding a useful and growing base of research (for example, Clark & Lyons, 2004; Clark, Nguyen, & Sweller, 2006; Jonassen, 2004; Mayer, 2001a, 2005a; Sweller, 1999). Our goal is not to review every e-learning study, but rather to summarize some exemplary studies that represent the best-established findings. In this section, we want to help you recognize high-quality research in your role as a consumer or designer of e-learning courseware. Table 2.2 summarizes three roads to research—informal studies, controlled studies, and clinical trials.

Table 2.2. Three Types of Research.

Research Type	Definition	Example
Informal Studies	Conclusions based on feedback from and observations of students	e-Lesson revisions are based on evaluation sheets completed during pilot test.
Controlled Studies	Conclusions based on outcome comparisons of randomly assigned participants to groups with different treatments	Learning from two identical lessons (one with and one without music) is compared in a laboratory setting.
Clinical Trials	Conclusions based on outcomes of lessons taken in actual learning settings	A particular e-learning program is selected based on outcomes from two hundred supervisors.

Informal Studies

Informal studies (or observational studies) involve observing people as they learn or asking them about their learning. For example, we might develop an e-learning course and ask people what they like and don't like about it. Based on this feedback, we can adjust some features of the course. The process of making changes based on learner feedback is called *formative evaluation*. Alternatively, we can use the feedback along with post-test learning data to summarize the positive and negative features of the course. The process of making an end-of-project evaluation is called *summative evaluation*. Although informal studies can play a useful role in course development, they do not meet the high scientific standards we have set for the science of instruction.

Controlled Studies

Controlled studies (or experimental studies) involve comparing the learning process and/or outcomes of two or more groups of learners. In measuring the learning process and/or outcomes (which can be called the *dependent* measures), we recommend measuring how deeply people have learned. This can be accomplished by asking them to apply what was taught to new situations, rather than simply asking them to recall lesson content. In setting up the groups, we recommend keeping all the conditions the same except for one variable (which can be called the *independent* variable). For example, we can compare a group that receives an e-learning course that has background music to an identical course that lacks the music. The learners must be equivalent in the two groups—a feat that is best ensured by randomly assigning people to the groups. This is a controlled study because all features of the learning situation are the same (that is, controlled) except for the feature being studied (that is, the independent variable, which in this case is background music).

In an analysis of research methods in education, Phye, Robinson, and Levin (2005) conclude that experimental research methods offer the strongest evidence that student learning is caused by a particular educational intervention. Large-scale application of the experimental method to research with humans has been one of the greatest scientific achievements of the 20th Century. This is our preferred research method for the purposes of this book.

Clinical Trials

Clinical trials (or controlled field testing) involve comparing the learning process and outcome of people who learn from a targeted e-learning course versus people who learn from some other venue (such as a different e-learning course). Clinical trials use the experimental method, as described previously, but do so by examining whether the e-learning course works in the field, that is, in the real-world context for which it was intended. Clinical trials are useful because they evaluate outcomes in real-world contexts. However, the results are limited by the many extraneous variables that can impact learning in the field. Mosteller and Boruch (2002) have shown that clinical trials have been used successfully in medical research and argue that clinical trials can also be useful in determining the impact of educational programs on learning.

Although we believe that clinical trials are an important component in the development of effective e-learning courses, our focus in this book is on more basic design principles that are best discovered in controlled studies.

How Can You Identify Relevant Research?

You might wonder how we selected the research we include in this book or how you could determine whether a given research study is applicable to your design decisions. The following list summarizes five questions to consider when reading research studies:

1. How similar are the learners in the research study to your learners? Research conducted on children may be limited in its applicability to adult populations. More relevant studies use subjects of college age or beyond.

2. Are the conclusions based on an experimental research design? Look for subjects randomly assigned to test and control groups.

3. Are the experimental results replicated? Look for reports of research in which conclusions are drawn from a number of studies that essentially replicate the results. The *Review of Educational Research* and *Educational Psychology Review* are good sources, as are handbooks such as the *Cambridge Handbook of Multimedia Learning* (Mayer, 2005a), *the Handbook of Research on Educational Communications and Technology* (Jonassen, 2004), and the *Handbook of Educational Psychology* (Alexander & Winne, 2006).

4. Is learning measured by tests that measure application? Research that measures outcomes with recall tests may not apply to workforce learning goals in which the learning outcomes must be application, not recall, of new knowledge and skills.

5. Does the data analysis reflect practical significance as well as statistical significance? With a large sample size, even small learning differences may have statistical significance yet may not justify the expense of implementing the test method. Look for statistical significance of .05 or less and effect sizes of .5 or more. (See our explanation of effect sizes in the paragraphs to follow.)

All of these questions relate to the applicability of the research to your learning audience and desired outcomes or the confidence you can put in the results based on the validity of the study. Throughout this book we report the results of statistical tests of the research we summarize. Therefore, we briefly summarize how to interpret those tests in the next section.

How Do You Interpret Research Statistics?

Suppose you read a study comparing two groups of students—a test group and a control group. The control group received a basic multimedia lesson that explains content with graphics and audio narration. We call this the no-music group. The test group received the same lesson with background music added to the narration. We call this the music group. Suppose the no-music group averaged 90 percent correct on a test of the material and the music group averaged 80 percent on the same test. Averages are also called means (for example, 90 percent versus 80 percent). Also suppose the scores were not very spread out, so most of the no-music students scored close to 90 and most of the music students scored close to 80. Standard deviation tells you how spread out the scores are, or how much variation there is in the results. Powerful instructional methods should yield high averages and low standard deviations. In other words, high scores are achieved and nearly all learners score close to the average so that there is high consistency in outcomes among the learners.

As illustrated in Figure 2.4, let's suppose the standard deviation is 10 for the no-music group and 10 for the music group. Based on these means and standard deviations, can we conclude that background music hurts learning? Generally, when the difference between the score averages is high (90 percent versus 80 percent in our example) and the standard deviations are low (10 percent in our example), the difference is real. However, to accurately decide that issue requires statistical tests. Two common statistical measures associated with research studies we present in this book are probability and effect size. As you read research, look for results in which the probability is less than .05 ($p < .05$) and show an effect size of .5 or greater.

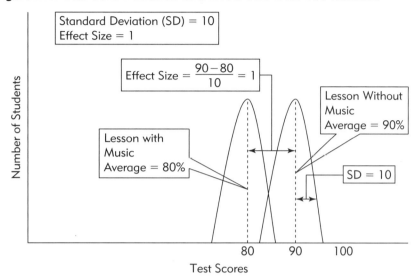

Figure 2.4. Standard Deviation and Effect Size from Two Lessons.

PROBABILITY AND EFFECT SIZE: DETAILS

Some statistical tests yield a measure of probability such as p < .05 (which is read, "probability less than point oh five"). In the case of our background music study, this means that there is less than a 5 percent chance that the difference between 90 percent and 80 percent does NOT reflect a real difference between the two groups. In other words, there is a 95 percent chance that the difference in scores is real—not just a chance result. Thus we can conclude that the difference between the groups is statistically significant. In general, when the probability is less than .05, researchers conclude that the difference is real, that is, statistically significant.

EFFECT SIZE: HOW BIG IS THE DIFFERENCE IN PRACTICAL TERMS?

Even if music has a statistically significant effect, we might want to know how strong the effect is in practical terms. We could just subtract one mean score from the other, yielding a difference of 10 in our music study. However, to tell whether 10 is a big dif-ference, we can divide this number by the standard deviation of the control group (or of both groups pooled together). This tells us how many standard deviations one group is more than the other and is called effect size (ES). In this case, the ES is 1, which is generally regarded as a strong effect. What this means is that an individual learner in the control group would have a 1 standard deviation increase (10 points in our example) if he or she were to study with a lesson that omitted music. If the ES had been .5 in our example, an individual learner in the control group would have a .5 standard deviation increase. When the ES is less than .2, the practical impact of the experimental treatment is a bit too small to worry about, an ES of .5 is moderate, and when it climbs to .8 or above, it is large enough to get very excited about (Cohen, 1988).

What We Don't Know About Learning

The study of learning has a long history in psychology, but until recently most of the research involved contrived tasks in laboratory settings such as how hungry rats learned to run a maze or how humans learned a list of words. Within the last twenty-five years, however, learning researchers have broadened their scope to include more complex kinds of learning tasks, including e-learning. What is needed is more high-quality research that is methodologically rigorous, theoretically based, and grounded in realistic e-learning situations. In short, we need research-based principles of e-learning (Mayer, 2001, 2005a). This book provides you with a progress report on research-based principles that are consistent with the current state of research in e-learning.

DESIGN DILEMMA: RESOLVED

Your HR director wanted to launch an e-learning program with popular new technological features such as games, simulations, and animations. However, you were concerned that an unbalanced focus on technology would be counter productive. We considered the following options:

A. Online applications such as games, simulations, and blogs are engaging and should be a central feature of all new e-learning initiatives.

B. Online applications such as games, simulations, and blogs may interfere with human learning processes and should be avoided.

C. We don't know enough about human learning to make specific recommendations about how to use new technology features.

D. Not sure which options are correct.

Based on the evidence in this chapter, we believe that the right question is NOT whether popular online features such as games or simulations are good or bad ideas. Instead, we recommend that you take a learner-centered approach and consider how all technology features from graphics to games can be used in ways that support cognitive processes of selection, rehearsal, load management, and retrieval. In this book we will address all major technology features from a learner-centered perspective.

A week later you stop by the HR director's office for a follow-up meeting. You make your case: "Using the corporate intranet for learning is not the same as using the Internet for entertainment or reference. We really need to shape the media to our purposes, not vice versa! It's going to cost a lot to develop this training and even more for the employees to take it. Can we risk spending that money on materials that violate research-proven principles for learning? Let's use e-learning as an opportunity to improve the quality of the training we have been providing by factoring in evidence of what works!"

WHAT TO LOOK FOR IN e-LEARNING

At the end of the remaining chapters, you will find in this section a checklist of things to look for in effective e-lessons. The checklists summarize teaching methods that support cognitive processes required for learning and have been proven to be valid through controlled research studies. In Chapter 16, as well as on the CD, we present a checklist that combines the guidelines from all of the chapters along with some sample e-learning course reviews.

ON *e-LEARNING AND THE SCIENCE OF INSTRUCTION* CD

In this new edition, we add examples of multimedia instruction that apply and fail to apply our guidelines. With the help of Alan Koenig, a doctoral student at Arizona State University, we have designed and programmed two sample lessons on how to construct a database. The example lesson applies most of our guidelines, while the counter-example lesson violates most of them. At the end of each chapter, we write specific commentary on how the example and counter-example relate to the guidelines of that chapter.

COMING NEXT

Two fundamental tools you have for teaching are visuals and words. Is there a value to using both visuals and words? In Chapter 3 we look at evidence regarding the instructional value of graphics and consider whether some types of graphics are more effective than others.

Suggested Readings

Alexander, P.A., & Winne, P.H. (Eds.). (2006). *Handbook of educational psychology* (2nd ed.). Mahwah, NJ: Lawrence Erlbaum.

Clark, R., Nguyen, F., & Sweller, J. (2006). *Efficiency in learning.* San Francisco, CA: Pfeiffer.

Jonassen, D.H. (Ed.). (2004). *Handbook of research on educational communications and technology* (2nd ed.). Mahwah, NJ: Lawrence Erlbaum.

Mayer, R.E. (2001). *Multimedia learning.* New York: Cambridge University Press.

Mayer, R.E. (Ed.). (2005). *The Cambridge handbook of multimedia learning.* New York: Cambridge University Press.

Mayer, R.E. (in press). *Learning and instruction* (2nd ed.) Upper Saddle River, NJ: Pearson Merrill Prentice Hall.

Phye, G.D., Robinson, D.H., & Levin, J. (Eds.). (2005). *Empirical methods for evaluating educational interventions*. San Diego, CA: Elsevier.

Shavelson, R.J., & Towne, L. (Eds.). (2002). *Scientific research in education*. Washington, DC: National Academy Press.

CHAPTER OUTLINE

3

Applying the Multimedia Principle

USE WORDS AND GRAPHICS RATHER
THAN WORDS ALONE

IN THE FIRST EDITION we summarized evidence for learning gains that result from combining text and relevant graphics in e-lessons. In the past few years, we have seen a growing body of research focusing on the types of visuals that best promote learning. For example, studies are comparing learning from animated and from static visuals. Flash animations are popular additions to contemporary e-learning courses. How effective are these animations? In addition, we have growing evidence that well-designed visuals and text can particularly benefit learners with less experience in the lesson content.

DESIGN DILEMMA: YOU DECIDE

The new vice president of corporate learning and performance is anxious to get started with the company's new e-learning initiative. She wants to show results quickly to offset upper management's impression that e-learning development is so slow that, by the time it's released, it's already out-of-date. She has committed to an asynchronous lesson on building databases to be ready in the next month. "After all," she says to Matt, the project lead, "we already have the content from our current instructor-led course, so let's quickly convert it into e-learning!"

Ben, the project programmer, works quickly putting the classroom lecture notes into HTML. He proudly shows the team his first-draft storyboards, such as the one shown in Figure 3.1.

Figure 3.1. A Screen from Ben's First Draft of the Database Course.

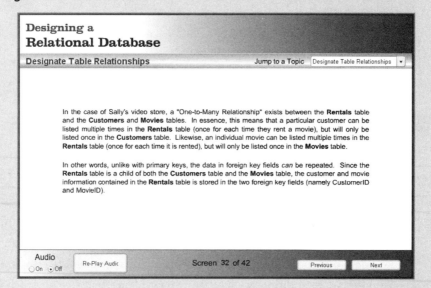

Reshmi, one of the course designers, reacts negatively: "Hey, Ben, it's great that you got a draft together quickly since we don't have much development time. But this looks pretty boring to me! In e-learning the computer screen is our main connection with the students, and screens filled with text will turn them off right away. We need this first project to be engaging. We need to add graphics and animations!" "Yeah," Ben replies, "graphics are great, but we don't have a graphic artist, so I'll have to download some clip art. And that will add development time. Finding clip art about databases won't be that easy!" "Clip art is cheesy," Reshmi replies. "Let's contract with an artist to create some custom Flash animations for us so we can really show what e-learning can do." Matt, the project manager, jumps in: "It will take time to get a contract set up and get the artist up-to-speed—time we don't have. Let's just start simple on this first project by going with mostly text with some clip art here and there to add interest. We can try for a graphic artist on future projects. After all, basically our goal is to explain about databases, and we can do that effectively with words." Based on your own experience or intuition, which of the following options is correct:

A. Matt is right. Learning will be just as effective from good textual explanations as from text plus graphics.

B. Ben is right. Adding clip art to a few screens will make the lesson more interesting.

C. Reshmi is right. Customized visuals including animations to illustrate the content will add appeal and improve learning.

D. Not sure which options are correct.

Do Visuals Make a Difference?

In training, it is customary to use words—either in printed or spoken form—as the main vehicle for conveying information. Words are quick and inexpensive to produce. The question is whether there is any return on investment for supplementing words with pictures—either static graphics such as drawings or photos, or dynamic graphics such as animation or video. In particular, do people learn more deeply from words and graphics than from words alone? This is the issue we want to explore with you in this chapter.

Include Both Words and Graphics

Based on cognitive theory and research evidence, we recommend that e-learning courses include words and graphics, rather than words alone. By words, we mean printed text (that is, words printed on the screen that people read) or spoken text (that is, words presented as speech that people listen to through earphones or speakers). By graphics, we mean static illustrations such as drawings, charts, graphs, maps, or photos, and dynamic graphics such as animation or video. We use the term "multimedia presentation" to refer to any presentation that contains both words and graphics. For example, if you are given an instructional message that is presented in words alone, such as shown in Figure 3.1, we recommend you convert it into a multimedia presentation consisting of words and pictures, such as shown in Figure 3.2. As you complete the job and content analysis, you should visualize how the instructional message can be communicated using both words and relevant pictures.

Figure 3.2. A Revision of Figure 3.1 with Visuals Added.

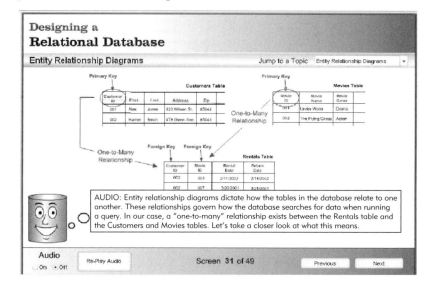

The rationale for our recommendation is that people are more likely to understand material when they can engage in active learning—that is, when they engage in relevant cognitive processing such as attending to the relevant material in the lesson, mentally organizing the material into a coherent cognitive representation, and mentally integrating the material with their existing knowledge. Multimedia presentations can encourage learners to engage in active learning by mentally representing the material in words and in pictures and by mentally making connections between the pictorial and verbal representations. In contrast, presenting words alone may encourage learners—especially those with less experience or expertise—to engage in shallow learning, such as not connecting the words with other knowledge.

There are many examples of e-learning environments that contain window after window of text and more text. Some may even have graphics that decorate the page, but do not help you understand the text. For example, Figure 3.3 from a military course on ammunition presents scrolling text and a picture of a general as a decorative element. As you can see, the general graphic does not support the text, but rather simply serves to fill screen space.

Figure 3.3. A Decorative Graphic That Does Not Improve Learning.

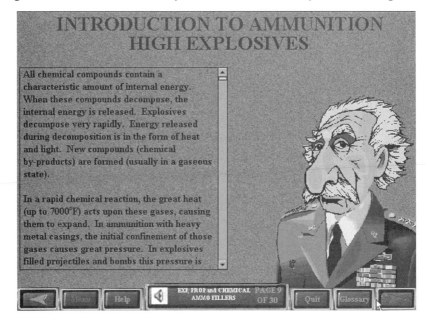

Select Graphics That Support Learning

Instead of presenting words alone, we recommend presenting words and graphics. However, not all kinds of graphics are equally helpful. For example, let's consider several possible functions of graphics:

1. Decorative graphics serve to decorate the page without enhancing the message of the lesson, such as a photo or a video of a person riding a bicycle in a lesson on how bicycle tire pumps work;

2. Representational graphics portray a single element, such as a photo of the bicycle tire pump along with a caption, "bicycle tire pump";

3. Relational graphics portray a quantitative relation among two or more variables, such as a line graph showing the relation between years of age on the x-axis and probability of being in a bicycle accident on the y-axis;

4. Organizational graphics depict the relations among elements, such as a diagram of a bicycle tire pump with each part labeled or a matrix giving a definition and example of each of three different kinds of pumps;

5. Transformational graphics depict changes in an object over time, such as a video showing how to fix a flat tire, or a series of annotated frames showing steps in how a bicycle tire pump works; and

6. Interpretive graphics illustrate invisible relationships such as an animation of the bicycle pump that includes small dots to show the flow of air into and out of the pump.

Based on this analysis, we recommend that you minimize graphics that decorate the page (called decorative graphics) or simply represent a single object (called representational graphics), and that you incorporate graphics that help the learner understand the material (called transformational and interpretive graphics) or organize the material (called organizational graphics). For example, Table 3.1 is an organizational graphic that gives the name, definition, and example of six functions of graphics in the form of a matrix. When the text describes a quantitative relationship, then a relational graphic is warranted; and when the text describes changes over time, then a transformational graphic is warranted.

Table 3.1. An Organizational Graphic of Graphic Types.

Adapted from Clark and Lyons, 2004.

Graphic Type	Description	Examples
Decorative	Visuals added for aesthetic appeal or for humor	1. The general in Figure 3.3 2. A person riding a bicycle in a lesson on how a bicycle pump works 3. Baseball-related icons as a game theme in a lesson on product knowledge
Representational	Visuals that illustrate the appearance of an object	1. The sample tables in Figure 3.2 2. A photograph of equipment in a maintenance lesson 3. A screen capture in a computer application lesson
Organizational	Visuals that show qualitative relationships among content	1. A matrix such as this table 2. A concept map 3. A tree diagram
Relational	Visuals that summarize quantitative relationships	1. A bar graph or pie chart 2. A map with circles of different sizes representing location and strength of earthquakes
Transformational	Visuals that illustrate changes in time or over space	1. An animated demonstration of a computer procedure 2. A video of how volcanoes erupt 3. A time-lapse animation of seed germination
Interpretive	Visuals that make intangible phenomena visible and concrete	1. Drawings of molecular structures 2. A series of diagrams with arrows that illustrate the flow of blood through the heart 3. Pictures that show how data is transformed and transmitted through the Internet

In Chapter 2, we summarized the dual channels principle that learners have separate channels for processing visual material and auditory material. We see the job of an instructional professional as not just to present information—such as presenting text that contains everything the learner needs to know—but rather to leverage both channels in ways that enable the learner to make sense out of the material. Providing relevant graphics with text is a proven method of fostering deeper cognitive processing in learners. In short, learning is facilitated when the graphics and text work together to communicate the instructional message.

Some Ways to Use Graphics to Promote Learning

Helping you determine how to create the best types of graphics to meet your instructional goals requires a book topic in itself. In fact, just such a book is *Graphics for Learning* by Ruth Colvin Clark and Chopeta Lyons. Here we offer just a few examples of the ways to use graphics that serve instructional rather than decorative roles: to teach content types, as topic organizers, and as lesson interfaces.

Graphics to Teach Content Types

Clark (2007) has identified five different kinds of content: fact, concept, process, procedure, and principle. Table 3.2 briefly describes each content type and lists graphic types commonly used to teach specific lesson content such as facts, concepts, processes, procedures, and principles.

Since 63 percent of computer-systems training is delivered by e-learning (Industry Report, 2006), many e-learning graphics are screen captures. A screen capture is a graphic that is a replication of an actual software screen. For example, Figure 3.4 is a screen capture from a synchronous e-learning class on Excel. At this point in the lesson, the instructor uses application sharing features of the virtual classroom to demonstrate how to use formulas in Excel. Another content type that profits from graphic support is process. A process is a step-by-step description of how a system works, including business, scientific, and mechanical systems. Process information is effectively visualized with a series of static frames or, in some cases, animations. Figure 3.5 is a screen from an animated graphic showing how the AIDS virus infects cells.

Table 3.2. Graphics to Teach Content Types.

Adapted from Clark, 2007.

Content Type	Description	Useful Graphic Types	Example
Facts	Unique and isolated information such as specific application screens, forms, or product data	Representational Organizational	A screen capture of a spreadsheet, as in Figure 3.4 A table of parts' names and specifications
Concepts	Groups of objects, events, or symbols designated by a single name	Representational Organizational Interpretive	Diagrams of database tables as in Figure 3.2 A tree diagram of biological species Three Excel formulas to illustrate formatting rules
Process	A description of how something works	Transformational Interpretive Relational	Animations of how the heart pumps blood Still diagrams to illustrate how a bicycle pump works An animation showing how a virus invades a cell as in Figure 3.5
Procedure	A series of steps resulting in completion of a task	Transformational	An animated illustration of how to use a spreadsheet as in Figure 3.4 A diagram with arrows showing how to install a printer cable
Principle	Guidelines that result in completion of a task; cause-and-effect relationships	Transformational Interpretive	A video showing two effective sales approaches An animation showing genes passing from parents to offspring

Figure 3.4. A Transformation Visual of an Excel Screen Projected
          Through Application Sharing in Synchronous e-Learning.

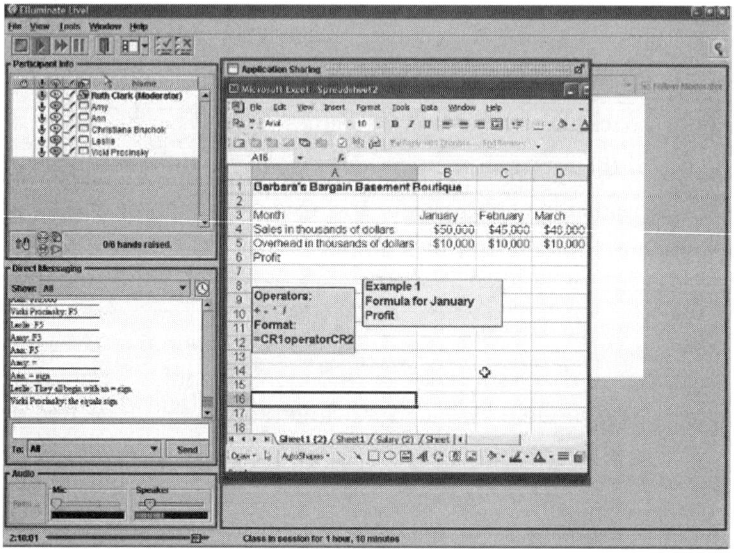

Figure 3.5. A Transformational Graphic Illustrating Process of
          AIDS Infection.

With permission of Roche, Basel, Switzerland.
www.roche-hiv.com/front.cfm

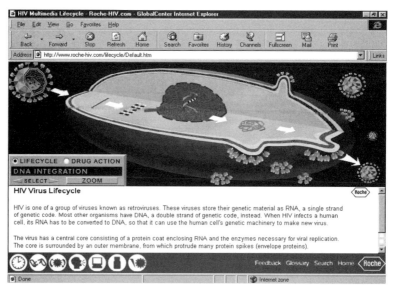

Graphics as Topic Organizers

In addition to illustrating specific content types, graphics such as topic maps can serve an organizational function by showing relationships among topics in a lesson. For example, Figure 3.6 shows a screen with a series of coaching topics mapped in the left-hand bar, including where to coach, when to coach, how long to coach, and so on. When the mouse is placed over each of the topics in the graphic organizer, a different illustration appears on the right side of the screen. In this example, the topic of formal and informal coaching sessions is reinforced with text and photographs.

Figure 3.6. An Organizational Graphic on Coaching Topics.

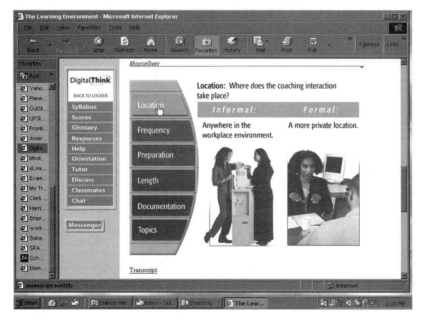

Graphics to Show Relationships

Graphics in the form of dynamic and static graphs can make invisible phenomena visible and show relationships. Imagine an e-learning lesson to teach fast-food workers safe cooking and food-handling practices. An animated line graph with numbers on the vertical axis and time on the horizontal axis illustrates changes in bacterial growth in food cooked at different temperatures or handled in safe and unsafe ways. The lesson includes an interactive simulation in which the learner adjusts the cooking temperature and sees the impact on a dynamic line graph called a "germ meter." A geographic map can illustrate population density by adding a small red dot to represent five thousand individuals. If made interactive, the map could include a slider bar that accessed different time periods, allowing the viewer to see population shifts over time.

Graphics as Lesson Interfaces

Finally, courses designed using a guided discovery approach often use a graphical interface as a backdrop to present case studies. For jobs that are conducted in office settings, a generic office like the one shown in Figure 3.7 illustrates a number of resources for the learner to use while working on a simulated job assignment. In this lesson, bank loan agents can use the computer, telephone, fax machine, and bookshelf to research a commercial loan application. For additional information on the use of graphics in instruction, see Clark and Lyons (2004).

Figure 3.7. The Graphic Interface Provides Resources for Researching a Bank Loan Applicant.
With permission from Moody's Investment Service.

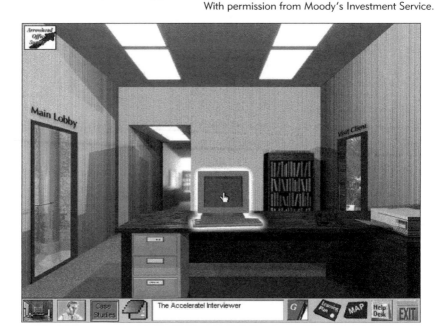

Psychological Reasons for the Multimedia Principle

Perhaps the single greatest human invention is language, and the single greatest modification of this invention is printed language. Words allow us to communicate effectively, and printed words allow us to communicate effectively across miles and years. (So does recorded speech, by the way, which is yet another modification of the great invention of language.) Therefore, it makes sense to use words when we provide training or instruction. For thousands of years, the main format for education has been words—first in spoken form and more recently in printed form. Words are also the most efficient and effective way of producing e-learning because words can convey a lot of information and are easier to produce than graphics.

This line of thinking is based on the information acquisition theory, in which teaching consists of presenting information and learning consists of acquiring information, as summarized in the middle of Table 2.1. Information can be delivered in many forms—such as printed words, spoken words, illustrations, photos, graphs, animation, video, and narration. Over the years, it has become clear that words are an efficient and effective method for presenting information, so based on this view, in most situations instruction should involve simply presenting words. According to the information acquisition theory, the format of the information (for example, words versus pictures) does not matter, as long as the information is delivered to the learner.

In our opinion, the information acquisition theory is based on an inadequate conception of how people learn. Instead, we favor a knowledge construction theory in which learning is seen as a process of active sense-making and teaching is seen as an attempt to foster appropriate cognitive processing in the learner, as summarized in the bottom of Table 2.1. According to this learning metaphor, it is not good enough to deliver information to the learner; instructors must also guide the learner's cognitive processing during learning, thereby enabling and encouraging learners to actively process the information. An important part of active processing is to mentally construct pictorial and verbal representations of the material and to mentally connect them. This goal is more likely to be achieved with multimedia lessons with both words and corresponding pictures that depict the same to-be-learned content. Adding relevant graphics to words can be a powerful way to help learners engage in active learning. Overall, your view of the cognitive stages of learning (as summarized in Table 2.1) can influence your decisions about how to design instruction (Mayer, 2003).

Evidence for Using Words and Pictures

There is consistent evidence that people learn more deeply from words and pictures than from words alone, at least for some simple instructional situations. In eleven different studies, researchers compared the test performance of students who learned from animation and narration versus narration alone or from text and illustrations versus text alone (Mayer, 1989b; Mayer & Anderson, 1991, 1992; Mayer, Bove, Bryman, Mars, & Tapangco, 1996; Mayer & Gallini, 1990; Moreno & Mayer, 1999b, 2002b). The lessons taught scientific and mechanical processes, including how lightning works, how a car's braking system works, how pumps work, and how electrical generators work. For example, in one study students read an accurate verbal description of how a bicycle pump works (as shown in Figure 3.8), while others read the same verbal description and viewed a diagram depicting the same steps (as shown in Figure 3.9).

Figure 3.8. How a Bicycle Pump Works Explained with Words Alone.

How a Bicycle Pump Works
"As the rod is pulled out, air passes through the piston and fills the area between the piston and the outlet valve. As the rod is pushed in, the inlet valve closes and the piston forces air through the outlet valve."

In all eleven comparisons, students who received a multimedia lesson consisting of words and pictures performed better on a subsequent transfer test than students who received the same information in words alone. Across the eleven studies, people who learned from words and graphics produced between 55 percent to 121 percent more correct solutions to transfer problems than people who learned from words alone. Across all studies, a median percentage gain of 89 percent was achieved with an effect size of 1.50. Recall

Figure 3.9. How a Bicycle Pump Works Explained with Words and Graphics.

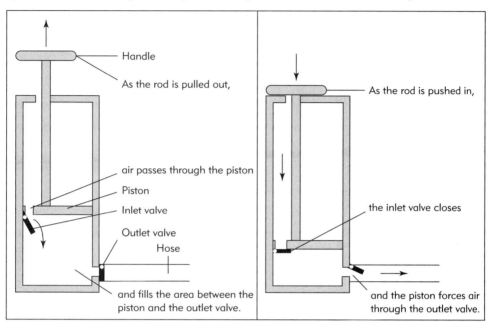

from our discussion in Chapter 2 that effect sizes over .8 are considered large. Figure 3.10 shows a result from one of these experiments.

Figure 3.10. Learning Is Better from Words Plus Graphics Than from Words Alone.

Adapted from Mayer, 2001a.

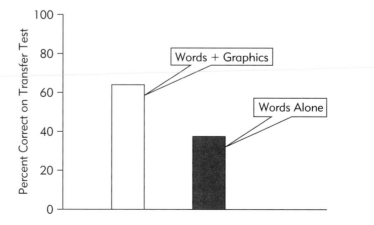

We call this finding the multimedia effect—people learn more deeply from words and graphics than from words alone. In a recent review, Fletcher and Tobias (2005, p. 128) concluded: "The multimedia principle, which suggests that learning and understanding are enhanced by adding pictures to text rather than presenting text alone, appears to be well supported by findings from empirical research." The multimedia effect is the starting point for our discussion of best instructional methods for e-learning because it establishes the potential for multimedia lessons to improve human learning.

Complementary results come from research on graphic advance organizers—pictorial material presented at the start of a lesson intended to help the learner understand the material (Mayer, 1989b). For example, in one study (Mayer, 1983) students read a lesson on how radar works and then answered questions. Students performed much better on the test if they saw a graphic representation of the steps in radar (as a ball being thrown, bouncing off an object, and returning to the source) before the lesson was presented. In this lesson, using a ball bouncing off a wall served as an interpretive graphic to illustrate the invisible phenomenon of radar.

In a related study involving interactive multimedia, Moreno and Mayer (1999b) developed a mathematics computer game intended to teach students how to add and subtract signed numbers (such as $2 - 3 =$ _____). Some students learned from drill-and-practice problems, whereas others worked on the same problems, but as feedback also saw a bunny hop along a number line to represent each problem (such as starting at 2, turning to face the left, hopping backward three steps, and landing on 5). Students learned better with symbols and graphics than from symbols alone.

In the remainder of this section, we consider two addition research questions, concerning for whom the multimedia principle works (novices versus experts) and where the multimedia principle works (static illustrations versus animations).

The Multimedia Principle Works Best for Novices

Does the multimedia principle apply equally to all learners? There is increasing evidence that our recommendation to use words and graphics is particularly important for learners who have low knowledge of the domain (whom we can call novices), rather than learners who have high knowledge of the domain (whom we can call experts). For example, in a series of three experiments involving lessons on brakes, pumps, and generators, Mayer and Gallini (1990) reported novices learned better from text and illustrations (such as shown in Figure 3.9) than from words alone (such as shown in Figure 3.8), but experts learned equally well from either condition. Apparently, the more experienced learners are able to create their own mental images as they read the text about how the pump works, for example, whereas the less experienced learners need help in relating the text to a useful pictorial representation.

In a related study, Ollershaw, Aidman, and Kidd (1997) presented text lessons on how pumps work to learners who had low or high knowledge of the domain. Low-knowledge learners benefited greatly when animation was added to the text, whereas high-knowledge learners did not. These and related results (Kalyuga, Chandler, & Sweller, 1998, 2000; Mayer & Gallini, 1990; Ollerenshaw, Aidman, & Kidd, 1997) led Kalyuga, Ayres, Chandler, and Sweller (2003) and Kalyuga (2005) to propose the expertise reversal effect— the idea that instructional supports that help low-knowledge learners may not help (and may even hurt) high-knowledge learners. Overall, we recommend that you be sensitive to the level of prior knowledge of your learners, so that you can provide needed supports—such as multimedia instruction—to low-knowledge learners. If you are working on a course for a less advanced group of learners—beginning trainees, for example—you should be especially careful to supplement text-based instruction with coordinated graphics. If you have a more advanced group of learners—such as medical residents or engineers experienced in the topic you are presenting—they may be able to learn well mainly from text or even mainly from graphics.

Should You Change Static Illustrations into Animations?

If it is important to add graphics to words, is it better to use animations or static illustrations? Flash animations are currently very popular additions to many e-learning lessons. At first glance, you might think that animations are best because they are an active medium that can depict changes and movement. Similarly, you might think that static illustrations are a poorer choice because they are a passive medium that cannot depict changes and movement in as much detail as animations can. In spite of these impressions, a number of research studies have failed to find that animations are more effective than a series of static frames depicting the same material (Betrancourt, 2005; Hegarty, Kriz, & Cate, 2003; Mayer, Hegarty, Mayer, & Campbell, 2005; Tversky, Morrison, & Betrancourt, 2002).

Let's consider two ways to use multimedia to explain how lightning storms develop—a paper-based lesson of a series of static illustrations with printed text (as shown in Figure 3.11) or a computer-based lesson of narrated animations in which the words are spoken and the transitions between frames are animated. On a transfer test, students in the paper group performed 32 percent better than students in the computer group, yielding an effect size of .55 (Mayer, Hegarty, Mayer, & Campbell, 2005). In four such comparisons—involving lessons on lightning, ocean waves, hydraulic brakes, and toilet tanks—the illustrations-and-text group always performed better than the animation-and-narration group, yielding a median effect size of .57. Presumably, the so-called passive medium of illustrations and text actually allowed for active processing because the learners had to mentally animate the changes from one frame to the next and learners were able to control the order and pace of their processing. In contrast, the so-called active medium of animations and narration may foster passive learning because the learners did not have to mentally animate and could not control the pace and order of the presentation. In addition, animation may overload the learners' working memory because the images are so rich in detail and are so transitory that they must be held in memory. In contrast, a series of static frames does not impose extra cognitive load because the learners can always review a previous frame.

In spite of these results, there may be some content that is particularly suited to animation or video rather than static frames of illustrations or photos, such as descriptions of how to perform a motor skill. For example, ChanLin (1998) reported that animation was more effective than static diagrams in helping students learn to make paper flowers through paper folding. Additionally, animations can serve an interpretive function when designed with special effects that reveal relationships not otherwise visible. Hegarty (2004) suggests

Figure 3.11. A Series of Static Visuals to Teach How Lightning Forms.

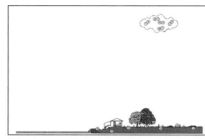

"The charge results from the collision of the cloud's rising water droplets against heavier, falling pieces of ice."

"The negatively charged particles fall to the bottom of the cloud, and most of the positively charged particles rise to the top."

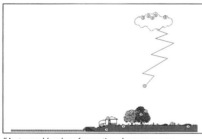

"A stepped leader of negative charges moves downward in a series of steps. It nears the ground."

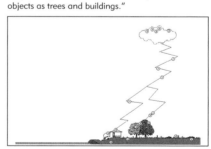

"A positively charged leader travels up from such objects as trees and buildings."

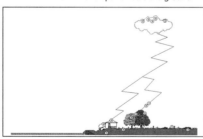

"The two leaders generally meet about 165-feet above the ground."

"Negatively charged particles then rush from the cloud to the ground along the path created by the leaders. It is not very bright."

"As the leader stroke nears the ground, it induces an opposite charge, so positively charged particles from the ground rush upward along the same path."

"This upward motion of the current is the return stroke. It produces the bright light that people notice as a flash of lightning."

that "dynamic displays can distort reality in various ways, such as slowing down some processes and speeding up others, showing an object or phenomenon from different or changing viewpoints, augmenting the display with cues to draw viewers' attention to the most relevant parts, or having moving objects leave a trace or wake" (p. 345). A time-lapse video of seed germination or a slow-motion video of hummingbirds in flight are two examples of how special effects can make phenomena visible.

Animations can cost more to develop than static diagrams, so it makes sense to use a series of static frames as our default graphic. Overall, our recommendation is to use static illustrations unless there is a compelling instructional rationale for animation. In particular, when you have an explanative illustration, we recommend presenting a series of static frames to depict the various states of the system rather than a lock-step animation.

What We Don't Know About Visuals

We have good evidence that relevant visuals promote learning. Now it's time to find out more about what types of visuals are most effective for different learners and instructional goals. Some of the unresolved issues around graphics include:

A. When is an animation more effective than a static graphic?

B. Most of our research data measures learning immediately after taking the lesson. We need more information on the effectiveness of visuals for longer-term learning.

C. Explanatory visuals can be time-consuming to produce and require an investment in graphic design resources. When are such investments warranted? What are the cost benefits for creating customized visuals to illustrate technical content?

D. Do polished color visuals improve learning and motivation more than simpler formats? Many of the visuals used in experiments are relatively simple line drawings like the one shown in Figure 3.9. Some commercial e-learning programs use highly realistic and detailed visuals, such as the one shown in Figure 3.7. What are the tradeoffs in learning and in motivation between simple line drawings and highly polished art? Consistent with earlier research, Ricer, Filak, and Short (2005) found that medical students showed no difference in learning or subjective rating of lessons on cancer screening whether the lesson used static black-and-white figures or slides containing animated computer-generated graphics. We need more research on how the surface features of a visual rendering affect learning and motivation.

DESIGN DILEMMA: RESOLVED

In our chapter introduction, you considered the following options for use of graphics in the database course:

A. Matt is right. Learning will be just as effective from good textual explanations as from text plus graphics.

B. Ben is right. Adding clip art to a few screens will make the lesson more interesting.

C. Reshmi is right. Customized visuals, including animations to illustrate the content, will add appeal and improve learning.

D. Not sure which options are correct.

Based on the evidence we presented in this chapter, we believe that Reshmi is on the right track. e-Learning is a visual medium and relevant graphics will add appeal and improve learning. However, animations are not likely to add much value in this situation. Learning will be as effective with static graphics to illustrate database concepts. Ben's idea to add decorative graphics in the form of clip art will most likely not contribute to learning and, in fact, as we will see in Chapter 7, may even detract from learning. We recommend that the team engage a graphic designer to create a few simple but functional visuals to support the lesson concepts—including visuals that serve organizational, transformational, and interpretive functions. Even if a few extra days are required, the improvement in instructional quality and appeal is worth the investment.

WHAT TO LOOK FOR IN e-LEARNING

☐ Graphics and text are used to present instructional content.

☐ Graphics are relevant to the instructional purpose, rather than decorative.

☐ Representative graphics are used to illustrate concrete facts, concepts, and their parts.

☐ Animations are limited and used to illustrate content that cannot as readily be shown with a series of static visuals.

☐ Organizational graphics are used to show relationships among ideas or lesson topics or where the parts are located within a whole structure.

☐ Relational graphics are used to show quantitative relationships among variables.

☐ Transformational graphics, such as a video showing how to operate equipment, are used to show changes over time.

☐ Interpretive graphics, such as a series of static frames, are used to explain how a system works or to make invisible phenomena visible.

☐ Graphics are used as a lesson interface for case studies.

ON e-LEARNING AND THE SCIENCE OF INSTRUCTION CD

You can compare the visuals in our example database lesson with our counter-example. You will notice that in the example version most of the screens include relevant visuals that illustrate the concepts and steps involved in constructing a database. In contrast, the counter-example is either missing relevant visuals or uses decorative visuals that do not contribute to learning.

COMING NEXT

In this chapter we have seen that learning is improved by the use of relevant graphics combined with words to present instructional content. In the next chapter, we will build on this principle by examining the contiguity principle that addresses the best ways to position graphics and related text on the screen.

Suggested Readings

Clark, R.C., & Lyons, C. (2004). *Graphics for learning*. San Francisco, CA: Pfeiffer.

Fletcher, J.D., & Tobias, S. (2005). The multimedia principle. In R.E. Mayer (Ed.), *The Cambridge handbook of multimedia learning* (pp. 117–134). New York: Cambridge University Press.

Mayer, R.E. (1989b). Systematic thinking fostered by illustrations in scientific text. *Journal of Educational Psychology, 81,* 240–246.

Mayer, R.E., & Anderson, R.B. (1992). The instructive animation: Helping students build connections between words and pictures in multimedia learning. *Journal of Educational Psychology, 84,* 444–452.

Mayer, R.E., & Anderson, R.B. (1991). Animations need narrations: An experimental test of a dual-processing system in working memory. *Journal of Educational Psychology, 90,* 312–320.

Mayer, R.E., & Gallini, J.K. (1990). When is an illustration worth ten thousand words? *Journal of Educational Psychology, 88,* 64–73.

Mayer, R. E., Hegarty, M., Mayer, S., & Campbell, J. (2005). When static media promote active learning: Annotated illustrations versus narrated animations in multimedia instruction. *Journal of Experimental Psychology: Applied, 11,* 256–265.

Robinson, D.H. (2002). Spatial text adjuncts and learning. *Educational Psychology Review,* 14(1).

CHAPTER OUTLINE

Contiguity Principle 1: Place Printed Words Near Corresponding Graphics

Violations of Contiguity Principle 1

Separation of Text and Graphics on Scrolling Screens

Separation of Feedback from Questions or Responses

Covering Lesson Screens with Linked Windows

Presenting Exercise Directions Separate from the Exercise

Displaying Captions at the Bottom of Screens

Using a Legend to Indicate the Parts of a Graphic

Contiguity Principle 2: Synchronize Spoken Words with Corresponding Graphics

Violations of Contiguity Principle 2

Separation of Graphics and Narration Through Icons

Separation of Graphics and Narration in a Continuous Presentation

Psychological Reasons for the Contiguity Principle

Evidence for Presenting Printed Words Near Corresponding Graphics

Evidence for Presenting Spoken Words at the Same Time as Corresponding Graphics

What We Don't Know About Contiguity

4

Applying the Contiguity Principle

ALIGN WORDS TO CORRESPONDING GRAPHICS

SOMETIMES IN e-LEARNING that uses on-screen text to explain graphics, a scrolling screen reveals the text, followed by the graphic further down the screen. Alternatively, often a storyboard template will place all of the text into a box at the bottom of the screen. The result is a physical separation of the text and the graphic. Alternatively, audio narration may be presented before or after the graphics it describes. In this chapter we summarize the empirical evidence for learning gains resulting from presenting text and graphics in an integrated fashion, compared to the same information presented separately. The psychological advantage of integrating text and graphics results from a reduced need to search for which parts of a graphic correspond to which words, which allows the user to devote limited cognitive resources to understanding the materials.

In our new edition, we retain an emphasis on the need to embed printed words near the graphic they describe—which constitutes contiguity of printed words and graphics on the screen. A new topic in this chapter focuses on the benefits of coordinating spoken words and graphics so that the learner can look at the part of the graphic that is being described by spoken words. In short, a new form of contiguity involves concurrently listening to spoken words while viewing the corresponding material in a graphic—which constitutes contiguity of spoken words and graphics in time.

DESIGN DILEMMA: YOU DECIDE

The e-learning design team is reviewing storyboards for their course on designing databases. To accommodate different learning styles, they have decided to include both text and audio options in the lessons. To apply the multimedia principle discussed in Chapter 3, Ben has added some simple but relevant visuals to illustrate the concepts. For example, to show the value of databases, he plans a demonstration in which he asks learners to find information in different sections of a spreadsheet. As shown in Figure 4.1, he gives directions in text on one screen (A) and asks learners to view the spreadsheet containing the answers on the following screen (B).

In reviewing the screens, Reshmi feels that the text directions and the visuals should be on the same screen. "I recall reading an article that mentioned research proving that it is better to place text close to a relevant graphic," she comments. "That's a good idea in many situations," Ben replies. "However, we need to make the graphics large so they can view an entire spreadsheet for this demonstration. There is no room for the text and the graphic on the same screen!" Based on your own experience or intuition, which of the following options is best:

A. Ben is right. For visibility, he needs to use most of the screen real estate for the visual. The text directions should be placed on the preceding screen.

Figure 4.1. Ben's First Draft Storyboards.

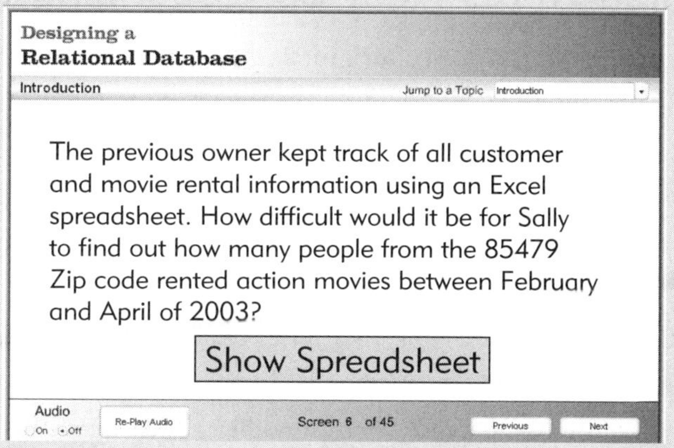

Designing a
Relational Database

Introduction   Jump to a Topic Introduction

The previous owner kept track of all customer
and movie rental information using an Excel
spreadsheet. How difficult would it be for Sally
to find out how many people from the 85479
Zip code rented action movies between February
and April of 2003?

Show Spreadsheet

Audio   Re-Play Audio   Screen 6 of 45   Previous   Next
On   Off

Screen A

Designing a
Relational Database

Introduction   Jump to a Topic Introduction

Video Store Movie Rentals

Audio   Re-Play Audio   Screen 6 of 45   Previous   Next
On   Off

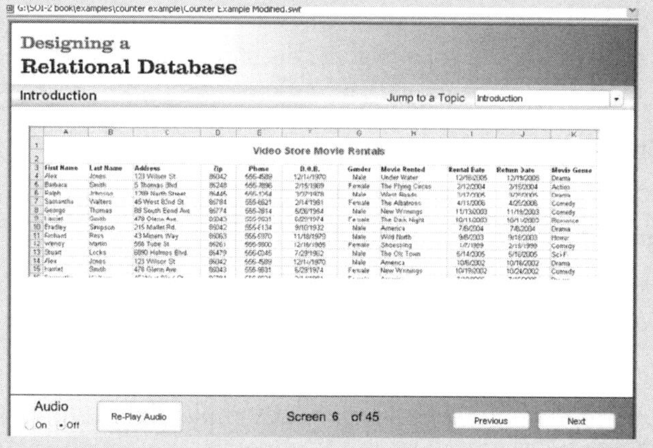

Screen B

B. Reshmi is right. Learning is more efficient when visuals and text are integrated. The text directions should be placed on the same screen as the visual

C. Both ideas could be accommodated by placing text directions in a rollover box on the spreadsheet activated by the mouse.

D. Not sure which option is best.

Place Printed Words Near Corresponding Graphics

The first version of the contiguity principle involves the need to coordinate printed words and graphics. In this chapter, we focus on the idea that on-screen words should be placed near the parts of the on-screen graphics to which they refer. We recommend that corresponding graphics and printed words be placed near each other on the screen (that is, contiguous in space).

In designing or selecting e-learning courseware, consider how on-screen text is integrated with on-screen graphics. In particular, when printed words refer to parts of on-screen graphics, make sure the printed words are placed next to the part of a graphic to which they refer. For example, when the graphic is a diagram showing the parts of an object, the printed names of the parts should be placed near the corresponding parts of the diagram, using a pointing line to connect the name to the part. Similarly, when a lesson presents words that describe actions (or states) depicted in the series of still frames, make sure that text describing an action (or state) is placed near the corresponding part of the graphic, using a pointing line to connect the text with the graphic.

When there is too much text to fit on the screen, the text describing each action or state can appear as a small pop-up message that appears when the mouse touches the corresponding portion of the graphic. This technique is called a mouse-over or rollover. For example, Figure 4.2 shows an application screen that uses the rollover technique. When learners place their cursors over different sections of the application screen, a text caption appears that explains that section. In Figure 4.2 the mouse has rolled over section 1 and the text window below it appears as long as the mouse remains in that area of the screen. Rollovers are transient. The text box disappears when the cursor moves to a different location on screen.

Violations of Contiguity Principle 1

Violations of the contiguity principle are all too common. The following list gives some of the most common violations (although there are more) of this principle that are frequently seen in e-learning courseware:

Figure 4.2. A Screen Rollover Integrates Text Below Section 1 of Graphic.
From Clark and Lyons, 2004.

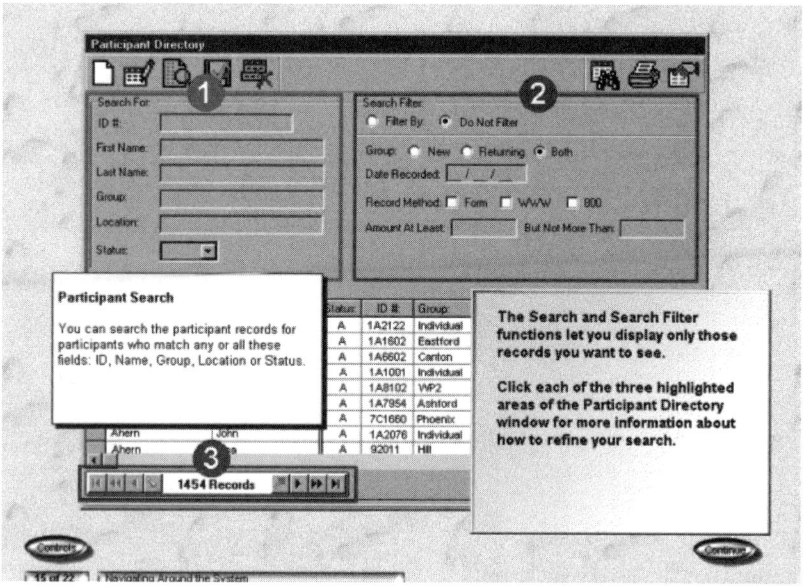

- In a scrolling window, graphics and corresponding printed text are separated, one before the other, and partially obscured because of scrolling screens.

- Feedback is displayed on a separate screen from the practice or question.

- Links leading to an on-screen reference appear in a second browser window that covers the related information on the initial screen (that is, printed text is in one window and graphics are in another window).

- Directions to complete practice exercises are placed on a separate screen from the application screen in which the directions are to be followed.

- All text is placed at the bottom of the screen away from graphics.

- Key elements in a graphic are numbered, and a legend at the bottom of the screen includes the name for each numbered element.

Separation of Text and Graphics on Scrolling Screens

Sometimes scrolling screens are poorly designed so that text is presented first and the visual illustration appears further down the screen, as illustrated in

Figure 4.3. Text and Graphic Separated on Scrolling Screen.

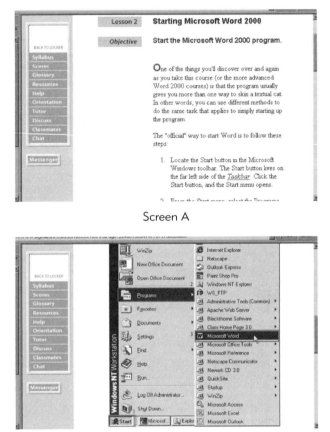

Screen A

Screen B

Figure 4.3. As the user scrolls down to view the graphic, the text is no longer visible and vice versa. This is a common problem we see in many courses that use scrolling screens to present instructional content. This problem can be remedied by integrating text and visuals on a scrolling screen, as shown in Figure 4.4. Alternatively, fixed screen displays can be used when it is important to see the text and graphic together. On a fixed screen, the graphic can fill the screen, and text boxes can be placed over the graphic near the element of the screen being described. Another remedy to the scrolling screen problem is to use text boxes that pop up over graphics when the graphic is touched by the cursor (as shown in Figure 4.2).

Figure 4.4. Text and Graphic Visible Together on a Scrolling Screen.

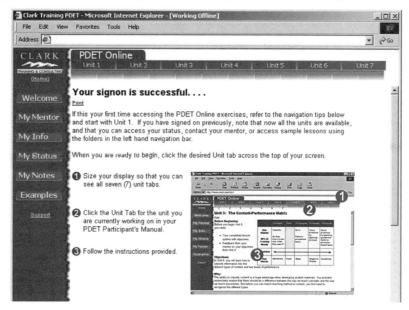

Separation of Feedback from Questions or Responses

Another common violation of the contiguity principle is feedback placed on a screen separate from the question or from the learner's answers. This requires the learner to page back and forth between the question and the feedback, adding cognitive load to learning. For example, in Figure 4.5 from our database counter-example on the CD, a multiple-select question (not shown) requires the learner to review the spreadsheet and select appropriate items. When the learner clicks "done" he or she is routed to Feedback A screen that shows the correct answer. In order to compare his or her answer with the correct answer, the learner must page back to the question screen. A better solution is shown in the Feedback B screen. In this screen, the learner's answers (in black box) have been carried over from the question screen and placed next to the correct answer, allowing a quick and easy comparison without paging back.

Covering Lesson Screens with Linked Windows

The use of links to lead to adjunct information is common in e-learning. However, when the linked information covers related information on the primary screen, this practice can create a problem. For example, a link of

Figure 4.5. Ineffective (A) and Effective (B) Placement of Feedback.
From the *e-Learning and the Science of Instruction* CD.

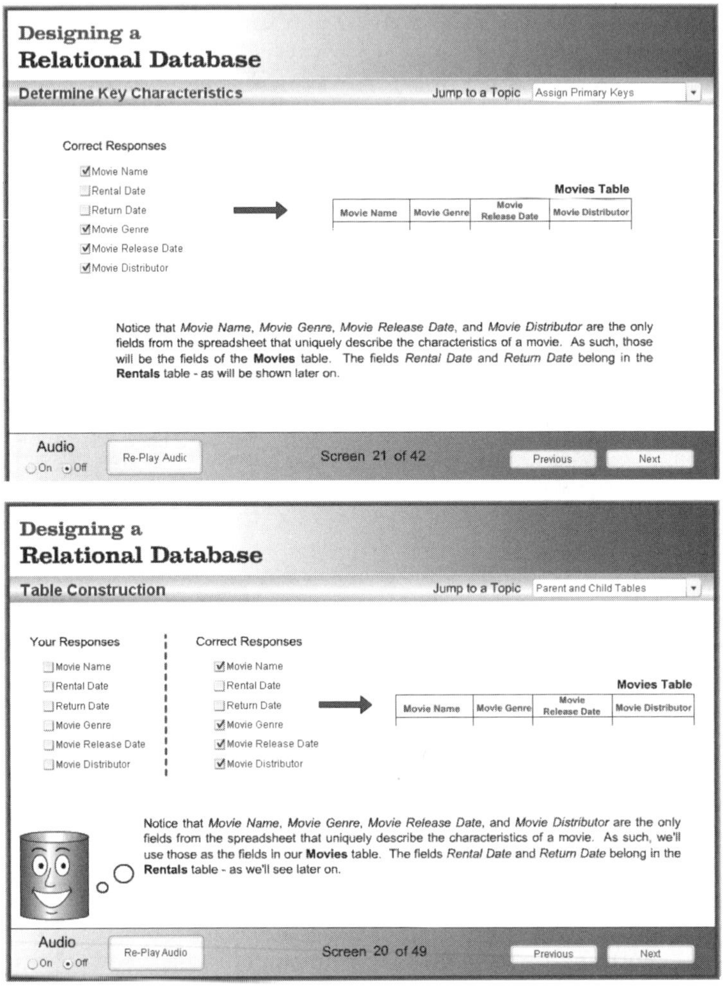

an application screen leads to a window containing a job aid. Having access to reference material is a good idea for memory support. However, if the resulting window covers the graphic example that it describes, the contiguity principle is violated. A better solution is to link to a window that is small, can be moved around on the main screen, and/or can be printed.

Presenting Exercise Directions Separate from the Exercise

Another common violation of the contiguity principle is presenting exercise directions in text separated from the screens on which the actions are to be taken. For example, in Figure 4.6 we see textual directions for a case study from an Excel e-learning lesson. When moving to the spreadsheet on the next screen, the learner no longer has access to the directions. A better alternative is to put the step-by-step directions in a box that can be minimized on the application screen.

Figure 4.6. Separating Exercise Directions from Application Screen Adds Extraneous Memory Load.

Displaying Captions at the Bottom of Screens

For consistency, many e-learning designs place all text in a box at the bottom of the screen, such as the frame shown in Figure 4.7A. The problem with this layout is that the learner needs to scan back and forth between the words at the bottom of the screen and the part of the graphic they describe. A better arrangement is to relocate the text closer to the visual as well as to insert lines to connect the text and visual, as shown in Figure 4.7B.

Using a Legend to Indicate the Parts of a Graphic

Suppose you wanted students to learn about the parts in a piece of equipment. You could show them an illustration in which each equipment part

Figure 4.7. Text Placed at Bottom of Screen (A) vs. Next to Visual (B)

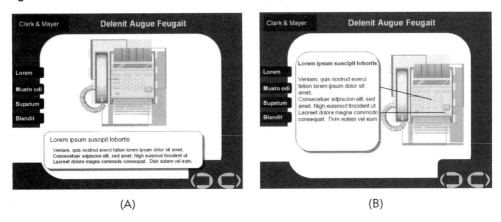

(A)   (B)

is numbered, and a legend below the illustration describes each one. The problem with this layout is that the learner must scan between the number and the legend—which creates wasted cognitive processing. A more efficient design would place the name and part description in a separate box near the corresponding part on the visual. The text could be placed in a rollover box or in a fixed display on the screen.

CONTIGUITY PRINCIPLE 2

Synchronize Spoken Words with Corresponding Graphics

Another version of the contiguity principle deals with the need to coordinate spoken words and graphics. In this section, we focus on the idea that spoken words (narration) that describe an event should play at the same time as the graphic (animation or video) is depicting the event. In short, we recommend that corresponding graphics and spoken words be presented at the same time (that is, contiguous—next to each other—in time).

When e-learning courseware contains narration and corresponding graphics (animation or video), you should consider how spoken words are integrated with on-screen graphics. In particular, when spoken words describe actions that are depicted in the on-screen graphics, make sure the corresponding spoken words and graphics are presented at the same time. For example, when the graphic is an animation showing the steps in a process, the narration describing a particular step should be presented at the same time that the step is shown on the screen. When the graphic is a video showing how to perform a task, the narration describing each step should be presented at the same time as the action shown on the screen.

Violations of Contiguity Principle 2

Violations of the contiguity principle include the following:

- A link to audio is indicated by one icon and a link to video is indicated by another icon.

- A segment provides a narrated introduction followed by animation or video.

Separation of Graphics and Narration Through Icons

Suppose you click on "How the Heart Works" in an online encyclopedia, and two buttons appear—a speaker button indicating that you can listen to a short narration about the four steps in the heart cycle—and a movie button indicating that you can watch a short animation, as illustrated in Figure 4.8. You click on the speaker button and listen to a description of the four steps in the heart cycle. Then you click on the movie button and watch a narration showing the four steps in the heart cycle. You might think this is an excellent presentation because you can select which mode of presentation you prefer. You might like the idea that you listen to the explanation first and then watch, or vice versa, thereby giving you two complementary exposures to the same material.

What's wrong with this situation? The problem is that when a lesson separates corresponding words and graphics, learners experience a heavier load on working memory—leaving less capacity for deep learning. Consider the learner's cognitive processing during learning when a narration is followed by an animation. After listening to the narration, the learner needs to hold all the relevant words in working memory and then match up each segment with the corresponding segment of the animation. However, having to hold so much information in working memory can be overwhelming, so

Figure 4.8. Narration Is Presented Separately from Animation.

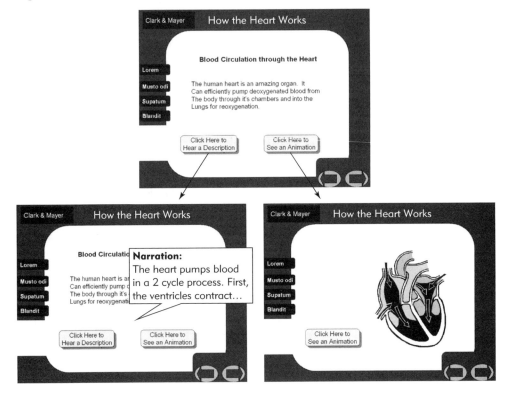

the learner may not be able to engage in other cognitive processes needed for deep learning. This is the type of load we called extraneous processing in Chapter 2. Extraneous processing refers to mental load that does not contribute to learning. Therefore, we recommend that you avoid e-learning lessons that present narration and graphics separately.

Separation of Graphics and Narration in a Continuous Presentation

Even when a lesson presents graphics and narration as a continuous unit, a lesson may be designed so that an introduction is presented as a brief narration that is followed by graphics, such as an animation, video, or series of still frames depicting the same material. For example, consider a multimedia presentation on "How the Heart Works" that begins with a narrator describing the four steps in the heart cycle, followed by four still frames depicting the four steps in the heart cycle.

At first glance, you might like this arrangement because you get a general orientation in words before you inspect a graphic. Yet, like the previous scenario, this situation can create cognitive overload because the learner has to mentally hold the words in working memory until the graphic appears—thereby creating a form of extraneous cognitive processing. To overcome this problem, we recommend presenting the narration at the same time the static frames are presented. In this situation, the learner can more easily make mental connections between corresponding words and graphics.

Psychological Reasons for the Contiguity Principle

As we have reviewed in the examples shown in the previous sections, it is not unusual to see (a) corresponding printed text and graphics physically separated in e-lessons or (b) corresponding narration and graphics presented at different times in e-lessons. The physical separation may occur because of vertical placement of printed text and graphics (one on top of the other), which separates them when the screen is scrolled, or by placing related information on separate fixed screen displays. The temporal separation may occur because a narrated introduction precedes a graphic or because graphics and narration are accessed through clicking on different icons.

Some designers separate words and pictures because they haven't stopped to think about whether it's an effective way to present information. Others reason that presenting the same material in two different places on the page or at two different times allows learners to choose the format that best suits their needs or even to experience the same information in two different ways. We recommend against separating words and pictures, even for environments with high traffic and low bandwidth, because it is not based on an accurate understanding of how people learn. Rather than being copy machines that record incoming information, humans are sense-makers who try to see the meaningful relations between words and pictures. When words and pictures are separated from one another on the screen or in time, people must use their scarce cognitive resources just to match them up. This creates what can be called *extraneous processing*—cognitive processing that is unrelated to the instructional goal. When learners use their limited cognitive capacity for extraneous processing, they have less capacity to use to mentally organize and integrate the material.

In contrast, when words and pictures are integrated, people can hold them together in their working memories and therefore make meaningful connections between them. This act of mentally connecting corresponding words and pictures is an important part of the sense-making process that leads to meaningful learning. As we saw in Chapter 2, it is in working memory that the related incoming information is organized and integrated with existing knowledge in long-term memory. When the learner has to do the added work of coordinating corresponding words and visual components that are separated on the screen or in time, the limited capacity of working memory is taxed—leading to cognitive overload. Ayres and Chandler (2005) argue that putting corresponding words and pictures far apart from each other (or presenting them at different times) creates what they call *split attention,* which forces the learner to use limited working memory capacity to coordinate the multiple sources of information. You should avoid instructional designs that cause split attention because they force the learner to waste precious cognitive processing on trying to coordinate two disparate sources of information.

Evidence for Presenting Printed Words Near Corresponding Graphics

Our first recommendation—presenting corresponding printed text and graphics near each other on the screen—is not only based on cognitive theory, but it is also based on several relevant research studies (Mayer, 1989b; Mayer, Steinhoff, Bower, & Mars, 1995; Moreno & Mayer, 1999a). In five different tests involving lessons on lightning formation and how cars' braking systems work, learners received printed text and illustrations containing several frames (or on-screen text with animation). For one group of learners (integrated group), text was placed near the part of the illustration that it described, as you can see in Figure 4.9A. For another group (separated group), the same text was placed under the illustration as a caption, as you can see in Figure 4.9B. In five studies, the integrated group performed

Figure 4.9. Screens from Lightning Lesson with Integrated Text and Graphics (A) and Separated Text and Graphics (B).
Adapted from Mayer, 2001, 2005c. © Cambridge University Press 2005.
Reprinted with the permission of Cambridge University Press.

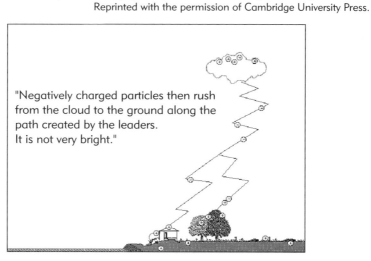

(A)

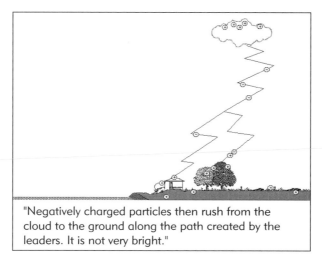

(B)

Figure 4.10. Learning Is Better from Integrated Text and Graphics Than from Separated Text and Graphics.
Adapted from Mayer, 2001a, 2005,b. © Cambridge University Press 2005.
Reprinted with the permission of Cambridge University Press.

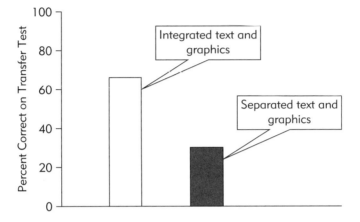

better on problem-solving transfer tests than the separated group. Overall, the integrated group produced between 43 and 89 percent more solutions than the separated group. The median gain across all the studies was 68 percent for an effect size of 1.12, which, as mentioned in Chapter 2, is a large effect. Figure 4.10 summarizes the results from one of the experiments.

Similar results have been found with training programs for technical tasks (Chandler & Sweller, 1991; Paas & Van Merrienboer, 1994; Sweller & Chandler, 1994; Sweller, Chandler, Tierney, & Cooper, 1990). Additional evidence comes from eye-movement studies involving text and corresponding diagrams. Successful learners tended to read a portion of the text, then search the diagram for the object being described in the text, then read the next portion of text and search the diagram for the object being described, and so on (Hegarty, Carpenter, & Just, 1996). It seems reasonable that we can simplify this process for all learners by breaking text into chunks, and by placing each chunk of text near the part of the graphic that it describes. Overall, there are numerous studies that support our recommendation.

Evidence for Presenting Spoken Words at the Same Time as Corresponding Graphics

Our second recommendation—presenting corresponding speech and graphics at the same time—is also based on research evidence (Mayer & Anderson, 1991, 1992; Mayer & Sims, 1994; Mayer, Moreno, Boire, & Vagge, 1999). In one experiment, some students (integrated group) viewed a 30-second narrated animation that explained how a bicycle tire pump works, in which the spoken words described the actions taking place on the screen. For example, when the narrator's voice said, "… the inlet valve opens …," the animation on the screen showed the inlet valve moving from the closed to the open position. Other students (separated group) listened to the entire narration and then watched the entire animation (or vice versa). On a subsequent transfer test, the integrated group generated 50 percent more solutions than did the separated group, yielding an effect size greater than 1, which is considered large.

Overall, across eight different experimental comparisons involving pumps, brakes, lightning, and lungs, students who received integrated presentations generated 60 percent more solutions on a transfer test than did students who received a separated presentation. The median effect size across all eight experiments was 1.30, which is considered a large effect in practical terms. Figure 4.11 summarizes the results from one such experiment. Research by Baggett (1984) and Baggett and Ehrenfeucht (1983) shows that learners experience difficulty in learning from a narrated video, even when corresponding words and graphics are separated by a few seconds. As you can see, when you have a narrated animation, narrated video, or even a narrated series of still frames, there is consistent evidence that people learn best when the words describing an element or event are spoken at the same time that the animation (or video or illustration) depicts the element or event on the screen.

What We Don't Know About Contiguity

Overall, our goal is to reduce the need for learners to engage in extraneous processing by helping them see the connection between corresponding words and graphics. Two techniques we explored in this chapter are (1) to present

Figure 4.11. Learning Is Better from Integrated Audio and Graphics
Than from Separated Audio and Graphics.

Adapted from Mayer and Anderson, 1991.

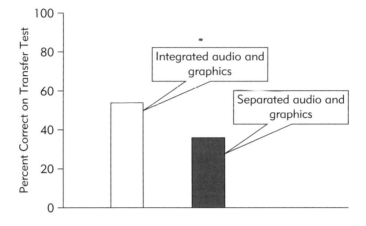

printed words near the part of the graphic they refer to and (2) to present spoken text at the same time as the portion of graphic they refer to. Some unresolved issues concern:

A. How much detail should be in the graphics and in the words?

B. When it is better to use printed words and when is it better to use spoken words?

C. How does the conversational style of the words affect learning?

D. How do characteristics of the voice affect learning with spoken words?

These issues are addressed in Chapters 5, 7, and 8.

DESIGN DILEMMA: RESOLVED

Ben and Reshmi are debating the best placement of text in the database lesson. Some alternatives raised were:

A. Ben is right. For visibility, he needs to use most of the screen real estate for the visual. The text directions should fall on the preceding screen.

B. Reshmi is right. Learning is more efficient when visuals and text are integrated. The text directions should be placed on the same screen as the visual.

C. Both ideas could be accommodated by placing text directions in a rollover box on the spreadsheet activated by the mouse.

D. Not sure which option is best.

We recommend Option B for most situations. Although rollovers can be a useful way to ensure contiguity between visuals and text, rollovers are transient, with the information disappearing when the cursor is moved. In the case of text that will be referred to over time, such as directions for an exercise, a more permanent display that integrates text and graphic will impose less mental load on learners.

WHAT TO LOOK FOR IN e-LEARNING

☐ Screens that place printed text next to the portion of the graphic it describes

☐ Feedback that appears on the same screen as the question and responses

☐ Directions that appear on the same screen in which the steps are to be applied

☐ Linked information does not obscure related information on the primary screen

☐ Text placed next to or within graphics, rather than below them

☐ Legend callouts are embedded within the graphic, rather than separated from it

☐ Narrated graphics in which corresponding words and graphics are presented at the same time

ON e-LEARNING AND THE SCIENCE OF INSTRUCTION CD

Our database counter-example includes a number of violations of contiguity. For example, on Screen 6, text directions for an exercise require viewing a spreadsheet.

However, the learner must click on a button to view the spreadsheet. While viewing the spreadsheet, the text directions are not visible. A similar break in contiguity is seen on Screen 17, in which the text describes a table that can only be viewed separately from the text. On Screen 20, the learner can respond to a multiple-select practice exercise. The correct answers appear on the next screen, requiring the learners to page back to compare the correct answers with their responses. These contiguity problems are corrected in the example lesson.

COMING NEXT

In this chapter, we have seen the importance of (a) the on-screen layout of printed text and graphics and (b) the coordination of corresponding narration and graphics. Next we will consider the benefits of presenting words in audio narration rather than in on-screen text. We know that audio adds considerably to file sizes and requires the use of sound cards and sometimes headsets. Does the use of audio add anything to learning? In the next chapter we examine the modality principle, which addresses this issue.

Suggested Readings

Ayres, P., & Sweller, J. (2005). The split-attention principle in multimedia learning. In R.E. Mayer (Ed.), *Cambridge handbook of multimedia learning* (pp. 135–146). New York: Cambridge University Press.

Mayer, R.E. (1989b). Systematic thinking fostered by illustrations in scientific text. *Journal of Educational Psychology, 81,* 240–246.

Mayer, R.E. (2005b). Principles for reducing extraneous processing in multimedia learning: Coherence, signaling, redundancy, spatial contiguity, and temporal contiguity. In R.E. Mayer (Ed.), *Cambridge handbook of multimedia learning* (pp. 183–200). New York: Cambridge University Press.

Mayer, R.E., & Anderson, R.B. (1991). Animations need narrations: An experimental test of a dual-coding hypothesis. *Journal of Educational Psychology, 83,* 484–490.

Mayer, R.E., & Anderson, R.B. (1992). The instructive animation: Helping students build connections between words and pictures in multimedia learning. *Journal of Educational Psychology, 84,* 444–452.

Mayer, R.E., Steinhoff, K., Bower, G.,& Mars, R. (1995). A generative theory of textbook design: Using annotated illustrations to foster meaningful learning of science text. *Educational Technology Research and Development, 43,* 31–43.

Moreno, R., & Mayer, R.E. (1999a). Cognitive principles of multimedia learning: The role of modality and contiguity. *Journal of Educational Psychology, 91,* 358–368.

CHAPTER OUTLINE

Modality Principle: Present Words as Speech, Rather Than On-Screen Text

Limitations to the Modality Principle

Psychological Reasons for the Modality Principle

Evidence for Using Spoken Rather Than Printed Text
Recent Reviews of Research on the Modality Effect

When the Modality Principle Applies

What We Don't Know About Modality

5

Applying the Modality Principle

PRESENT WORDS AS AUDIO NARRATION, RATHER
THAN ON-SCREEN TEXT

WHAT'S NEW IN THIS CHAPTER?

THE MODALITY PRINCIPLE has the most research support of any of the principles described in this book. Technical constraints on the use of audio in e-learning may lead consumers or designers of e-learning to rely on text to present content and describe visuals. However, when it's feasible to use audio, there is considerable evidence that presenting words in audio, rather than on-screen text, results in significant learning gains. In this chapter, we summarize the empirical evidence for learning gains that result from using audio rather than on-screen text to describe graphics. To moderate this guideline, we also describe a number of situations in which memory limitations require the use of text rather than audio. The psychological advantage of using audio results from the incoming information being split across two separate cognitive channels—words in the auditory channel and pictures in the visual channel—rather than concentrating both words and pictures in the visual channel. What is new in this chapter is an update to the evidence reported in the previous edition, including recent reviews of research on the modality principle. Overall, there continues to be strong and consistent support for using narration rather than on-screen text to describe graphics, especially when the material is complex or is presented at a fast pace.

DESIGN DILEMMA: YOU DECIDE

Now that they have agreed on the value of adding relevant visuals, as described in Chapter 3, the database design team has bogged down in discussions about how best to explain those graphics. Reshmi, the instructional designer, believes that providing words in text, as shown in Figure 5.1, allows learners to move at their own pace rather than have to wait for audio to play. "Besides that," she adds, "we must meet 508 compliance to accommodate learners with hearing loss. We must provide words in text!" Matt, the project leader, also prefers using text, since file sizes will be smaller and the team can save time and expense on audio recording. However, Michael, a graduate student in multimedia learning who is interning from the local university, disagrees strongly: "In our class last semester, the professor went on and on about the benefits of audio. You are losing a big learning opportunity if you rely on text alone!" Based on your experience or intuition, which option(s) do you select:

A. Reshmi and Matt are right. The advantages of explaining on-screen graphics with text outweigh the disadvantages.

B. Michael is right. Learning is much better when words are presented in audio narration.

C. Everyone can be accommodated by providing words in both text and audio.

D. Not sure which options are correct.

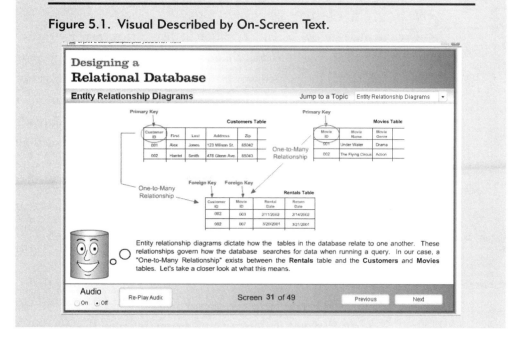

Figure 5.1. Visual Described by On-Screen Text.

MODALITY PRINCIPLE

MODALITY PRINCIPLE

Present Words as Speech, Rather Than On-Screen Text

Suppose you are presenting a verbal explanation along with an animation, video, or series of still frames. Does it matter whether the words in your multimedia presentation are represented as printed text (that is, as on-screen text) or as spoken text (that is, as narration)? What do cognitive theory and research evidence have to say about the modality of words in multimedia presentations? You'll get the answer to these questions in the next few sections of this chapter.

Based on cognitive theory and research evidence, we recommend that you put words in spoken form rather than printed form whenever the graphic (animation, video, or series of static frames) is the focus of the words and both are presented simultaneously. Thus, we recommend that you avoid e-learning courses that contain crucial multimedia presentations where all words are in printed rather than spoken form.

The rationale for our recommendation is that learners may experience an overload of their visual/pictorial channel when they must simultaneously process graphics and the printed words that refer to them. If their eyes must attend to the printed words, they cannot fully attend to the animation or graphics—especially when the words and pictures are presented concurrently and at a rapid pace. Since being able to attend to relevant words and pictures is a crucial first step in learning, e-learning courses should be designed to minimize the chances of overloading learners' visual/pictorial channel.

Figure 5.2 illustrates a multimedia course delivered on CD-ROM that effectively applies the modality principle. This section of the lesson is demonstrating how to use a new online telephone management system. As the

---

Figure 5.2. Audio Explains the Animated Demonstration of the Telephone System.

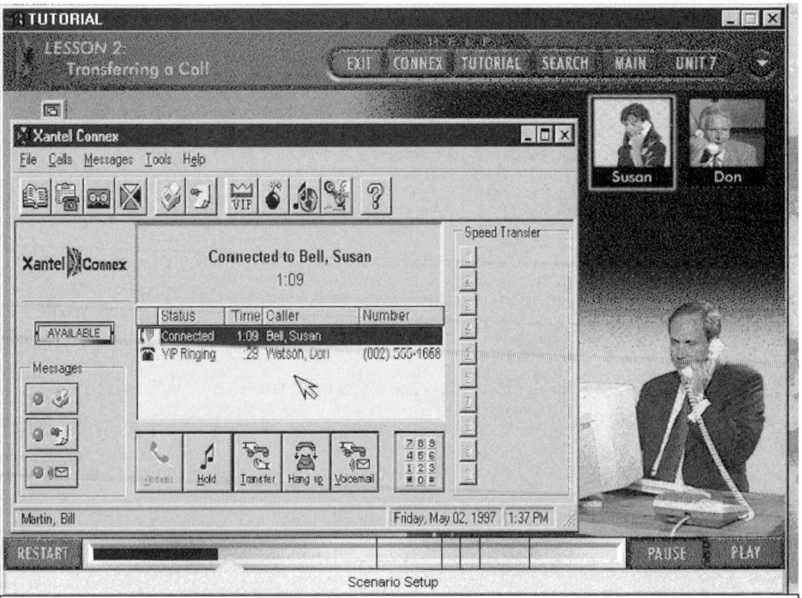

Audio: While Bill is talking to Don, Susan calls with a question. Bill knows that Susan needs to talk to Sally in the Art Department and decides to transfer her while he is talking to Don.

animation illustrates the steps on the computer screen, the audio describes the actions of the user. Another good example is seen in Figure 5.3 from our database sample lesson on the CD. Audio narration describes the visual illustration of database table relationships. In both of these examples, the visuals are relatively complex; therefore, using audio allows the learner to focus on the visual while listening to the explanation.

Figure 5.3. Visual Described by Audio Narration.

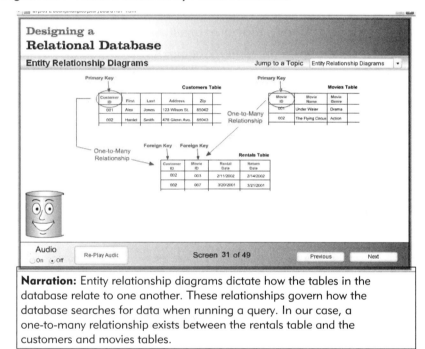

Narration: Entity relationship diagrams dictate how the tables in the database relate to one another. These relationships govern how the database searches for data when running a query. In our case, a one-to-many relationship exists between the rentals table and the customers and movies tables.

Limitations to the Modality Principle

When simultaneously presenting words and the graphics explained by the words, use spoken rather than printed text as a way of reducing the demands on visual processing. We recognize that in some cases it may not be practical to implement the modality principle, because the creation of sound may involve technical demands that the learning environment cannot meet (such as bandwidth, sound cards, headsets, and so on). Using sound also may add unreasonable expense or may make it more difficult to update rapidly changing information. We also recognize that the recommendation is limited to those situations in which the words and graphics are simultaneously presented, and thus does not apply when words are presented without any concurrent picture or other visual input.

Additionally, there are times when the words should remain available to the learner for memory support. For example, a mathematical formula may be part of an audio explanation of an animated demonstration, but because of its complexity, it should remain visible as on-screen text. Key words that identify the steps of a procedure may be presented by on-screen text and highlighted (thus used as an organizer) as each step is illustrated in the animation and discussed in the audio. Another common example involves the directions to a practice exercise. Thus, we see in Figure 5.4 (from an Excel virtual classroom session) that the instructor narration throughout most of the program is suspended when the learner comes to the practice screen. Instead, the directions to the practice remain in text in the box on the spreadsheet for reference as the learners complete the exercise.

Figure 5.4. Practice Directions Provided in On-Screen Text in Virtual Classroom Session.

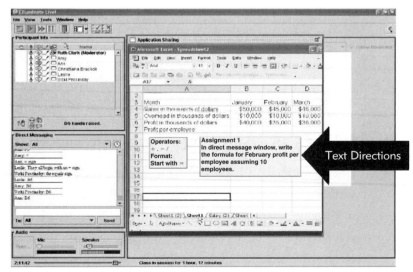

One advantage to virtual classrooms is the use of instructor speech to describe graphics projected on the whiteboard or through application sharing. In virtual classroom sessions, participants hear the instructor either through telephone conferencing or through their computers via voice-over-IP. However, virtual classroom facilitators should be careful to place text on their slides for instructional elements such as practice directions, memory support, and technical terms.

Psychological Reasons for the Modality Principle

If the purpose of the instructional program is to present information as efficiently as possible, then it does not matter whether you present graphics with printed text or graphics with spoken text. In both cases, identical pictures and words are presented, so it does not matter whether the words are presented as printed text or spoken text. This approach to multimedia design is suggested by the information acquisition view of learning—the idea that the instructor's job is to present information and the learner's job is to acquire information. Following this view, the rationale for using on-screen text is that it is generally easier to produce printed text rather than spoken text and that it accomplishes the same job—that is, it presents the same information.

The trouble with the information acquisition view is that it conflicts with much of the research evidence concerning how people learn. This book is based on the idea that the instructional professional's job is not only to present information, but also to present it in a way that is consistent with how people learn. Thus, we adopt the cognitive theory of multimedia learning, in which learning depends both on the information that is presented and on the cognitive processes used by the learner during learning.

Multimedia lessons that present words as on-screen text can conflict with the way the human mind works. According to the cognitive theory of learning—which we use as the basis for our recommendations—people have separate information processing channels for visual/pictorial processing and for auditory/verbal processing. When learners are given concurrent graphics and on-screen text, both must be initially processed in the visual/pictorial channel. The capacity of each channel is limited, so the graphics and their explanatory on-screen text must compete for the same limited visual attention. When the eyes are engaged with on-screen text, they cannot simultaneously be looking at the graphics; when the eyes are engaged with the graphics, they cannot be looking at the on-screen text. Thus, even though the information is presented, learners may not be able to adequately attend to all of it because their visual channels become overloaded.

In contrast, we can reduce this load on the visual channel by presenting the verbal explanation as speech. Thus, the verbal material enters the cognitive system through the ears and is processed in the auditory/verbal channel. At the same time, the graphics enter the cognitive system through the eyes and are processed in the visual/pictorial channel. In this way neither channel is overloaded, but both words and pictures are processed.

The case for presenting verbal explanations of graphics as speech is summarized in Figures 5.5 and 5.6. Figure 5.5 shows how graphics and on-screen text can overwhelm the visual channel, and Figure 5.6 shows how graphics and speech can distribute the processing between the visual and auditory channels. This analysis also explains why the case for presenting words as speech only applies to situations in which words and pictures are presented simultaneously. As you can see in Figure 5.5, there would be no overload in the visual channel if words were presented as on-screen text but there were no concurrent graphics that required the learner's simultaneous attention.

Figure 5.5. Overloading of Visual Channel with Presentation of Written Text and Graphics.

Adapted from Mayer, 2001a.

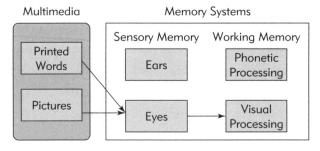

Figure 5.6. **Balancing Content Across Visual and Auditory Channels with Presentation of Narration and Graphics.**

Adapted from Mayer, 2001a.

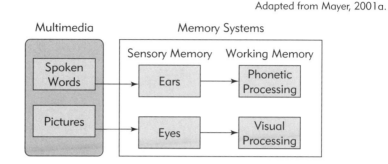

Evidence for Using Spoken Rather Than Printed Text

Do students learn more deeply from graphics with speech (for example, narrated animation) than from graphics with on-screen text (for example, animation with on-screen text blocks), as suggested by cognitive theory? Researchers have examined this question in several different ways, and the results consistently support our recommendation. Let's consider several recent studies that compare multimedia lessons containing animation with concurrent narration versus animation with concurrent on-screen text, in which the words in the narration and on-screen text are identical. Some of the multimedia lessons present an explanation of how lightning forms, how a car's braking system works, or how an electric motor works (Craig, Gholson, & Driscoll, 2002; Mayer, Dow, & Mayer, 2003; Mayer & Moreno, 1998; Moreno & Mayer, 1999a). Others are embedded in an interactive game intended to teach botany (Moreno, Mayer, Spires, & Lester, 2001; Moreno & Mayer, 2002b), and a final set are part of a virtual reality training episode concerning the operation of an aircraft fuel system (O'Neil, Mayer, Herl, Niemi, Olin, & Thurman, 2000).

For example, in one study (Moreno & Mayer, 1999a), students viewed an animation depicting the steps in lightning formation along with concurrent narration (Figure 5.7) or concurrent on-screen text captions (Figure 5.8). The words in the narration and the on-screen text were identical and they were presented at the same point in the animation. On a subsequent test in which students had to solve transfer problems about lightning, the animation-with-narration group

Figure 5.7. Screens from Lightning Lesson Explained with Audio Narration.

From Moreno and Mayer, 1999a.

"The charge results from the collision of the cloud's rising water droplets against heavier, falling pieces of ice."

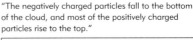

"The negatively charged particles fall to the bottom of the cloud, and most of the positively charged particles rise to the top."

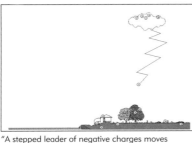

"A stepped leader of negative charges moves downward in a series of steps. It nears the ground."

"A positively charged leader travels up from such objects as trees and buildings."

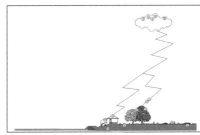

"The two leaders generally meet about 165-feet above the ground."

"Negatively charged particles then rush from the cloud to the ground along the path created by the leaders. It is not very bright."

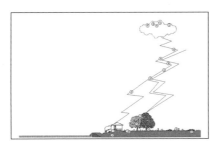

"As the leader stroke nears the ground, it induces an opposite charge, so positively charged particles from the ground rush upward along the same path."

"This upward motion of the current is the return stroke. It produces the bright light that people notice as a flash of lightning."

Figure 5.8. Screens from Lightning Lesson Explained with On-Screen Text.

From Moreno and Mayer, 1999a.

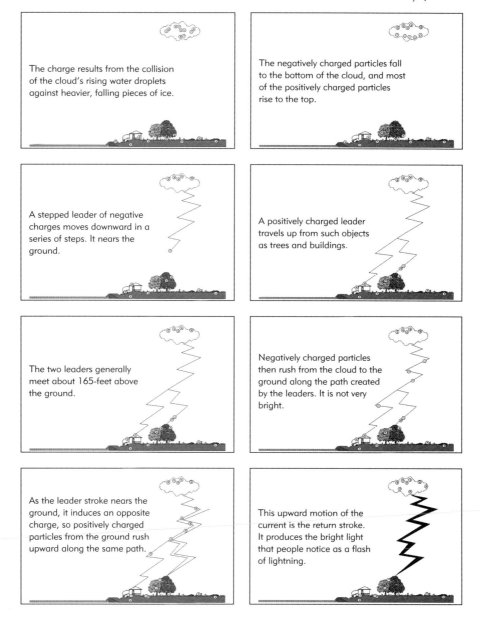

produced more than twice as many solutions to the problems as compared to the animation-with-text group, yielding an effect size greater than 1. The results are summarized in Figure 5.9. We refer to this finding as the modality effect— people learn more deeply from multimedia lessons when words explaining concurrent graphics are presented as speech rather than as on-screen text.

Figure 5.9. Better Learning When Visuals Are Explained with Audio Narration.

From Moreno and Mayer, 1999a.

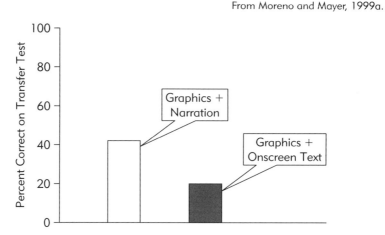

In a more interactive environment aimed at explaining how an electric motor works, students could click on various questions and for each see a short animated answer, along with narration or printed text delivered by a character named Dr. Phyz (Mayer, Dow, & Mayer, 2003). In the frame on the right side of the top screen in Figure 5.10, suppose the student clicks the question, "What happens when the motor is in the start position?" As a result, the students in the animation-with-text group see an animation along with on-screen text, as exemplified in the Response B frame on the bottom right side of Figure 5.10. In contrast, students in the animation-with-narration group see the same animation and hear the same words in spoken form as narration, as in the Response A frame on the bottom left side of Figure 5.10. Students who received narration generated 29 percent more solutions on a subsequent problem-solving transfer test, yielding an effect size of .85.

In a related study on the modality effect involving paper-based printed materials, Mousavi, Low, and Sweller (1995) presented worked-out examples

Figure 5.10. Responses to Questions in Audio Narration (A) or in On-Screen Text (B).
From Mayer, Dow, and Mayer, 2003.

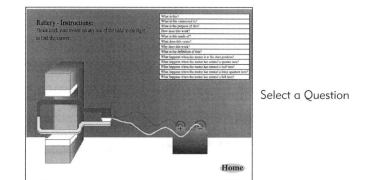

Select a Question

Response A   Response B

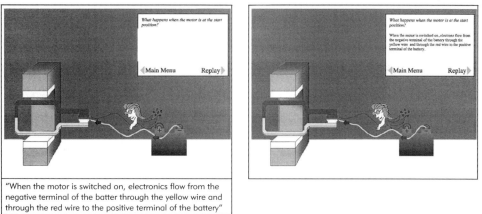

"When the motor is switched on, electronics flow from the negative terminal of the batter through the yellow wire and through the red wire to the positive terminal of the battery"

of geometry problems, described with a concurrent oral explanation or described with the same explanation printed on the page. When the words were spoken rather than printed, students performed much better on subsequent problem-solving tests involving geometry problems.

Recent Reviews of Research on the Modality Effect

In a recent review of research on modality, Mayer (2005c) identified twenty-one experimental comparisons of learning from printed text and graphics versus learning from narration and graphics, based on published research articles. The lessons included topics in mathematics, electrical engineering, environmental science, and aircraft maintenance, as well as explanations of how brakes work, how lightning storms develop, and how an electric motor works. In each of the twenty-one comparisons, there was a modality effect in which students who received narration and graphics performed better on solving transfer problems than did students who received on-screen text and graphics. The median effect size was .97, which is considered a large effect. Based on the growing evidence for the modality effect, we feel confident in recommending the use of spoken rather than printed words in multimedia messages containing graphics with related descriptive words.

In a somewhat more lenient review that included both published articles and unpublished sources (such as conference papers and theses) and a variety of learning measures, Ginns (2005) found forty-three experimental tests of the modality principle. Overall, there was strong evidence for the modality effect, yielding an average effect size of .72, which is considered moderate to large. Importantly, the positive effect of auditory modality was stronger for more complex material than for less complex material, and for computer-controlled pacing than for learner-controlled pacing. Apparently, in situations that are more likely to require heavy amounts of essential cognitive processing to comprehend the material—for example, lessons with complex material or fast pacing—it is particularly important to use instructional designs that minimize the need for extraneous processing.

When the Modality Principle Applies

Does the modality principle mean that you should never use printed text? The simple answer to this question is: Of course not. We do not intend for you to use our recommendations as unbending rules that must be rigidly applied in all situations. Instead, we encourage you to apply our principles in ways that are consistent with the way that the human mind works—that is, consistent with the cognitive theory of multimedia learning rather than the information delivery theory. As noted earlier, the modality principle applies in situations in which you present graphics and their verbal commentary at the same time, and particularly when the material is complex and presented at a rapid continuous pace. If the material is familiar to the learner or the learner has control over the pacing of the material, the modality principle becomes less important.

As we noted previously, in some cases words should remain available to the learner over time. When you present technical terms, list key steps in a procedure, or are giving directions to a practice exercise, it is important to present words in writing for reference support. When the learner is not a native speaker of the language of instruction or is extremely unfamiliar with the material, it may be appropriate to present printed text. Further, if you present only printed words on the screen (without any corresponding graphic) then the modality principle does not apply. Finally, in some situations people may learn better when you present both printed and spoken words. We describe these situations in the next chapter on the redundancy principle.

What We Don't Know About Modality

Overall, our goal in applying the modality principle is to reduce the cognitive load in the learner's visual/pictorial channel (through the eyes) by off-loading some of the cognitive processing onto the auditory/verbal channel (through the ears). Some unresolved issues concern:

A. When is it helpful to put printed words on the screen with a concurrent graphic?

B. Is it helpful to put concise summaries or labels for key components on the screen as printed words?

C. When it is not feasible to provide audio, how can we eliminate any negative effects of on-screen text?

D. Do the negative effects of on-screen text decline over the course of long-term training?

DESIGN DILEMMA: RESOLVED

The database design team was in a quandary about use of text and audio in their course. The options presented were:

A. Reshmi and Matt are right. There are many advantages to communicating words as on-screen text.

B. Michael is right. Learning is much better when words are presented in audio narration.

C. Everyone can be accommodated by providing words in both text and audio.

D. Not sure which options are correct.

We recommend that audio narration will promote better learning on screens that include important and detailed graphics, as shown in Figure 5.3. Therefore we select Option B. Although Option C might seem like a good compromise, as we will see in the next chapter, using both text and audio to explain a graphic can be problematic. Some elements in the database lesson should be presented as text, especially directions and feedback for practice exercises.

WHAT TO LOOK FOR IN e-LEARNING

☐ Use of audio narration to explain on-screen graphics or animations

☐ Use of text for information that learners will need as reference, such as technical terms or directions to practice exercises

---

ON e-LEARNING AND THE SCIENCE OF INSTRUCTION CD

You will note that in our example lesson, the default option for screens with graphics is audio. However, practice scenarios, directions, and feedback remain as on-screen text to allow learners to review these at their own pace. In our counter-example, we have violated the modality principle by using on-screen text to explain important visuals, such as the example shown in Figure 5.1.

COMING NEXT

In this chapter we have seen that learning is improved when graphics or animations presented in e-lessons are explained using audio narration rather than on-screen text. What would be the impact of including both text and narration? In other words, would learning be improved if narration were used to read on-screen text? We will address this issue in the next chapter.

Suggested Readings

Ginns, P. (2005). Meta-analysis of the modality effect. *Learning and Instruction, 15,* 313–331.

Low, R., & Sweller, J. (2005). The modality effect in multimedia learning. In R.E. Mayer (Ed.), *The Cambridge handbook of multimedia learning* (pp. 147–158). New York: Cambridge University Press.

Mayer, R.E. (2005c). Principles for managing essential processing in multimedia learning: Segmenting, pretraining, and modality principles. In R.E. Mayer (Ed.), *The Cambridge handbook of multimedia learning* (pp. 147–158). New York: Cambridge University Press.

Mayer, R.E., & Moreno, R. (1998). A split-attention effect in multimedia learning: Evidence for dual processing systems in working memory. *Journal of Educational Psychology, 90,* 312–320.

Moreno, R., & Mayer, R.E. (1999a). Cognitive principles of multimedia learning: The role of modality and contiguity. *Journal of Educational Psychology, 91,* 358–368.

Mousavi, S., Low, R., & Sweller, J. (1995). Reducing cognitive load by mixing auditory and visual presentation modes. *Journal of Educational Psychology, 87,* 319–334.

CHAPTER OUTLINE

Redundancy Principle 1: Do Not Add On-Screen Text to Narrated Graphics

Psychological Reasons for the Redundancy Principle

Evidence for Omitting Redundant On-Screen Text

Redundancy Principle 2: Consider Adding On-Screen Text to Narration in Special Situations

Psychological Reasons for Exceptions to the Redundancy Principle

Evidence for Including Redundant On-Screen Text

What We Don't Know About Redundancy

6

Applying the Redundancy Principle

EXPLAIN VISUALS WITH WORDS IN AUDIO
OR TEXT: NOT BOTH

SOME e-LEARNING DESCRIBES graphics using words in both on-screen text and audio narration in which the audio repeats the text. We call this technique *redundant* on-screen text because the printed text (on-screen text) is redundant with the spoken text (narration or audio). In this chapter, we summarize empirical evidence that people learn better from concurrent graphics and audio than from concurrent graphics, audio, and on-screen text. In this chapter we update research and theory that has appeared since the previous edition of this book, but the overall message remains the same: In general, do not add printed text to a narrated graphic. The psychological advantage of presenting words in audio alone is that you avoid overloading the visual channel of working memory. There are also certain situations that benefit from the use of redundant on-screen text. We describe those here as well.

DESIGN DILEMMA: YOU DECIDE

Now that the database e-learning design team has decided to add relevant visuals, as described in Chapter 3, their focus is on how best to explain those visuals. Reshmi, the instructional designer, recommends explaining visuals with a combination of text and audio: "I've reviewed the latest storyboards and I'm concerned. We know some people have visual learning styles and some are auditory learners so we need to accommodate both. Also 508 compliance requires us to accommodate learners who have visual and hearing deficits, so we have to provide words in a visual format with on-screen text and also in an auditory format with narration of that text. That way we cover all our bases!" Figure 6.1 shows one of Reshmi's revised storyboards. Charlene, the graphic artist who has been contracted to help with visuals, protests: "We've discussed this issue before and we decided to go with

Figure 6.1. Visual Described by On-Screen Text and Narration.
From *e-Learning and the Science of Instruction* CD.

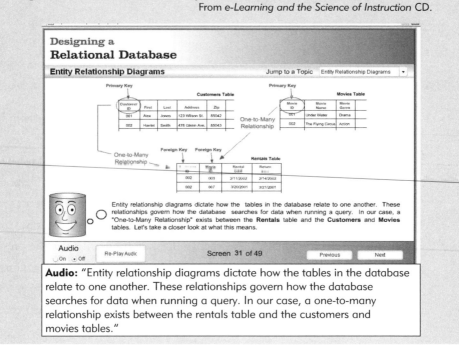

Audio: "Entity relationship diagrams dictate how the tables in the database relate to one another. These relationships govern how the database searches for data when running a query. In our case, a one-to-many relationship exists between the rentals table and the customers and movies tables."

audio narration to describe the visuals. I've designed large visuals and there is no screen real estate reserved for lengthy text passages!" Based on your experience or intuition, which options are best:

A. Communicate words in both on-screen text and audio narration to accommodate different learning styles and to meet 508 compliance.

B. Explain visuals with audio alone to promote best learning per the modality principle described in Chapter 5.

C. Let the learner select either audio or text as part of the course introduction.

D. Not sure which options are correct.

Do Not Add On-Screen Text to Narrated Graphics

If you are planning a multimedia program consisting of graphics (such as animation, video, or even static pictures or photos) explained by narration, should you also include on-screen text that duplicates the audio? We explore this question in this section.

Based on research and theory in cognitive psychology, we recommend that you avoid e-learning courses that contain redundant onscreen text presented at the same time as onscreen graphics and narration. Our reason is that learners might pay so much attention to the printed words that they pay less attention to the accompanying graphics. When their eyes are on the printed words, learners cannot be looking at the on-screen graphics. In addition, learners may try to compare and reconcile on-screen text and the narration, which requires cognitive processing extraneous to learning the content. For example, Figure 6.2 shows a screen from a lesson on ammunition safety that uses video to illustrate an explosion. Note that the on-screen text is the same as the narration, so we call it redundant on-screen text. In contrast, Figure 6.3 shows a screen from an animated demonstration of how to use a new computerized telephone system. The procedural steps are narrated with audio. Note the absence of on-screen text that duplicates the narration.

Figure 6.2. Graphics Explained Using Identical Text and Audio Narration.

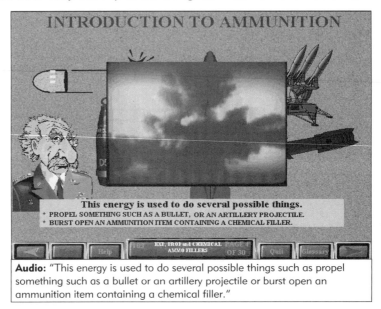

Audio: "This energy is used to do several possible things such as propel something such as a bullet or an artillery projectile or burst open an ammunition item containing a chemical filler."

Figure 6.3. Graphics Explained Using Audio Alone.

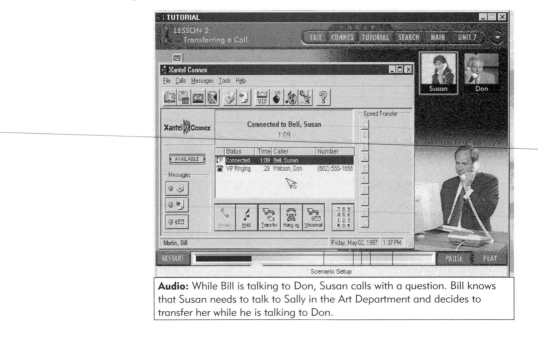

Audio: While Bill is talking to Don, Susan calls with a question. Bill knows that Susan needs to talk to Sally in the Art Department and decides to transfer her while he is talking to Don.

Psychological Reasons for the Redundancy Principle

There is a common belief that some people have visual learning styles, while others have auditory learning styles. Therefore, it seems that words should always be presented in both spoken and printed form so that learners can choose the presentation format that best matches their learning preference. We call this idea the *learning styles hypothesis* because it plays on the common sense argument that instruction should be flexible enough to support different learning styles. Accommodating different learning styles may seem appealing to e-learning designers who are fed up with the "one-size-fits-all" approach and to clients who intuitively believe there are visual and auditory learners.

The learning styles hypothesis is based on the information acquisition theory of multimedia learning, which holds that learning consists of receiving information. In our Design Dilemma section, the multimedia lesson illustrated in Figure 6.1 provides three delivery routes for information—by pictures (in the illustrations), by spoken words (in the narration), and by written words (in the on-screen text). In contrast, you could drop the third route and describe graphics with words in audio, but not with words both in audio and on-screen text. According to the information acquisition theory, three ways of delivering the same information is better than two, especially if one or two of the routes do not work well for some learners. Therefore, the information acquisition theory predicts that students will learn more deeply from multimedia presentations when redundant on-screen text is included rather than excluded.

The learning styles view—and the information acquisition theory upon which it is built—seems to make sense, but let's look a little deeper. What's wrong with the information acquisition theory? Our major criticism is that it makes unwarranted assumptions about how people learn. For example, it assumes that people learn by adding information to memory, as if the mind were an empty vessel that needs to be filled with incoming information. In contrast, the cognitive theory of multimedia learning is based on the assumptions that (a) all people have separate channels for processing verbal and pictorial material, (b) each channel is limited in the amount of processing that can take place at one time, and (c) learners actively attempt to build pictorial and verbal models from the presented material and build connections between them. These assumptions are consistent with theory and research in cognitive science and represent a consensus view of how people learn.

According to the cognitive theory of multimedia, adding redundant on-screen text to a multimedia presentation could overload the visual channel. For example, Figure 6.4 summarizes the cognitive activities that occur for a presentation containing animation, narration, and concurrent on-screen text. As you can see, the animation enters the learner's cognitive system through the eyes and is processed in the visual/pictorial channel, whereas the narration enters the learner's cognitive system through the ears and is processed in the auditory/verbal channel. However, the on-screen text also enters through the eyes and must be processed (at least initially) in the visual/pictorial channel. Thus, the limited cognitive resources in the visual channel must be shared in processing both the animation and the printed text. If the pace of presentation is fast and learners are unfamiliar with the material, learners may experience cognitive overload in the visual/pictorial channel. As a result, some important aspects of the animation may not be selected and organized into a mental representation.

Now consider what happens when only narration and animation are presented. The animation enters through the eyes and is processed in the visual/pictorial channel, whereas the narration enters through the ears and is processed in the auditory/verbal channel. The chances for overload are minimized, so the learner is more able to engage in appropriate cognitive processing. Thus, the cognitive theory of multimedia learning predicts that learners will learn more deeply from multimedia presentations in which redundant on-screen text is excluded rather than included.

Figure 6.4. Overloading of Visual Channel with Graphics Explained by Words in Audio and Written Text.

Adapted from Mayer, 2001a.

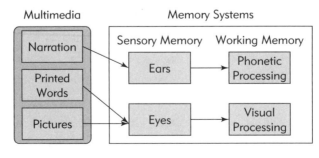

Mayer and Moreno (2003) and Mayer (2005b) describe another potential problem with adding redundant on-screen text. Learners may waste precious cognitive resources in trying to compare the printed words with the spoken words as they are presented. We refer to this wasted cognitive processing as *extraneous cognitive processing.* According to the cognitive theory of multimedia learning, learners have limited cognitive capacity so, if they use their cognitive capacity to reconcile printed and spoken text, they can't use it to make sense of the presentation.

Evidence for Omitting Redundant On-Screen Text

Several researchers have put these two competing predictions to a test. In a recent set of studies (Craig, Gholson, & Driscoll, 2002; Mayer, Heiser, & Lonn, 2001; Moreno & Mayer, 2002a), some students (non-redundant group) viewed an animation and listened to a concurrent narration explaining the formation of lightning. Other students (redundant group) received the same multimedia presentation, but with concurrent, redundant on-screen text. In this series of four comparisons, students in the non-redundant group produced more solutions (ranging between 43 to 69 percent more) on a problem-solving transfer test than did students in the redundant group. The median effect size was greater than 1, which is considered to be large. Figure 6.5 shows the results from one of these studies.

Figure 6.5. Better Learning When Visuals Are Explained by Audio Alone.
From Moreno and Mayer, 1999a.

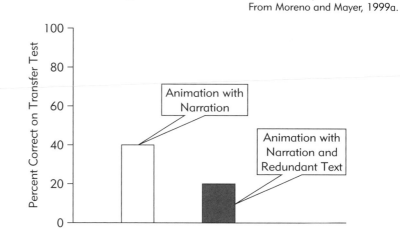

Kalyuga, Chandler, and Sweller (1999, 2000) provide complementary evidence. One group (non-redundant) received training in soldering (that is, techniques for joining metals) through the use of static diagrams presented on a computer screen along with accompanying speech, whereas another group (redundant group) received the same training along with on-screen printed text duplicating the same words as the audio. On a problem-solving transfer test involving troubleshooting, the non-redundant group outperformed the redundant group—producing an effect size of .8 in one study and greater than 1 in another. More recently, Kalyuga, Chandler, and Sweller (2004) found similar results in three additional experiments involving technical trainees learning how to set controls on power machinery for cutting. In this case, simply presenting the text after presenting the narration resulted in better test performance than presenting them at the same time, yielding a median effect size of .8.

Finally, Moreno and Mayer (2002b) also found a redundancy effect within the context of an educational computer game, both when played on a desktop computer and within a virtual reality version using a head-mounted display. An on-screen agent explained the mechanics of plant growth using speech or speech and on-screen text while an animation was presented. Although students who received animation and narration performed better on subsequent tests than did students who learned with animation, narration, and on-screen text, the effect sizes were much smaller—approximately .2, which is considered a small effect. Perhaps students were better able to ignore some of the on-screen text in the game environment, although it was still a mild detriment to learning.

Mayer (2005b) refers to this result as a *redundancy effect* to reflect the idea that adding redundant on-screen text to narrated graphics tends to hurt learning. Overall, these kinds of results support the conclusion that, in some cases, less is more. Because of the limited capacity of the human information processing system, it can be better to present less material (graphics with corresponding narration) than more material (graphics with corresponding narration and printed text).

REDUNDANCY PRINCIPLE 2

Consider Adding On-Screen Text to Narration in Special Situations

Are there any situations in which e-learning courses would be improved by adding redundant on-screen text? Although we recommend omitting redundant on-screen text in most e-learning programs, consider using it in special situations that will not overload the learner's visual information processing system, such as when:

- There is no pictorial presentation (for example, when the screen contains no animation, video, photos, graphics, illustrations, and so on);

- There is ample opportunity to process the pictorial presentation (for example, when the on-screen text and corresponding graphics are presented sequentially or when the pace of presentation is sufficiently slow); or

- The learner must exert much greater cognitive effort to comprehend spoken text than printed text (for example, for learners who are not native speakers or who have specific learning disabilities, or when the verbal material is long and complex or contains unfamiliar key words).

REDUNDANT ON-SCREEN TEXT: WHEN TO LOSE IT AND WHEN TO USE IT

Avoid narrating on-screen text when:

Words and pictures are presented simultaneously at a fast pace

Consider narrating on-screen text when:

There are no pictures

The learner has ample time to process the pictures and words

The learner is likely to have difficulty processing spoken words

Figure 6.6. When No Visuals Are Present, Content Can Be Presented with Text and Redundant Narration.

From *e-Learning and the Science of Instruction* CD.

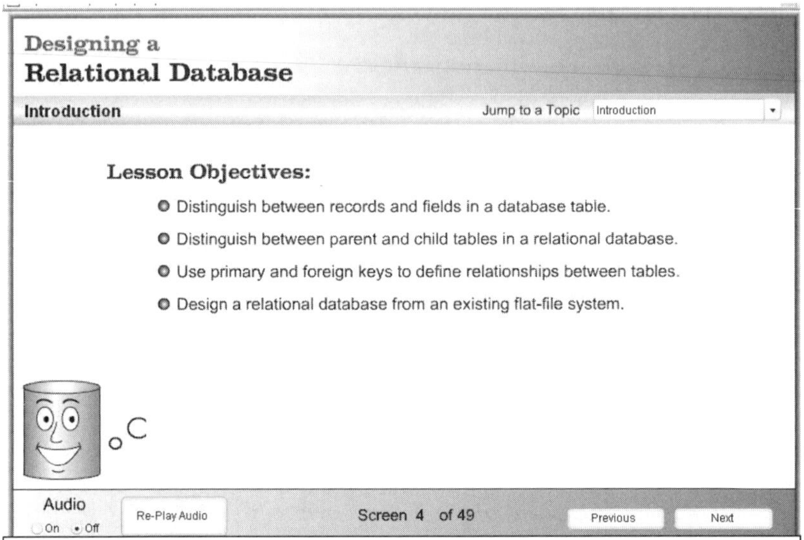

Audio: At the end of this lesson you will be able to distinguish between records and fields in a database table, and between parent and child tables in a relational database. You will be able to use primary and foreign keys to define relationships between tables and to design a relational database from an existing flat-file system.

For example, Figure 6.6 is an introductory screen that presents the learning objectives of a multimedia lesson. Since there are no graphic illustrations, narration of the objectives presented in text on the screen should not depress learning. As described in Chapter 5, situations in which learners need to refer to information over time (such as directions to exercises) are best presented as text alone.

Psychological Reasons for Exceptions to the Redundancy Principle

The major exceptions to the redundancy principle occur in special situations in which on-screen text either does not add to the learner's processing demands or actually diminishes them. For example, consider the situation in which an instructional presentation consists solely of spoken words with no graphics—such as in a pod-cast. In this case, information enters through the ears so the verbal channel is active, but the visual channel is not active. Now, consider what happens in the learner's cognitive system when you use redundant on-screen text, for example, presented as text on a computer screen using the same words as the narration. In this case, spoken words enter through the ears and text words enter through the eyes, so neither channel is overloaded. Using dual modes of presentation can be helpful when the spoken material may be hard to process, or if seeing and hearing the words provides a benefit (such as learning a technical subject or a foreign language).

Similarly, consider a situation in which the lesson is presented at a slow pace or is under learner control. For example, presenting concurrent narration, on-screen text, and static graphics under learner control is less likely to cause cognitive overload in the visual channel, because the learner has time to process all of the incoming material. Similarly, printing unfamiliar technical terms on the screen may actually reduce cognitive processing because the learner does not need to grapple with decoding the spoken words.

Evidence for Including Redundant On-Screen Text

In the previous section, we summarized research in which people learned less about the process of lightning formation when the presentation included animation with redundant on-screen text than when the presentation included animation with concurrent narration alone. In this section, we explore special situations in which adding redundant on-screen text has been shown to help learning.

Research shows that in certain situations learners generate approximately three times as many correct answers on a problem-solving transfer test from presentations containing concurrent spoken and printed text than from spoken text alone (Moreno & Mayer, 2002a). In these studies, there were no graphics on the screen and thus the visual system was not overloaded. In another study, the animation presentation was broken into a series of sixteen short animation clips, with each clip preceded by a corresponding sentence. Thus, the learner sees and hears a sentence, then views ten seconds of animation corresponding to it, then sees and hears the next sentence, then views ten seconds of corresponding animation, and so on. In this way, the learner can view the animation without any interference from printed text. In this situation, learners who received redundant on-screen text and spoken text generated an average of 79 percent more correct answers on a problem-solving test than learners who received only spoken text (Moreno & Mayer, 2002a). Of course, this choppy sequential presentation is somewhat unusual and therefore is not likely to be applicable to most e-learning situations.

Based on the research and theory presented in this chapter, we offer the redundancy principle: When the instructional message includes graphics, explain the graphics with narration alone. Do not add redundant on-screen text. When there is limited graphic information on the screen or when the words are technical or the audience has language difficulties, consider the use of redundant on-screen text. As described in Chapter 5, use on-screen text without narration to present information that needs to be referenced over time, such as directions to complete a practice exercise.

Overall, the theme of this chapter is that e-learning should not add redundant on-screen text (that is, the same words that are being spoken) when attending to the text could distract the learner from viewing important graphics that are being presented at the same time. However, when spoken text is presented alone (that is, without concurrent graphics), you can help the learner process the words by providing concurrent printed text.

What We Don't Know About Redundancy

Research is needed to determine the situations in which the redundancy principle does not hold—including the kinds of learners, materials, and presentation methods that do not create a redundancy effect:

- *Kinds of learners*—Does adding redundant on-screen text to a narrated graphic not hurt (or even help) non-native speakers or learners with very low prior knowledge?

- *Kinds of material*—Does adding redundant on-screen text to a narrated graphic not hurt (or even help) when the on-screen material is technical terms, equations, or brief headings?

- *Kinds of presentation methods*—Does adding redundant on-screen text to a narrated graphic not hurt (or even help) when the presentation pace is slow, when the presentation pace is under learner control, when the narration precedes the on-screen text, or when the learner is given pre-training in names and characteristics of the key concepts?

It would be particularly helpful to pinpoint situations in which some form of redundancy helps learning.

DESIGN DILEMMA: RESOLVED

The database team members disagreed about how best to describe the visuals they decided to add. To accommodate the modality principle described in Chapter 5, they decided to use audio. But some team members wanted to also add on-screen text to accommodate different learning styles and to meet 508 compliance. The options were:

A. Communicate words in both on-screen text and audio narration to accommodate different learning styles and to give multiple learning opportunities.

B. Explain visuals with audio alone to promote best learning, per the modality principle described in Chapter 5.

C. Let the learner select either audio or text as part of the course introduction.

D. Not sure which options are correct.

It's a common misconception that learning is better from adding redundant on-screen text to audio that describes visuals. However, we have reviewed evidence in this chapter that learning is generally improved by using audio alone to describe graphics. Therefore we select Option B. However, what about 508 compliance? We recommend that your e-learning program default to audio describing visuals. However, to accommodate learners who for various reasons may not be able to access audio, offer an "audio off" button. When the "audio off" button is activated, narration is replaced by on-screen text as shown in Figure 6.7. In this arrangement, the learners receive words in audio narration as the default but can also access words via text when audio is turned off. However, they do not have the option for both audio narration and text.

Figure 6.7. Visual Explained by On-Screen Text When Audio Off Is Selected.

From e-*Learning and the Science of Instruction* CD.

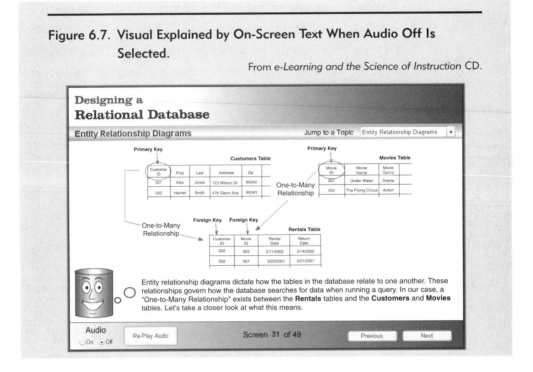

WHAT TO LOOK FOR IN e-LEARNING

☐ Graphics are described by words presented in the form of audio narration, not by concurrent narration and redundant text.

☐ On-screen text can be narrated when the screens do not include graphics.

☐ When language is challenging, words are presented as text.

ON e-*LEARNING AND THE SCIENCE OF INSTRUCTION* CD

In our example lesson, you will see that the default version uses audio to describe on-screen visuals. However, when you select audio off, on-screen text replaces the narration. You are unable to access simultaneous on-screen text and audio. In the counter-example, many screens with graphics violate the redundancy principle by describing on-screen graphics with both on-screen text and audio narration, such as the example shown in Figure 6.1.

COMING NEXT

In the previous four chapters we have described a number of principles for best use of text, audio, and graphics in e-learning. We have seen that the appropriate use of these media elements can improve learning. However, there are circumstances when too much of these elements can actually depress learning. In the next chapter we review how to apply the *coherence* principle to your e-learning decisions.

Suggested Readings

Mayer, R.E. (2005c). Principles for reducing extraneous processing in multimedia learning: Coherence, signaling, redundancy, spatial contiguity, and temporal contiguity. In R.E. Mayer (Ed.), *The Cambridge handbook of multimedia learning* (pp. 183–200). New York: Cambridge University Press.

Mayer, R.E., Heiser, J., & Lonn, S. (2001). Cognitive constraints on multimedia learning: When presenting more material results in less understanding. *Journal of Educational Psychology, 93,* 187–198.

Moreno, R., & Mayer, R.E. (2002a). Verbal redundancy in multimedia learning: When reading helps listening. *Journal of Educational Psychology, 94,* 151–163.

CHAPTER OUTLINE

Coherence Principle 1: Avoid e-Lessons with Extraneous Audio

Psychological Reasons to Avoid Extraneous Audio in e-Learning

Evidence for Omitting Extraneous Audio

Coherence Principle 2: Avoid e-Lessons with Extraneous Graphics

Psychological Reasons to Avoid Extraneous Graphics in e-Learning

Evidence for Omitting Extraneous Graphics

Coherence Principle 3: Avoid e-Lessons with Extraneous Words

Psychological Reasons to Avoid Extraneous Words in e-Learning

Evidence for Omitting Extraneous Words Added for Interest

Evidence for Omitting Extraneous Words Added to Expand on Key Ideas

Evidence for Omitting Extraneous Words Added for Technical Depth

What We Don't Know About Coherence

7

Applying the Coherence Principle

ADDING INTERESTING MATERIAL CAN HURT LEARNING

PERHAPS OUR SINGLE MOST IMPORTANT recommendation is to keep the lesson uncluttered. In short, according to the coherence principle, you should avoid adding any material that does not support the instructional goal. The *coherence principle* is important because it is commonly violated, is straightforward to apply, and can have a strong impact on learning. Mayer and Moreno (2003) use the term *weeding* to refer to the need to uproot any words, graphics, or sounds that are not central to the instructional goal of the lesson. In spite of our calls for conciseness, you might be tempted to embellish lessons in an effort to motivate learners. For example, in order to counter high e-learning dropout rates, some designers attempt to spice up their

133

materials by adding entertaining or motivational elements such as dramatic stories, pictures, or background music. Our advice is: Don't do it! In this chapter we summarize the empirical evidence for excluding rather than including extraneous information in the form of background sound, added text, and added graphics. What is new in this chapter is some updating of the growing research base, but the main conclusion remains the same: Adding interesting but unnecessary material to e-learning can harm the learning process.

DESIGN DILEMMA: YOU DECIDE

"This database lesson is pretty boring. We are dealing with the MTV and video game generation here. They are used to high-intensity multimedia. But don't worry! I've added some really important information that everyone should know about databases and I've energized the information with some visual effects. Take a look at this example. On this screen (Figure 7.1), I'm giving them some key information about privacy violations resulting from databases."

Figure 7.1. A Screen to Add Interest to the Database Lesson.
From *e-Learning and the Science of Instruction* CD.

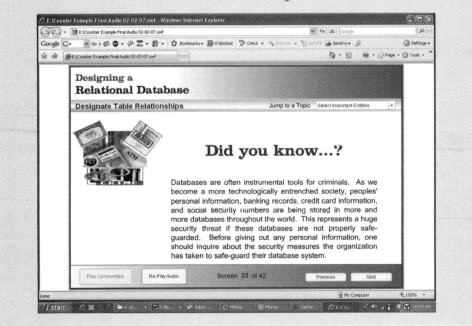

Ben, the team programmer, has challenged the idea of a simple e-learning program—specially for younger learners. Reshmi, the instructional designer, agrees: "Ben is right. We know that dropout rates from asynchronous e-learning are high. By adding some interesting information about databases throughout the lesson, we can hold everyone's interest. In fact, I learned in an accelerated learning class that soft background classical music helps people retain information better. Could we add a soft instrumental to the narration?"

Matt, the project manager, interjects: "How much will the extra visual and audio effects add to the budget and delay our timeline?" Shouldn't we just stick to the basics?" Based on your intuition or experience, which of the following options do you choose:

A. Ben is correct. Adding some interesting words and visuals about databases will improve interest and learning, especially among younger learners.

B. Reshmi is correct. Learning is better in the presence of soft music, especially classical music.

C. Matt is right. Less is more for most learners.

D. Not sure who is correct.

The added sounds, graphics, and words, such as those in Figure 7.1, are examples of *seductive details,* interesting but irrelevant material added to a multimedia presentation in an effort to spice it up (Garner, Gillingham, & White, 1989). The following three sections explore the merits of adding extra sounds, pictures, and words that are intended to make multimedia environments more interesting to the learner.

COHERENCE PRINCIPLE 1

Avoid e-Lessons with Extraneous Audio

First, consider the addition of background music and sounds to a narrated animation. You can see an example of this type of treatment in our database counter-example lesson on the CD. Is there any theoretical rationale for adding or not adding music and sounds, and is there any research evidence? These questions are addressed in this section.

Based on the psychology of learning and the research evidence summarized in the following paragraphs, we recommend that you avoid e-learning courseware that includes extraneous sounds in the form of background music or environmental sounds. Like all recommendations in this book, this one is limited. Recommendations should be applied based on an understanding of how people learn from words and pictures rather than a blind application of rules in all situations.

Background music and sounds may overload working memory, so they are most dangerous in situations in which the learner may experience heavy cognitive load, for example, when the material is unfamiliar, when the material is presented at a rapid rate, or when the rate of presentation is not under learner control. More research is needed to determine whether there are some situations in which the advantages of extraneous sounds outweigh the disadvantages. At this point, our recommendation is to avoid adding extraneous sounds, especially in situations in which the learner is likely to experience heavy cognitive processing demands.

For example, Figure 7.2 shows a screen from a military multimedia lesson on ammunition. As the lesson illustrates the different types of ammunition

Figure 7.2. Sounds of Explosion and Bullets Added to Narration of On-Screen Text.

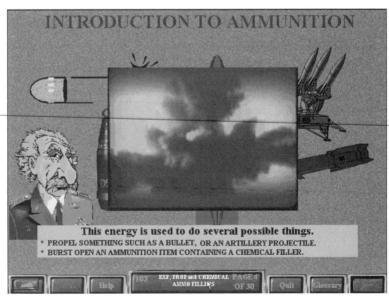

that workers may encounter, background sounds such as bullets flying, bombs exploding, and tanks firing are included. These sounds are extraneous to the points being presented and are likely to prove distracting. Figure 7.3 shows a screen from the same program that invites the learners to select the type of background music they want to hear during the course introduction. Again, the addition of extra sounds in the form of music is likely to depress learning.

Figure 7.3. Learners Can Select Music During Course Introduction.

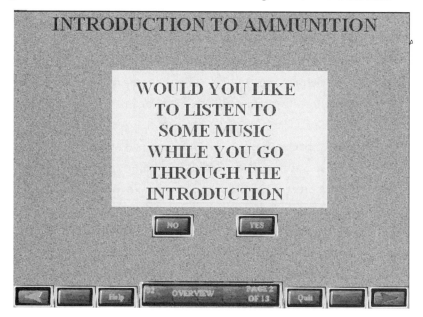

Psychological Reasons to Avoid Extraneous Audio in e-Learning

For some learners, e-learning can seem boring, and you might be concerned with reports that claim high dropout rates in e-learning (Svetcov, 2000). Therefore, developers may feel compelled to spice up their materials to arouse the learner's interest. Similarly, consumers may feel that a "jazzier" product is especially important for the new generation of learners raised on high-intensity multimedia such as MTV and video games. This is the premise underlying *arousal theory,* the idea that entertaining and interesting embedded effects cause learners to become more emotionally aroused and therefore they work harder to learn the material. In short, the premise is that emotion (for example, arousal caused by emotion-grabbing elements) affects cognition (for example, higher cognitive engagement). Arousal theory predicts that students will learn more from multimedia presentations that contain interesting sounds and music than from multimedia presentations without interesting sounds and music.

Arousal theory seems to make sense, so is there anything wrong with it? As early as 1913, Dewey argued that adding interesting adjuncts to an otherwise boring lesson will not promote deep learning: "When things have to be made interesting, it is because interest itself is wanting. Moreover, the phrase is a misnomer. The thing, the object, is no more interesting than it was before" (pp. 11–12). The theoretical rationale against adding music and sounds to multimedia presentations is based on the cognitive theory of multimedia learning, which assumes that working memory capacity is highly limited. Background sounds can overload and disrupt the cognitive system, so the narration and the extraneous sounds must compete for limited cognitive resources in the auditory channel. When learners pay attention to sounds and music, they are less able to pay attention to the narration describing the relevant steps in the explanation. The cognitive theory of multimedia learning predicts that students will learn more deeply from multimedia presentations that do not contain interesting but extraneous sounds and music than from multimedia presentations that do.

Evidence for Omitting Extraneous Audio

Can we point to any research that examines extraneous sounds in a multimedia presentation? Moreno and Mayer (2000a) began with a three-minute narrated animation explaining the process of lightning formation and a forty-five-second narrated animation explaining how hydraulic braking systems work. They created a music version of each by adding a musical loop to the background. The music was an unobtrusive instrumental piece, played at low volume that did not mask the narration nor make it less perceptually discernable. Students who received the narrated animation remembered more of the presented material and scored higher on solving transfer problems than students who received the same narrated animation along with background music. The differences were substantial—ranging from 20 to 67 percent better scores without music—and consistent for both the lightning and brakes presentations. Clearly, adding background music did not improve learning, and in fact, substantially hurt learning.

Moreno and Mayer (2000a) also created a background sound version of the lightning and brakes presentations by adding environmental sounds. In the lightning presentation, the environmental sounds included the sound of a gentle wind (presented when the animation depicted air moving from the ocean to the land), a clinking sound (when the animation depicted the top portion of cloud forming ice crystals), and a crackling sound (when the animation depicted charges traveling between ground and cloud). In the brakes presentation, the environmental sounds included mechanical noises (when the animation depicted the piston moving forward in the master cylinder) and grinding sounds (when the animation depicted the brake shoe pressing against the brake drum). On the lightning presentation, students who received the narrated animation without environmental sounds performed as well on retention and transfer as students who received the narrated animation with environmental sounds; on the brakes presentation, students who received narrated animation performed better on retention and transfer than students who received the narrated animation with environmental sounds.

For both lightning and brakes presentations, when students received both background music and environmental sounds, their retention and transfer performance was much worse than when students received neither—ranging between 61 to 149 percent better performance without the extraneous sounds and music. The average percentage gain from all the studies was 105 percent, with a very high effect size of 1.66. Figure 7.4 shows a result from one of these studies.

Related evidence points to the mental toll that can be levied by extraneous sounds. Kenz and Hugge (2002) compared learning from a seven-page text read in a quiet environment with learning from reading the same text in the presence of irrelevant conversational background speech. Recall of text ideas was significantly better among those reading in a silent environment.

Figure 7.4. Learning Is Better When Sounds and Music Are Excluded.
Adapted from Mayer, 2001a.

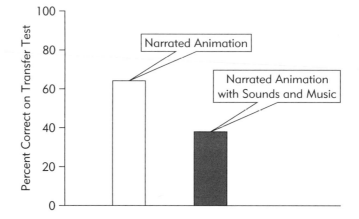

Ransdell and Gilroy (2001) compared the quality and efficiency of essay writing in the presence of music (vocal and instrumental) with writing in a quiet environment. They found that the quality of the essays was similar in all conditions, but that those working in the presence of music required significantly more time. To maintain quality, writers slow down their production in the presence of background music. The research team recommends that: "For all those college students who listen to music while they write on a computer, the advice from this study is clear. One's writing fluency is likely to be disrupted by both vocal and instrumental music" (p. 147).

COHERENCE PRINCIPLE 2

Avoid e-Lessons with Extraneous Graphics

The previous section shows that learning is depressed when we add extraneous sounds to a multimedia presentation, so perhaps we should try another way to spice up our lessons, namely interspersing interesting video clips. For example, in the database lesson we could insert some news video discussing recent database thefts from government agency computers. What is the learning impact of adding related but not directly relevant pictures and video clips to e-learning lessons?

Based on what we know about human learning and the evidence we summarize next, we offer a second version of the coherence principle: Avoid adding extraneous pictures. This recommendation does not mean that interesting graphics are harmful in all situations. Rather, they are harmful to the extent that they can interfere with the learner's attempts to make sense of the presented material. Extraneous graphics can be distracting and disruptive of the learning process. In reviews of science and mathematics books, most illustrations were found to be irrelevant to the main theme of the accompanying lesson (Mayer, 1993; Mayer, Sims, & Tajika, 1995). In short, when pictures are used only to decorate the page or screen, they are not likely to improve learning. As an example of irrelevant graphics, Figure 7.5 shows a screen from a lesson on ammunition safety that includes extensive video about the history of ammunition. Some of the information is quite interesting but not related to the tasks involved in handling ammunition. We recommend excluding this type of information.

Figure 7.5. Interesting But Unrelated Historical Information Should Be Excluded.

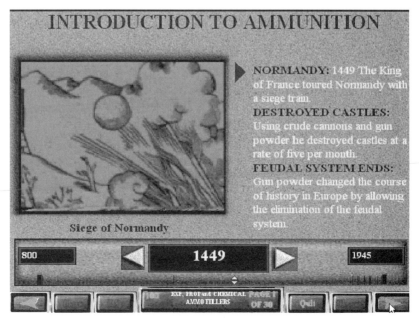

Psychological Reasons to Avoid Extraneous Graphics in e-Learning

Pictures—including color photos and action video clips—can make a multimedia experience more interesting. This assertion flows from arousal theory—the idea that students learn better when they are emotionally aroused. In this case, photos or video segments are intended to evoke emotional responses in learners, which in turn are intended to increase their level of cognitive engagement in the learning task. Thus, pictures and video are emotion-grabbing devices that make the learner more emotionally aroused, and therefore more actively involved in learning the presented material. Arousal theory predicts that adding interesting but extraneous pictures will promote better learning.

What's wrong with this justification? The problem—outlined in the previous section—is that interest cannot be added to an otherwise boring lesson like some kind of seasoning (Dewey, 1913). According to the cognitive theory of multimedia learning, the learner is actively seeking to make sense of the presented material. If the learner is successful in building a coherent mental representation of the presented material, the learner experiences enjoyment. However, adding extraneous pictures can interfere with the process of sense-making because learners have a limited cognitive capacity for processing incoming material. According to Harp and Mayer (1998), extraneous pictures (and their text captions) can interfere with learning in three ways:

- *Distraction*—by guiding the learner's limited attention away from the relevant material and toward the irrelevant material;

- *Disruption*—by preventing the learner from building appropriate links among pieces of relevant material because pieces of irrelevant material are in the way; and

- *Seduction*—by priming inappropriate existing knowledge (suggested by the added pictures), which is then used to organize the incoming content.

Thus, adding interesting but unnecessary material—including sounds, pictures, or words—to e-learning can harm the learning process by preventing the learner from processing the essential material. The cognitive theory of multimedia learning, therefore, predicts that students will learn more deeply from multimedia presentations that do not contain interesting but extraneous photos, illustrations, or video.

Evidence for Omitting Extraneous Graphics

What happens when entertaining but irrelevant video clips are placed within a narrated animation? Mayer, Heiser, and Lonn (2001) asked students to view a three-minute narrated animation on lightning formation, like the one described in the previous section. For some students, the narrated animation contained six ten-second video clips intended to make the presentation more entertaining, yielding a total presentation lasting four minutes. For example, one video clip showed trees bending against strong winds, lightning striking into the trees, an ambulance arriving along a path near the trees, and a victim being carried in a stretcher to the ambulance near a crowd of onlookers. At the same time, the narrator said: "Statistics show that more people are injured by lightning each year than by tornadoes and hurricanes combined." This video clip and corresponding narration were inserted right after the narrated animation describing a stepped leader of negative charges moving toward the ground. Thus, the narrated video was related to the general topic of lightning strikes but was not intended to help explain the cause-and-effect chain in lightning formation.

Students who received the lightning presentation without the inserted video clips performed better on solving transfer problems than students who received the lightning presentation with inserted video clips—producing about 30 percent more solutions, which translated into an effect size of .86. Mayer, Heiser, and Lonn (2001, p. 187) note that this result is an example of "when presenting more material results in less understanding."

Harp and Mayer (1997) found a similar pattern of results using a paper-based medium. Some students were asked to read a 550-word, six-paragraph passage containing six captioned illustrations. The passage described the cause-and-effect sequence leading to lightning formation, and the captioned illustrations depicted the main steps (with captions that repeated the key events from the passage). Each illustration was placed to the left of the paragraph it depicted. Other students read the same illustrated passage, along with six color pictures intended to spice up the presentation. Each picture was captioned and was placed to the right of a paragraph to which it was related. For example, next to the paragraph about warm moist air rising, there was a color photo of an airplane being hit by lightning accompanied by the following text: "Metal airplanes conduct lightning very well, but they sustain little damage because the bolt, meeting no resistance, passes right through." In another section of the lesson, a photo of a burned uniform from a football player stuck by lightening was included. Figure 7.6 shows an example of one of these visuals.

Figure 7.6. Interesting But Unrelated Graphics Added to Lightning Lesson.
Adapted from Harp and Mayer, 1998.

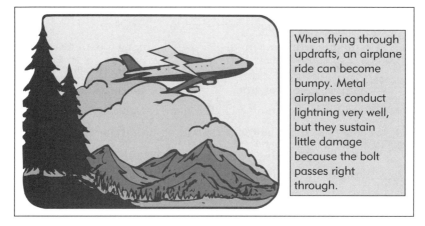

When flying through updrafts, an airplane ride can become bumpy. Metal airplanes conduct lightning very well, but they sustain little damage because the bolt passes right through.

Students who received the lightning passage without added color photos performed better on retention and transfer tests than students who received the lightning passage with color photos, generating about 52 percent more solutions on the transfer test, which translates into an effect size greater than 1. This is another example of how adding interesting but irrelevant graphics can result in less learning from a multimedia presentation. In each of four follow-up experiments, Harp and Mayer (1998) found that adding interesting but irrelevant captioned illustrations to the lightning lesson tended to hurt student performance on subsequent transfer tests, yielding effect sizes greater than 1.

For those who argue that these guidelines won't apply to the new generation raised on high-intensity media, we should mention that all of the above research was conducted with young adults. The subjects in these experiments were college-aged students ranging in age from eighteen to twenty-two years.

Therefore we cannot agree that members of the younger generation are less susceptive to mental overload as a result of intensive multimedia exposure.

More recently, Sanchez and Wiley (2006) found that adding irrelevant illustrations to scientific text hurt learning, particularly for students who have difficulty in processing information. (For example, if we read a short list of words to these low-ability learners, they would make mistakes reciting the words back to us.) Apparently, the low-ability students were more easily overloaded by the extraneous material. In a follow-up study involving eye tracking, low-ability students spent more time looking at irrelevant illustrations than did high-working-memory students, indicating that extraneous graphics can be particularly distracting for learners with low ability. Overall, it appears that good design principles—such as the coherence principle—are particularly important for the most at-risk learners.

An important implication of the coherence principle is that illustrations should not be embellished to make them look more realistic than they need to be. In some cases simple line drawings can be more effective than detailed color drawings or photos (Butcher, 2006; Parkhurst & Dwyer, 1983). For example, Butcher (2006) asked students to study a lesson on the human heart that contained text and simple illustrations or text and detailed illustrations. On subsequent tests of understanding of how the heart works, the students who had learned with text and simple drawings performed better than those who had learned with text and detailed drawings. During learning, students who studied text and simple illustrations made more integration inferences—indicating an attempt to understand how the heart works—than did students who studied text and complex illustrations. Perhaps studying a simplified visual actually promotes more mental processing by learners, who will fill in the visual gaps to understand the meaning of the diagram. This research sounds a cautionary note to those considering highly realistic learning or simulation interfaces.

COHERENCE PRINCIPLE 3

Avoid e-Lessons with Extraneous Words

So far we have tried and failed twice to improve a narrated animation by adding a few pieces of interesting material, such as sounds or pictures. In this, our third attempt, the database team considers adding some interesting text about the history of databases, as shown in Figure 7.7. What is the learning impact of adding extra words to a presentation? We answer this question in this section.

Figure 7.7. Text on History of Databases Added to Lesson.
From *e-Learning and the Science of Instruction* CD.

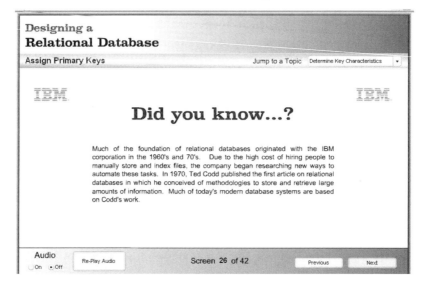

Our third version of the coherence principle recommends that you avoid adding extraneous words to lessons. When the goal is to promote learning of the target material—such as the workings of a cause-and-effect system—adding interesting but extraneous words may result in poorer learning. Cute little stories and interesting pieces of trivia may seem like harmless embellishments, but the research reviewed in this chapter shows that such devices may not produce the intended effects.

This guideline is helpful when limited screen real estate and bandwidth suggest shorter rather than longer narrations. Rather than fully embellished textual or narrative descriptions, stick to basic and concise descriptions of the content. It also helps implement the modality principle effectively. By keeping the narration on each screen concise, learners won't become as frustrated waiting for lengthy audio segments to play. Figure 7.8 shows a screen

Figure 7.8. Extensive Text Elaborates on Database Concepts.
From *e-Learning and the Science of Instruction* CD.

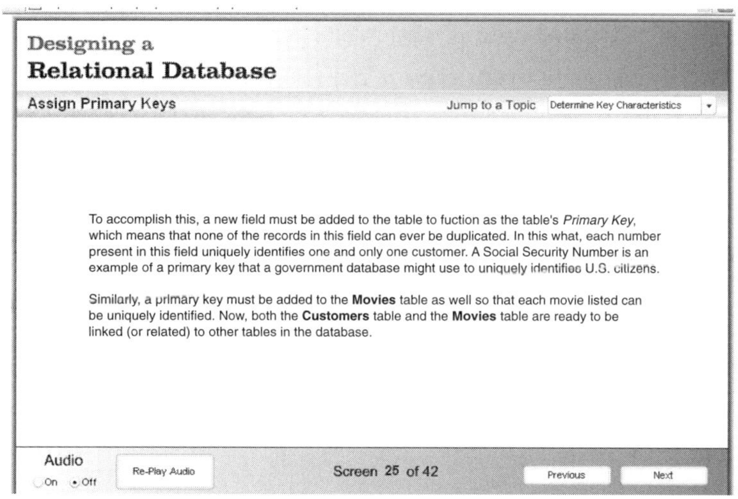

that includes a great deal of text added to provide detailed explanation of the concept of a primary key in the database lesson. Compare this treatment with the screen shown in Figure 7.9 that limits words to the essential points and uses a relevant visual to illustrate the concept.

Figure 7.9 . Lean Text and Relevant Visual Explains Database Concepts.
From *e-Learning and the Science of Instruction* CD.

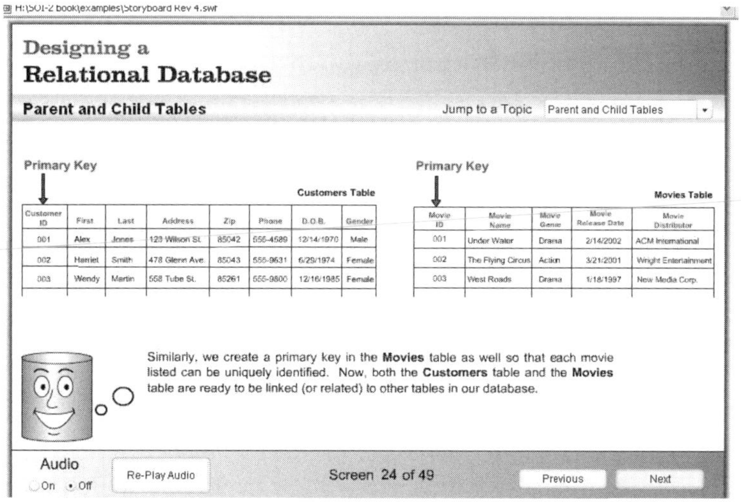

Psychological Reasons to Avoid Extraneous Words in e-Learning

For the same reasons that extraneous sounds and graphics can be distracting, adding extra words can interfere with the learning process. We address three types of extraneous wording. First, additional words may be added for interest. The extra words are related to the topic but are not relevant to the primary instructional goal. Second, extra words may be added to expand on the key ideas of the lesson. A third purpose for extra words is to add technical details that go beyond the key ideas of the lesson. Subject-matter experts like to incorporate considerable amounts of technical information that expands on the basics. We recommend against extraneous words added for interest, for elaboration, or for technical depth.

Evidence for Omitting Extraneous Words Added for Interest

Do students learn more deeply from a narrated animation when interesting verbal information is added to the narration? To address this question, Mayer, Heiser, and Lonn (2001) asked some students to view a three-minute narrated animation about lightning formation, like the one described in the previous section. Other students viewed the same three-minute presentation, but with six additional narration segments inserted at various points. The narration segments were short and fit within the three-minute presentation at points that otherwise were silent. For example, after saying that water vapor forms a cloud, the narrator added: "On a warm cloudy day, swimmers are sitting ducks for lightning." Similarly, after saying that electrical charges build in a cloud, the narrator added: "Golfers are vulnerable targets because they hold metal clubs, which are excellent conductors of electrical charge." Students who received the lightning presentation without additional narration segments performed better on transfer tests than students who received the lightning presentation with added narration segments—generating about 34 percent more solutions on the transfer test, which translated into an effect size of .66. Again, these results show that adding interesting but irrelevant material does not help learning, and in this case even hurts learning.

Evidence for Omitting Extraneous Words Added to Expand on Key Ideas

In a more extreme version of this research (Mayer, Bove, Bryman, Mars, & Tapangco, 1996), students read the standard lightning passage like the one described above (that is, with six hundred words and five captioned illustrations) or a summary consisting of five captioned illustrations. The captions described the main steps in the lightning formation, and the corresponding illustrations depicted the main steps. Approximately eighty words—taken from the standard passage—were used in the captioned illustrations. In three separate experiments, students who read the summary performed better on tests of retention and transfer than students who received the whole passage—in some cases, producing twice as many steps in the causal chain on the retention test and twice as many solutions on the transfer test. Figure 7.10 shows results from one of the experiments in this study. Mayer, Bove, Bryman, Mars, and Tapangco (1996, p. 64) conclude that this research helps show "when less is more."

Figure 7.10. Learning Is Better When Non-Essential Text Is Excluded.
Adapted from Mayer, 2001a.

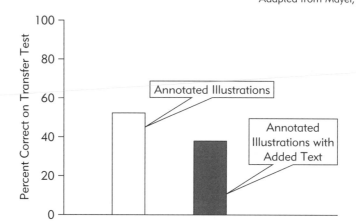

Evidence for Omitting Extraneous Words Added for Technical Depth

In a more recent experiment, Mayer and Jackson (2005) compared learning from a multimedia lesson on how ocean waves work in concise form with one that included additional technical information. The embellished version contained additional words and graphics about computational details, such as how to apply formulas related to ocean waves. The versions with additional quantitative details depressed performance on a subsequent problem-solving transfer test focusing on conceptual understanding—yielding effect sizes of .69 for a computer-based lesson and .97 for a paper-based lesson. Mayer and Jackson (2005, p. 13) conclude, "The added quantitative details may have distracted the learner from constructing a qualitative model of the process of ocean waves."

In short, when tempted to add more words, ask yourself whether additional verbiage is really needed to achieve the instructional objectives. If not, weed out extra words!

What We Don't Know About Coherence

As you can see in this chapter, there is strong and consistent support for the coherence effect. In the latest review, Mayer (in press) listed positive results for eliminating extraneous materials in thirteen out of fourteen experiments, with a median effect size near 1. In spite of this initial body of useful research evidence, there is still much we do not know about the coherence principle. Much of the research reported in this chapter deals with short lessons delivered in a controlled lab environment. Does the coherence effect also apply to longer-term instruction presented in an authentic learning environment, such as a training program? It would be useful to determine whether students can learn to ignore irrelevant material or whether lessons can be redesigned to highlight relevant material—a technique that can be called *signaling* (Mautone & Mayer, 2001; Mayer, 2005b; Mayer & Moreno, 2003). Signaling includes using headings, bold, italics, underlining, capital letters, larger font, color, white space, arrows, and related techniques to draw the learner's attention to specific parts of the display or page. Preliminary research (Harp & Mayer, 1997; Mautone & Mayer, 2001) shows that signaling can improve learning from multimedia lessons, but additional research is needed.

In addition, we do not know much about how individual characteristics of learners are related to the effectiveness of the coherence principle. Most of the research reported in this chapter is based on learners who are novices—that is, who lack prior knowledge in the domain of the lesson. Does the coherence effect also apply to high-knowledge learners? Research on the expertise reversal effect (Kalyuga, 2005) suggests that instructional design techniques that are effective for beginners may not be effective for more experienced learners. For example, Mayer and Jackson (2005) found that adding computational details hurt learning for beginners, but it is possible that students who had extensive physics backgrounds might have benefited from the added material. Similarly, research by Sanchez and Wiley (2006) provides preliminary evidence that adding irrelevant material can be particularly damaging for lower-ability learners. In short, research is needed to determine for whom the coherence principle applies.

Finally, you should not interpret the coherence principle to mean that lessons should be boring. There is ample evidence that students learn better when they are interested in the material (Hidi & Renninger, 2006). However, the challenge for instructional professionals is to stimulate interest without adding extraneous material that distracts from the cognitive objective of the lesson. Is there a way to add interesting words or graphics that serve to support the instructional goal while at the same time promote interest? Research is needed on how to interest learners and at the same time be sensitive to limits on their cognitive processing capacity.

DESIGN DILEMMA: RESOLVED

In an effort to accommodate younger learners used to high-intensity media, the database team considered adding interesting visuals, audio, and words to the basic lesson. The options we considered were:

A. Ben is correct. Adding some interesting words and visuals about databases will improve interest and learning, especially among younger learners.

B.   Reshmi is correct. Learning is better in the presence of soft music, especially classical music.

C.   Matt is right. Less is more for most learners.

D.   Not sure who is correct.

Based on the evidence presented in this chapter, we vote for Option C. The project manager will be happy because resources needed to create interesting visuals and narrations will not be needed, since evidence suggests their effects are deleterious to learning. Because the evidence for the coherence principle is based on performance of college-aged subjects, we reject the generational argument. We suggest that the team consider other ways to make the lesson engaging, such as using examples and practice exercises that are relevant to the work tasks that learners will face on the job and making the benefits of databases explicit in the process.

We recommend that you make a distinction between *emotional interest* and *cognitive interest*. Emotional interest occurs when a multimedia experience evokes an emotional response in a learner, such as reading a story about a life-threatening event or seeing a graphic video. There is little evidence that emotion-grabbing adjuncts—which have been called seductive details—promote deep learning (Garner, Gillingham, & White, 1989; Renninger, Hidi, & Krapp, 1992). In short, attempts to force excitement do not guarantee that students will work hard to understand the presentation. In contrast, cognitive interest occurs when a learner is able to mentally construct a model that makes sense. As a result of attaining understanding, the learner feels a sense of enjoyment. In summary, understanding leads to enjoyment. The achievement of cognitive interest depends on active reflection by the learner, rather than exposure to entertaining but irrelevant sights and sounds.

Overall, the research and theory summarized in this chapter show that designers should always consider the cognitive consequences of adding interesting sounds, pictures, or words. In particular, designers should consider whether the proposed additions could distract, disrupt, or seduce the learner's process of knowledge construction.

WHAT TO LOOK FOR IN e–LEARNING

☐ Lessons that do not contain extraneous sounds in the form of background music or sounds

☐ Lessons that do not use illustrations, photos, and video clips that may be interesting but are not essential to the knowledge and skills to be learned

☐ Lessons that do not contain interesting stories or details that are not essential to the instructional goal

☐ Lessons that present the core content with the minimal amount of words and graphics needed to help the learner understand the main points.

ON e-LEARNING AND THE SCIENCE OF INSTRUCTION CD

You will note periodic "Did You Know" screens in the database counter-example lesson. These screens give related information about databases, as well as include visual effects. Although related to databases, they are not relevant to the instructional goal. These screens do not appear in the example lesson. Likewise, soft background music and gratuitous sound effects added to the counter-example are omitted in the example lesson version.

COMING NEXT

We have seen in this chapter that sounds, graphics, and textual details added for interest can depress learning compared to more concise lessons. In the next chapter on the personalization principle, we ask about the learning effects of formal versus informal language in e-lessons and preview an area of emerging research on the use of virtual coaches.

Suggested Readings

Avoid Adding Extraneous Sounds

Moreno, R., & Mayer, R.E. (2000). A coherence effect in multimedia learning: The case for minimizing irrelevant sounds in the design of multimedia instructional messages. *Journal of Educational Psychology, 92,* 117–125.

Avoid Adding Extraneous Pictures

Mayer, R.E., Heiser, J., & Lonn, S. (2001). Cognitive constraints on multimedia learning: When presenting more material results in less understanding. *Journal of Educational Psychology, 93,* 187–198.

Avoid Adding Extraneous Words

Harp, S.F., & Mayer, R.E. (1998). How seductive details do their damage: A theory of cognitive interest in science learning. *Journal of Educational Psychology, 90,* 414–434.

Mayer, R.E., Heiser, J., & Lonn, S. (2001). Cognitive constraints on multimedia learning: When presenting more material results in less understanding. *Journal of Educational Psychology, 93,* 187–198.

Renninger, K.A., Hidi, S., & Krapp. A. (Eds.). (1992). *The role of interest in learning and development.* Mahwah, NJ: Lawrence Erlbaum.

CHAPTER OUTLINE

Personalization Principle 1: Use Conversational Rather Than Formal Style

Psychological Reasons for the Personalization Principle

Evidence for Using Conversational Style

Promote Personalization Through Voice Quality

Promote Personalization Through Polite Speech

Personalization Principle 2: Use Effective On-Screen Coaches to Promote Learning

What Are Pedagogical Agents?

Do Agents Improve Student Learning?

Do Agents Need to Look Real?

Do Agents Need to Sound Real?

Personalization Principle 3: Make the Author Visible to Promote Learning

What Is a Visible Author?

Psychological Reasons for Using a Visible Author

Evidence for the Visible Author

What We Don't Know About Personalization

8

Applying the Personalization Principle

USE CONVERSATIONAL STYLE AND VIRTUAL COACHES

WHAT'S NEW IN THIS CHAPTER?

SOME e-LEARNING LESSONS rely on a formal style of writing to present information. In this chapter we summarize the empirical evidence that supports using a conversational style of writing (including using first- and second-person language). Since the first edition of this book, the research base for using conversational style has grown, and new evidence has emerged concerning the role of the speaker's voice. The personalization principle is particularly important for the design of pedagogical agents—on-screen characters who help guide the learning processes during an instructional episode. While research on agents is somewhat new, we present evidence—including new evidence since the previous edition—for the learning gains achieved in the presence of an agent as well as for the most effective ways to design and use agents. A new topic we've added to this edition focuses on what we call "the visible author." We will define, give examples, and show evidence for the benefits of a visible author. The psychological advantage of conversational style, pedagogical agents, and visible authors is to induce the learner to engage with the computer as a social conversational partner.

DESIGN DILEMMA: YOU DECIDE

Reshmi has been working on the script for the database lesson. As a former classroom instructor, she is convinced that a more relaxed instructional environment leads to better learning. Therefore she is writing in a conversational rather than a formal style. She also has designed an on-screen coach to guide learners through the lesson. "The agent adds a personal touch that leads to a more friendly learning environment," she claims as she shows her draft storyboard (Figure 8.1).

Figure 8.1. An Informal Approach Uses an Agent and Conversational Language.

From *e-Learning and the Science of Instruction* CD.

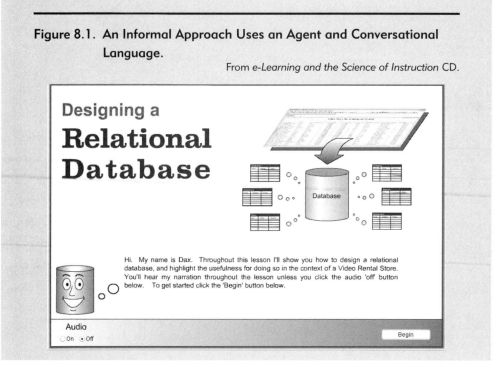

Matt, the project manager, has his doubts: "I don't think Legal is going to approve of this approach. And neither will the communications department. They are going to require us to use the official corporate communication standards. No contractions—no slang! That new VP is pretty traditional. He will think the character—what did you call it? An agent? Well, anyway, he will think it's a cartoon. I suggest for our first e-learning we follow the corporate tradition with something more like this" (Figure 8.2).

Figure 8.2. A Formal Approach Omits the Agent and Drops First- and Second-Person Language.

From *e-Learning and the Science of Instruction* CD.

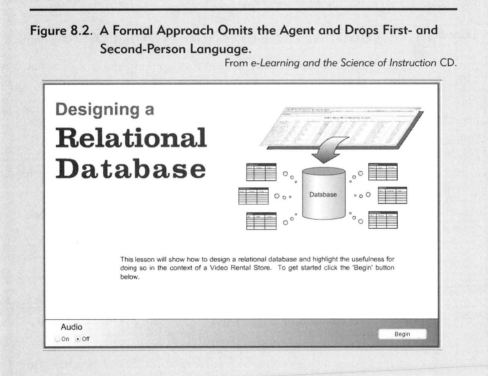

The database e-learning team is divided over the tone of the lesson, including the use of an agent. Based on your own experience or intuition, which of the following options would you select?

A.   Reshmi is correct. A more informal approach plus an agent will lead to better learning.

B.   Matt is correct. A more formal tone will fit the corporate image better, leading to a more credible instructional message.

C.   The tone of the lesson should be adjusted for the learners. Women will benefit from more informality and men will find a formal approach more credible.

D.   Not sure which option is correct.

PERSONALIZATION PRINCIPLE 1

Use Conversational Rather Than Formal Style

Does it help or hurt to change printed or spoken text from formal style to conversational style? Would the addition of a friendly on-screen coach distract from or promote learning? In this chapter, we explore research and theory that directly address these issues.

Consider the lesson introduction shown in Figure 8.1. As you can see, an on-screen agent uses an informal conversational style to introduce the lesson. This approach resembles human-to-human conversation. Of course, learners know that the character is not really in a conversation with them, but they may be more likely to act as if the character is a conversational partner. Now, compare this with the introduction shown in Figure 8.2. Here the overall feeling is quite impersonal. The agent is gone and the tone is more formal. Based on cognitive theory and research evidence, we recommend that you create or select e-learning courses that include some spoken or printed text that is conversational rather than formal.

Let's look at a couple of e-learning examples. The screen in Figure 8.3 summarizes the rules for calculating compound interest. Note that the on-screen text is quite formal. How could this concept be made more conversational? Figure 8.4 shows a revised version. Rather than passive voice, it uses second-person active voice and includes a comment about how this concept relates to the learner's job. It rephrases and segments the calculation procedure into four directive steps. The overall result is a more user-friendly tone.

Figure 8.3. Passive Voice Leads to a Formal Tone in the Lesson.

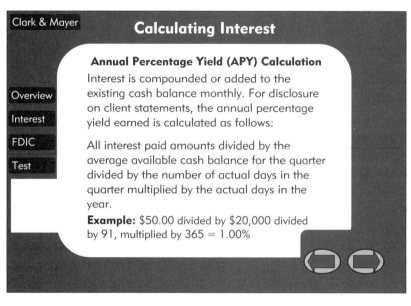

Figure 8.4. Use of Second Person and Informal Language Lead to a Conversational Tone in the Lesson.

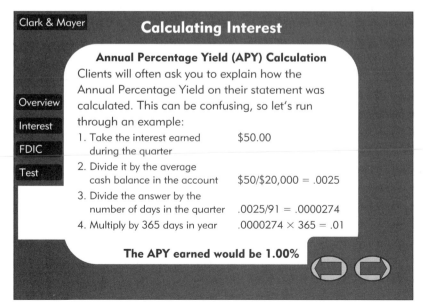

Psychological Reasons for the Personalization Principle

Let's begin with a common sense view that we do not agree with. The rationale for putting words in formal style is that conversational style can detract from the seriousness of the message. After all, learners know that the computer cannot speak to them. The goal of a training program is not to build a relationship, but rather to convey important information. By emphasizing the personal aspects of the training—by using words like "you" and "I"—you convey a message that training is not serious. Accordingly, the guiding principle is to keep things simple by presenting the basic information.

This argument is based on an *information delivery* view of learning in which the instructor's job is to present information and the learner's job is to acquire the information. According to the information delivery view, the training program should deliver information as efficiently as possible. A formal style meets this criterion better than a conversational style.

Why do we disagree with the call to keep things formal and the information delivery view of learning on which it is based? Although the information delivery view seems like common sense, it is inconsistent with how the human mind works. According to cognitive theories of learning, humans strive to make sense of presented material by applying appropriate cognitive processes. Thus, instruction should not only present information but also prime the appropriate cognitive processing in the learner. Research on discourse processing shows that people work harder to understand material when they feel they are in a conversation with a partner, rather than simply receiving information (Beck, McKeown, Sandora, Kucan, & Worthy, 1996). Therefore, using conversational style in a multimedia presentation conveys to the learners the idea that they should work hard to understand what their conversational partner (in this case, the course narrator) is saying to them. In short, expressing information in conversational style can be a way to prime appropriate cognitive processing in the learner.

According to cognitive theories of multimedia communication (Mayer, 2005d), Figure 8.5 shows what happens within the learner when a lesson contains conversational style and when it does not contain conversational style. On the top row, you can see that instruction containing social cues (such as conversational style) activates a sense of social presence in the learner

Figure 8.5. How the Presence or Absence of Social Cues Affects Learning.

How Social Cues Prime Deeper Learning

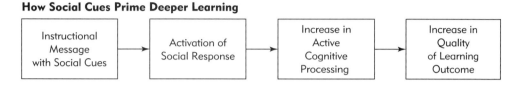

| Instructional Message with Social Cues | → | Activation of Social Response | → | Increase in Active Cognitive Processing | → | Increase in Quality of Learning Outcome |

How Lack of Social Cues Does Not Prime Deeper Learning

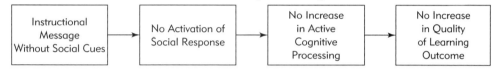

| Instructional Message Without Social Cues | → | No Activation of Social Response | → | No Increase in Active Cognitive Processing | → | No Increase in Quality of Learning Outcome |

(a feeling of being in a conversation with the author). The feeling of social presence, in turn, causes the learner to engage in deeper cognitive processing during learning (by working harder to understand what the author is saying), which results in a better learning outcome. In contrast, when an instructional lesson does not contain social cues, the learner does not feel engaged with the author and therefore will not work as hard to make sense of the material. The challenge for instructional processionals is to avoid over-using conversational style to the point that it becomes distracting to the learner.

Evidence for Using Conversational Style

Although this technique as it applies to e-learning is just beginning to be studied, there is already preliminary evidence concerning the use of conversational style in e-learning lessons. In a set of five experimental studies involving a computer-based educational game on botany, Moreno and Mayer (2000b, 2004) compared versions in which the words were in formal style with versions in which the words were in conversational style. For example, Figure 8.6 gives the introductory script spoken in the computer-based botany game; the top portion shows the formal version and the bottom shows the personalized version. As you can see, both versions present the same basic information, but in the personalized version the computer is talking directly to the learner. In five out of five studies, students who learned with personalized text performed better on subsequent transfer tests than students who learned with formal text. Overall, participants

---

Figure 8.6. Formal vs. Informal Lesson Introductions Compared in Research Study.

From Moreno and Mayer, 2000b.

> **Formal Version:**
> "This program is about what type of plants survive on different planets. For each planet, a plant will be designed. The goal is to learn what type of roots, stems, and leaves allow the plant to survive in each environment. Some hints are provided throughout the program."
>
> **Personalized Version:**
> "You are about to start a journey where you will be visiting different planets. For each planet, you will need to design a plant. Your mission is to learn what type of roots, stems, and leaves will allow your plant to survive in each environment. I will be guiding you through by giving out some hints."

in the personalized group produced between 20 to 46 percent more solutions to transfer problems than the formal group, with effect sizes all above 1. Figure 8.7 shows results from one study where improvement was 46 percent and the effect size was 1.55, which is considered to be large.

People can also learn better from a narrated animation on lightning formation when the speech is in conversational style rather than formal style

---

Figure 8.7. Better Learning from Personalized Narration.

From Moreno and Mayer, 2000b.

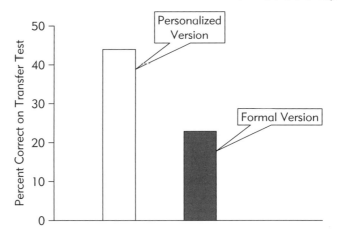

(Moreno & Mayer, 2000b). For example, consider the last sentence in the lightning lesson: "It produces the bright light that people notice as a flash of lightning." To personalize, we can simply change "people" to "you." In addition to changes such as this one, Moreno and Mayer (2000b) added direct comments to the learner, such as, "Now that your cloud is charged up, let me tell you the rest of the story." Students who received the personalized version of the lightning lesson performed substantially better on a transfer test than those who did not, yielding effect sizes greater than 1 across two different experiments.

These results also apply to learning from narrated animations involving how the human lungs work (Mayer, Fennell, Farmer, & Campbell, 2004). For example, consider the final sentence in the lungs lesson: "During exhaling, the diaphragm moves up, creating less room for the lungs, air travels through the bronchial tubes and throat to the nose and mouth, where it leaves the body." Mayer, Fennell, Farmer, and Campbell (2004) personalized this sentence by changing "the" to "your" in five places, turning it into: "During exhaling, your diaphragm moves up, creating less room for your lungs, air travels through your bronchial tubes and throat to your nose and mouth, where it leaves your body." Overall, they created a personalized script for the lungs lesson by changing "the" to "your" in eleven places. Across three experiments, this fairly minor change resulted in improvements on a transfer test yielding a median effect size of .79.

These results should not be taken to mean that personalization is always a useful idea. There are cases in which personalization can be overdone. For example, consider what happens when you add too much personal material, such as, "Wow, hi dude, I'm here to teach you all about…, so hang onto your hat and here we go!" The result can be that the advantages of personalization are offset by the disadvantages of distracting the learner and setting an inappropriate tone for learning. Thus, in applying the personalization principle it is always useful to consider the audience and the cognitive consequences of your script—you want to write with sufficient informality so that the learners feel they are interacting with a conversational partner, but not so informally that the learner is distracted or the material is undermined. In fact, implementing the personalization principle should create only a subtle change in the lesson; a lot can be accomplished by using a few first- and second-person pronouns.

Promote Personalization Through Voice Quality

Recent research summarized by Reeves and Nass (1996) shows that, under the right circumstances, people "treat computers like real people." Part of treating computers like real people is to try harder to understand their communications. Consistent with this view, Mayer, Sobko, and Mautone (2003) found that people learned better from a narrated animation on lightning formation when the speaker's voice was human rather than machine-simulated, with an effect size of .79. More recently, Atkinson, Mayer, and Merrill (2005) presented online mathematics lessons in which an on-screen agent named Peedy the parakeet explained the steps in solving various problems. Across two experiments, students performed better on a subsequent transfer test when Peedy spoke in a human voice rather than a machine voice, yielding effect sizes of .69 and .78. We can refer to these findings as the voice principle: People learn better from narration with a human voice than from narration with a machine voice. Nass and Brave (2005) have provided additional research showing that characteristics of the speaker's voice can have a strong impact on how people respond to computer-based communications.

There is also some preliminary evidence that people learn better from a human voice with a standard accent rather than a foreign accent (Mayer, Sobko, & Mautone, 2003), but this work is limited by focusing only on a Russian accent used over a short presentation. There is also some preliminary evidence that both men and women prefer to learn from female voices for female-stereotyped subjects such as human relationships and to learn from male voices for male-stereotyped subjects such as technology (Nass & Brave, 2005). However, more work is needed to determine whether the gender of the voice affects learning outcomes.

Promote Personalization Through Polite Speech

A related implication of the personalization principle is that on-screen agents should be polite. For example, consider an instructional game in which an on-screen agent gives you feedback. A direct way to put the feedback is for the agent to say, "Click the ENTER key," and a more polite wording is, "You may want to click the ENTER key" or "Do you want to click on the ENTER key?" or "Let's click the ENTER key." A direct statement is, "Now use the quadratic formula to solve this equation," and a more polite version is "What about using the quadratic formula to solve this equation?" or "You could use the quadratic formula to solve this equation," or "We should use the quadratic formula to solve this equation." According to Brown and Levinson's (1987) politeness theory, these alternative wordings help to save face—by allowing the learner to have some freedom of action or by allowing the learner to work cooperatively with the agent. Mayer, Johnson, Shaw, and Sandhu (2006) found that students rated the reworded statements as more polite than the direct statements, indicating that people are sensitive to the politeness tone of feedback statements. Students who had less experience in working with computers were most sensitive to the politeness tone of the on-screen agent's feedback statements.

Do polite on-screen agents foster deeper learning than direct agents? A preliminary study by Wang, Johnson, Mayer, Rizzo, Shaw, and Collins (2006) indicates that the answer is yes. Students interacted with an on-screen agent while learning about industrial engineering by playing an educational game called Virtual Factory. On a subsequent problem-solving transfer test, students who had learned with a polite agent performed better than those who learned with a direct agent, yielding an effect size of .70. Overall, there is evidence that student learning is not only influenced by what on-screen agents say but also by how they say it.

These results have important implications for virtual classroom facilitators. In many virtual classrooms, only the instructor's voice is transmitted. The virtual classroom instructor can apply these guidelines by using polite conversational language as one tool to maximize the benefits of social presence on learning.

PERSONALIZATION PRINCIPLE 2

Use Effective On-Screen Coaches to Promote Learning

In the previous section, we provided evidence for writing with first- and second-person language, speaking with a friendly human voice, and using polite wording to establish a conversational tone in your training. In some of the research described in the previous section, the instructor was an on-screen character who interacted with the learner. A related new area of research focuses specifically on the role of on-screen coaches, called pedagogical agents, on learning.

What Are Pedagogical Agents?

Personalized speech is an important component in animated pedagogical agents developed as on-screen tutors in educational programs (Cassell, Sullivan, Prevost, & Churchill, 2000; Moreno, 2005; Moreno, Mayer, Spires, & Lester, 2001). Pedagogical agents are on-screen characters who help guide the learning process during an e-learning episode. Agents can be represented visually as cartoon-like characters, as talking-head video, or as virtual reality avatars; they can be represented verbally through machine-simulated voice, human recorded voices, or printed text. Agents can be representations of real people using video and human voice or artificial characters using animation and computer-generated voice. Our major interest in agents concerns their ability to employ sound instructional techniques that foster learning.

On-screen agents are appearing frequently in e-learning. For example, Figure 8.8 introduces Jim in a lesson on reading comprehension. Throughout

Figure 8.8. On-Screen Coach Used to Give Reading Comprehension Demonstrations.

With permission from Plato Learning Systems.

profile

JIM

Hey there. I'm Jim and I'm taking a class to help me prepare for the GED. Each week my instructor assigns the class literature to read and discuss.

Since I have to remember a lot of stories, I learned how to find what's important in each one. I'll show you how I do it and then I'll give you a strategy for finding what's important on your own.

the lesson, Jim demonstrates techniques he uses to understand stories, followed by exercises that ask learners to apply Jim's guidelines to comprehension of stories.

Figure 8.9 shows a screen from a guided discovery e-learning game called Design-A-Plant in which the learner travels to a planet with certain environmental features (such as low rainfall and heavy winds) and must choose the roots, stem, and leaves of a plant that could survive there. An animated pedagogical agent named Herman-the-Bug (in lower left corner of Figure 8.9) poses the problems, offers feedback, and generally guides the learner through the game. As you can see in the figure, Herman is a friendly little guy, and research shows that most learners report liking him (Moreno & Mayer, 2000b; Moreno, Mayer, Spires, & Lester, 2001).

Figure 8.9. Herman the Bug Used in Design-A-Plant Instructional Game.
From Moreno, Mayer, Spires, and Lester, 2001.

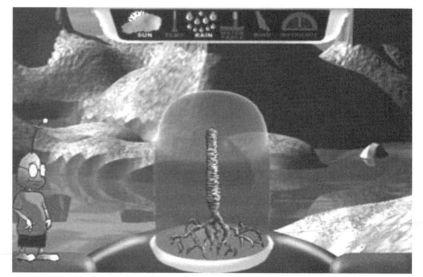

In another program, an animated pedagogical agent is used to teach students how to solve proportionality word problems (Atkinson, 2002; Atkinson, Mayer, & Merrill, 2005). In this program, an animated pedagogical agent named Peedy provides a step-by-step explanation of how to solve each problem. Although

Peedy doesn't move much, he can point to relevant parts of the solution and make some simple gestures as he guides the students. Peedy and Herman are among a small collection of agents who have been examined in controlled research studies.

Computer scientists are doing a fine job of producing life-like agents who interact well with humans (Cassell, Sullivan, Prevost, & Churchill, 2000). For example, an on-screen agent named Steve shows students how to operate and maintain the gas turbine engines aboard naval ships (Rickel & Johnson, 2000); an on-screen agent named Cosmo guides students through the architecture and operation of the Internet (Lester, Towns, Callaway, Voerman, & Fitzgerald, 2000); and an on-screen agent named Rea interacts with potential home buyers, takes them on virtual tours of listed properties, and tries to sell them a house (Cassell, Sullivan, Prevost, & Churchill, 2000).

In spite of the continuing advances in the development of on-screen agents, research on their effectiveness is just beginning (Atkinson, 2002; Moreno & Mayer, 2000b; Moreno, Mayer, Spires, & Lester, 2001). Let's look at some important questions about agents in e-learning courses and see how the preliminary research answers them.

Do Agents Improve Student Learning?

An important primary question is whether adding on-screen agents can have any positive effects on learning. Even if computer scientists can develop extremely lifelike agents that are entertaining, is it worth the time and expense to incorporate them into e-learning courses? In order to answer this question, researchers began with an agent-based educational game, called Design-A-Plant, described previously (Moreno, Mayer, Spires, & Lester, 2001). Some students learned by interacting with an on-screen agent named Herman-the-Bug (agent group), whereas other students learned by reading the identical words and viewing the identical graphics presented on the computer screen without the Herman agent (no-agent group). Across two separate experiments, the agent group generated 24 to 48 percent more solutions in transfer tests than did the no-agent group.

In a related study (Atkinson, 2002), students learned to solve proportionality word problems by seeing worked-out examples presented via a computer screen. For some students, an on-screen agent spoke, giving a step-by-step explanation for the solution (agent group). For other students, the same explanation was printed as on-screen text without any image or voice of an agent (no-agent group). On a subsequent transfer test involving different word problems, the agent group generated 30 percent more correct solutions than the no-agent group. Although these results are preliminary, they suggest that it might be worthwhile to consider the role of animated pedagogical agents as aids to learning.

Do Agents Need to Look Real?

As you may have noticed in the previously described research, there were many differences between the agent and no-agent groups, so it is reasonable to ask which of those differences has an effect on student learning. In short, we want to know what makes an effective agent. Let's begin by asking about the looks of the agent, such as whether people learn better from human-looking agents or cartoon-like agents. To help answer this question, students learned about botany principles by playing the Design-A-Plant game with one of two agents—a cartoon-like animated character named Herman-the-Bug or a talking-head video of a young male who said exactly the same words as Herman-the-Bug (Moreno, Mayer, Spires, & Lester, 2001). Overall, the groups did not differ much in their test performance, suggesting that a real character did not work any better than a cartoon character. In addition, students learned just as well when the image of the character was present or absent, as long as the students could hear the agent's voice. These preliminary results (including similar findings by Craig, Gholson, & Driscoll, 2002) suggest that a lifelike image is not always an essential component in an effective agent.

Do Agents Need to Sound Real?

Even if the agent may not look real, there is compelling evidence that the agent has to sound conversational. First, across four comparisons (Moreno, Mayer, Spires, & Lester, 2001; Moreno & Mayer, 2004), students learned better in the Design-A-Plant game if Herman's words were spoken rather than presented as on-screen text. This finding is an indication that the modality effect (as described in Chapter 5) applies to on-screen agents. Second, across three comparisons (Moreno & Mayer, 2000b), as reported in the previous section, students learned better in the Design-A-Plant game if Herman's words were spoken in a conversational style rather than a formal style. This finding is an indication that the personalization effect applies to on-screen agents. Finally, as reported in the previous section, Atkinson and colleagues (Atkinson, 2002; Atkinson, Mayer, & Merrill, 2005) found some preliminary evidence that students learn to solve word problems better from an on-screen agent when the words are spoken in a human voice rather than a machine-simulated voice. Overall, these preliminary results show that the agent's voice is an important determinant of instructional effectiveness.

Although it is premature to make firm recommendations concerning on-screen pedagogical agents, we are able to offer some suggestions based on the current state of the field. We suggest that you consider using on-screen agents, and that the agent's words be presented as speech rather than text, in conversational style rather than formal style, and with human-like rather than machine-like articulation. Although intense work is underway to create entertaining agents who display human-like gestures and facial expressions, their educational value is yet to be demonstrated.

We further suggest that you use agents to provide instruction rather than for entertainment purposes. For example, an agent can explain a step in a demonstration or provide feedback to a learner's response to a lesson question. In contrast, the cartoon general in Figure 8.10 is not an agent, since he is never used for any instructional purpose. Likewise, there is a common unproductive tendency to insert theme characters from popular games and movies who are added only for entertainment value and serve no instructional role. These embellishments are likely to depress learning, as discussed in Chapter 7.

Based on the cognitive theory and research we have highlighted in this chapter, we can propose the personalization principles. First, present words in conversational style rather than formal style. In creating the script for a narration or the text for an on-screen passage, you should use some first- and second-person constructions (that is, involving "I," "we," "me," "my," "you," and/or "your") to create the feeling of conversation between the course and

Figure 8.10. The General Character Plays No Instructional Role So Is Not an Agent.

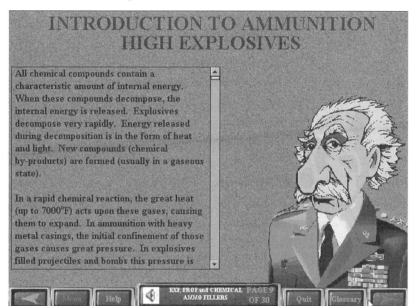

the learner. However, you should be careful not to overdo the personalization style because it is important not to distract the learner. Second, use on-screen agents to provide coaching in the form of hints, worked examples, demonstrations, and explanations.

PERSONALIZATION PRINCIPLE 3

Make the Author Visible to Promote Learning

What Is a Visible Author?

Instructional text is often written in a formal and impersonal style, in which the author seems invisible. Invisible authors do not tell you anything about themselves, whereas visible authors reveal information about themselves and highlight their personal perspectives (Nolen, 1995; Paxton, 2002). Converting an invisible author to a visible one can be called giving a voice to the text (Beck, McKeown, & Worthy. 1995). Take a minute to review the two descriptions of Mayer's multimedia research shown in Figure 8.11. Sample A is a factual summary of Mayer's multimedia research. Sample B discusses similar material but uses an interview format. In Sample B, Mayer speaks directly to the reader in a personal style. In Sample B, the author is visible, whereas in Sample A the author is invisible.

Figure 8.11. Invisible (A) vs. Visible (B) Author in Summaries of Mayer's Research.

> **A. Review of Richard Mayer's Research by Kiewra and Creswell, 2000**
>
> "Another example of Mayer's systematic approach to writing review articles is seen in his article 'Multimedia Learning: Are We Asking the Right Questions?' (Mayer, 1997). Here Mayer reviews research showing that (a) multimedia delivery systems are better than verbal explanations alone, (b) instructional methods involving coordinated verbal and visual explanations are better than explanations separated by time or space (c) effects are strongest for students with low prior knowledge and high spatial ability" (p.144)
>
> **B. Interview of Richard Mayer by Suomala & Shaughnessy**
>
> Q: What are you currently researching?
> A: For the past decade, my colleagues and I at Santa Barbara have been studying multimedia learning. Multimedia learning occurs when material is presented in more than one format, such as in words and in pictures. In particular we have been tracking down the conditions under which multimedia presentations concerning scientific explanations lead to meaningful, constructivist learning. We have found, for example, that adding animation to narration improves learners' understanding, and we have identified six principles for how to combine visual and verbal materials (p. 478)

In a statistics lesson on correlation, visible authors might include themselves in an example (Nolen, 1995, p. 61): "Yet, lest anyone become too hopeful that correlation represents a magic method for unambiguous identification of cause, consider the relationship between my age and the price of gasoline during the past ten years. The correlation is nearly perfect, but no one would suggest any assignment of cause." As another example from a history lesson on the fall of Rome, visible authors might reveal personal beliefs (Paxton, 2002, p. 244): "To those of us looking back at the ancient past, Julius Caesar remains one of the most controversial figures. I, for one, still have a hard time determining if he was a great leader, or a terrible dictator. Other historians have the same problem. Let's see what you think." One final example involves providing transcripts (or video clips) of interviews with famous scholars, so they can describe their ideas in their own words (Inglese, Mayer, & Rigotti, in press).

The visible author principle can be applied in both synchronous and asynchronous forms of e-learning. For example, compare the narration in the two virtual classroom sessions shown in Figures 8.12 and 8.13. The lesson topic is branding. Figure 8.12 applies the visible author principle when the instructor reveals his favorite brand by typing it into the chat window. In contrast, the instructor in Figure 8.13 describes the concept of branding without making any personal references.

Figure 8.12. The Instructor Makes Himself Visible by Typing His Favorite Brand in the Direct Message Window.

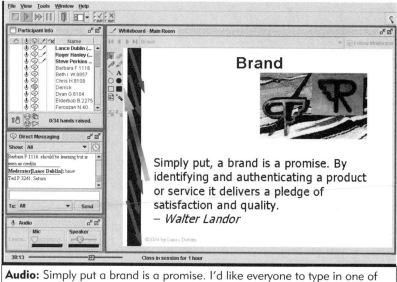

Audio: Simply put a brand is a promise. I'd like everyone to type in one of your favorite brands. I'm typing in mine. Think of a product that you are committed to – a brand that you will always select due to your confidence...

Figure 8.13. The Instructor Remains Invisible to the Learners.

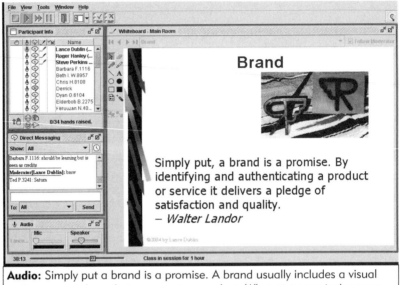

Audio: Simply put a brand is a promise. A brand usually includes a visual and a name or logo that represents a product. What company is the most recognized brand in the world? Type in your ideas.

Psychological Reasons for Using a Visible Author

The main rationale for using a visible author style is to promote learner motivation. For example, Nolen (1995, p. 47) suggests that when authors are visible, students might see the author as "a personal guide through an otherwise difficult domain." Paxton (2002, p. 202) proposes that "a human-to-human relationship between author and reader is encouraged by the presence of a visible author." Consistent with Mayer's (2005d) extension of the cognitive theory of multimedia learning shown in Figure 8.5, the visible author technique can help prime a sense of social presence in the learner—a feeling of being in a conversation with the author. The activation of social presence, in turn, encourages the learner to engage in deeper cognitive processing during learning, leading to a better learning outcome. The underlying rationale for the visible author approach is that people work harder to understand a lesson when they feel they are in a conversation with the author. However, the danger of over-emphasis on the author's self-revealing remarks is that they can become seductive details, which distract the learner (and violate the coherence principle described in the previous chapter). Good instructional design involves adding just the right amount of social cues to prime a sense of social presence in the learner, without adding so much that the learner is distracted.

Evidence for the Visible Author

There is some preliminary evidence that using the visible author style can promote deeper engagement in some learners. Paxton (2002) asked high school students to read a history lesson that featured an anonymous author (one who writes in the third person, revealing little about personal beliefs or self) or a visible author. On a subsequent essay writing task, students in the visible author group worked harder—as is indicated by writing longer essays that showed greater sensitivity to the audience. Inglese, Mayer, and Rigotti (2007) asked students at an Italian-speaking university to view online video clips and read online transcripts of various scholars in a course on political theory. On subsequent tests, non-native speakers wrote more and provided richer answers concerning visible authors than for scholars whose theories had been described without any interviews, whereas the effects of author visibility were not as strong for native speakers. These results suggest that making authors visible may be particularly effective for students who might otherwise be losing interest in the course. At this time, there is not a strong database to support the widespread use of the visible author technique, but we anticipate more research on this potentially useful technique in the future.

What We Don't Know About Personalization

Although personalization can be effective in some situations, additional research is needed to determine when it becomes counterproductive by being distracting or condescending. Further work also is needed to determine conditions—if any—under which the visible author technique can be effective. Perhaps the most exciting application of the personalization principle involves the design of pedagogical agents, so research is needed to determine which features of an agent promote learning. In addition, we do not know whether specific types of learners benefit more than others from the personalization principle. For example, would there be any differences between novice and experienced learners, learners who are committed to the content versus learners who are taking required content, male versus female learners? Finally, research is needed to determine the long-term effects of personalization, that is, does the effect of conversational style (or politeness) diminish as students spend more time with the course?

DESIGN DILEMMA: RESOLVED

The database team was debating the tone of their lesson defined by the language used and by adding a learning agent. The options considered were:

A. Reshmi is correct. A more informal approach plus an agent will lead to better learning.

B. Matt is correct. A more formal tone will fit the corporate image better, leading to a more credible instructional message.

C. The tone of the lesson should be adjusted for the learners. Women will benefit from more informality and men will find a formal approach more credible.

D. Not sure which option is correct.

Based on the evidence reviewed in this chapter, we would select Option A. Until we have more research on individual differences in response to the personalization principle, we cannot make any comment about Option C. We recommend that Matt make a case to the legal department as well as to communications showing the evidence for learning benefits from an e-learning environment in which social presence is heightened through the use of second-person constructions and an on-screen agent who guides the learning process.

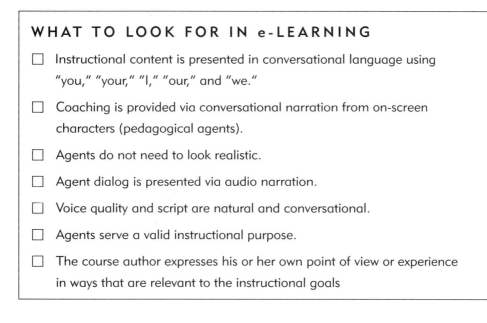

WHAT TO LOOK FOR IN e-LEARNING

☐ Instructional content is presented in conversational language using "you," "your," "I," "our," and "we."

☐ Coaching is provided via conversational narration from on-screen characters (pedagogical agents).

☐ Agents do not need to look realistic.

☐ Agent dialog is presented via audio narration.

☐ Voice quality and script are natural and conversational.

☐ Agents serve a valid instructional purpose.

☐ The course author expresses his or her own point of view or experience in ways that are relevant to the instructional goals

ON *e-LEARNING AND THE SCIENCE OF INSTRUCTION* CD

As you compare the example and counter-example, you will immediately notice the absence of the on-screen agent in the counter-example. You will also see that in the counter-example, most second-person constructions have been dropped in favor of more formal language.

COMING NEXT

The next chapter on segmenting and pretraining completes the basic set of multimedia principles in e-learning. These principles apply to training produced to inform as well as to increase performance; in other words they apply to all forms of e-learning. After reading the next chapter, you will have topped off your arsenal of basic multimedia instructional design principles described in Chapters 3 through 9.

Suggested Readings

Mayer, R.E. (2005). Principles based on social cues: Personalization, voice, and image principles. In R.E. Mayer (Ed.), *The Cambridge handbook of multimedia learning* (pp. 201–212). New York: Cambridge University Press.

Mayer, R.E., Sobko, K., & Mautone, P.D. (2003). Social cues in multimedia learning: Role of speaker's voice. *Journal of Educational Psychology, 95,* 419–425.

Moreno, R., & Mayer, R.E. (2000). Engaging students in active learning: The case for personalized multimedia messages. *Journal of Educational Psychology, 93,* 724–733.

Moreno, R., & Mayer, R.E. (2004). Personalized messages that promote science learning in virtual environments. *Journal of Educational Psychology, 96,* 165–173.

Moreno, R., Mayer, R.E., Spires, H., & Lester, J. (2001). The case for social agency in computer-based teaching: Do students learn more deeply when they interact with animated pedagogical agents? *Cognition and Instruction, 19,* 177–214.

Nass, C., & Brave, S. (2005). *Wired for speech: How voice activates and advances the human–computer relationship.* Cambridge, MA: MIT Press.

Reeves, B., & Nass, C. (1996). *The media equation: How people treat computers, television, and new media like real people and places.* New York: Cambridge University Press.

CHAPTER OUTLINE

Segmenting Principle: Break a Continuous Lesson into Bite-Size Segments

Psychological Reasons for the Segmenting Principle

Evidence for Breaking a Continuous Lesson into Bite-Size Segments

Pretraining Principle: Ensure That Learners Know the Names and Characteristics of Key Concepts

Psychological Reasons for the Pretraining Principle

Evidence for Providing Pretraining in Key Concepts

What We Don't Know About Segmenting and Pretraining

9

Applying the Segmenting and Pretraining Principles

MANAGING COMPLEXITY BY BREAKING
A LESSON INTO PARTS

WHAT'S NEW IN THIS CHAPTER?

IN SOME OF THE PREVIOUS CHAPTERS, you learned how to reduce extraneous processing (processing caused by poor instructional design) by eliminating extraneous words and pictures (Chapter 7), by placing corresponding words and illustrations near each other on the screen (Chapter 4), or by refraining from adding redundant on-screen text to a narrated animation (Chapter 6). In Chapter 2, we introduced the concept of *essential cognitive processing* that results from the complexity of the material. In this chapter we focus on situations in which learners must engage in so much essential processing that their cognitive systems are overwhelmed. In particular, in this chapter we focus on techniques for managing essential processing, including segmenting (breaking a lesson into manageable segments) and pretraining (providing pretraining in the names and characteristics of key concepts). This chapter is a new addition to the book and represents the small but growing research base in techniques for managing the learning of complex material.

DESIGN DILEMMA: YOU DECIDE

The database lesson team is working on their lesson design. They have completed their job analysis and identified five key steps involved in designing a relational database. Sergio, the subject-matter expert, offers the team an outline. "Here," he says, "let me save you some time. This is the outline I use when I teach in the classroom. (See Sergio's outline in Figure 9.1.) It works really well because I teach one step at a time." "Thanks, Serg, it really helps to have the content broken out," Reshmi replies. "But after I reviewed our job analysis, I came up with a slightly different sequence. Take a look." (See Reshmi's outline in Figure 9.1.). After reading Reshmi's outline, Sergio reacts: "Wow, Reshmi! I think your outline is confusing. My plan places all of the key concepts with each step. That way they learn each concept in the context in which they will use it! We can use that new screen capture tool to run my slides continuously while the narration plays." Reshmi is not convinced by Sergio's argument: "Yes, but your plan lumps a lot of content together.

Figure 9.1. Two Organizational Sequences for the Database Lesson.

Sergio's Outline	Reshmi's Outline
I. Introduction	I. Introduction
II. Step 1 – Select Important Entities	II. What Are Entities and Tables?
A. What are entities?	III. Table Construction
III. Step 2 – Determine Key Characteristics	I. Fields and records
A. What are key characteristics?	IV. Parent and Child Tables
IV. Step 3 – Assign Primary Keys	I. Primary and foreign keys
A. What are primary keys?	V. Entity Relationship Diagrams
V. Step 4 – Assign Foreign Keys	VI. Steps to Design a Relational Database
A. What are foreign keys?	
VI. Step 5 – Designate Table Relationships	
A. What are entity-relationship diagrams?	

I think it will overwhelm people new to databases; and our learners will be new to databases."

Sergio and Reshmi disagree about the sequence of content as well as its display. Based on your own experience or intuition, which of the following options would you select?

A. Sergio's plan is better because it teaches all content in context of the procedure.

B. Reshmi's plan is better because she has separated the key concepts from the procedure.

C. It is better to let the lesson "play" like a video so learners receive a continuous picture of the entire procedure.

D. It is better to let the learners control the sequence by selecting screens in small bites so they can work at their own rates.

E. Not sure which options are correct.

SEGMENTING PRINCIPLE

Break a Continuous Lesson into Bite-Size Segments

How can you tell that material is so complex that it will overload the learner's cognitive system? A good way to gauge the complexity of a lesson is to tally the number of elements (or concepts) and the number of interactions between them. For example, consider a narrated animation on how a bicycle tire pump works that has the script: "When the handle is pulled up, the piston moves up, the inlet valve opens, the outlet valve closes, and air enters the cylinder. When the handle is pushed down, the piston moves down, the inlet valve closes, the outlet valve opens, and air exits from the cylinder through the hose." In this case there are five main elements—handle, piston, cylinder, inlet valve, and outlet valve. The relations among them constitute a simple chain in which a change in one element causes a change in the next element, and so on. Overall, this is a fairly simple lesson that probably requires just two segments—one showing what happens when the handle is pulled up and one showing what happens when the handle is pushed down.

Next, consider a lesson on lightning formation, such as shown in Figure 9.2. This is a much more complex lesson because it has many more elements—warm and cold air, updrafts and downdrafts, positive and negative particles in the cloud, positive and negative particles on the ground, leaders, and so on. This lesson can be broken into sixteen segments, each describing one or two major steps in the causal chain, such as, "Cool moist air moves over a warmer surface and becomes heated." Each of the frames shown in Figure 9.2 constitutes a segment—involving just a few elements and relations between them.

As training professionals, you have probably worked with content that was relatively simple as well as with content that was more complex. For example, if you are teaching a class on editing text in MSWord, you need to teach a four-step procedure. First the learner must use the mouse to select the text to edit. Second he or she must click on the scissors icon to cut the text from its present location. These first two steps are illustrated in Figure 9.3. Next the writer places the cursor at the insertion point and clicks on the paste icon. This software procedure is quite linear and relatively simple. It is made easier by having only a few steps and by using on-screen icons that call up familiar metaphors such as scissors for cutting. However, in many cases, your content is more complex than this example. Even an introductory Excel class offers greater degrees of complexity. As you can see in Figure 9.4, constructing a formula in Excel can be quite complex for someone new to spreadsheets and to Excel. One of the key concepts involves the construction of a formula that uses the correct formatting conventions to achieve the desired calculation. For someone new to Excel, we would rate this as a more complex task than the word processing editing task.

When the material is complex, you can't make it simpler by leaving out some of the elements or steps in the explanation, because that would destroy the accuracy of the lesson. However, you can help the learner manage the complexity by breaking the lesson into manageable segments—parts that convey just one or two or three steps in the process or procedure or describe just one or two or three major relations among the elements. We recommend that you break a complex lesson into smaller parts, which are presented one at a time. We call this recommendation the *segmenting principle.*

Figure 9.2. Screens from Lightning Lesson.

From Moreno and Mayer, 1999a. © Cambridge University Press 2005.
Reprinted with the permission of Cambridge University Press.

"The charge results from the collision of the cloud's rising water droplets against heavier, falling pieces of ice."

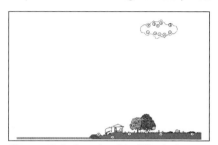

"The negatively charged particles fall to the bottom of the cloud, and most of the positively charged particles rise to the top."

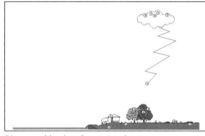

"A stepped leader of negative charges moves downward in a series of steps. It nears the ground."

"A positively charged leader travels up from such objects as trees and buildings."

"The two leaders generally meet about 165-feet above the ground."

"Negatively charged particles then rush from the cloud to the ground along the path created by the leaders. It is not very bright."

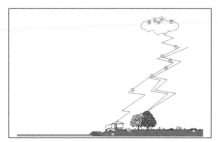

"As the leader stroke nears the ground, it induces an opposite charge, so positively charged particles from the ground rush upward along the same path."

"This upward motion of the current is the return stroke. It produces the bright light that people notice as a flash of lightning."

Figure 9.3. Cutting and Pasting Text in MSWord Is a Simple Task.

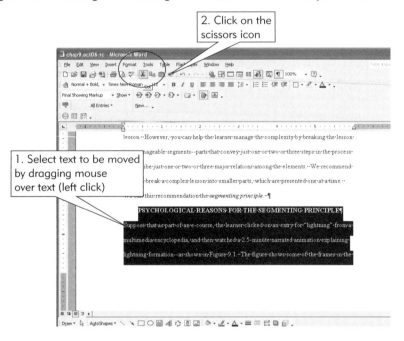

Figure 9.4. Constructing a Formula in Excel Is a Complex Task.

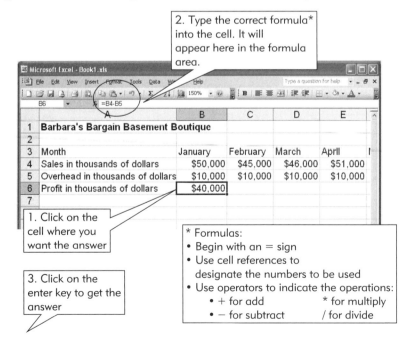

Psychological Reasons for the Segmenting Principle

Suppose that, as part of an e-course, the learner clicked on an entry for "lightning" from a multimedia encyclopedia, and then watched a 2.5-minute narrated animation explaining lightning formation—as shown in Figure 9.2. The figure shows some of the frames in the animation along with the complete spoken script, indicated in quotation marks at the bottom of each frame. As you can see, the lesson is complex—with many interacting elements—and is presented at a fairly rapid pace. If a learner misses one point, such as the idea that a cloud rises to the point that the top is above the freezing level and the bottom is below, the entire causal chain will no longer make sense. If a learner is unfamiliar with the material, he or she may need time to consolidate what was just presented. In short, when an unfamiliar learner receives a continuous presentation containing a lot of interrelated concepts, the likely result is that the cognitive system becomes overloaded—too much essential processing is required. In short, the learner does not have sufficient cognitive capacity to engage in the essential processing required to understand the material.

One solution to this dilemma that we recommend is to break the lesson into manageable parts, such as sixteen segments with a "Continue" button in the bottom right corner of each. Figure 9.5 shows an example of a frame from one of

---

Figure 9.5. Adding a Continue Button Allows Learners to Progress at Their Own Rate.

From Moreno and Mayer, 1999a. © Cambridge University Press 2005.
Reprinted with the permission of Cambridge University Press.

"Cool moist air moves over a warmer surface and becomes heated."

the segments. As you can see, the learner receives a short clip approximately ten seconds in length, along with one sentence describing the actions that are depicted. The learner can completely digest this link in the causal chain before clicking on the "Continue" button to go on to the next segment. This technique—which can be called *segmenting*—allows the learner to manage essential processing. Thus, the rationale for using segmenting is that it allows the learner to engage essential processing without overloading the learner's cognitive system.

Evidence for Breaking a Continuous Lesson into Bite-Size Segments

The previous section tells a nice story, but is there any evidence that segmenting helps people learn better? The answer is yes. Mayer and Chandler (2001) carried out the study described in the previous section. They found that learners who received the segmented presentation on lightning formation performed better on transfer tests than the learners who received a continuous presentation, even though identical material was presented in both conditions.

In another set of studies (Mayer, Dow, & Mayer, 2003), students learned how an electric motor works by watching a continuous narrated animation or by watching a segmented version. In the segmented version, the learner could click on a question and then see part of the narrated animation, click on another question and see the next part, and so on. The material was identical for both the continuous and segmented versions, but learners performed much better on transfer tests if they had received the segmented lesson. Overall, in three out of three studies the results provided strong positive effects for segmenting, yielding a median effect size of about 1. We conclude that there is tantalizing preliminary evidence in favor of segmenting, but additional research is needed.

PRETRAINING PRINCIPLE

Ensure That Learners Know the Names and Characteristics of Key Concepts

Segmenting appears to be a promising way to address the situation in which the learner is overloaded by the need to engage in essential processing—

that is, the learner is overwhelmed by the amount of essential processing required to understand a complex lesson. In this section, we examine a related technique, which can be called the *pretraining principle*: Provide pretraining in the names and characteristics of the key concepts in a lesson. For example, before viewing a narrated animation on how the digestive system works, learners could receive pretraining in which they learn the names and locations of key body parts such as the esophagus, epiglottis, trachea, pharynx, upper esophageal sphincter, lower esophageal sphincter, and stomach.

We mentioned previously that, for a new student or instructor, using the various facilities in the virtual classroom can be overwhelming. Therefore we recommend a quick orientation session at the start of a virtual classroom session that applies the pretraining principle. During the orientation, the instructor can show the different parts of the virtual classroom, as in Figure 9.6, followed by some introductory exercises during which each student uses those facilities. We also categorized learning how to use

Figure 9.6. Pretraining Illustrates the Parts and Functions of the Virtual Classroom Interface.

From Clark & Kwinn, 2007.

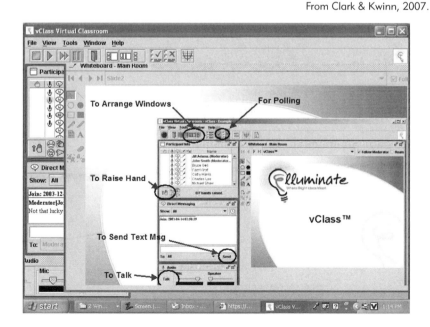

Figure 9.7. Pretraining Teaches Formula Format Before Procedure.
From Clark and Kwinn, 2007.

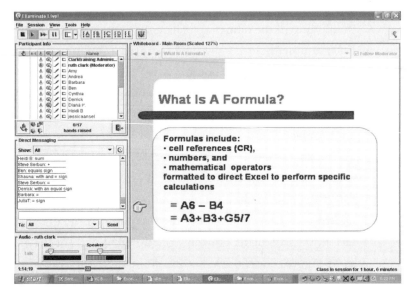

Excel formulas as another complex task. To apply the pretraining principle, the lesson shown in Figure 9.7 begins by teaching formula formatting conventions. Following this portion of the lesson, the instructor demonstrates the procedure of how to enter a formula into a spreadsheet.

Psychological Reasons for the Pretraining Principle

The pretraining principle is relevant in situations in which trying to process the essential material in the lesson would overwhelm the learner's cognitive system. In these situations involving complex material, it is helpful if some of the processing can be done in advance. When you see a narrated animation on how the digestive system works, for example, you need to build a cause-and-effect model of how a change in one part of the system causes a change in the next part and so on, and you need to understand what each part does. We can help the learner understand the cause-and-effect chain by making sure the learner already knows the name and characteristics of each part. When you hear a term like "upper esophageal sphincter" in a narrated animation, you need to try to figure out what this term refers to and how it works. Learners who are more familiar with the content area may not need pretraining because they already know the names and characteristics of key concepts. In short, pretraining can help beginners to manage their processing of complex material by reducing the amount of essential processing they do at the time of the presentation. If they already know what terms like "upper esophageal sphincter" mean, they can devote their cognitive processing to building a mental model of how that component relates to others in the causal chain. Thus, the rationale for the pretraining principle is that it helps manage the learner's essential processing by redistributing some of it to a pretraining portion of the lesson.

To implement the pretraining principle, evaluate the procedures and processes you need to teach. If they are complex for your audience, then identify key concepts and concept features that could be sequenced prior to teaching the process or procedure. You could follow your lesson introduction with a short section on the key concepts, even including a practice exercise on them. Then you can move into the process or procedure that is the main focus of your lesson.

Evidence for Providing Pretraining in Key Concepts

Suppose we asked some learners to watch a sixty-second narrated animation on how a car's braking system works (no pretraining condition), containing the script: "When the driver steps on a car's brake pedal, a piston moves forward in the master cylinder. The piston forces brake fluid out of the master cylinder, through the tubes to the wheel cylinders. In the wheel cylinders, the increase in fluid pressure makes a smaller set of pistons move. Those smaller pistons activate the brake shoes. When the brake shoes press against the drum, both the drum and the wheel stop or slow down." Figure 9.8 shows part of the animation that goes with this script. As you can see, this lesson is somewhat complex, partly because it contains some unfamiliar terms. It describes interactions among many parts such as brake pedal, piston in master cylinder, brake fluid in tube, pistons in wheel cylinders, brake shoes, drum, and wheel. The learner must learn the relations among the parts as well as the characteristics of the parts themselves.

What can be done to provide some pretraining so the learner can be relieved of some of the essential processing during the narrated animation?

Figure 9.8. Part of a Multimedia Presentation on How Brakes Work.
From Mayer, Mathias, and Wetzell (2002). © Cambridge University Press 2005.
Reprinted with the permission of Cambridge University Press.

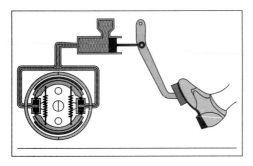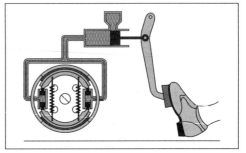

Figure 9.9. Pretraining on How Brakes Work.
From Mayer, Mathias, and Wetzell, 2002. © Cambridge University Press 2005.
Reprinted with the permission of Cambridge University Press.

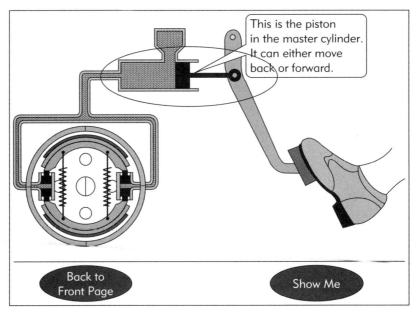

Mayer, Mathias, and Wetzell (2002) constructed a short pretraining episode in which learners saw a labeled diagram of the braking system on the screen and could click on any part, as shown in Figure 9.9. When they clicked on a part, they were told the name of the part and its main characteristics. In three

Figure 9.10. Pretraining Version Resulted in Better Learning.
Based on data from Mayer, Mathias, and Wetzell, 2002.

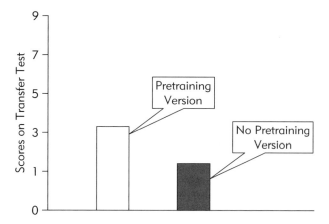

separate studies, learners who received this kind of pretraining performed better on transfer tests than did learners who did not receive pretraining, yielding a median effect size of .9. The results from one of these studies is shown in Figure 9.10

In another set of studies (Pollock, Chandler, & Sweller, 2002), electrical engineering trainees took a course that included a multimedia lesson on conducting safety tests for electrical appliances. The no-pretraining group was shown how all the electrical components worked together within an electrical system. The pretraining group first was shown how each component worked individually. Across two separate experiments, the pretraining group outperformed the no-pretraining group on transfer tests, yielding effect sizes greater than 1. Overall, there is encouraging preliminary evidence for the pretraining principle, but additional research is warranted.

What We Don't Know About Segmenting and Pretraining

Research on segmenting and pretraining is not as well developed as research supporting other principles in this book, so we need a larger research base that examines whether the effects replicate with different materials, learners, and learning contexts. We do not yet know how large a segment should be, that is, we need to determine how much information should be in a bite-sized chunk. Should a segment last for ten seconds, thirty seconds, sixty seconds, or more? How do you determine where to break a continuous lesson into meaningful segments? The issue of how much learner control is optimal is examined in Chapter 13, but also is not a resolved issue. We also do not yet know how best to identify key concepts that should be included in pretraining, or how extensive the pretraining needs to be. Is it enough for learners to simply know the names and locations of the key components in a to-be-learned system?

DESIGN DILEMMA: RESOLVED

The database e-learning team was debating the best way to sequence and to display their content. The options considered were:

   A.   Sergio's plan is better because it teaches all content in context of the procedure.

   B.   Reshmi's plan is better because she has separated the key concepts from the procedure.

   C.   It is better to let the lesson "play" like a video so learners receive a continuous picture of the entire procedure.

   D.   It is better to let the learners see the lesson in small bites so they can work at their own rates.

   E.   Not sure which options are correct.

Our first question is whether constructing a relational database is a complex task. We believe it is complex for those who are new to databases. There are a number of concepts to consider and to weigh in the design of an effective database. Given a complex instructional goal, we recommend applying the segmenting and pretraining principles suggested in Options B and D. We do agree that it's a good idea to teach the supporting concepts in job context and recommend that these concepts be shown in the context of constructing a sample database; in this case, the team used a video store example as their context.

WHAT TO LOOK FOR IN e-LEARNING

☐ Material is presented in manageable segments (such as short clips of narrated animation) controlled by the learner, rather than as a continuous unit (such as a long clip of narrated animation).

☐ Technical terms are defined and exemplified before the lesson.

☐ Key concepts are named and their characteristics are described before presenting the processes or procedures to which the concepts are linked.

ON e-LEARNING AND THE SCIENCE OF INSTRUCTION CD

You can compare the organization of our example and counter-example lessons to see application of the pretraining principle. One quick way to compare these is to look at the lesson pull-down menus for each, located in the upper-right section of the screen. The example version teaches the major concepts first and then shows how to apply them in some examples and practice exercises. The counter-example lumps the concepts in with the steps, potentially leading to student overload. Both examples apply the segmenting principle, since both allow the learners to proceed at their own rate by pressing the continue button.

COMING NEXT

One of the most popular and powerful instructional techniques is the example. Just about all effective lessons incorporate examples. What is the best way to use examples in your e-lessons? How can examples actually accelerate learning? In the next chapter you will learn important guidelines and the evidence behind the guidelines for the best design, placement, and layout of examples in your e-learning.

Suggested Readings

Mayer, R.E., (2005). Principles for managing essential processing in multimedia learning: Segmenting, pretraining, and modality principles. In R.E. Mayer (Ed.), *The Cambridge handbook of multimedia learning* (pp. 169–182). New York: Cambridge University Press.

Mayer, R.E., & Chandler, P. (2001). When learning is just a click away: Does simple user interaction foster deeper understanding of multimedia messages? *Journal of Educational Psychology, 93,* 390–397.

Mayer, R.E., Mathias, A., & Wetzell, K. (2002). Fostering understanding of multimedia messages through pretraining: Evidence for a two-stage theory of mental model construction. *Journal of Experimental Psychology: Applied, 8,* 147–154.

CHAPTER OUTLINE

Worked Examples: Fuel for Learning

How Worked Examples Work

How to Leverage Worked Examples: Overview

Worked Example Principle 1: Transition from Worked Examples to Problems via Fading

Worked Example Principle 2: Promote Self-Explanations of Worked-Out Steps

Worked Example Principle 3: Supplement Worked Examples with Explanations

Worked Example Principle 4: Apply Multimedia Principles to Examples

Worked Example Principle 5: Support Learning Transfer

Design Guidelines for Near-Transfer Learning

Design Guidelines for Far-Transfer Learning

What We Don't Know About Worked Examples

10

Leveraging Examples in e-Learning

IN OUR FIRST EDITION we recommended that you replace some practice with worked examples to make learning more efficient and effective. Of all of our chapters from the first edition, the design of worked examples is among those topics that have generated a large amount of new research. In our update, we find that worked examples continue to be a powerful proven instructional method. We now can recommend new research-based techniques for transitioning from worked examples to full problem exercises via a fading process. We also offer new suggestions for encouraging deep mental processing of worked examples by way of questions that require learners to explain worked-out steps to themselves.

As in our first edition, we recommend application of the multimedia principles to worked examples as well as design techniques to promote near or far transfer. However, we add new evidence for techniques to get the most of examples designed to promote far transfer by requiring learners to actively compare pairs of examples to derive their common principles.

DESIGN DILEMMA: YOU DECIDE

In the database lesson, Reshmi plans to give an explanation and then show one example, followed by several practice exercises that involve different situations that would benefit from a database. She is tired of e-learning that is nothing more than page turning. She wants a learning environment that is rich with problem-solving practice. Matt, however, is concerned about the amount of time required to develop the practice exercises and associated feedback, as well as the amount of time that the learners will need to devote to the lessons. He feels that the team could save time and money by using more examples and fewer practice problems. Based on your own experience or intuition, which of the following options would you select:

A. Reshmi is correct. The explanation should be followed by a good example and then by multiple practice problems.

B. Matt is correct. Learning could be faster and more effective if the lesson included more examples and less practice.

C. Both Reshmi's and Matt's approaches could be incorporated in a lesson that alternates examples with practice.

D. Both Reshmi's and Matt's concerns could be addressed by a series of interactive examples.

E. Not sure which options are best.

Worked Examples: Fuel for Learning

Worked examples are one of the most powerful methods you can use to build new cognitive skills, and they are popular with learners. Learners often bypass verbal descriptions in favor of examples. For example, learners in a LISP programming tutorial ignored verbal descriptions of LISP procedures in favor of worked examples (Anderson, Farrell, & Sauers, 1984). LeFevre and Dixon (1986) evaluated learners who were free to study either textual descriptions or worked examples to help them complete problem assignments. The information in the text was deliberately written to contradict the examples. By evaluating the learners' solutions, it was clear that the learners used the examples, not the text, as their preferred resource.

What Are Worked Examples?

In this chapter we write about a specific type of example called a worked example. A worked example is a step-by-step demonstration of how to perform a task or solve a problem. Worked examples are designed to help learners build procedural skills such as how to use a spreadsheet or strategic skills such as how to conduct a negotiation. In Figure 10.1 we show a three-step worked example used in a statistics lesson to illustrate calculation of probability. In Figure 10.2 we show a screen capture from part of a worked example from our sample database lesson on the CD. While worked examples are not new, today we have research providing guidelines on the most effective type, sequencing, and layout of examples to result in faster and better learning.

Figure 10.1. A Worked Example of a Probability Problem.

From Atkinson, Renkl, and Merrill, 2003.

Problem: From a ballot box containing 3 red balls and 2 white balls, two balls are randomly drawn. The chosen balls are not put back into the ballot box. What is the probability that the red ball is drawn first and a white ball is second?

First Solution Step	Total number of balls: 5 Number of red balls: 3 Probability of red ball first $3/5 = .6$

Second Solution Step	Total number of balls after first draw: 4(2 red and 2 white balls) Probability of a white ball second: $2/4 = .5$

Third Solution Step	Probability that a red ball is drawn first and a white ball is second: $3/5 \times 1/2 = 3/10 = .3$ Answer: The probability that a red ball is drawn first and white ball is second is 3/10 or .3.

Next

Figure 10.2. A Worked Example from a Database Lesson.
From *e-Learning and the Science of Instruction* CD.

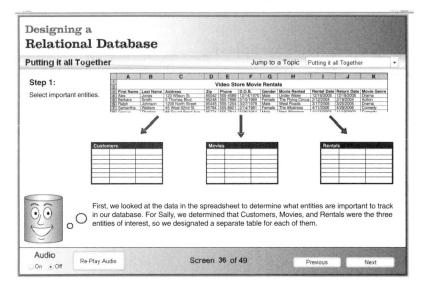

How Worked Examples Work

In Chapter 2, we summarized the central role of working memory in learning processes that build new knowledge in long-term memory. We've all heard the expression, "Practice makes perfect." It's a common assumption that the best way to learn is to work lots of practice problems. However, solving problems demands a great deal of working memory resource. During the early stages of learning, limited worked memory capacity is most productively allocated to building new knowledge. When working practice problems, so much working memory capacity is used up that there is little available resource remaining for knowledge construction.

Instead of following the traditional practice of showing a single example followed by a great deal of practice, learning is more efficient with a greater reliance on worked examples. While studying a worked example (in contrast to solving a problem), working memory is relatively free for learning. As learning progresses, new knowledge forms. At that point, practice does become beneficial to help learners automate the new knowledge. In other words, most efficient learning starts with lessons that initially use worked examples that manage cognitive load and then transition into practice.

Evidence for the Benefits of Worked Examples

Sweller and Cooper (1985) used algebra to compare the learning outcomes of studying examples to working multiple practice problems. One lesson version assigned learners eight practice problems. The second lesson version assigned learners a worked example followed by a practice exercise four times. Both groups were exposed to eight problems, with the worked example group only solving four of the eight. Following the lesson, learners took a test with six new problems similar to those used in the lessons. The results are shown in Table 10.1. It's not surprising that those who worked all eight problems took a lot longer to complete the lesson—almost six times longer! Notice, however, that the number of errors during training and in the test was higher for the all practice groups. This was the first of many experiments demonstrating the benefits of replacing some practice with worked examples.

Table 10.1. Worked Example Problem Pairs Result in Faster Learning and Performance.

From Sweller and Cooper, 1985.

Outcome	Worked Examples/ Practice Pairs	All Practice
Training Time (Sec)	32.0	185.5
Training Errors	0	2.73
Test Time	43.6	78.1
Test Errors	.18	.36

What If Examples Are Ignored?

A potential problem with worked examples is that many learners either ignore them altogether or review them in a very shallow manner. Either way, the learners fail to leverage the examples in a way that will build new knowledge. A comparison of how high-success and low-success learners processed worked examples found that better learners reviewed worked examples by explaining to themselves the principles reflected in the examples. For example, when studying the worked example shown in Figure 10.1, a shallow processor might be thinking: "To get the answer they multiplied 3/5 by 1/2." In contrast, a deeper processor might be thinking: "To determine the probability of two events, you have to multiply the probability of the first event by the probability of the second event, assuming the first event happened." The shallow processor more or less repeats the content of the example, in contrast to the deeper processor, who focuses on the principles being illustrated.

To overcome this potential limitation of worked examples, you can encourage your learners to process examples in a meaningful way by asking them to respond to questions about the worked-out steps. In this chapter we show you how to design effective worked examples and to promote their processing.

How to Leverage Worked Examples: Overview

In our first edition, we showed evidence that replacing some practice with worked examples results in more efficient and effective learning. To ensure that learners actively process worked examples, we suggested that some worked examples be designed as "completion" problems that require the learner to fill in some of the steps. We can update these recommendations with the following new guidelines:

Principle 1: Transition from worked examples to full problems via fading.

Principle 2: Include self-explanation questions with your worked examples.

Principle 3: Supplement worked examples with effective explanations.

Regarding the formatting of worked examples, we continue to recommend that you apply the multimedia principles, including multimedia, modality, redundancy, contiguity, and chunking, to the design of your worked examples:

Principle 4: Apply the multimedia principles to the design of your examples.

Last, the context you use for your examples will affect the transferability of the new knowledge that learners build from the examples. In other words, how you construct your example scenarios will influence the degree to which learners are able to apply new skills learned from them after the training. As in the first edition, we offer guidance for the design of examples to promote near transfer or procedural skills, as well as those for building far-transfer skills. We add new suggestions for helping learners gain the most from diverse examples designed for far-transfer learning.

Principle 5: Support learning transfer through effective design of context of worked examples.

WORKED EXAMPLE PRINCIPLE 1

Transition from Worked Examples to Problems via Fading

Although worked examples are proven to be the most effective path during the initial stages of learning, as learners gain more expertise, worked examples can actually impede learning. This phenomenon is an example of the *expertise reversal effect*. The reason for expertise reversal is that novices benefit from the cognitive load relief of studying an example rather than working a problem as the basis for initial learning. However, once the new knowledge is stored in memory, studying a worked example adds no value. In fact, the worked example may conflict with the learner's unique approach to completing the task. At that point, learners need to practice in order to automate their new skills. A fading process accommodates the growth of expertise by starting with full worked examples and progressing gradually into full problem assignments.

What Is Fading?

In fading, the first example is a worked example provided completely by the instruction, similar to the examples in Figures 10.1 and 10.2. The first fully worked example is followed by a second example, in which most of the steps are worked out but the learner is asked to complete one or two of them. As examples progress, the learner gradually completes more of the steps. Eventually the learner solves a practice problem completely on his or her own. Figure 10.3 illustrates the concept of fading. The gray area represents steps the instruction works and the white area represents steps completed by the learner. Suppose, for example, you were teaching probability calculations in a statistics class. Figure 10.1 shows a fully worked example as represented by the all gray circle on the left in Figure 10.3. In Figure 10.4, you can see the first faded example in the probability examples series. In this

---

Figure 10.3. Fading from a Full Worked Example to a Practice Problem.

From Clark, Nguyen, and Sweller, 2006.

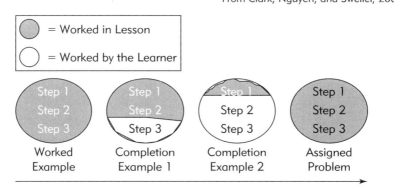

Figure 10.4. A Faded Worked Probability Problem.

From Atkinson, Renkl, and Merrill, 2003.

Problem: The bulb of Mrs. Dark's dining room table is defective. Mrs. Dark had 6 spare bulbs on hand. However, 3 of them are also defective. What is the probability that Mrs. Dark first replaces the original defective bulb with another defective bulb before then replacing it with a functioning one?

First Solution Step	Total number of spare bulbs: 6 Number of defective spare bulbs: 3 Probability of a defective bulb first $3/6 = 1/2 = .5$

Second Solution Step	Total number of spare bulbs After a first replacement trial: 5(2 defective and 3 functioning spares) Probability of a functioning bulb second: $3/5 = .6$

Third Solution Step	Probability of first replacing the original defective dining room bulb with a defective bulb first and then replacing it with a functioning one:	Please enter the numerical answer below:

Next

example, the first two steps are worked by the instruction and the learner is required to complete the final step. This example matches the second circle in Figure 10.3. Following this worked example, a third probability problem demonstrates the first step and asks the learner to complete Steps 2 and 3. A fourth probability problem is assigned to the learner as a practice problem to work alone. In progressing through a series of faded worked examples, the learner gradually assumes more and more of the mental work until at the end of the sequence he or she is working full practice problems.

Evidence for Benefits of Fading

A number of experiments have demonstrated better learning from faded worked examples compared to learning from worked example-problem pairs. For example, Atkinson, Renkl, and Merrill (2003) designed lessons on probability to include three-step faded worked examples like those shown in Figures 10.1 and 10.4. The first example was a full worked example, followed by examples in which learners had to complete an increasing number of steps until they worked the full problem themselves.

Half of the participants were assigned to lessons with faded worked examples, while the other half were assigned to lessons with worked examples paired with problems. The amount of study time was the same in both groups. As you can see in Figure 10.5, learning was better among those who used the faded examples than among those with the example-problem pairs. The differences showed an effect size of .27, which is a small effect.

WORKED EXAMPLE PRINCIPLE 2

Promote Self-Explanations of Worked-Out Steps

Principle 1 stated that learning is better with a series of faded worked examples, compared to learning from a series of example-problem pairs. However, as we mentioned at the start of the chapter, if learners ignore the worked-out steps or give them only superficial attention, much of the potential of a worked example is lost. In our first edition, we recommended that you teach your learners how to self-explain. Based on recent research, we revise our

Figure 10.5. Faded Examples Result in Better Learning Than Problem-Example Pairs.

From Experiment 1, Near Transfer Learning, Atkinson, Renkl, and Merrill, 2003.

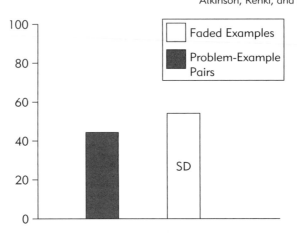

recommendation, suggesting that you require your learners to self-explain worked-out steps by asking them meaningful questions about them.

What Are Self-Explanation Questions?

A self-explanation question is an interaction—usually multiple choice in multimedia—that requires the learner to review the worked-out step(s) and identify the underlying principles or concepts behind them. Note that the worked example we show in Figure 10.6 includes a multiple-choice question next to the first worked step. The learner is required to identify the principle that supports each step demonstrated in the worked example by selecting one of the probability rules or principles. The goal of the self-explanation question is two-fold. First, it discourages bypassing the worked example, since an overt response is required. Second, because learners are asked to identify the principles that underlie each step, they are encouraged to process that step in a meaningful way.

Evidence for Benefits of Self-Explanation Questions

Atkinson, Renkl, and Merrill (2003) compared the learning of high school students from faded worked examples that included self-explanation questions

Figure 10.6. A Self-Explanation Question on First Solution Step.

From Atkinson, Renkl, and Merrill, 2003.

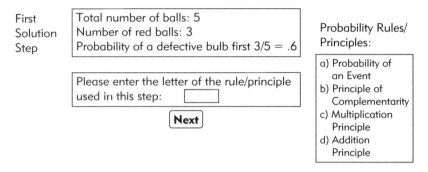

Problem: From a ballot box containing 3 red balls and 2 white balls, two balls are randomly drawn. The chosen balls are not put back into the ballot box. What is the probability that a red ball is drawn first and a white ball is second?

First
Solution
Step

Total number of balls: 5
Number of red balls: 3
Probability of a defective bulb first 3/5 = .6

Probability Rules/
Principles:

a) Probability of
   an Event
b) Principle of
   Complementarity
c) Multiplication
   Principle
d) Addition
   Principle

Please enter the letter of the rule/principle used in this step:

Next

like the one in Figure 10.6 with the same faded worked examples without questions. As you can see in Figure 10.7, adding the questions resulted in greater learning from the worked examples. The effect size was .42, which is a moderate effect.

Figure 10.7. Worked Examples with Self-Explanation Questions Result in Better Learning Than Worked Examples Without Questions.

From Experiment 2, Near Transfer Learning, Atkinson, Renkl, and Merrill, 2003.

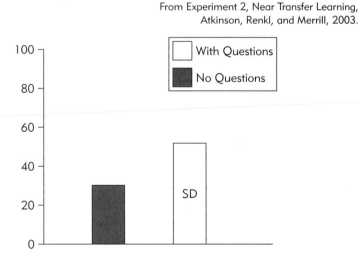

Supplement Worked Examples with Explanations

So far, we have seen that learning can be significantly improved if you transition from examples to practice through a series of faded worked examples and if you encourage processing of the worked-out steps with self-explanation questions. These techniques free working memory to focus on processing examples in ways that will build new knowledge.

However, when reviewing a worked example, the learners may not really understand the steps shown. Then when required to respond to a self-explanation question, they are likely to get stuck. When you present your worked example, you can accompany the worked-out steps with an explanation of the example. Your explanation would provide the underlying principles and rationale for the steps. You could make the explanation of the example available only when the learner requests it or in response to errors to a self-explanation question.

Tips for Design of Explanations to Support Worked Examples

We have consistent evidence that providing explanations to support worked out steps aids learning (Reed, Demptster, & Ettinger, 1985; Renkl, 2002). We do not yet know when it is better to provide a more detailed explanation or a shorter explanation. We also do not know when it is better to incorporate the explanation as a part of the worked example or to make it available on learner demand or in response to an error to a self-explanation question. Until we have more evidence on these issues, we recommend the following:

- Provide detailed explanations of initial worked examples for novice learners;

- As the lesson progresses, make explanations shorter and available on demand OR in response to an error to a self-explanation question;

- Write explanations that make the connection between the steps and underlying principles clear; and

- Position explanations close to the location of the worked step that is being explained, that is, apply the contiguity principle.

Apply Multimedia Principles to Examples

In Chapters 3 through 9, we presented Mayer's multimedia principles pertaining to the use of graphics, text, audio, and content sequencing. Some of the earliest research on worked examples found that they failed to have a positive effect when the multimedia principles were violated. For example, if the contiguity principle was violated by separating text steps from a relevant visual, split attention resulted. Since split attention added extraneous cognitive load, the potential of worked examples to reduce cognitive load was negated. To maximize the cognitive load benefits of worked examples, it is important that you apply the multimedia principles to their design. In this section we show you how.

Illustrate Worked Examples with Relevant Visuals: Multimedia Principle

We saw in Chapter 3 that relevant visuals benefit learning in contrast to lessons that use text alone to present content. The same guideline applies to design of worked examples. Where possible, include relevant visuals to illustrate the steps. For example in Figures 10.8 and 10.9, we show Step 2 in

Figure 10.8. A Worked Example Step with a Relevant Visual.

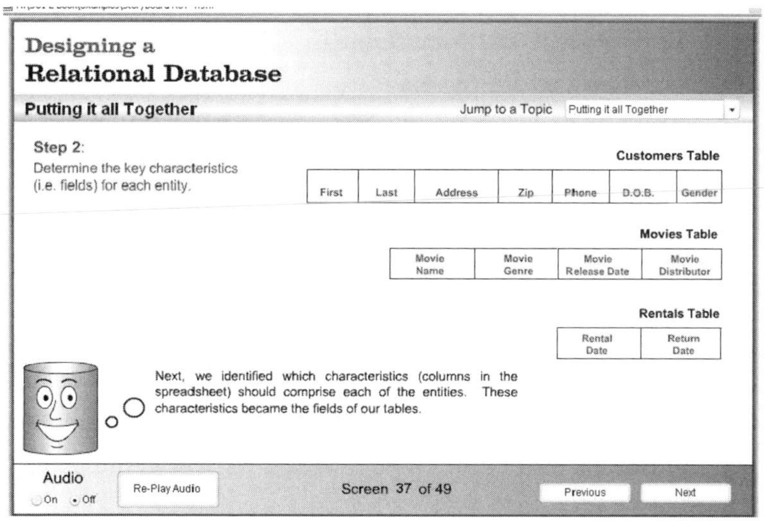

Figure 10.9. A Worked Example Step Without a Relevant Visual.
From *The e-Learning and Science of Instruction* CD.

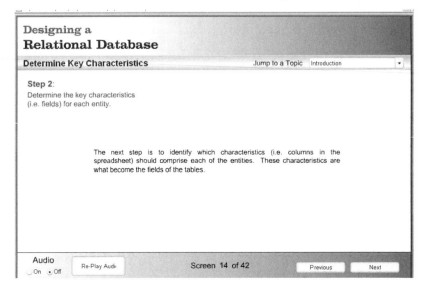

a worked example from the database lesson. Figure 10.8 illustrates the fields associated with the three entities for the video store example. In contrast, Figure 10.9 summarizes the step in text only.

Present Steps with Audio—NOT Audio and Text: Modality and Redundancy Principles

In Chapters 5 and 6 we summarized research showing that learning is better when a relevant visual is explained with words presented in audio rather than text or audio and text. The same guideline applies to worked examples. Leahy, Chandler, and Sweller (2003) compared learning from a worked example of how to calculate temperature changes from the graph shown in Figure 10.10. Three different modality combinations were used to present the steps: audio, text, and text plus audio. They found that, for complex problems where cognitive load would be the highest, learning was better when the graph was explained with audio alone.

Keep in mind, however, that applying the modality principle sometimes creates more cognitive load than it saves. For example, you should not use

Figure 10.10. A Worked Example with Steps Integrated into Visual.
Adapted from Leahy, Chandler, and Sweller, 2003.

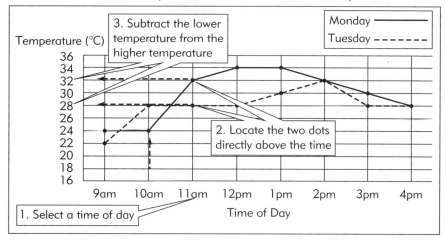

audio in situations in which the learners need to refer to words at their own pace. For example, when presenting a faded worked example that requires the learner to complete some of the steps, all steps should be presented in text so the learner can review those steps at his or her own pace in order to complete those that are faded. In addition, when including self-explanation questions, it will also be better to present the steps and the question in text, permitting flexible review of those steps in order to correctly identify the appropriate principle. (See Chapter 5 for a more detailed discussion of the modality principle.)

Present Steps with Integrated Text: Contiguity Principle

We recommend that you make audio the default modality option in multimedia lessons when presenting steps related to a visual. However, to accommodate learners who may have hearing impairments, who are not native speakers of the language used in the instruction, or who may not have access to technology that can deliver sound, as well as to help learners review steps in faded worked examples or in self-explanation questions, examples should be presented in text. When using text to present steps pertaining to a visual, implement the contiguity principle by placing the text close to the relevant visual, as shown in Figure 10.10.

You will notice in our sample database lesson that most of our worked examples require some response in the form of a self-explanation question or a completed step. Therefore we have used text to present these examples.

Present Steps in Conceptually Meaningful Chunks

Often worked examples may include ten or more steps. Learners may follow each step individually, failing to see the conceptual rationale for the steps or for combinations of steps. For example, in the probability problems shown in Figures 10.1 and 10.4, the steps are grouped into three segments, each segment illustrating the application of a probability principle. Atkinson and Derry (2000) showed that, in multimedia, better learning results from worked examples in which each step is presented on a new screen, rather than when the steps are presented together. Your challenge is to group your steps into meaningful chunks and draw learner attention to those chunks by visually isolating them, by building them through a series of screens, or by surrounding related steps with boxes to signal the underlying principles.

Present Worked Example Steps Under Learner Control of Pacing: Segmenting Principle

In Chapter 9 we showed that, for complex content, learning was better when learners could move through screens at their own pace by clicking on the "continue" button, rather than viewing the content in a non-stop video manner. This guideline also applies to worked examples that are complex. After each step, the learner should have control over pacing and click continue when ready to move to the next screen.

Tips for Design of Worked Examples

In summary, the goal of worked examples is to minimize extraneous cognitive load so that learners can allocate limited working memory resources to learning. If you violate one or more of the multimedia principles in the presentation of your worked examples, you add load and thus neutralize the potential effectiveness of your worked example. Therefore when designing your examples:

- Provide relevant visual illustrations;

- Use audio to present steps related to a visual; use text to present steps when there is no accompanying visual;

- Use integrated text to present steps for faded worked examples or when including self-explanation questions;

- Provide explanations of worked examples in text;

- Avoid presenting words in both text and audio;

- Segment worked examples with many steps into conceptually meaningful chunks and use labels to highlight the chunks; and

- Allow learners to access each chunk at their own pace, rather than playing all of the steps continuously.

WORKED EXAMPLE PRINCIPLE 5

Support Learning Transfer

In our first edition, we offered guidelines for designing the context of your examples to support near or far transfer. Here we repeat those guidelines and add a new guideline based on recent research related to far-transfer learning.

What Are Near and Far Transfer?

In some training situations, the main goal is to teach learners procedures, tasks that are performed pretty much the same way each time they are completed. Accessing your email or filling out a customer order form are two typical examples. When teaching procedures, your goal is to help learners achieve *near transfer*. In other words, your goal is to help learners apply steps learned in the training to similar situations in the work environment.

However, often your training goal is to build job skills that will require the worker to use judgment in order to adapt strategies to new work situations. In a sales setting, for example, the product, the client, and the situation will vary each time. It is not productive to teach sales skills as an invariant set of steps because each situation will require adaptation. Rather, you need to teach learners a set of strategies. Your goal is to help learners adapt strategies learned in the training to the work environment, where each situation will vary. When teaching strategies, your goal is to help learners achieve *far transfer*. Management training, customer service training, and non-routine troubleshooting are all examples of tasks that require far-transfer skills.

Design Guidelines for Near-Transfer Learning

You won't be surprised to learn that you need to design worked examples in different ways for near-transfer goals than for far-transfer goals. In this section we will review evidence-based guidelines for constructing worked examples in ways that best support near-transfer learning.

The Psychology of Near Transfer

Suppose we asked you to state aloud the months of the year. No problem. However, what if we asked you to state aloud the months of the year in alphabetical order? That would likely take you a bit of time to sort out. Why? Because you learned the calendar chronologically, your retrieval cues stored in long-term memory are chronological cues. This is an example of what psychologists call *encoding specificity*. Encoding specificity states that the cues you will use to retrieve information after learning must be embedded at the time of learning!

Design to Support Near-Transfer Learning

To apply the encoding specificity principle, it's important that, for near-transfer learning, your worked examples incorporate the same context that workers will encounter on the job. We typically call these types of worked examples *demonstrations*. For example, if you are teaching a new computer skill, it will be important that your instruction incorporate visuals of the same screens that workers will see on the job. By emulating the work environment in the training interface, learners will encode new skills in the same context in which they will be retrieved later.

Design Guidelines for Far-Transfer Learning

When it comes to far-transfer learning, the learner will need more flexible knowledge based on strategic knowledge that can be adapted to many different job situations. In this section we review the psychology, evidence, and guidelines for using worked examples in ways that promote far-transfer learning.

The Psychology of Far Transfer

Experts can size up a problem in their domain by identifying the underlying principles that are not apparent to a novice. For example, an expert physicist is able to look at a problem that involves pulleys and realize the problem is really about the conservation of linear momentum. To a novice, it would appear to be simply a "pulley problem." Experts gain the ability to see under the surface of a problem to identify its type through experience with hundreds of different real problems encountered in their specialty fields. Over time, experts abstract flexible strategies that they can apply to new problems they face on a regular basis. The first thing someone needs to figure out when faced with a problem is: "What kind of a problem is this?" Once the problem is categorized, the appropriate solution procedures can be applied.

How can you design examples in e-learning that will help learners build strategies that will transfer to new and diverse situations?

Recall that encoding specificity states that the retrieval cues must be encoded at the time of learning. This works fine for near-transfer tasks that have predictable application environments. We simply need to replicate the environment in our examples. However, we face a different challenge in far transfer. Here we will need more flexible knowledge—knowledge that can only be derived from multiple examples with different contexts or story lines but with the same underlying principles.

Deep Versus Surface Features of Examples

Take a minute to review the tumor problem displayed on the next page.

THE TUMOR PROBLEM

Suppose you are a doctor faced with a patient who has a malignant tumor in his stomach. It is impossible to operate on the patient, but unless the tumor is destroyed, the patient will die. There is a kind of ray that at a sufficiently high intensity can destroy the tumor. Unfortunately, at this intensity, the healthy tissue that the rays pass through on the way to the tumor will also be destroyed. At lower intensities, the rays are harmless to healthy tissue, but will not affect the tumor either. How can the rays be used to destroy the tumor without injuring the healthy tissue? (Duncker, 1945).

What are some possible solutions to this problem? This problem was used in an experiment reported by Gick and Holyoak (1980) in which different groups had different pre-work assignments. One group read a story about a general who captured a mined fortress by splitting up his troops and attacking from different directions. Another group read the fortress story, plus a story about putting out a fire on an oil rig. A single hose was not large enough to disperse sufficient foam, so the fire was put out by directing many small hoses toward the middle of the fire. In these three stories, the surface features—the contexts—are quite different. One is about a medical problem, another is about a fire, and a third is about a fortress. However, the underlying principle—convergence principle—is the same. The convergence principle illustrates the *deep structure* of the stories.

Gick and Holyoak (1980) found that most individuals who tried to solve the tumor problem without any other stories did not arrive at the convergence solution. Even those who read the fortress problem prior to the tumor problem did not have much better luck. But the group that read both the fire and the fortress stories had much better success. That is because, by studying two examples with different surface features that reflect the same principle, learners were able to abstract the underlying principle that connected them.

Our challenge in far-transfer learning is to help learners build strategies that can be retrieved and applied to new problems that emerge in the work environment. In the next section we show you how.

Design to Support Far-Transfer Learning

In the tumor problem experiment, we saw that, when participants were presented with two stories that varied regarding their surface features (fire fighting and fortress) but were similar regarding the deep structure (convergence principle), many participants were able to solve the tumor problem. The best way to help learners build strategies is to present several varied context worked examples. In this section we will offer guidelines for creating varied context worked examples and for encouraging learners to engage with those worked examples in ways that promote strategic knowledge.

What Are Varied Context Worked Examples

Varied context worked examples are several worked examples that illustrate some common set of principles in which you vary the cover story but keep the relevant solution methods or principle the same. Take a look at the examples in Figures 10.1 and 10.4. Both of these worked examples demonstrate how to solve basic probability problems. However, they vary on surface features. First, one is about red and white balls and the other is about defective and operative light bulbs. In other words, the cover stories have changed in each problem. Second, the number of items in the two examples differs. The example in Figure 10.1 involves three red balls and two white balls, whereas the light bulb example involves three defective and three good bulbs. However, the basic solution principles (multiplication and probability) are applied in the same way in each example. Since the number of objects differs in each problem, so will the numbers differ in the calculation steps.

When teaching far-transfer skills, build several (at least two) worked examples in which you vary the cover story but illustrate the same guidelines in each.

Evidence for Varied Context Worked Examples

Quilici and Mayer (1996) created examples to illustrate three statistical tests of t-test, correlation, and chi-square. Each of these test types requires a different mathematical procedure and they are most appropriately applied to different types of data. For each test type they created three examples. Some example sets used the same surface story. For example, the three t-test problems used data regarding experience and typing speed; the three correlation examples used data regarding temperature and precipitation; and the three chi-square examples included data related to fatigue and performance. The example sets that used the same cover story were called *surface emphasizing* examples. An alternative set of examples varied the cover story. For example, the t-test was illustrated by one example that used experience and typing speed, a second example about temperature and precipitation, and a third example about fatigue and performance. This set of examples was called *structure emphasizing* examples.

After reviewing the examples, participants sorted a new set of problems into groups (Experiment 2) or selected which set of calculations they should use to implement the appropriate statistical test (Experiment 3). As shown in Figure 10.11, the structure-emphasizing examples led to significantly greater discrimination among the test types.

Figure 10.11. Varied Context Worked Examples Resulted in More Correct Discrimination of Test Type.
From Experiment 3, Quilici and Mayer, 1996.

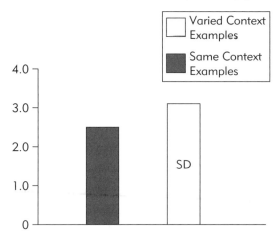

Paas and Van Merrienboer (1994) gave learners math problems in the form of either worked examples or problem assignments. The examples and problems used were either all quite similar or used a varied context design that presented examples with different surface features. Consistent with the Quilici and Mayer results, they found better far-transfer learning occurred with varied context examples, but only when those examples were presented in the form of worked examples rather than problem assignments. The varied contexts helped learners build more robust knowledge that could apply to different problems on the test. However, using example sets with varied surface features will impose greater cognitive load than problems with the same surface features. Only when that additional load is offset by using worked examples will the varied contexts pay off in better far-transfer learning. Therefore we see that worked examples are especially important in building strategic knowledge to offset the additional cognitive load imposed by the varied contexts of the examples.

Engage Learners in Comparisons of Varied Context Worked Examples

We mentioned previously that often learners either bypass worked examples or attend to them in a shallow manner. We recommended that you use self-explanation questions to maximize the potential of worked examples. We extend this guideline by recommending that for far-transfer learning, you engage learners in a comparison of two or more worked examples in which the surface features change but the principles remain the same.

Present your first worked example using self-explanation questions, as we described previously. Then maintain a summary of the solution for the first worked example on the screen and display a second worked example with a different surface feature next to the solution summary of the first. To promote an active comparison, ask the learner to state or identify the common guidelines shared by the two worked examples.

Evidence for Benefits of Active Comparisons of Varied Context Worked Examples

Gentner, Loewenstein, and Thompson (2003) designed a lesson on negotiation skills in which they emphasized the benefits of a negotiated agreement that uses a safeguard solution, rather than a less effective tradeoff solution. They presented one worked example of negotiation that involved a conflict between a Chinese and an American company over the best way to ship parts. They illustrated both the tradeoff (less effective) and the safeguard (more effective) negotiation strategies. In the next part of the lesson, they provided a different worked example involving a conflict between two travelers over where to stay on a planned trip. On the same page as the traveler negotiation example, the learner can see a diagrammed summary of the safeguard shipping solution next to a blank diagram the learner must complete using the traveler's scenario. To complete the blank diagram, the learner must study the second example closely and compare it with the solution summary from the first example. This interaction encourages learners to abstract the deep structure from the cover stories of the two examples.

To evaluate learning, three lesson versions illustrated in Figure 10.12 were studied. In one lesson (separate examples) participants saw the shipping and traveling examples, each on a separate page. After reading the examples, participants were asked questions about each case such as, "What is going on in this negotiation?" In this lesson version, learners reviewed each example separately, rather than make a comparison between them. In a second lesson version (comparison), participants saw both examples displayed on the same page and were directed to think about the similarities between the two situations. A third group (active comparison) presented the first example

Figure 10.12. Alternative Placement of Negotiation Strategy Examples in Three Lessons.

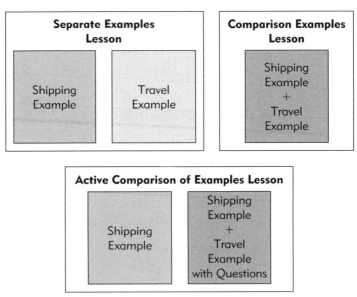

on one page. The solution to this example is carried to a second page that presents the second example and asks learners to actively respond to questions about the second case. A fourth group received no training.

Following the training, all participants interacted in a role-played face-to-face negotiation over salary. In the role play they assumed the role of a job recruiter negotiating with a job candidate who wanted more salary than was offered. Judges scored the resulting job contract awarding a higher score if the contract reflected the safeguard solution illustrated in the lessons. As you can see in Figure 10.13, the lesson that required an active comparison of the two examples resulted in best learning, followed by the lesson in which both examples were displayed on the same page and participants were directed to compare them. The groups that were encouraged to make comparisons (comparison) and that were engaged in a comparison activity (active comparison) applied the new skill significantly more than those who did not draw comparisons (separate examples and control group). The active comparison lessons were more effective than the passive comparisons.

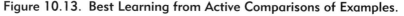

Figure 10.13. Best Learning from Active Comparisons of Examples.
Adapted from Gentner, Loewenstein, and Thompson, 2003.

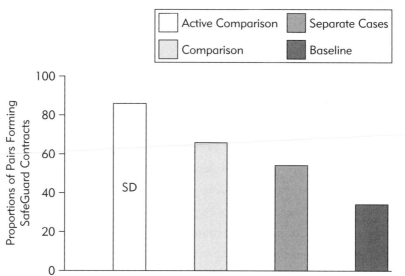

Tips for Design of Worked Examples for Near and Far Transfer

In summary we recommend that you:

- Incorporate the environment of the job as closely as possible in worked examples designed to support learning of near-transfer tasks;

- Include at least two worked examples that vary their cover stories but embody similar principles to support learning of far-transfer tasks; and

- Promote active comparisons of far-transfer worked examples by a contiguous display of the examples, plus interactions that require the learners to focus on the common principles.

What We Don't Know About Worked Examples

We have learned a great deal in the past few years about the most effective way to design worked examples to maximize learning. Still, a number of issues remain to be resolved.

1. How to best fade multi-step worked examples. In worked examples with a few steps, such as the probability problems in Figures 10.1 and 10.4, it is easy to create a sequence of a few examples that start with a full worked example and end with a complete problem with two or three intervening faded examples. However, many tasks require multiple steps. If such examples are faded one step at a time, many worked examples would be needed. We need more data on how best to apply fading techniques to multi-step examples.

2. When to drop worked examples in favor of practice. We mentioned that worked examples are best for early learning and should be abandoned in favor of multiple practice assignments once the basic knowledge is acquired. Presumably, different learners would benefit from different numbers of worked examples to complete the initial learning stage. Some early work has been initiated on how to use a rapid adaptive testing technique to assess learner expertise and

determine when to transition to full problem assignments (Clark, Nguyen, & Sweller, 2006). However, the implementation of adaptive testing can be quite labor-intensive, and it would be helpful to have alternative guidelines to determine when to move from worked examples to full problem assignments.

3. How to design worked examples for ill-defined domains. Most of the research has used mathematical domains. This is because there are clear-cut correct and incorrect answers, making it easy to assess learning in an experiment. Except for the negotiation skills research described previously, we lack examples of how to best construct worked examples in more ill-defined arenas such as sales, communication skills, and management training.

DESIGN DILEMMA: RESOLVED

We summarized a debate between Reshmi and Matt on the best ratio and placement of examples and practice exercises with the following options:

A. Reshmi is correct. The explanation should be followed by a good example and then by multiple practice problems.

B. Matt is correct. Learning could be faster and more effective if the lesson included more examples and less practice.

C. Both Reshmi's and Matt's approaches could be incorporated in a lesson that alternates examples with practice.

D. Both Reshmi's and Matt's concerns could be addressed by a series of interactive examples.

Based on evidence reviewed in this chapter, we recommend option D. We recommend a series of faded worked examples in which the learner works an increasingly larger number of steps as he or she progresses through the examples. Worked-out steps can be made more effective by requiring the learner to respond to self-explanation questions. Together, these techniques will result in a series of interactive examples that end with full practice problems.

WHAT TO LOOK FOR IN e-LEARNING

☐ Worked examples that fade from a full worked example into a full problem assignment

☐ Worked examples in which self-explanation questions are attached to worked steps

☐ Worked examples that provide instructional explanations of the worked steps

☐ Worked examples that minimize cognitive load by applying appropriate multimedia principles

   ☐ Use relevant visuals

   ☐ Explain visuals with audio or text – not both

   ☐ Integrate explanatory text close to relevant visual

   ☐ Segment worked examples into chunks that focus attention to underlying principles

   ☐ Present complex examples under learner control of pacing

☐ Worked examples that mirror the work environment for near-transfer tasks

☐ Multiple varied-context worked examples for far-transfer tasks

☐ Interactions that encourage learners to actively compare sets of varied context examples for far-transfer learning

ON e-LEARNING AND THE SCIENCE OF INSTRUCTION CD

You can see an example of a faded worked example on our example database lesson. From the drop-down menu, select "Putting It All Together." The first worked example appears on screens 36 through 40. Note self-explanation questions on screens 38 and 39. The next worked example on screens 41 through 47 is faded. For each step, the instruction completes part and the learner finishes it. The final example starting on screen 48 is a full problem that the learner works alone. In the counter-example lesson, we do not include fading or self-explanation questions.

COMING NEXT

Although we recommend that you replace some practice with worked examples, you will still need to include effective practice in your training. In the next chapter we offer evidence for the number, type, design, and placement of practice, along with new guidelines on design of practice feedback that will optimize learning.

Suggested Readings

Gentner, D., Loewenstein, J., & Thompson, L. (2003). Learning and transfer: A general role for analogical encoding. *Journal of Educational Psychology, 95*(2), 393–408.

Renkl, A. (2005). The worked-out examples principle in multimedia learning. In R.E. Mayer (Ed.), *The Cambridge handbook of multimedia learning*. New York: Cambridge University Press.

CHAPTER OUTLINE

What Is Practice in e-Learning?

> Practice Formats in e-Learning

The Paradox of Practice

How to Leverage Practice: Overview

Practice Principle 1: Mirror the Job

Practice Principle 2: Provide Explanatory Feedback

> What Is Explanatory Feedback?
>
> Evidence for Benefits of Explanatory Feedback
>
> Tips for Feedback

Practice Principle 3: Adapt the Amount and Placement of Practice to Job Performance Requirements

> The Benefits of Practice
>
> Practice Benefits Diminish Rapidly
>
> Adjust the Amount of Practice in e-Learning Based on Task Requirements
>
> Distribute Practice Throughout the Learning Environment
>
> Tips for Determining the Number and Placement of Practice Events

Practice Principle 4: Apply Multimedia Principles

> Modality and Redundancy Principles
>
> Contiguity Principle
>
> Coherence Principle
>
> Tips for Applying the Multimedia Principles to Your Interactions

Practice Principle 5: Transition from Examples to Practice Gradually

> An Example of Faded Worked Examples
>
> Why Faded Worked Examples Are Efficient

What We Don't Know About Practice

11

Does Practice Make Perfect?

IN OUR FIRST EDITION, we recommended that you design practice to build job-relevant skills and adjust the amount and placement of practice to match proficiency requirements. These guidelines are still valid today. There has been a moderate amount of new research on practice since our first edition. In our update we focus on proven conditions that make practice exercises effective, including feedback. As discussed in Chapter 10, we recommend that you manage cognitive load by transitioning from examples to full practice assignments gradually.

As described in our first edition, you should distribute interactions throughout the instructional environment and apply Mayer's multimedia principles to the design and layout of e-learning interactions.

DESIGN DILEMMA: YOU DECIDE

Reshmi, Sergio, and Ben have very different ideas about how to design practice for the database lesson. Sergio and Ben want to add a Jeopardy-type game like the one shown in Figure 11.1. They feel that most of the learners will find the database topic very dry and that adding some fun games will increase engagement and motivation. Reshmi does not like the game idea. She would prefer to include short scenarios about situations that can benefit from databases and incorporate questions about them.

Figure 11.1. A Jeopardy Game Design for the Database Lesson.

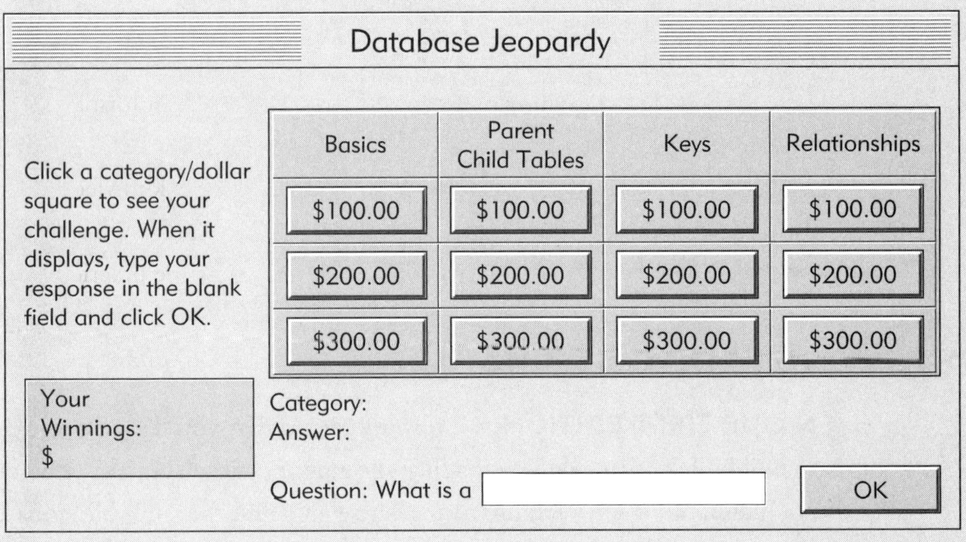

When it comes to feedback, Reshmi and Ben disagree about what kind of feedback to include. Reshmi wants to tell participants whether they answered correctly or incorrectly and explain why. Ben feels they can save a lot of development time by simply using the automatic program feature of their authoring tool that tells learners whether they are correct or incorrect. Otherwise the team will have to devote a large block of time to writing tailored explanations for all correct and incorrect response options. Based on your own experience or intuition, which of the following options would you select:

A. Adding some familiar and fun games like Jeopardy will make the lesson more engaging for learners and lead to better learning.

B. It would be better to use scenarios as the basis for interactions.

C. The extra time invested in writing feedback explanations for practice responses won't pay off in increased learning.

D. Time invested in writing tailored feedback will pay off in improved learning.

E. Not sure which options are best.

What Is Practice in e-Learning?

Effective e-learning engages learners with the instructional environment in ways that foster the selection, organization, integration, and retrieval of new knowledge. First, attention must be drawn to the important information in the training. Then the instructional words and visuals must be integrated with each other and with prior knowledge. Finally, the new knowledge and skills that are built in long-term memory must be retrieved from long-term memory after the training when needed on the job. Effective practice exercises support all of these psychological processes. In this chapter we will review research and guidelines for optimizing learning from online practice.

Practice Formats in e-Learning

One path to engagement is through overt learner responses to lesson practice exercises. Practice exercises, often referred to as *interactions* in computer learning environments, assume a variety of formats. Some interactions use formats similar to those used in the classroom, such as selecting the correct answer in a list or indicating whether a statement is true or false. Other interactions use formats that are unique to computers, such as drag and drop and simulations in asynchronous e-learning and whiteboard marking or typing into a chat window in synchronous e-learning.

However, the psychological effectiveness of a practice exercise is more important than its format. For example, consider the questions shown in Figures 11.2 and 11.3. Both questions use a multiple-choice format. However, to respond to the question in 11.2, the learner need only recognize the definition provided in the lesson. We call these kinds of interactions

Figure11.2. This Multiple-Choice Question Requires the Learner to Recognize the Definition of a Field.

A Field is:
A. An instance of data located in a cell of the table
B. A class of data located in the column of the table
C. A row of data related to one instance

Figure 11.3. This Multiple-Choice Question Requires the Learner to Apply the Concept of a Field to an Example.

From *e-Learning and the Science of Instruction* CD.

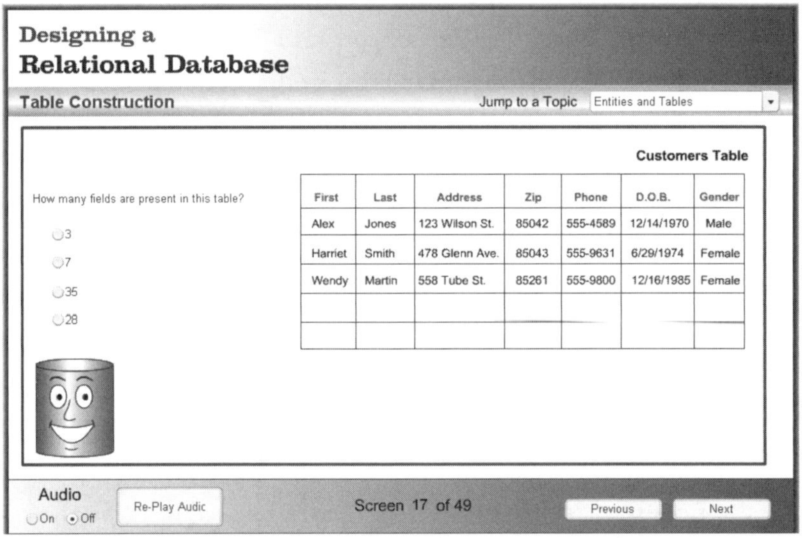

Designing a
Relational Database

Table Construction   Jump to a Topic   Entities and Tables

Customers Table

How many fields are present in this table?

First	Last	Address	Zip	Phone	D.O.B.	Gender
Alex	Jones	123 Wilson St.	85042	555-4589	12/14/1970	Male
Harriet	Smith	478 Glenn Ave.	85043	555-9631	6/29/1974	Female
Wendy	Martin	558 Tube St.	85261	555-9800	12/16/1985	Female

○ 3
○ 7
○ 35
○ 28

Audio   Re-Play Audio   Screen 17 of 49   Previous   Next
○ On ◉ Off

"regurgitative." They don't demand much thought. In contrast, to respond to the question in 11.3, the learners need to apply their understanding of the concept to an actual example. This question requires a deeper level of processing than the question shown in Figure 11.2.

The Paradox of Practice

We've all heard the expression that "practice makes perfect." But how important is practice to skill acquisition? Studies of top performers in music, chess, and sports point to the criticality of practice in the development of expertise.

Sloboda, Davidson, Howe, and Moore (1996) compared the practice schedules of higher-performing and lower-performing teenage music students of equal early musical ability and exposure to music lessons. All of the students began to study music around age six. The higher performers had devoted much more time to practice. By age twelve higher performers were practicing about two hours a day, compared to fifteen minutes a day for the lower performers. The researchers concluded that "There was a very strong relationship between musical achievement and the amount of formal practice undertaken" (Sloboda, Davidson, Howe, & Moore, 1996, p. 287). In fact, musicians who had reached an elite status at a music conservatory had devoted over 10,000 hours to practice by the age of twenty!

In contrast, no relationship was found between college student grade-point average and the amount of time devoted to study (Plant, Ericsson, Hill, & Asberg, 2005). The research team concluded that the amount of study by college students has no relationship to academic performance. Similarly, we have all met individuals of average proficiency in an avocation such as golf or music who spend a considerable amount of time practicing with little improvement. Based on studies of expert performers in music and sports, Ericsson (2006) concludes that practice is a necessary but not sufficient condition to reach high levels of competence. What factors differentiate practice that leads to growth of expertise from practice that does not?

Ericsson (2006) refers to practice that leads to expertise as *deliberate practice*. He describes deliberate practice as tasks presented to performers that "are initially outside their current realm of reliable performance, yet can be mastered within hours of practice by concentrating on critical aspects and by gradually refining performance through repetitions after feedback. Hence, the requirement for concentration sets deliberate practice apart from both mindless, routine performance and playful engagement"(p. 692). To maximize the payoff from practice, we recommend the following factors: (1) practice that focuses on specific skill gaps; (2) explanatory corrective feedback; (3) practice in distraction-free environments; as well as (4) practice that builds skills that will transfer from learning environments to work environments.

How to Leverage Practice: Overview

In our first edition, we showed evidence that practice should be job-relevant, distributed throughout the learning environment, and that more practice leads to improved performance. We update and extend these recommendations with the following guidelines:

Principle 1: Mirror the job.

Principle 2: Provide explanatory corrective feedback.

Principle 3: Determine the amount of practice based on job performance requirements; distribute practice throughout the learning environment.

Principle 4: Apply the multimedia principles to the design of your practice questions.

Principle 5: Transition from examples to practice gradually via fading.

PRACTICE PRINCIPLE 1

Mirror the Job

Design interactions that require learners to respond in a job-realistic context. Questions that ask the learner to merely recognize or recall information presented in the training will not promote learning that transfers to the job.

Begin with a job and task analysis in order to define the specific cognitive and physical processing required in the work environment. Then create *transfer appropriate interactions*—activities that require learners to respond in similar ways during the training as they would in the work environment. In Chapter 10 we described the *encoding specificity* principle that tells us that the cues of transfer must be encoded at the time of learning. The more the features of the job environment are integrated into the interactions, the more likely the right cues will be encoded into long-term memory for later transfer. The Jeopardy game shown in Figure 11.1 requires only recall of information. Neither the psychological nor the physical context of the work environment is reflected in the game. In contrast, the question shown in Figure 11.3 requires learners to process new content in a job-realistic context and therefore is more likely to support transfer of learning.

For the most part, avoid e-learning with interactions that require simple regurgitation of information provided in the training program. These questions do not support the psychological processes needed to integrate new information with existing knowledge. They can be answered without any real understanding of the content, and they don't implant the cues needed for retrieval on the job. Instead, as you design your course, keep in mind the ways that your workers will apply new knowledge to their job tasks.

Table 11.1 summarizes our recommendations for the best types of interactions for training of procedural (near transfer) tasks, strategic (far transfer) tasks, processes, concepts, and facts (Clark, 2007).

Table 11.1. Interactions for Five Types of Content in e-Learning.

Based on Clark, 2007.

Content Type	Interaction Description	Example: Web-Page Creation
Fact	Use the fact to complete a task; provide a job aid for memory support	Use the codes on your reference aid to access the application
Concept	Identify a new instance of the concept	Select the web page that applies effective text design features
Process	Solve a problem or make a decision	Predict the impact of a miscoded page property specification on the final web page output
Procedure	Perform a task by following steps	Enter text specifications into the text properties screen
Principle	Perform a task by applying guidelines	Design an effective web page

Provide Explanatory Feedback

Feedback provides knowledge of practice results. It tells learners whether they answered the question correctly. But feedback can do much more! We recommend that, in addition to telling learners that their answers are correct or incorrect, you provide a short explanation of why a given response is correct or incorrect. In this section we provide examples and research on feedback to help you maximize learning from interactions.

What Is Explanatory Feedback?

Take a look at the two feedback responses to the incorrect question response shown in Figures 11.4 and 11.5. The feedback in Figure 11.4 tells you that your answer is wrong. However, it does not help you understand why your answer is wrong. The feedback in Figure 11.5 provides a much better opportunity for learning because it incorporates an explanation. A missed question is a teachable moment. The learner is open to a brief instructional

---

Figure 11.4. This Feedback Tells the Learner That His or Her Response Is Incorrect.

From e-*Learning and the Science of Instruction* CD.

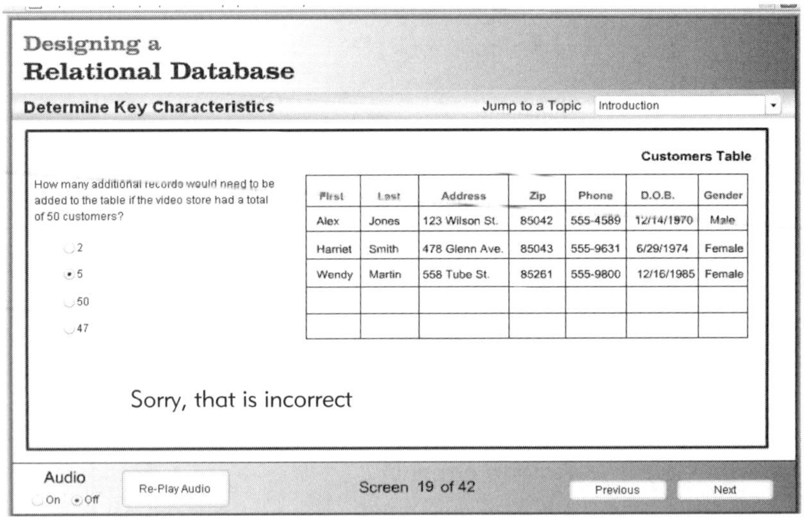

Figure 11.5. This Feedback Tells the Learner That His or Her Response Is Incorrect and Provides an Explanation.

From *e-Learning and the Science of Instruction* CD.

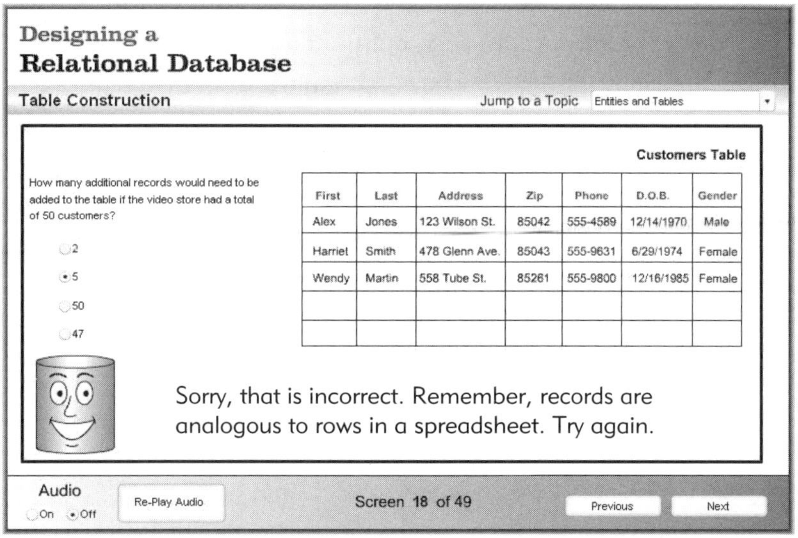

explanation that will help build the right mental model and/or correct misconceptions. Although the benefits of explanatory feedback seem obvious, crafting explanatory feedback is much more labor-intensive than corrective feedback, which can be automated in many authoring tools with only a few key strokes. What evidence do we have that explanatory feedback will give a return sufficient to warrant the investment?

Evidence for Benefits of Explanatory Feedback

Moreno (2004) compared learning from two versions of a computer botany game called Design-A-Plant. In the game, participants construct plants from a choice of roots, leaves, and stems in order to build a plant best suited to an imaginary environment. The object of the game is to teach the adaptive benefits of plant features for specific environments, such as heavy rainfall, sandy soil, and so forth. In the research study, either *corrective* or *explanatory feedback* was offered by a pedagogical agent in response to a plant design. For explanatory feedback, the agent made comments such as: "Yes, in a low sunlight environment, a large leaf has more room to make food by photo-synthesis" (for a correct answer) or "Hmmm, your deep roots will not help your plant collect the scarce rain that is on the surface of the soil" (for an incorrect answer). Corrective answer feedback told the learners whether they were correct or incorrect, but did not offer any explanation. As you can see in Figure 11.6, better learning resulted from explanatory feedback, with an effect size of 1.16. Students rated the version with explanatory feedback as more helpful than the versions with corrective feedback. Motivation and interest ratings were the same in both versions.

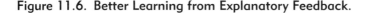

Figure 11.6. Better Learning from Explanatory Feedback.

From data in Experiment 1, Moreno, 2004.

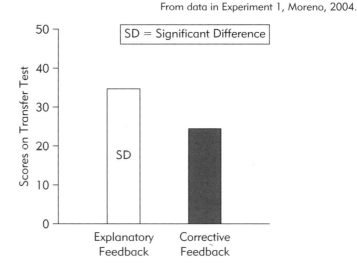

Moreno and Mayer (2005) reported similar results using the same botany game environment in a follow-up study. They found that explanatory feed-back resulted in much better learning than corrective feedback, with a very high effect size of 1.87. Learners in the explanatory feedback group gave fewer wrong answers than those in the correct feedback group, with an effect size of .94.

Debowski, Wood, and Bandura (2001) compared learning an electronic search task from a guided and an unstructured practice session. All par-ticipants attended an initial class that explained and demonstrated several principles for conducting effective online searches. Following the instruction, participants were assigned to conduct practice searches on five topics. Half the participants were randomly assigned to an unstructured practice in which they could search on the five topics in any order or use topics of their own choice. Participants in the unstructured group were encouraged to explore and practice using the skills they learned in their training. The guided practice group was assigned the five search tasks in a sequence from easier to more difficult. If they made an error in the search steps, they were reminded of the correct procedure and given a demonstration of the correct approach. Therefore, the guided practice group received a practice sequence from easier to more difficult problems in addition to immediate explanatory feedback. After the practice session, both groups completed two test searches during which they were monitored and rated for the quality of their search strategy, wasted effort, total effort, depth and breadth of search, and final performance, measured by the number of relevant records retrieved by the final search statement. The guided practice was more effective in building learner confidence and in satisfaction with learning. Additionally, learners who practiced under structured conditions demonstrated better quality search strategies and retrieved more relevant records.

Search tasks offer little in the way of natural feedback. A novice would have no way to know whether there are additional relevant records that were not retrieved. The research team concludes that "for complex, ill-structured tasks that provide low fidelity feedback, the evidence suggests that guided mastery training plus extended guided exploration during practice is needed to build initial competencies before the benefits of self-guided exploration will be realized" (p. 1139).

Taken together, there is strong evidence for increased learning efficiency, better learning, and higher learner satisfaction from environments that provide explanatory feedback during practice.

Tips for Feedback

We believe your lesson will benefit from the following tips:

- After the learner responds to a question, provide feedback in text that tells the learner whether the answer is correct or incorrect and provides a succinct explanation.

- Position the feedback so that the learner can see the question, his or her response to the question, and the feedback in close physical approximation to maintain contiguity.

- For a question with multiple answers, such as the example in Figure 11.7, show the correct answers next to the learner's answers and include an explanation for the correct answers.

Figure 11.7. A Multiple-Select Question and Its Feedback.
From the example lesson on *e-Learning and the Science of Instruction* CD.

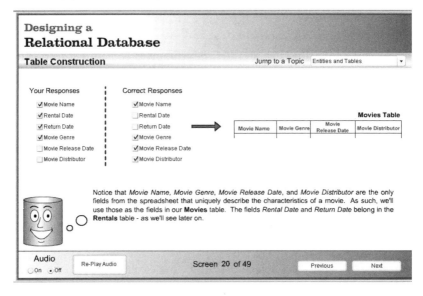

Adapt the Amount and Placement of Practice to Job Performance Requirements

Practice exercises are expensive. First, they take time to design and to program. Even more costly will be the time learners invest in completing the practice. How much practice is necessary and where should the practice be placed? In this section we describe evidence that will help you determine the optimal amount and placement of practice in your e-learning environments.

The Benefits of Practice

Some e-learning courses in both synchronous and asynchronous formats include little or no opportunities for overt practice. In Chapters 1 and 2 we classified these types of courses as *receptive*. Can learning occur without practice? How much practice is needed?

Moreno and Mayer (2005) compared learning from the Design-A-Plant game described previously in this chapter from interactive versions in which the learner selected the best plant parts to survive in a given environment with the same lesson in which the learning agent selected the best parts. As you can see in Figure 11.8, interactivity improved learning with an effect size of .63, which is considered moderate. In the same research report, a second form of interactivity asked learners to explain why an answer was correct or not correct to promote reflection on responses. Asking learners to provide an explanation proved beneficial when the agent rather than the learners selected the plant parts. In fact, learner explanations promoted learning only when learners explained correct answers rather than their own answers, which may have been incorrect. From these results, we conclude that interactions are beneficial to far-transfer learning but that one form of interaction (either selecting the plant parts OR giving an explanation for correct selections made by the program) is probably sufficient.

Figure 11.8. Better Learning from e-Learning with Interactions.
Based on data from Experiment 2, Moreno and Mayer, 2005.

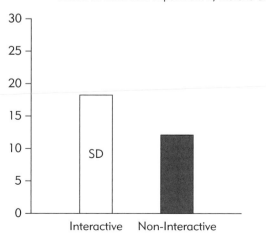

Practice Benefits Diminish Rapidly

Practice can improve performance indefinitely, although at diminishing levels. Timed measurements of workers using a machine to roll cigars found that, after thousands of practice trials conducted over a four-year period, proficiency continued to improve (Crossman, 1959). Proficiency leveled off only after the speed of the operator exceeded the physical limitations of the equipment. In plotting time versus practice for a variety of motor and intellectual tasks, a logarithmic relationship has been observed between amount of practice and time to complete tasks (Rosenbaum, Carlson, & Gilmore, 2001). Thus the logarithm of the time to complete a task decreases with the logarithm of the amount of practice. This relationship, illustrated in Figure 11.9, is called the *power law of practice*. As you can see, while the greatest proficiency gains occur on early trials, even after thousands of practice sessions, incremental improvements continue to accrue. Practice likely leads to improved performance in early sessions as learners find better ways to complete the tasks and in later practice sessions as automaticity increases efficiency.

**Figure 11.9. The Power Law of Practice: Speed Increases with More
              Practice.**

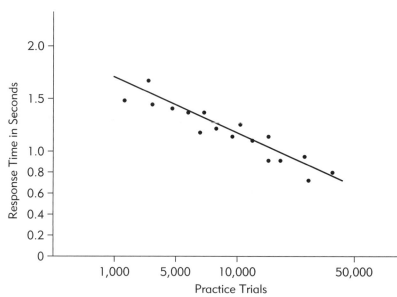

Adjust the Amount of Practice in e-Learning Based on Task Requirements

More directly relevant to e-learning, Schnackenberg and others compared learning from two versions of computer-based training, one offering more practice than the other (Schnackenberg, Sullivan, Leader, & Jones, 1998; Schnackenberg & Sullivan, 2000). In their experiment, two groups were assigned to study from a full-practice version lesson with 174 information screens and sixty-six practice exercises or from a lean practice version with the same 174 information screens and twenty-two practice exercises. Participants were divided into high-ability and low-ability groups based on their grade point averages and randomly assigned to complete either the full or lean practice version. Outcomes included scores on a fifty-two-question test and average time to complete each version. Table 11.2 shows the results.

Table 11.2. Better Learning with More Practice.

From Schnackenberg, Sullivan, Leader, and Jones, 1998.

	66 Practices		22 Practices	
Ability Level	Low	High	Low	High
Test Scores	32.25	41.82	28.26	36.30
Time to Complete (minutes)	146	107	83	85

As expected, higher-ability learners scored higher and the full version took longer to complete. The full version resulted in higher average scores, with an effect size of .45, which is considered moderate. The full-practice version resulted in increased learning for both higher-ability and lower-ability learners. The authors conclude: "When instructional designers are faced with uncertainty about the amount of practice to include in an instructional program, they should favor a greater amount of practice over a relatively small amount if higher student achievement is an important goal" (Schnackenberg, Sullivan, Leader, & Jones, 1998, p. 14).

Notice that lower-ability learners required 75 percent longer to complete the full-practice version than the lean-practice version, for a gain of about 4 points on the test. Does the additional time spent in practice warrant the learning improvement? To decide how much practice your e-learning courses should include, consider the nature of the job task and the criticality of job proficiency to determine whether the extra training time is justified by the improvements in learning.

After many practice exercises, new skills can be executed without using any capacity from working memory. We refer to these skills as *automatic*. Some job tasks must be learned to *automaticity* to ensure safe job performance the first time these tasks are performed. Landing an airplane is one example. These types of tasks benefit from repetitive drills that over time result in automaticity. Other tasks benefit from automaticity of skills, but the automaticity can be developed through practice on the job. Yet other types of tasks will depend more on understanding the underlying concepts and principles to apply to problem-solving situations than on automatic responses. In these environments, more attention to the quality of practice than to the quantity of practice may be warranted.

Distribute Practice Throughout the Learning Environment

The earliest research on human learning, conducted by Ebbinghaus in 1913, showed that distributed practice yields better long-term retention. According to the National Research Council, "The so-called spacing effect—that practice sessions spaced in time are superior to massed practices in terms of long-term retention—is one of the most reliable phenomena in human experimental psychology. The effect is robust and appears to hold for verbal materials of all types as well as for motor skills" (1991, p. 30). As long as eight years after an original training, learners whose practice was spaced showed better retention than those who practiced in a more concentrated time period (Bahrick, 1987).

The spacing effect, however, does not result in better immediate learning. It is only after a period of time that the benefits of spaced practice are realized. Since most training programs do not measure delayed learning, the benefits of spaced practice would typically not be noticed. Only in long-term evaluation would this advantage be seen. Naturally, practical constraints will dictate the amount of spacing that is feasible.

Since our first edition, there are at least two studies that continue to support the benefits of distributed practice. Both studies focused on reading skills. Seabrook, Brown, and Solity (2005) showed that recall of words in a laboratory experiment that included various age groups was better for words in a list that were repeated after several intervening words than for words that were repeated in sequence. To demonstrate the application of this principle to instructional settings, they found that phonics skills taught in reading classes scheduled in three two-minute daily sessions showed an improvement six times greater than those practicing in one six-minute daily session.

Rawson and Kintsch (2005) compared learning among groups of college students who read a text once, twice in a row, or twice with a week separating the readings. As you can see in Figure 11.10, reading the same text twice in a row (massed practice) improves performance on an immediate test, whereas reading the same text twice with a week in between readings (distributed practice) improves performance on a delayed test.

Figure 11.10. Best Learning on Delayed Test from Spaced Readings.
Data from Experiment 1, Rawson and Kintsch, 2005.

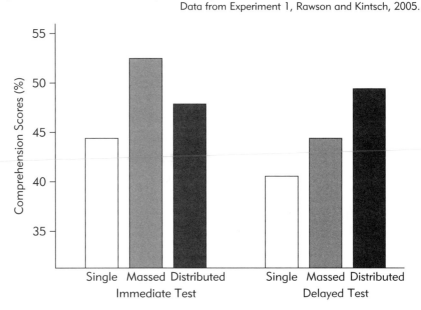

Taken together, evidence continues to recommend practice that is scheduled throughout a learning event, rather than concentrated in one time or place. To apply this guideline, incorporate review practice exercises among the various lessons in your course, and within a lesson distribute practice over the course of the lesson rather than all in one place.

Tips for Determining the Number and Placement of Practice Events

We have consistent evidence that interactions promote learning. However, the greatest amount of learning accrues on the initial practice events. Large amounts of practice will build automaticity, but offer diminishing performance improvements. We also know that greater long-term learning occurs when practice is distributed throughout the learning environment rather than all at once. To summarize our guidelines for practice, we recommend that you:

- Analyze the desired result for task performance requirements: Is automatic task performance needed? If so, is automaticity required immediately or can it develop during job performance? Does the task require an understanding of concepts and processes along with concomitant reflection?

- For less critical tasks or for tasks that do not require automaticity, incorporate fewer practice sessions.

- For tasks that require high degrees of accuracy and/or automaticity, incorporate large numbers of practice sessions.

- For tasks that require automatic responses, use the computer to measure response accuracy and response time. Once automated, responses will be both accurate and fast.

- Distribute practice among lessons in the course and within any given lesson.

- In synchronous e-learning courses, extend learning by designing several short sessions of one to two hours with asynchronous practice assigned between sessions.

Apply Multimedia Principles

In Chapters 3 through 8, we presented six principles for design of multimedia pertaining specifically to the use of graphics, text, and audio in e-learning. Here are some suggestions for ways to apply those principles to the design of practice interactions.

Modality and Redundancy Principles

According to the modality principle described in Chapter 5, audio should be used to explain visuals in your lesson. However, audio is too transient for practice exercises. Learners need to refer to the directions while responding to questions. Any instructions or information learners need in order to answer a question should remain in text on the screen while the learner formulates a response.

Previously in this chapter, we focused on the importance of explanatory feedback. Feedback should also be presented in text so that learners can review the explanations at their own pace. Based on the redundancy principle described in Chapter 6, use text alone for most situations. Do not narrate on-screen text directions, practice questions, or feedback.

Contiguity Principle

According to the contiguity principle, text should be closely aligned to the graphics it is explaining to minimize extraneous cognitive load. Since you will be using text for your questions and feedback, the contiguity principle is especially applicable to design of practice questions. Clearly distinguish response areas by placement, color, or font and place them adjacent to the question. In addition, when laying out practice that will include feedback to a response, leave an open screen area for feedback near the question and as close to the response area as possible so that learners can easily align the feedback to their responses and to the question. In multiple-choice or multiple-select items, use color or bolding to show the correct options as part of the feedback.

In situations in which there are multiple responses to a lengthy practice question, the feedback may require considerable screen real estate. In these circumstances, show a correct answer on a different screen along with an explanation. However, when so doing, be sure to display the learner's responses next to the correct response and visible to the feedback, as shown in Figure 11.7.

Coherence Principle

In Chapter 7 we reviewed evidence suggesting that violation of the coherence principle imposes extraneous cognitive load and may interfere with learning. Specifically, we recommended that you exclude stories added for entertainment value, background music and sounds, and detailed textual descriptions. Our bottom line is "less is usually more."

We recommend that practice opportunities be free of extraneous visual or audio elements such as gratuitous animations or sounds (applause, bells, or whistles) associated with correct or incorrect responses. Research has shown that, while there is no correlation between the amount of study and grade point average in universities, there is a correlation between the amount of deliberate practice and grades. Specifically, study in distraction-free environments alone in a quiet room (rather than with a radio) or in a team leads to better learning (Plant, Ericsson, Hill, & Asberg, 2005; Kenz & Hugge, 2002). During virtual classroom synchronous sessions, the instructor should maintain a period of silence during practice events. In addition, the instructor should ask learners to display one of the response icons, such as the smiley face, when they have completed an exercise outside of the virtual environment, such as in a workbook. Multi-session virtual classroom courses can leverage the time in between sessions with homework assignments that may require a lengthy time of individual reflection.

Tips for Applying the Multimedia Principles to Your Interactions

In summary, the following tips will be helpful in designing your learning events:

- Include relevant visuals as part of your interaction design;
- Align directions, practice questions, and feedback in on-screen text; and
- Minimize extraneous text, sounds, or visuals during interactions.

PRACTICE PRINCIPLE 5

Transition from Examples to Practice Gradually

Completing practice exercises imposes a great deal of mental load. In Chapter 10, we showed evidence that using healthy doses of worked examples along with practice will result in more efficient learning. In fact, a proven strategy to impose load gradually as learners gain expertise is to use faded worked examples. Because we discussed the evidence for faded worked examples extensively in Chapter 10, we provide only a brief review here.

An Example of Faded Worked Examples

In our database lesson on the CD, after presenting several basic concepts, the lesson guides the learners to apply five database design steps. The first example is a full worked example in which all of the steps to construct a video store database are illustrated for the learner and briefly explained by the agent. To ensure that learners process this example, self-explanation questions are included at several of the steps. The second example is a faded example focusing on a database for a library. In the faded example, steps are partially worked out for the learner and the learner is asked to finish the steps. The final assignment requires the learner to construct a database on his or her own.

Why Faded Worked Examples Are Efficient

A number of research studies we reviewed in Chapter 10 have shown that using worked examples speeds learning and improves learning outcomes. When carefully observing and processing a demonstration, the learner can use limited working memory capacity to build a mental model. By gradually assuming more mental work in completing examples and then in working problems themselves, learners invest more mental effort after they have built an initial mental model.

What We Don't Know About Practice

We conclude that, while practice does not necessarily lead to perfect, deliberate practice that includes effective feedback does. We saw that explanatory feedback is more effective than feedback that merely tells learners whether their responses are correct or incorrect. We still need to know more about the best types of feedback to give. For example, should feedback be detailed or brief? We also need to know more about the best timing for feedback. Is feedback provided immediately after a response always most effective? Finally, it is easy for learners to bypass or give feedback only cursory attention. What are some techniques we can use to ensure that learners reflect on feedback? We look to future research on these questions.

Another question of interest involves the tradeoffs between overt practice and reflecting on the responses of others. In the Design-A-Plant experiment, both actively responding or giving explanations for the correct actions of others led to learning. Under which circumstances would one type of response be more effective and more efficient than the other? Would it be as valuable to ask learners to pause and think to themselves as it is to ask them to overtly type or select explanations?

DESIGN DILEMMA: RESOLVED

The database design team had disagreements about the type of practice and practice feedback to include in the database lesson, leading to the following options:

A. Adding some familiar and fun games like Jeopardy will make the lesson more engaging for learners and lead to better learning.

B. It would be better to use database scenarios as the basis for interactions.

C. The extra time invested in writing feedback explanations for practice responses won't pay off in increased learning.

D. Time invested in writing tailored feedback will pay off in improved learning.

E. Not sure which options are best.

Based on the research we have summarized in this chapter, we recommend Options B and D.

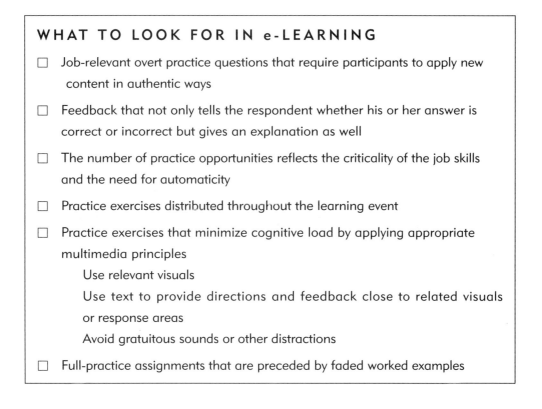

WHAT TO LOOK FOR IN e-LEARNING

☐ Job-relevant overt practice questions that require participants to apply new content in authentic ways

☐ Feedback that not only tells the respondent whether his or her answer is correct or incorrect but gives an explanation as well

☐ The number of practice opportunities reflects the criticality of the job skills and the need for automaticity

☐ Practice exercises distributed throughout the learning event

☐ Practice exercises that minimize cognitive load by applying appropriate multimedia principles

    Use relevant visuals

    Use text to provide directions and feedback close to related visuals or response areas

    Avoid gratuitous sounds or other distractions

☐ Full-practice assignments that are preceded by faded worked examples

ON e-LEARNING AND THE SCIENCE OF INSTRUCTION CD

Although both example and counter-example lessons include practice, the feedback and layout of practice in the example lesson applies our guidelines more effectively.

COMING NEXT

From discussion boards to blogs to breakout rooms, there are numerous computer facilities to promote to synchronous and asynchronous forms of collaboration among learners and instructors during e-learning events. There has been a great deal of research on how to best structure and leverage online collaboration to maximize learning. Unfortunately, we still have few solid guidelines from that research. In the next chapter we look at what we know about online collaboration and learning.

Suggested Readings

Debowski, S., Wood, R.E., & Bandura, A. (2001). Impact of guided exploration and inactive exploration on self-regulatory mechanisms and information acquisition through electronic search. *Journal of Applied Psychology, 86*(6), 1129–1141.

Moreno, R., & Mayer, R.E. (2005). Role of guidance, reflection, and interactivity in an agent-based multimedia game. *Journal of Educational Psychology, 97*(1), 117–128.

Plant, E.A., Ericsson, K.A., Hill, L., & Asberg, K. (2005). Why study time does not predict grade point average across college students: Implications of deliberate practice for academic performance. *Contemporary Educational Psychology, 30,* 96–116.

CHAPTER OUTLINE

What Is Computer-Supported Collaborative Learning (CSCL)?

Types of CSCL

Individual vs. Group Outcomes from CSCL

Factors That Make a Difference: Overview

Optimizing Individual Outcomes from CSCL

Optimizing Group Products from CSCL

Is Problem-Solving Learning Better with CSCL or Solo?

Virtual vs. Face-to-Face Group Decisions

Software Representations to Support Collaborative Work

Group Roles and Assignments in CSCL

Team-Building Skills and CSCL Outcomes

Collaborative Structures and CSCL Outcomes

Collaborative Group Techniques

Structured Controversy

Problem-Based Learning

CSCL: The Bottom Line

12

Learning Together Virtually

WE STATED IN OUR FIRST EDITION that the research base was insufficient to make firm recommendations regarding computer-mediated collaborative learning. Therefore, we summarized the research evidence available from face-to-face collaborative learning and speculated about ways this evidence might apply to e-learning environments.

Although there continues to be a great deal written about computer-supported collaborative learning (CSCL), we still do not have sufficient evidence to offer guidelines for its best use. However, due to the interest in this topic and to the emergence of *"social software"* in the form of synchronous collaboration tools, as well as blogs and wikis for asynchronous collaboration, we wanted to summarize the main issues being addressed in CSCL research. Design principles such as modality or contiguity featured in previous chapters are not yet available for CSCL. Still, our discussion of the issues and research surrounding computer-mediated collaboration will shape your ideas for applying collaborative techniques in ways that support workforce learning. We will review research on how the following factors may modify CSCL results: individual versus group outcomes, team composition, technology features, task assignments and instructions, participant roles, time to collaborate, and teamwork skills.

DESIGN DILEMMA: YOU DECIDE

The new vice president of corporate learning and performance is very keen on knowledge management strategies that capture organizational expertise and make it accessible via electronic repositories. She has indicated that she wants all project teams to integrate collaborative activities into both formal and informal learning programs. The database training project manager has directed the design team to integrate some effective collaboration techniques into the new course. Reshmi wants to incorporate collaborative projects. Specifically, she would like to assign teams to design a database that will improve an operational objective in their department. Matt thinks a team project of this type will require too much instructor mentoring time. And he is skeptical about the learning outcomes of group work for the resources invested. Instead, he suggests that they set up a company-wide discussion board to exchange ideas and applications relevant to databases. Both Matt and Reshmi wonder about the best collaborative approach to use. Would they get better results from synchronous activities or from asynchronous discussions? They also wonder about the best way to structure whatever collaborative assignments they decide to pursue. Based on your own experience or intuition, which of the following options is/are correct:

A. A team project assignment to create a real-world database will result in better individual learning than an individual project assignment.

B. A discussion board would have more far-reaching benefits than an end-of-class project.

C. A team project would be best accomplished through synchronous collaborative facilities using chat or audio.

D. Any collaborative assignments should include structured group roles and processes for best results.

E. Not sure which options are correct.

What Is Computer-Supported Collaborative Learning (CSCL)?

The first generations of e-learning were designed for solo learning. There were few practical ways to integrate multiple learners or instructors into asynchronous self-study e-learning. However, the emergence of *social software* has made both synchronous and asynchronous connections practical and easy. Table 12.1 summarizes common social software and some of their applications in e-learning. Chats, breakout rooms in virtual classrooms (shown in Figure 12.1), wikis (shown in Figure 12.2), blogs, and discussion boards (shown in Figure 12.3) offer a variety of channels for online collaboration. Tools such as wikis and blogs have emerged since our first edition.

Table 12.1. Online Facilities for Social Learning.

Facility	Description	Some e-Learning Applications
Blogs	A website where individuals write commentaries on an ongoing basis. Visitors can comment or link to a blog. Some writers use blogs to organize individual thoughts, while others command influential, worldwide audiences of thousands.	Learning journals Post-class application commentaries Informal updates on course skills and related topics Evaluation of course effectiveness
Breakout Rooms	A conferencing facility that usually supports audio, whiteboard, polling, and chat, used for small groups in conjunction with a virtual classroom event or online conference (see Figure 12.1)	Synchronous team work during a virtual classroom session Small group meetings

(Continued)

Table 12.1. (Continued).

Facility	Description	Some e-Learning Applications
Chats	Two or more participants communicating at the same time by text	Role-play practice Group decision making Group project work Pair collaborative study Questions or comments during a virtual presentation
Email	Two or more participants communicating at different times with messages received and managed at the individual's mail site	Group project work Instructor-student exchanges Pair collaborative activities
Message Boards	A number of participants communicate at different times by typing comments that remain on the board for others to read and respond to (see Figure 12.3)	Topic-specific discussions Case-study work Post-class commentaries
Online Conferencing	A number of participants online at once with access to audio, whiteboard, polling, media displays, and chat	Guest speakers Virtual classes Group project work
Wikis	A website that allows visitors to edit its contents; can be controlled for editing/viewing by a small group or by all (see Figure 12.2)	Collaborative work on a project document Ongoing updated repository of course information Collaborative course material construction

Figure 12.1. Synchronous Collaborative Learning with Chat, Audio, Whiteboard in Breakout Room.

From Clark & Kwinn, 2007.

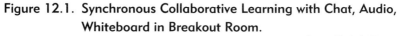

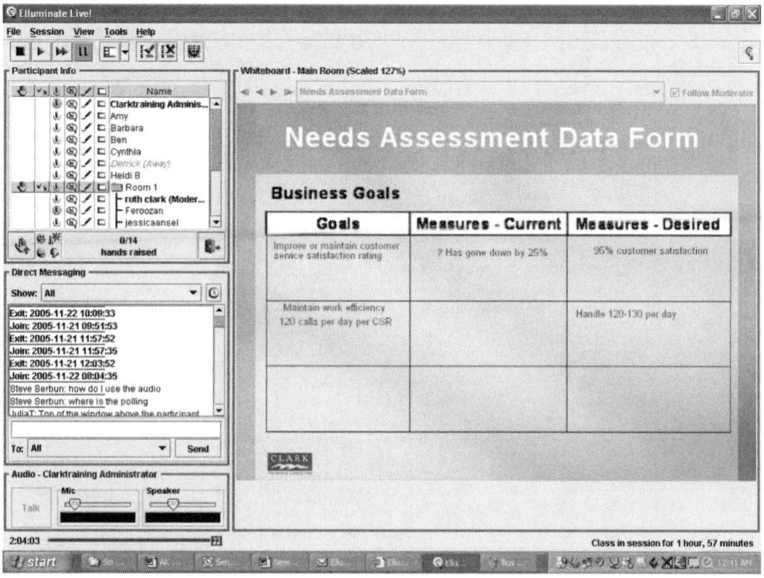

Figure 12.2. Asynchronous Collaborative Learning Using a Wiki.

Accessed from http://en.wikipedia.org, August 15, 2006.

**Figure 12.3. Asynchronous Collaborative Learning Using a
Discussion Board.**

With permission from The Australian Flexible Learning Framework 2006
and the e-Learning Networks Community Forum.

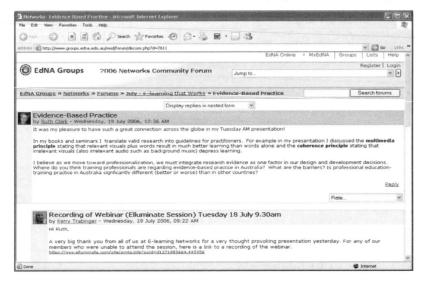

Other tools have expanded greatly in their use. For example, in large commercial organizations remote synchronous forms of instructor-led training make up 25 percent of the training delivery media (Dolezalek, 2005).

What do we really know about how various approaches to computer-mediated collaborative learning affect learning and performance? To answer that question we need to define what we mean by CSCL and how we measure its effectiveness.

Types of CSCL

By CSCL we refer to collaborative engagements among teams of two to five members using synchronous and/or asynchronous tool facilities in ways that support an instructional goal, such as to produce a joint product, resolve a case study, or complete an instructional worksheet. Other forms of CSCL that we will not address include knowledge management resources as a repository of community electronic documents, including templates, checklists, best-practice examples, and mentor contacts. These resources are generally available on the organization's website and are intended primarily for use as asynchronous guides for individual work assignments.

Individual vs. Group Outcomes from CSCL

Research studies have used different metrics to assess CSCL outcomes. To assess the applicability of a CSCL research report to your environment and goals, you need to identify what outcomes were measured. *Individual outcomes* from CSCL measure achievements of each member of a team that has worked collaboratively. For example, a team of four collaborates in a virtual classroom for several hours to solve a case problem. After the exercise, each team member is individually tested for his or her knowledge gained from the case. Individual outcome metrics include satisfaction ratings, technology usage logs, analysis of statements made by participants during the collaborative activities, and learning evaluated by traditional tests or by a product such as an essay, a design plan, or a problem solution.

In contrast, other research studies measure *group outcomes.* For example, a team of four works together over several hours to solve a case problem. The group solution to this exercise and the quality of the discussions are evaluated as the primary outcomes. Group outcomes include metrics such as group perceptions of learning, team test scores or team grades, products or decisions emerging from team collaboration, analysis of team dialog during collaboration, and logs to evaluate which technology features were used for what purposes. Each of these outcomes tells us different things, and no one measure tells the full story. For instructional purposes, learning outcomes are an important metric to guide our decisions.

We might assume that if a team outcome is good, the individuals who make up that team likewise benefited. This, however, may not always be the case. A meta-analysis of CSCL by Lou, Abrami, and d'Apollonia (2001) separated research that measured individual achievement outcomes from studies that measured group products. They found that group performance is not necessarily predictive of individual performance. In addition, factors that optimize individual performance from collaborative environments are different from those that optimize team performance.

Therefore, you will need to carefully examine the performance metrics cited in any claims regarding the effectiveness of CSCL. In addition, decide whether group performance or individual performance is more relevant to your goals. For example, a project team is assigned to develop a risk analysis for a costly new technology initiative the organization is considering. The team consists of experts from product design, manufacturing, engineering, consumer research, and finance. In this setting, the final group product is the main focus of interest and you would want to design collaborative environments that lead to best team performance. In contrast, in a class on risk analysis, project teams are assembled to work on a case study. Each team must produce a risk analysis report. Here the main focus of interest is individual learning and you would want design collaborative environments that lead to best individual performance.

In general, goals related to workplace performance products suggest a focus on group outcomes, whereas learning goals suggest a focus on individual performance outcomes.

Factors That Make a Difference: Overview

Early CSCL research compared outcomes from various forms of CSCL to outcomes from individual work. Unfortunately, little consensus emerged. As the field matures, a more productive question is: Under what circumstances will individual or group outcomes of a given type be best mediated by what type of online collaborative structures? However, we are unlikely to find guidelines that are universally applicable.

As summarized in Table 12.2, technology features, team assignments, performance evaluation plans, and team sizes are among a number of elements that can affect CSCL outcomes. Any unique combination of those factors may exert different effects. For example, the individual learning outcomes of a team of two working on a near-transfer task in a synchronous chat mode would likely be quite different from a group product outcome from a team of four working on a decision task in an asynchronous discussion environment. Alter any one of these factors, and the outcome may shift.

In this section we review meta-analysis and individual research studies that have addressed some of the factors listed in Table 12.2. A comprehensive review of all relevant reports on CSCL is a book in itself. Instead, we limit ourselves to a few recent reports that illustrate the range and diversity of ongoing research. From these reports you can get a glimpse of some of the factors that shape CSCL outcomes. However, until there is a much larger body of controlled research that measures learning and that systematically varies the factors listed in Table 12.2, we cannot make any broad generalizations about computer-mediated collaboration and learning.

Optimizing Individual Outcomes from CSCL

As mentioned previously, Lou, Abrami, and d'Apollonia (2001) synthesized the results of over 122 experiments that compared individual and/or group achievements from collaborative learning environments with individual learning from technology. They defined collaborative learning as: "Two or more students per computer on the same task in a face-to-face setting or two or more students collaborating either synchronously or asynchronously on the same task electronically versus learning with computers individually—one computer per student each working on his or her own task" (p. 457). Notice their definition for collaborative learning includes data from groups working with computers in a face-to-face environment as well as groups working through computers in either synchronous or asynchronous formats.

Lou, Abrami, and d'Apollonia (2001) find that, when optimal conditions are present, individual learning is better in collaborative compared to individual settings with an effect size of .66, which is considered of moderate practical significance. But the key to success lies in the details. What factors should be present to realize these positive gains? Lou, Abrami, and d'Apollonia (2001) recommend the following:

A. Provide team skills training for students who lack previous experience working in a team.

B. Use specific collaborative learning structures that ensure interdependence among members of a team and at the same time promote individual accountability. Some examples of collaborative learning structures are structured argumentation and problem-based learning (to be summarized later in this chapter).

Table 12.2. CSCL Factors That Make a Difference.

Factor	Description	Guidelines	Citation
Outcome of Collaboration	Individual vs. group metrics; discourse analysis	Group metrics may be independent of individual outcomes. Assumes that deeper discourse equals better learning	Lou, Abrami, & d'Apollonia (2001); meta-analysis; Jonassen, Lee, Yang, & Laffey (2005)
Group Composition	Size: from 2 to 5 Makeup: heterogeneous vs. homogeneous	Best size may depend on desired outcomes; heterogeneous compositions generally favored	Lou, Abrami, & d'Apollonia (2001); meta-analysis
Technology	Synchronous vs. asynchronous Tools to support collaboration	Tool features should match outcome goals. Asynchronous better for reflection and longer time periods; synchronous better for higher social presence. Many common tools lack capability to capture and display group thinking. Need better groupware.	Kirschner, Strijbos, Kreijns, & Beers (2004); Suthers, Vatrapu, Joseph, Dwyer, & Medina (2005); McGill, Nicol, Littlejohn, Gierson, Juster, & Ion (2005); Jonassen, Lee, Yang, & Laffey (2005)
Task Assignment	Near transfer Far transfer —well structured Far transfer —ill structured	CSCL lends itself well to far-transfer ill-structured problem solving with groups of three to five. Mixed results with near and well-structured far-transfer assignments.	Jonassen, Lee, Yang, & Laffey (2005); Yetter, Gutkin, Saunders, Galloway, Sebansky, & Song (2006); Kirschner, Strijbos, Kreijns, & Beers (2004); Uribe, Klein, & Sullivan (2003)

Category	Variations	Findings	References
Group Roles, Processes, and Instructions	Instructor or student moderator; Assigned roles; High or low structure process; Frequency of interaction	Student moderators may be better for groups of advanced learners when argumentation structures are used; Higher structures generally lead to better outcomes than low structure; Specific instructions lead to better outcomes than general instructions	DeWever, Van Winckle, & Valcke (2006); Nussbaum & Kardash (2005); Campbell & Stasser (2006); Nussbaum (2005)
Time	Limited vs. constrained	CSCL outcomes take longer than individual outcomes; CSCL outcomes can exceed individual outcomes if there is ample processing time	Campbell & Stasser (2006)
Team Skills Training	Yes or No	Teamwork training leads to better outcomes as long as the trained group remains intact	Prichard, Bizo, & Stratford (2006)
Learner Prior Knowledge	High vs. Low	Factors that mediate CSCL among high PK learners likely different from those most appropriate for low PK learners	Uribe, Klein, & Sullivan (2003)
Incentives	The basis for awarding of points or grades	Base points or grades on a synthesis of individual outcomes rather than a group product or individual products alone	Mayer, 2007; Slavin, Hurley, & Chamberlain (2003)

C. Create teams of heterogeneous pairs. Pairs maximize the involvement of each participant. The more experienced member of the pair benefits from tutoring the less experienced member, while the less experienced member benefits from being tutored.

D. Use collaborative teams when the learning tasks are relatively near transfer rather than ill-structured open-ended assignments.

In addition, based on extensive research on group learning in face-to-face settings summarized by Slavin (1983) and Slavin, Hurley, and Chamberlain (2003), we recommend that incentives such as grades or points be assigned to individuals based on the achievement of each individual in the group, rather than based on a single group product or on individual achievements unrelated to the achievements of other members in the team. For example, if a group works together on a case study project, rather than assigning the same grade to each individual based on the group product, team grades are based on an aggregation of individual outcomes to a test or other individual measure of learning related to the project. This evaluation strategy assures that each member of the group is accountable not only for his or her own performance but for that of teammates.

Optimizing Group Products from CSCL

When your goal is a performance product, groups can outperform individuals. Under optimal conditions, Lou, Abrami, and d'Apollonia (2001) found that group products are better than individual products, with an effect size of 2 or more, indicating a very high practical significance! The research team concludes: "When working together, the group is capable of doing more than any single member by comparing alternative interpretations and solutions, correcting each other's misconceptions, and forming a more holistic picture of the problem" (p. 479).

To optimize group performance:

A. Assign challenging tasks that can benefit from the perspectives and expertise of several participants; ill-defined far-transfer tasks are best.

B. Construct groups of three to five members to provide sufficient expertise to tackle a difficult task.

In the next section of this chapter we will look at research that evaluates how various factors, including task assignments, technology, time limits, group roles, and teamwork training can influence either group or individual outcomes. Our goal is not a comprehensive review of CSCL research. That would require a book in itself. Rather, we seek to illustrate the diversity in research questions, assigned tasks, outcome measures, and technologies reflected in some representative recent reports.

Is Problem-Solving Learning Better with CSCL or Solo?

Jonassen, Lee, Yang, and Laffey (2005) recommend that CSCL is best suited to complex ill-defined tasks for which there is no single correct solution. These types of tasks benefit from the collaboration of a group. Some examples include developing a patient treatment plan, designing a small business website, or troubleshooting a unique equipment failure. The study reviewed in this section evaluates learning a process to solve ill-defined problems as a result of practice via CSCL compared to solo practice.

RESEARCH THUMBNAIL

Problem Solving: Team Using Chat vs. Individual Solutions

Authors: Uribe, Klein, and Sullivan (2003)

Type of Study: Experimental

Task: Applying a structured problem-solving process to solve ill-structured problems

Outcome Measures: Individual scores of an essay describing a solution to an ill-defined assessment problem

Teams: Heterogeneous pairs of college students

Technology: Synchronous chat

Comparison: Assessment scores of individuals who solved a practice problem in a team via synchronous chat versus individuals who solved the problem alone

Result: Individuals working in pairs via synchronous chat learned more than individuals working alone

In an experimental study, Uribe, Klein, and Sullivan (2003) compared individual learning of a problem-solving process from pairs solving an assessment problem collaboratively using synchronous chat to individuals solving the assessment problem on their own. The study included three phases. First, each participant individually completed web-based self-study training on a four-step problem-solving process. After the instructional period, participants were tested individually with a knowledge quiz to ensure learning of the process. Quiz results were positive for all participants. In Phase 2, participants were assigned to solve an ill-structured practice problem, either alone or with a virtual partner using chat. In the third phase, each participant individually completed an essay test that asked questions about the assessment problem they solved in Phase 2. Individuals who worked with a partner scored higher on the essay questions (60 percent average) than individuals who had worked independently (50 percent average). The difference was significant, with a small effect size of .11.

Virtual vs. Face-to-Face Group Decisions

How can group decision making benefit from collaborative technology? In the study reviewed in this section, the decisions of teams working face-to-face were compared with decisions made in a collaborative virtual environment.

RESEARCH THUMBNAIL

Team Decision Quality: Virtual vs. Face-to-Face Collaboration

Authors: Campbell and Stasser, 2006

Type of Study: Experimental

Task: Identify the guilty suspect in a crime case for which there was a correct answer that could be derived only by sharing of information given to different team members

Outcome Measures: Accuracy of group solutions to a crime decision task

Teams: Trios of college students in which each member was provided different relevant case knowledge

Technology: Synchronous chat

Comparison: Synchronous chat versus face-to-face decision accuracy; ample versus constrained time during synchronous chat

Result: Synchronous collaborators with plenty of time produced more accurate decisions than face-to-face teams or synchronous collaborators with restricted time

Campbell and Stasser (2006) compared the accuracy of a decision task that had a correct answer from three-person groups collaborating in a face-to-face group with the accuracy of trios collaborating via synchronous chat. The decision task involved a fictional homicide investigation with three suspects. Each participant in the trios received a different packet of information about the crime and the suspects. A correct solution required that all three team members disclose and discuss the unique information that each had reviewed in his or her packet.

Overall, the computer-mediated groups arrived at more correct solutions (63 percent) than face-to-face groups (less than 20 percent), provided the computer team was allocated sufficient discussion time. Some computer teams were given only twenty minutes to solve the problem, whereas others were instructed to take as long as they needed. The time-restricted computer-mediated groups were much less accurate when compared to computer groups given ample discussion time. The computer-mediated groups required more time to arrive at their solutions than the face-to-face groups, resulting in higher solution accuracy. The research team concluded that computer-mediated discussions are more effective for decision making than face-to face groups, provided virtual groups have sufficient working time. They suggest that synchronous chat leads to more accurate decisions than face-to-face discussions due to parallel communications in chat, the ability to reference the group discussion maintained in the text of the chat, as well as the anonymity of the communications.

Software Representations to Support Collaborative Work

How can computer interfaces more effectively represent and support collaborative work? For example, the comments in a traditional discussion board are displayed chronologically. In a lengthy discussion it is challenging to infer shared agreement or to make knowledge gained explicit. If you join an ongoing discussion, it can be difficult to find relevant contributions, enter your own ideas into a relevant context, or to make a determination of the outcomes.

RESEARCH THUMBNAIL

Problem Solving with Different Collaboration Interfaces

Authors: Suthers, Vatrapu, Joseph, Dwyer, and Medina (2005)

Type of Study: Experimental

Task: Solving a science problem

Outcome Measures: Accuracy of individual solutions to a science problem, convergence of conclusions in essays

Technology: Asynchronous discussions

Teams: Pairs of college students

Comparison: Asynchronous discussions using discussion board, graphic representation, and both discussion board and graphic representation

Result: No differences in quality of solutions; greater idea convergence with graphic representations

Suthers, Vatrapu, Joseph, Dwyer, and Medina (2005) evaluated the effectiveness of three different interfaces to summarize and capture collaboration decisions and data. They compared a traditional discussion board, the graphic representation shown in Figure 12.4, and a mix of the discussion board and graphic. The graphic representation uses symbols and lines to

Figure 12.4. A Graphical Interface to Capture Group Problem-Solving Processes.

From Suthers, Vatrapu, Joseph, Dwyer, and Medina, 2005.
Reprinted with permission from D. Suthers.

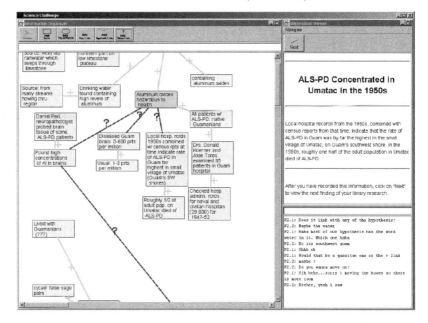

encode facts, state hypotheses, and link facts to hypotheses. The goal of the graphic interface is to represent a group discussion around scientific topics.

Pairs of college students were given science problems to solve along with a number of short articles with relevant information. Teams had up to 120 minutes to work asynchronously using one of the three different interfaces. An asynchronous environment was simulated by imposing filler activities during the 120-minute experimental period. Following the study period, each participant worked alone to write an essay about the problem he or she researched that stated the hypotheses considered, the evidence for or against the hypotheses, and the conclusion reached. The research team compared the solutions as well as the convergence in essay conclusions among teams working with different interfaces. They found best convergence among teams that used the graphic representation. However, there were no significant differences in correct solutions to the problem.

Group Roles and Assignments in CSCL

The outcomes in face-to-face team learning assignments are affected by the structure of the group process, including roles assigned to team members. In this section we summarize two studies that examine the influence of team member role assignments on CSCL interactions.

RESEARCH THUMBNAIL

Roles in Problem-Based Learning (PBL) Online Discussions

Authors: De Wever, Van Winckle, and Valcke (2006)

Type of Study: Quasi experimental

Task: Development of treatment plans for clinical pediatric cases

Outcome Measures: Depth of group discussions

Teams: Groups of four or five medical interns

Technology: Asynchronous discussions

Comparison: Student versus instructor discussion moderation and alternative treatment generation role

Results: Deeper case discussions with student moderators only when another student generated treatment alternatives

DeWever, Van Winckle, and Valcke (2006) report on adapting a problem-based learning program using asynchronous case discussions. Pediatric interns met weekly for face-to-face case reviews. More frequent case discussions were desired, but additional face-to-face meetings were not practical due to staff schedules and ward activities. To supplement the face-to-face meetings, the research team tested asynchronous discussions of authentic cases, each extending over a two-week period. A complete case with diagnosis was included, along with access to electronic information resources. For the first three days, each participant worked independently to develop a patient treatment plan. Starting on day four, individual posts were opened to everyone and each participant was required to post at least four additional messages in which they supported their treatment plans with rationale, data, and references.

Two different team roles were studied: moderator (student versus instructor) and alternatives generator (participant role versus no role). In some teams one of the interns served as a moderator, while in other teams the instructor moderated the discussions. A second variable was an assigned student role to review posted treatment suggestions and develop alternative treatments. Rather than direct measures of learning, the outcome measure was quality of discussions within the different teams.

DeWever, Van Winckle, and Valcke (2006) found that students who were assigned a moderator role were more likely to write higher-level contributions. Further, higher-knowledge construction was evident in groups moderated by a student, but only when one of the participants assumed the alternative treatment role. In the absence of this specialized role, there were no differences in the discussions of student-moderated or instructor-moderated discussions. The research team suggests that, when a student develops alternatives and the discussion is moderated by another student, there is greater freedom to critique and respond to one another than when an instructor is moderating.

In this study there were no direct measures of learning. The outcome measure was ratings of the quality of the discussions among the different teams. In addition, as medical interns, the background knowledge level of the participants was relatively high compared to other studies in which participants had little or no entry-level knowledge related to the experimental task. Different results might be seen among learners more novice to the content. This study suggests that discussions will differ depending on assigned roles within a team.

RESEARCH THUMBNAIL

Different Team Goal Assignments

Author: Nussbaum, 2005

Type of Study: Experimental

Task: Online debates of issues such as the relationship between watching television and violence in children

Outcome Measures: Type and complexity of group arguments during discussions

Teams: Trios of college students

Technology: Synchronous chat

Comparison: Different team goals such as persuade, explore, generate reasons, or no goal

Result: Persuade and generate reasons goals resulted in more argumentation claims

The type of assignment made to a collaborative group can affect group outcomes. Nussbaum (2005) compared the quality of arguments made by teams using synchronous chat responding to the question: "Does watching TV cause children to become more violent?" The type and complexity of team arguments were analyzed as outcomes. As in the DeWever research, the outcome was an analysis of the discussions of the group rather than individual learning.

Different teams were given different instructions. Some were assigned a general goal, such as *explore the question* or *write a persuasive discussion,* or no goal at all. Other teams were given specific goals, such as *give reasons* or *state counter-arguments.* The asynchronous discussion spanned five days, during which all participants were required to post two notes. The various goal assignments resulted in arguments of varying quality.

The author concludes that goals to persuade and generate reasons had the strongest effects, resulting in more argumentation claims. Specifically, the author recommends that students should be explicitly told to think of as many reasons as possible to support their positions.

In both the medical intern and the argumentation research summarized in this section, we see that CSCL outcomes are influenced by the instructions given to the team as well as by specific roles assigned within the team. Both studies measured the quality of the group discussions, so we do not know how individual learning outcomes were affected.

Team-Building Skills and CSCL Outcomes

In the Lou, Abrami, and d'Apollonia (2001) meta-analysis, better individual achievement outcomes are associated with better teamwork skills. A similar result is reported by a study conducted comparing a year-long face-to-face college course in which trained and untrained teams worked together to accomplish various course assignments.

RESEARCH THUMBNAIL

Team Skills Training

Authors: Prichard, Bizo, and Stratford (2006)

Type of Study: Naturalistic experimental

Task: Learning to report psychological research

Outcome Measures: Individual course scores and various individual ratings

Teams: Groups of five or six college students

Technology: Face-to-face teamwork

Comparison: Teams that had team skills training versus teams with no training

Result: Better outcomes for teams with teamwork training, only as long as the trained team remained intact

Prichard, Bizo, and Stratford (2006) found that individuals working in face-to-face teams that completed a one-day team skills training program earned end-of-semester scores that were 6 percent higher than untrained teams. The team-skills training included: setting objectives, problem solving, planning, decision making, and time management. The team-skills training benefits lasted as long as the teams that were trained together stayed together. However, when trained team members were reorganized into new teams the second semester, the outcomes of the new teams were no better than those of teams who had not been trained. In a follow-up experiment, another group of teams was provided team-skills training and, rather than being reorganized into new teams at the end of the semester, remained intact for the academic year. These intact teams maintained their improved learning outcomes. The authors suggest that team skills developed in a specific team may not transfer from one team to another. They conclude that "These findings provide empirical evidence that prior team-skills training has produced superior collaborative group work compared with that of students merely placed in unfacilitated groups"(p. 129).

This study focused on face-to-face collaborative learning. If specific elements of the teamwork training program such as setting objectives, problem solving, decision making, and so forth, could be translated into collaborative interfaces that supported those activities, perhaps the benefits of team training could be magnified in a collaborative environment.

Collaborative Structures and CSCL Outcomes

Research in face-to-face collaborative learning summarized by Slavin (1983), Slavin, Hurley, and Chamberlain (2003) and Mayer (2007), as well as the Lou, Abrami, and d'Apollonia (2001) meta-analysis of virtual collaboration, suggests that under appropriate conditions students can learn more together than individually. A structured collaborative assignment is one critical condition to maximize benefits from group work. A second is accountability for learning of each member of the team. Collaborative environments that give general instructions such as "Discuss these issues" and that reward group products rather than individual products may not lead to optimal results.

Collaborative Group Techniques

Collaborative structures that promote reliance of team members on each other and also foster individual accountability have proven most effective in face-to-face environments. In this section we review two structures that have been used extensively in face-to-face collaborative learning environments: *structured controversy* and *problem-based learning*. Structures such as these that have been evaluated in face-to-face collaborative settings can serve as starting points for the building of CSCL environments.

Structured Controversy

Wiley and Voss (1999) showed that individual learners assigned to write a pro and con argument learned more than learners asked to write either a narration or a summary. The deeper processing stimulated by synthesizing opposing aspects of an issue led to more learning than merely writing a summary. Developing alternative positions on an issue supported by facts is called *argumentation.* Johnson and Johnson (1992) developed a structured methodology for group argumentation called *structured controversy.*

The workflow for structured controversy is summarized in Figure 12.5. Learners are assigned to heterogeneous teams of four. The teams are presented with an issue or problem that lends itself to a pro-and-con position. The teams divide into pairs, each taking either the pro or con, and develop a strong position for their perspective. Later, the team of four reconvenes and one pair presents their argument to the other. After the presentation, the receiving pair must state back the argument adequately to the presenting pair to demonstrate their understanding of the presentation team's position. Then the pairs reverse roles. As a result, all team members develop an understanding of both perspectives. After the argumentation, the full team moves into a synthesis stage wherein the opposing perspectives are merged into a reasoned position that culminates in a group report or presentation.

Figure 12.5. Structured Argumentation Collaborative Learning Structure.

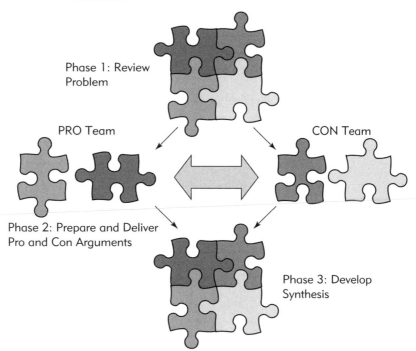

Phase 1: Review Problem

PRO Team

CON Team

Phase 2: Prepare and Deliver Pro and Con Arguments

Phase 3: Develop Synthesis

When comparing this structured controversy method with several alternative structures, including traditional debates, individual learning, or groups that stressed concurrence, the structured controversy method proved more effective, with effect sizes ranging from .42 to .77 (Johnson & Johnson, 1992).

The authors recommend the following elements for successful constructive controversy:

- Ensure a cooperative context where the goal is understanding the opposing views, followed by a synthesis of perspectives;
- Structure groups to include learners of mixed background knowledge and ability;
- Provide access to rich and relevant information about the issues;
- Ensure adequate social skills to manage conflict; and
- Focus group interactions on rational arguments.

Structured controversy can use a combination of asynchronous and synchronous facilities in a CSCL adaptation. For example, present an application problem or case that lends itself to two or more alternative positions. Provide links to relevant resources. Assign pairs to research and advocate for one of the positions. Each pair can work asynchronously through email or discussion boards to research their position and to develop their case, as well as synchronously via telephone or online conferencing. Next each pair posts their argument to an accessible online location and reviews opposing arguments. To verify understanding of alternative positions, pairs could post their summaries of the opposing arguments or state back the opposition positions in synchronous sessions. To complete the exercise, the entire team of four develops a project that represents a synthesis of all perspectives. Structured argumentation ported to CSCL could benefit from a combination of asynchronous research and reflection coupled with synchronous discussions.

Problem-Based Learning

A number of universities have adopted a specialized form of collaborative learning called problem-based learning (PBL). Most PBL teams follow a structured process whereby the team reviews a case together, each member works on it individually, and then the team reconvenes to apply lessons learned to the case. For example, the University of Maastricht in the Netherlands follows the following team process after reading a presented case such as the Life of a Miserable Stomach, shown in Figure 12.6:

1. Clarify unknown terms and concepts.

2. Define the problem in the case.

3. Use brainstorming to analyze the problem by identifying plausible explanations.

4. Critique the different explanations produced and work to draft a coherent description of the problem.

5. Define the learning issues.

6. Engage in self-directed study to fill the gaps specified by the learning issues.

7. Meet with the team to share learning and develop a final problem solution.

Figure 12.6. A Case Problem Used in PBL.

From Schmidt and Moust, 2000.

The Miserable Life of a Stomach

The protagonist of our story is the stomach of a truck driver who used to work shifts and who smokes a lot. The stomach developed a gastric ulcer and so the smoking stopped. Stomach tablets are not a regular part of the intake.

While on the highway in Southern Germany, our stomach had to digest a heavy German lunch. Half an hour later, a severe abdominal pain developed. The stomach had to expel the meal. Two tablets of acetylsalicylic acid were inserted to relieve the pain.

A second extrusion some hours later contained a bit of blood. In a hospital in Munich an endoscope was inserted. The stomach needed to be operated upon in the near future. Explain.

Research reviews conclude that there is no clear evidence that PBL offers significant learning advantages over traditional instructional approaches. However, PBL medical students consistently report more positive attitudes than students engaged in traditional courses (Hmelo-Silver, 2004).

How can PBL be adapted to CSCL? Valaitis, Sword, Jones, and Hodges (2005) evaluated a PBL lesson for nursing students that used both asynchronous and synchronous chat sessions. The focus of the lesson was Fetal Alcohol Spectrum Disorder (FASD). Students begin the lesson by viewing an online video of a pregnant patient being interviewed by the nurse. Students had access to a number of resources, including a patient history (shown in Figure 12.7), a multimedia description of early fetal development, and related articles and websites. In addition, students could email a variety of experts on FASD, including a public health nurse, a neonatologist, and a legal guardian of two children with FASD. Figure 12.8 shows the email interface to these resources. Student reactions to the case experts was very positive. One participant commented: "So, having a real person with real experience; that was really good," noting that Ann Guardian was more genuine than the characters in the PBL case videos (Valaitis, Sword, Jones, & Hodges, 2005, p. 242).

Figure 12.7. A Patient History from a PBL Case.

With permission from Ruta Valaitis. Accessed December 7, 2005, from www.fhs.mcmaster.ca/pblonline/scenarios.htm

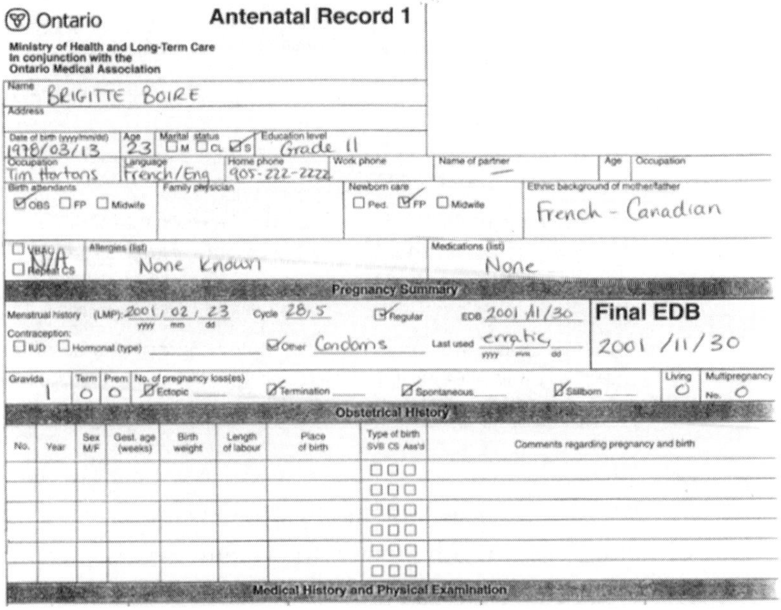
Ontario
Antenatal Record 1
Ministry of Health and Long-Term Care
in conjunction with the
Ontario Medical Association
Name: BRIGITTE BOIRE
Address
Date of birth (yyyy/mm/dd): 1978/03/13 | Age: 23 | Marital status: ☐ M ☐ CL ☑ S | Education level: Grade 11
Occupation: Tim Hortons | Language: French/Eng | Home phone: 905-222-2222 | Work phone | Name of partner: — | Age | Occupation
Birth attendants: ☑ OBS ☐ FP ☐ Midwife | Family physician | Newborn care: ☐ Ped. ☑ FP ☐ Midwife | Ethnic background of mother/father: French - Canadian
☐ VBAC ☐ Repeat CS: N/A | Allergies (list): None Known | Medications (list): None
Pregnancy Summary
Menstrual history (LMP): 2001 / 02 / 23 (yyyy mm dd) | Cycle 28, 5 | ☑ Regular | EDB 2001 /11/30 | Final EDB 2001 /11/30
Contraception: ☐ IUD ☐ Hormonal (type) ☑ Other Condoms | Last used erratic (yyyy mm dd)
Gravida 1 | Term 0 | Prem 0 | No. of pregnancy loss(es): ☑ Ectopic ☑ Termination ☑ Spontaneous ☑ Stillborn | Living 0 | Multipregnancy No. 0
Obstetrical History

No.	Year	Sex M/F	Gest. age (weeks)	Birth weight	Length of labour	Place of birth	Type of birth SVB CS Ass'd	Comments regarding pregnancy and birth
							☐ ☐ ☐	
							☐ ☐ ☐	
							☐ ☐ ☐	
							☐ ☐ ☐	
							☐ ☐ ☐	
							☐ ☐ ☐	

Medical History and Physical Examination

Figure 12.8. Asynchronous Access to Experts During PBL Lesson.

Accessed December 7, 2005, from www.fhs.mcmaster.ca/pblonline/scenarios.htm

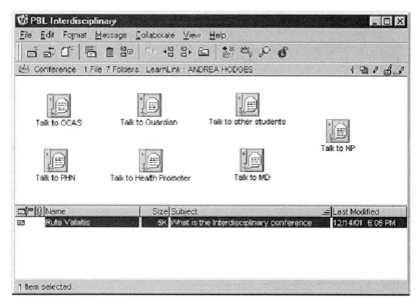

CSCL: The Bottom Line

Jonassen, Lee, Yang, and Laffey (2005) conclude their review of CSCL research as follows: "More is unknown about the practice than is known. CSCL will constitute one of the pivotal research issues of the next decade" (p. 264). We do have evidence that under optimal conditions, learning collaboratively can result in better outcomes than learning alone. Likewise, work products and projects can, under some conditions, benefit from a collaborative approach. However, what constitutes optimal conditions for one set of learners, desired outcomes, and technology features is likely different from what is appropriate for a different set. We can point to the following enablers that may promote better individual or group outcomes from collaborative environments:

A. Group process structures that foster the accountability and participation of each member of the team

B. Assignment of far-transfer problems to small heterogeneous groups composed of three to five members

C. Use of asynchronous facilities for outcomes that benefit from reflection and independent research; use of representational mechanisms such as text or diagrams to maintain a record of the communications, allow for parallel input, encode group agreements, and support greater anonymity of discussions

D. Team-skill training for groups that have not had previous teamwork experience

E. Group assignments and participant roles that promote deeper processing

F. Clear guidance and objectives for team processes to avoid extraneous mental processing

DESIGN DILEMMA: RESOLVED

In our chapter introduction, you considered the following options for collaborative work in the database course:

A. A team project assignment to create a real-world database will result in better individual learning than an individual project assignment.

B. A discussion board would have more far-reaching benefits than an end-of-class project.

C. A team project would be best accomplished through synchronous collaborative facilities using chat or audio.

D. Any collaborative assignments should include structured group roles and processes for best results.

E. Not sure which options are correct.

Constructing an effective database is a far-transfer task because the generic steps will require adaptation to each unique situation. Option A to assign a collaborative case study is a good idea. The database created by a well-structured collaborative team will likely be better than one designed by an individual working alone. However, in addition to evaluating the database constructed by a team as a whole, to motivate mutual support to each participant's learning, the instructor should base group assessments on some measures of individual learning. A team score should reflect some synthesis of individual scores.

Asynchronous discussions, as suggested in Option B, if appropriately structured, can result in deep communications. Likewise, a discussion board can provide a community resource for ongoing learning after a class. However, we do not have evidence to support the cost benefits of a discussion board compared to other CSCL alternatives such as a group project.

Option C recommends synchronous collaborative facilities. However, a team project would likely benefit from at least some asynchronous work, since constructing a database requires reflection and research. A combination of synchronous and asynchronous collaboration might yield the best results.

Option D is correct. The course outcomes will be well served by adding structured roles and processes into whatever CSCL options they choose.

At this stage in the evolution of CSCL, we lack sufficient evidence on which to predicate an ideal collaborative environment or even to know when resources invested in such an environment will yield any significant organizational return.

WHAT TO LOOK FOR IN e-LEARNING

☐ In classes that focus on far-transfer outcomes, group projects or case assignments that incorporate some asynchronous work to allow time for reflection and individual research

☐ Small teams with participants of diverse prior knowledge and background

☐ Structured collaborative team processes that encourage individual participation and accountability to the team outcome

☐ Use of CSCL when there is adequate learning time to support team discussions and product generation

☐ Student evaluations that reflect the accomplishments of each member of the team to encourage interdependence

COMING NEXT

Asynchronous forms of e-learning can use navigational devices such as menus and links that grant learners many choices over elements of the course. In Chapter 13, we review the options and benefits of offering control over pacing, lesson topics, and instructional methods such as practice. How do these levels of freedom affect learning? Who benefits most from learner control? How should synchronous forms of e-learning that are more limited in learner control options compensate for additional extraneous cognitive load? These are some of the issues we review in Chapter 13.

Suggested Readings

Campbell, J., & Stasser, G. (2006). The influence of time and task demonstrability on decision making in computer-mediated and face-to-face groups. *Small Group Research, 37* (3), 271–294.

Jonassen, D.H., Lee, C.B., Yang, C-C., & Laffey, J. (2005). The collaboration principle in multimedia learning. In R.E. Mayer (Ed.), *The Cambridge handbook of multimedia learning.* Newyork: Cambridge University Press.

Laboratory for Interactive Learning Technologies: lilt.ics.hawaii.edu/lilt/software/ belvedere/index.html

Lou, Y., Abrami, P.C., & d'Apollonia, S. (2001). Small group and individual learning with technology: A meta-analysis. *Review of Educational Research, 71*(3), 449–521.

Uribe, D., Klein, J.D., & Sullivan, H. (2003). The effect of computer-mediated collaborative learning on solving ill-defined problems. *Educational Technology Research and Development, 51*(1), 5–19.

CHAPTER OUTLINE

Learner Control Versus Program Control

    Three Types of Learner Control

    Popularity of Learner Control

Do Learners Make Good Instructional Decisions?

    Do You Know What You Think You Know? Calibration Accuracy

    How Calibration Is Measured

    Illusions of Knowing: Evidence for Poor Calibrations

    Practice and Examples Improve Calibration Accuracy

    Do Learners Like Lesson Features That Lead to Learning?

    Psychological Reasons for Poor Learner Choices

Four Principles for Learner Control: Overview

Learner Control Principle 1: Give Experienced Learners Control

    Who Learns What Best Under Learner Control?

    Evidence for Benefits of Program Control

    Evidence for Learner Control Later in Learning

Learner Control Principle 2: Make Important Instructional Events the Default

Learner Control Principle 3: Consider Adaptive Control

    Four Formats for Adaptive Control

    Dynamic Adaptive Control vs. Program Control

    Adaptive Advisement vs. Adaptive Control

    Shared Control

Learner Control Principle 4: Give Pacing Control

    Manage Cognitive Load When Pacing Is Program-Controlled

Navigational Guidelines for Learner Control

    Use Headings and Introductory Statements

    Use Links Sparingly

    Use Course Maps

    Provide Basic Navigation Options

What We Don't Know About Learner Control

13

Who's in Control?

GUIDELINES FOR e-LEARNING
NAVIGATION

WHAT'S NEW IN THIS CHAPTER?

LEARNER CONTROL is implemented by navigational features such as menus and links that allow learners to select the topics and instructional elements they prefer. In our first edition, we recommended that you adjust the amount of learner control in asynchronous e-learning based on the prior knowledge of your learners and the criticality of your training goals. There has been relatively little new research on learner control since our first edition. In our update, we summarize new research on adaptive control and adaptive advisement designs in which instructional elements are dynamically personalized based on learner performance. We introduce shared control as a new approach to learner control in which both the program and the learner make decisions.

Based on the segmentation principle summarized in Chapter 9, we recommend that in asynchronous e-learning, you always allow learners control over pacing. Pacing control allows participants to progress forward or backward at their own rates. Learner control is one of the features that distinguishes asynchronous from synchronous forms of e-learning. Since synchronous e-learning is instructor-led, by default it is usually under instructor control. Instructor-controlled lessons have a greater potential to overload learners. Therefore in virtual classroom events it is especially important to apply multimedia principles that manage cognitive load.

DESIGN DILEMMA: YOU DECIDE

The e-learning design team is discussing the navigation controls for the database training currently under development:

Ben: "Here's my first cut at the navigation controls. (See Figure 13.1.) We'll set it up so the learner can jump to any topic she wants and can skip lesson topics she doesn't find relevant. And I'm adding a lot of links so the learner can jump to the practice exercises or examples if she wants them or skip them if she feels she understands the concepts. I'll also put in links so learners can branch to definitions and to other relevant websites. That's

Figure 13.1. Navigational Elements Designed for High Learner Control.

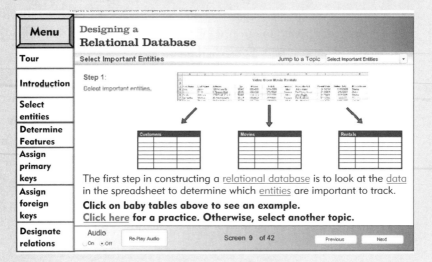

what people expect on the Internet. They are used to going where they want and doing what they want."

Reshmi: "But Ben, learning a new skill is not the same as surfing for information. We are building the lessons and topics in a logical sequence and including worked examples and practice exercises that should not be skipped. I think all those navigational features you've designed jeopardize the integrity of our training design. Having to make so many choices will only confuse the learners."

Ben: "The new generation of learners is used to make these kinds of choices. They know how to Google for any information they want! You instructional folks have to quit holding learners by the hand. And they will like the training much better if they can make their own choices. The whole point of the online world is choices—take those away and you lose the power of e-learning!

Based on your own experience or intuition, which of the following options would you select:

A. Ben is correct. The "digital natives" are used to high levels of learner control and will be turned off by excessive guidance.

B. Reshmi is correct. Learners do not make good decisions about what to study and what to skip. Program control will result in better learning.

C. Reshmi and Ben can compromise by providing learner control and at the same time giving learners guidance about what options they should select.

D. Not sure which options are best.

Control over the content and pace of a lesson is a common feature of asynchronous e-learning. Certainly the underlying scheme of the Internet is freedom of choice. How effective is learner control in training? What are the tradeoffs between learner control and program control? Fortunately, we have evidence from research and from cognitive theory to guide our decisions.

Learner Control Versus Program Control

In contrast to classroom and synchronous e-learning, asynchronous e-learning can be designed to allow learners to select the topics they want, control the pace at which they progress, and decide whether to bypass some lesson elements such as examples or practice exercises. e-Learning programs that offer these choices are considered high in *learner control.* In contrast, when the course and lesson offer few learner options, the instruction is under *program control.* Most synchronous forms of e-learning operate in program control mode—also called *instructional control.* Instructor-led virtual classrooms typically progress at a single pace, follow a linear sequence, and use one set of teaching techniques. The instructor facilitates a single learning path. On the other hand, asynchronous e-learning can offer many or few options and thus can be designed to be learner controlled or program controlled.

Three Types of Learner Control

Although the term "learner control" is often used generically, the actual type of control varies. Thus, two courses that are depicted as "high in learner control" may in fact offer quite different learner control options. In general, control options fall into three arenas:

1. *Content Sequencing.* Learners can control the order of the lessons, topics, and screens within a lesson. Many e-courses, such as the design in Figure 13.1, allow content control through a course menu from which learners select topics in any sequence they wish. Likewise, links placed in lessons can lead to additional pages in the course or to alternative websites with related information.

2. *Pacing.* Learners can control the time spent on each lesson page. With the exception of short video or audio sequences, a standard adopted in virtually all asynchronous e-learning, allows learners to progress through the training at their own rate, spending as much or as little time as they wish on any given screen. Likewise, options to move backward or to exit are made available on every screen. A more extensive form of pacing control allows learners to use slider bars or rollers to move through the content or includes fast forward, rewind, pause, and play buttons.

3. *Access to Learning Support.* Learners can control instructional components of lessons such as examples or practice exercises. Within a given lesson, navigation buttons, links, or tabs lead to course objectives, definitions, additional references, coaches, examples, help systems, or practice exercises. In contrast, a program-controlled lesson provides most of these instructional components by default as the learners click the forward button.

Figure 13.2 shows a screen for an asynchronous course that allows control over all three of these arenas. At the bottom right of the screen, the directional arrows provide for movement forward or backward at the learner's own pace. The course uses Microsoft standard control buttons in the upper-right-hand corner of the screen as well as an on-screen button to exit. In the left-hand frame, the course map allows learners to select lessons in any sequence. Within the central lesson frame, the learner can decide to study the examples by clicking on the thumbnail sample screens to enlarge them. Learners can also select a practice exercise by either clicking on the link above the examples or on the navigational tab on the right-hand side. In addition,

Figure 13.2. A Lesson with Multiple Navigational Control Elements.
With permission from Element K.

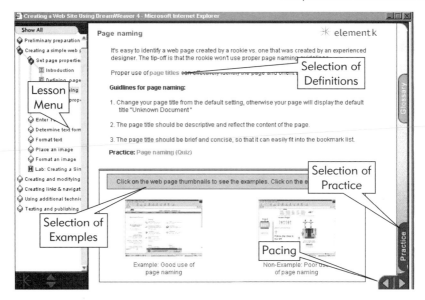

embedded links lead to definitions of terms. Table 13.1 summarizes the most common techniques used to implement various forms of learner control in asynchronous e-learning.

Table 13.1. Common Navigational Techniques Used in Asynchronous e-Learning.

Technique	Description	Examples
Course and lesson menus in left-hand frame, pull-down window, or section tabs	Allow learners to select specific lessons and topics within a lesson or a course	Figures 13.1 and 13.2 both use left window menu lists
Links placed within teaching frame	Allow learners to access content from other sites on the Internet or from other sections within the course	Figures 13.1 and 13.2 include links leading to definitions or practice exercises
Pop-ups or mouse-overs	Provide additional information without having when the learner to leave the screen	Figure 13.3 includes rollover functionality; clicks on a screen icon, a small window explains its functions
Buttons to activate forward, backward, and quit options	Permit control of pacing within a lesson and are standard features in asynchronous e-learning; more sophisticated buttons allow for fast forward, rewind, pause, and play	The database lesson shown in Figure 13.1 includes buttons for audio controls, movement forward, backward, and exit
Guided tours	Overviews of course resources accessible from the main menu screen	Typically used in courses that offer very high learner control, such as game-type interfaces with multiple paths and interface options

Figure 13.3. A Rollover Explains Screen Functionality.

Credit: Mark A. Palmer.

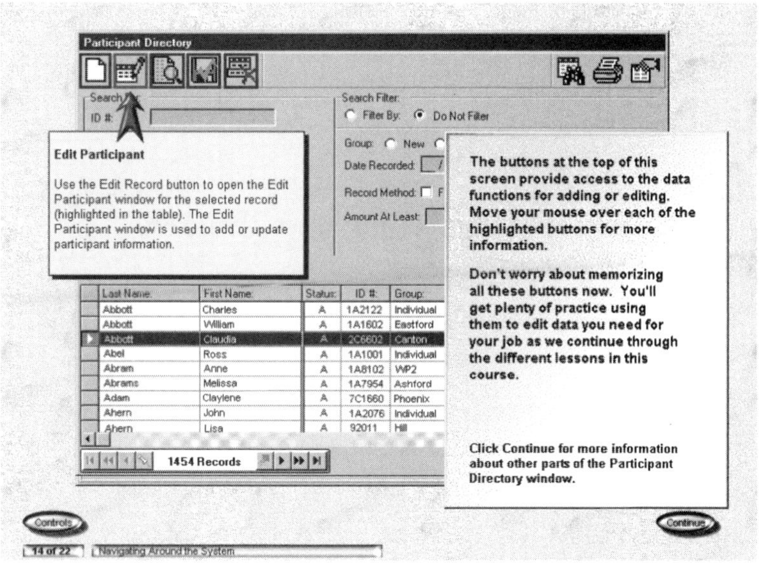

Popularity of Learner Control

Learners like learner control! To the extent that student appeal is a major goal of your instructional projects, learner control is a definite satisfier. Given the high control features inherent on the Internet, it is likely that learners will expect the same kind of freedom in e-learning courses.

Rather than advocate for or against learner control, we provide guidelines and illustrations for when and how learner control is best used. Additionally, we summarize both the evidence and the psychological reasons for these guidelines to help you adapt them to your own unique situations. Learner control can be effective if learners are able to make accurate decisions about their learning needs. If learners have a good sense of what they know and what learning support they need to reach their goals, they can make good use of navigation options. However, you might wonder, how accurate are learner self-assessments?

Do Learners Make Good Instructional Decisions?

The extent to which learners make accurate determinations of their existing knowledge will influence the kinds of decisions they make in a highly learner-controlled environment. For example, if learners can accurately assess which topics they do and do not comprehend, they can make good selections about topics to study and how much time and effort to put into studying those topics. In short, they are capable of good achievement under conditions of learner control. We have two lines of evidence addressing this question: calibration accuracy and student lesson ratings.

Do You Know What You Think You Know? Calibration Accuracy

Suppose you have to take a test on basic statistics. Prior to taking the test, you are asked to estimate your level of confidence in your knowledge. You know that even though you took statistics in college, you are a little rusty on some of the formulas, but you figure that you can score around 70 percent. After taking the test, you find your actual score is 55 percent. The correlation between your confidence estimate and your actual performance is called *calibration*. Had you guessed 55 percent, your calibration would have been perfect. Test your own calibration now by answering this question: What is the capital of Australia? As you state your answer, also estimate your confidence in your answer as high, medium, or low. We will return to this example later.

How Calibration Is Measured

In a typical calibration experiment, learners read a text and then make a confidence rating about their accuracy in responding to test questions about the text. The correlation between their confidence ratings, typically on a 1 to 6 scale, and their actual test score is the calibration metric. If there is no relationship between confidence and accuracy, the correlation is close to 0. Calibration is an important skill. If learners are well-calibrated, they can make accurate estimates of their knowledge and should be able to make appropriate instructional decisions in courses high in learner control. The focus of calibration measurement is not so much on what we actually know, but on the accuracy of what we think we know. If you don't think you know much and in fact your test score is low, you have good calibration.

Illusions of Knowing: Evidence for Poor Calibrations

Although most of us may feel we have a general sense of what we do and do not know, our specific calibration accuracy tends to be poor (Stone, 2000). Glenberg and his associates (1987) found calibration correlations close to 0, concluding that "contrary to intuition, poor calibration of comprehension is the rule, rather than the exception" (p. 119). Eva, Cunnington, Reiter, Keane, and Norman (2004) report poor correlations between medical students' estimates of their knowledge and their test scores. When comparing knowledge estimates among year 1, year 2, and year 3 medical students, there was no evidence that self-assessments improved with increasing seniority. The team concludes that "Self-assessment of performance remains a poor predictor of actual performance" (p. 222). Glenberg, Wilkinson, and Epstein (1992) refer to the subjective assessment of knowledge as "illusions of knowing."

By the way, the capital of Australia is not Sydney, as many people guess with high confidence. It is Canberra. If you guessed Sydney with low confidence OR if you guessed Canberra with high confidence, your calibration is high!

Practice and Examples Improve Calibration Accuracy

In comparing calibration of individuals before and after taking a test, accuracy is generally better after responding to test questions than before. Therefore, providing questions in training should lead to more accurate self-assessments. Walczyk and Hall (1989) confirmed this relationship by comparing the calibration of learners who studied using four resources: text alone, text plus examples, text plus questions, and text plus examples and questions. Calibration was best among those who studied from the version with examples and questions. Along similar lines, a pretest that matches the knowledge and skills of post-tests has been reported to improve calibration (Glenberg, Sanocki, Epstein, & Morris, 1987).

Do Learners Like Lesson Features That Lead to Learning?

Is there a correlation between actual learning and learner ratings of how much they learned and liked the instruction? Dixon (1990) compared course ratings with actual learning for more than 1,400 employees who participated in classroom training on implementation of a new manufacturing process. At the end of the class, learners completed a rating form in which they assessed the amount of new information they learned, rated their enjoyment of the session, and rated the skill of the instructor. These ratings were then correlated with the amount of actual learning determined by a valid post-test. The result? There was no correlation between ratings and actual learning.

Do students learn more when matched to their preferences in lesson features? Schnackenberg, Sullivan, Leader, and Jones (1998) surveyed participants before taking a course regarding their preferences for amount of practice—high or low. Participants were assigned to two e-learning courses—one with many practice exercises and a second identical course with half the amount of practice. Half the learners were matched to their preferences and half mismatched. Regardless of their preference, those assigned to the full practice version achieved significantly higher scores on the post-test than those in the shorter version. The authors conclude that "the results are more consistent with past evidence that students' preferences and judgments often may not be good indicators of the way they learn best" (p. 14).

Psychological Reasons for Poor Learner Choices

Metacognition refers to learners' awareness and control of their own learning processes, such as how well they understand a lesson or how best to study the material in a lesson. Metacognition is the mind's operating system. In short, metacognition supports mental self-awareness. Individuals with high metacognitive skills set realistic learning goals and use effective study strategies. They have high levels of learning management skills. For example, if faced with a certification test, they would plan a study schedule. Based on accurate self-assessments of their current strengths and weaknesses, they would focus their time and efforts on the topics most needed for achievement. They would use appropriate study techniques based on an accurate assessment of the certification requirements. In contrast, learners with poor metacognitive skills are prone to poor understanding of how they learn, which will lead to flawed decisions under conditions of high learner control.

Four Principles for Learner Control: Overview

How can you best apply the evidence and the psychology behind learner control to your design of effective e-courses? Based on empirical evidence, we recommend four guidelines for the best use of learner control to optimize learning:

1. Use learner control for learners with high prior knowledge and good metacognitive skills as well as in advanced lessons or courses.

2. When learner control is used, design the default navigation options to lead to important instructional course elements.

3. Design some form of adaptive control that tailors learning to individual needs.

4. Apply the Segmentation Principle described in Chapter 9 by allowing control over pacing in asynchronous e-learning; manage cognitive load in instructor-controlled environments such as synchronous e-learning.

LEARNER CONTROL PRINCIPLE 1

Give Experienced Learners Control

As we have seen, learners prefer full control over their instructional options, but often don't make good judgments about their instructional needs—especially those who are novice to the content and/or who lack good metacognitive skills. Hence the instructional professional must consider the multiple tradeoffs of learner control, including learner satisfaction, the profile of the target learners, the cost of designing learner-controlled instruction, and the criticality of skills being taught. Fortunately, there are design options that can provide both learner control and instructional effectiveness!

Who Learns What Best Under Learner Control?

A review of research on learner versus program control concludes that learners with little prior knowledge of the subject as well as poor metacognitive skills are likely to do better with program control—especially in high-complexity courses (Steinberg, 1989). Learner control is more likely to be successful when:

- Learners have prior knowledge of the content and skills involved in the training;

- The training is a more advanced lesson in a course or a more advanced course in a curriculum;

- Learners have good metacognitive skills; and/or

- The course is of low complexity.

Evidence for Benefits of Program Control

Gay (1986) found that low-prior-knowledge students learned more under program control. Figure 13.4 shows learning outcomes from high- and low-prior-knowledge students under learner and program control. In this experiment, individuals in the learner control version could control topic sequencing, presentation mode (video, audio, graphics, or text), number of examples, amount of practice, and depth of study. Those in program control could control their pacing only. As you can see, while low-prior-knowledge learners had low scores under learner control, high-prior-knowledge learners did well under either

Figure 13.4. Low-Prior-Knowledge Students Learn Least Under Learner Control.

Based on data from Gay, 1986.

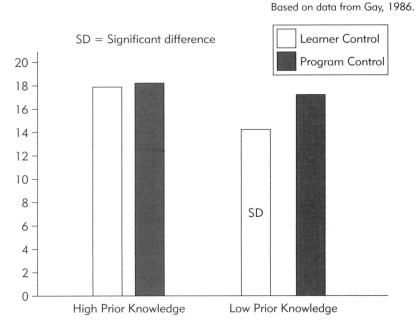

condition. Gay (1986) concludes: "The results demonstrate that not all subjects were capable of making appropriate decisions. The low-knowledge students practiced too little and emphasized areas with which they already had familiarity. In summary, low-prior-knowledge subjects did not use good learning strategies and made poor sequencing decisions under learner controlled treatment"(p. 227).

Young (1996) compared outcomes of learners with high and low self-regulatory (metacognitive) skills who took four e-lessons in either a learner-control or program-control mode. Under learner control, participants could select or bypass definitions, examples, and practice exercises, whereas those in the program-controlled version were presented with all the above options. Those in the learner-controlled version looked at less than 50 percent of the total number of screens available. As summarized in Table 13.2, Young found that learners with low metacognitive skills learned less in the learner-controlled mode than any of the other three groups.

Table 13.2. Test Scores of High and Low Metacognitive Learners Studying Under Learner or Program Control.

From Young, 1996.

	Learner-Controlled	Program-Controlled
Low Metacognitive Skill	20 percent	79 percent
High Metacognitive Skill	60 percent	82 percent

Overall, there is a consistent pattern in which too much learner control can be detrimental to learners with either low prior knowledge or metacognitive skill.

Evidence for Learner Control Later in Learning

A computer-based lesson in chemistry compared learning from program control and learner control over the sequence of tasks and number of practice exercises completed (Lee & Lee, 1991). Learning was compared during early stages of learning versus later stages of learning, when learners would have acquired a knowledge base. Program control gave better results during initial learning, while learner control was more effective at later stages. This outcome supports our conclusion that learners with greater prior knowledge are able to make more appropriate decisions under conditions of learner control. Based on evidence to date, we recommend that, when selecting or designing courseware for novice learners, look for courses with greater program control—at least in the beginning lessons in a course.

Make Important Instructional Events the Default

We saw in Chapter 11 that practice is an important instructional method that leads to expertise. We also know that learners prefer learner control, and in many e-learning environments, they can easily drop out if not satisfied. Therefore, if you opt for high learner control, set the default navigation option to lead to important instructional elements such as practice exercises. In other words, require the learner to make a deliberate choice to bypass practice.

Research by Schnackenberg and Sullivan (2000) supports this guideline. Two navigational versions of the same lesson were designed. As illustrated in Figure 13.5, in one version pressing "continue" bypassed practice, while in the other version pressing "continue" led to practice. In the "more practice"

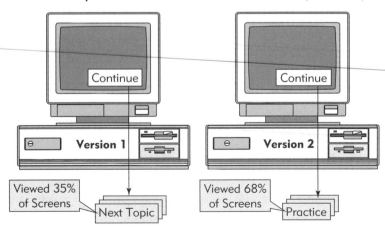

Figure 13.5. Default Navigation Options That Bypass Practice (Version 1) Compared to Those That Lead to Practice (Version 2).

default (Version 2), participants viewed nearly twice as many of the screens as those in version 1 and scored higher on the final test.

Programs that make a high amount of practice available as the default route are more likely to result in higher achievement than those that make less practice available as the default route. Schnackenberg and Sullivan (2000) suggest that since learner-controlled programs (a) have no instructional advantages, (b) have been shown in other studies to be disadvantageous for low-ability learners, and (c) cost more than program control, program control should be a preferred mode.

However, their learner population consisted of students taking a required university course. In environments in which learners have greater freedom about whether to take or complete e-learning, a designer cannot downplay user preferences to the extent recommended in this study. When designing programs with high learner control, set navigation controls so that critical aspects of the program (such as examples or practice exercises) are the default options.

LEARNER CONTROL PRINCIPLE 3

Consider Adaptive Control

In *adaptive control* (also called *personalized instruction* or *user modeling*), the program dynamically adjusts lesson content based on an evaluation of learner responses. If learners do better on an exercise, the program offers more challenging exercises. Conversely, if learners do poorly, the program offers more instruction or easier exercises. Adaptive control has proven to yield higher achievement than learner control (Tennyson, Tennyson, & Rothen, 1980).

Four Formats for Adaptive Control

Four ways to implement adaptive control are illustrated in Figure 13.6. An early type of adaptive control still used today involves branching learners to different lessons or topics based on pretest results. We refer to this form of adaptive control as *static* adaptive control. Static adaptive control defines learner needs based on a single event—a pretest for example. More recent forms of adaptive control are *dynamic*. That is, they adjust instructional elements based on an ongoing assessment of learner progress.

Figure 13.6. Four Forms of Adaptive Control.

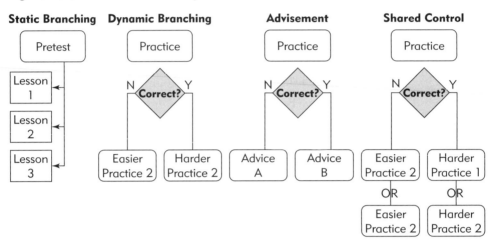

Dynamic Adaptive Control vs. Program Control

Salden, Paas, Broers, and Van Merrienboer (2004) confirmed the advantages of dynamic adaptive e-learning. They compared the effectiveness of program control and dynamic adaptive control on learning of simulated air traffic control situations displayed on radar screens. Program control assigned each learner twenty practice tasks selecting two tasks at each of ten complexity levels. Dynamic adaptive control adjusted number and complexity of practice tasks based on learners' performance on practice tasks. There were no differences in learning on the final test between program and adaptive groups. However, the program-controlled version required the greatest time to complete. In the program-controlled version all learners received twenty tasks, whereas learners in adaptive lessons completed an average of ten tasks.

The team concludes that "dynamic task selection leads to more efficient training than a fixed, predetermined training sequence that is not adjusted to the individual student. Although the fixed condition did attain the same performance score as the... dynamic conditions, its costs in terms of time and mental effort to achieve this performance level were substantially higher" (p. 168).

Adaptive Advisement vs. Adaptive Control

Advisement is a variation of adaptive control that leaves learner control in place. Advisement may be *generic* or *adaptive.* Generic advise offers general learning tips such as "We recommend that you take these topics in the order listed." All learners receive the same advice. In adaptive advisement, the computer program assesses learners' needs based on their responses, similar to the adaptive control designs described previously. However, rather than automatically branching learners to appropriate sections of the instruction, the program makes recommendations regarding what the learner should select next. In the end, the learner maintains control and is free to ignore or heed the advice.

Bell and Kozlowski (2002) compared learner control to adaptive guidance on a radar tracking simulation similar to the air traffic control tasks described previously. Both learner-control and adaptive-guidance lessons provided feedback regarding performance after each practice session. However, in the adaptive-guidance lessons, students received recommendations regarding what actions they could take to improve deficiencies based on their performance on the practice task. Specifically, they were told what areas needed improvement and how to best sequence learning and practice. The team found that learners in adaptive guidance spent over 25 percent more time studying and practiced almost twice as many relevant topics, compared to those in the learner-controlled program. Those in the adaptive-guidance lessons performed better on the final test on far-transfer tasks, although not on basic-knowledge items.

There are two main advantages to adaptive instruction with advisement. First, adaptive instruction leads to better learning outcomes than learner control and more efficient instruction than program control. Second, you still keep the popular learner-control features. The disadvantage of adaptive advisement is the time required to construct and validate decision logic, as well as to write appropriate recommendations.

We recommend that you consider the cost benefit of building advisement programs in terms of the criticality of the learning and the potential savings in learning time. If your training tasks have high criticality and/or your learner population is heterogeneous, adaptive designs may have cost benefit. However, when most of the audience is likely to be novice and development budgets or time is limited, we recommend program control or learner control with generic advisement.

Shared Control

We saw that, by using adaptive advisement, you can give learners full control and they will make better decisions based on personalized advice. Another control alternative is *shared control*. In shared control, the program makes some decisions and leaves others to the learner. For example, based on learner performance on practice questions, the program may assign the learner to tasks of a higher or lower level of complexity or to practice exercises with greater or lesser amounts of instructional support. Within those levels, however, the learner may be given a choice of alternative tasks with diverse context or surface features.

Corbalan, Kester, and Van Merrienboer (2006) tested a shared control approach in a course on dietetics. The program included a database containing tasks of varied complexity, varying levels of instructional support, and different surface features such as different people with varied genders, weight, age, energy intake, diet, and so forth. Based on a dynamic calculation of learner expertise, the program offers several tasks, each at the appropriate level of complexity and support. The task options vary regarding surface features such as the specifics of the client's diet, weight, and so forth. The learner can select the task he or she prefers. In shared control, the program makes decisions regarding task complexity and support and the learner makes decisions regarding the specific task. In a pilot study, the research team found that those working with shared control learned more than those working under full adaptive control. The effect sizes, however, were small, suggesting relatively little gain for the resources invested.

The concept of shared control offers some flexible options for a balance of program and learner control. A disadvantage to shared control is the number of tasks that must be created. Having to create multiple surface feature tasks for varying levels of task complexity and instructional support will require additional resources, compared to a pure adaptive guidance approach or to program control. We will need more evidence showing the benefits of shared control before recommending this approach.

Give Pacing Control

Most asynchronous e-learning programs allow learners to proceed at their own pace by pressing the "forward" button. Video or animated demonstrations typically have slider bar controls indicating progress as well as "replay" and "quit" options. Recent research by Mayer and Chandler (2001), Mayer, Dow, and Mayer (2003), and Mayer and Jackson (2005) summarized in Chapter 9 recommends that asynchronous e-learning be divided into small chunks that learners access at their own pace. In Chapter 9 we refer to this guideline as the Segmentation Principle.

Manage Cognitive Load When Pacing Is Program-Controlled

Pacing control is an important feature that distinguishes asynchronous from synchronous e-learning. Just as in the face-to-face classroom, the rate of lesson progress in virtual classrooms is typically controlled by the instructor. Based on the research on learner control of pacing, these environments pose a higher risk of cognitive overload than self-paced media. Therefore, those engaged in design and delivery of virtual classrooms should pay special attention to the multimedia principles we summarized throughout the book. For more details on managing cognitive load in the virtual classroom, see *The New Virtual Classroom* by Clark and Kwinn (2007).

Navigational Guidelines for Learner Control

Screen titles, embedded topic headers, topic menus, course maps, links, and movement buttons (forward, backward, and exit) are common navigational elements that influence comprehension. What evidence do we have for the benefits of various navigational elements commonly used in e-learning?

Use Headings and Introductory Statements

Content representations such as headings and introductory sentences improve memory and comprehension in traditional text documents. For example,

Lorch, Lorch, Ritchey, McGovern, and Coleman (2001) asked readers to provide summaries of texts that included headings for half of the paragraphs. They found that the summaries included more content from paragraphs with headers and less from paragraphs lacking headers. Mayer (2005b) refers to headings as a form of signaling—providing cues concerning the important information in a lesson. We recommend that similar devices be used in e-learning programs. Screen headings, for example, might include the lesson title followed by the topic. On-screen text blocks and visuals should likewise be signaled with brief descriptive labels similar to paper documents.

Use Links Sparingly

Links that take the learner off the teaching screen as well as links leading to important instructional events should be used sparingly. By definition, links signal to the user that the information is adjunct or peripheral to the site. Learners will bypass many links. Based on the research described previously, we discourage using links for access to essential skill building elements such as worked examples or practice, especially with novice audiences.

Neiderhauser, Reynolds, Salmen, and Skolmoski (2000) presented two related concepts in two separate lessons. In each lesson, links led learners to correlated information about the concept in the other lesson. For example, if reading about the benefits of Concept A in Lesson 1, a link would bring up benefits of Concept B in Lesson 2 for purposes of contrast. They found that nearly half the learners frequently made use of these links. The other half either never used the links or used them briefly before abandoning them in favor of a more linear progression where they moved through one lesson from start to finish before moving to the other. Contrary to the authors' expectations, they found that extensive use of the links was negatively related to learning. They attribute their findings to adverse impact of hypertext navigation on cognitive load.

These findings may reflect another example of the contiguity principle discussed in Chapter 4, where learning suffers from separated information that requires the learners to perform the integration themselves. The action of selecting a link and relating contrasting information to the primary instructional material may increase extraneous cognitive load similar to asking learners to integrate explanatory text with pictures that are physically separated.

Use Course Maps

A course map is a type of menu or concept map that graphically represents the topics included in a course or lesson. Nilsson and Mayer (2002) define a concept map as "a graphic representation of a hypertext document, in which the pages of the document are represented by visual objects and the links between pages are represented by lines or arrows connecting the visual objects" (p. 2). Figure 13.7 shows three different formats for course maps.

Figure 13.7. Three Map Layouts.
From Potelle and Rouet, 2003. © Cambridge University Press 2005. Reprinted with the permission of Cambridge University Press and H. Potelle.

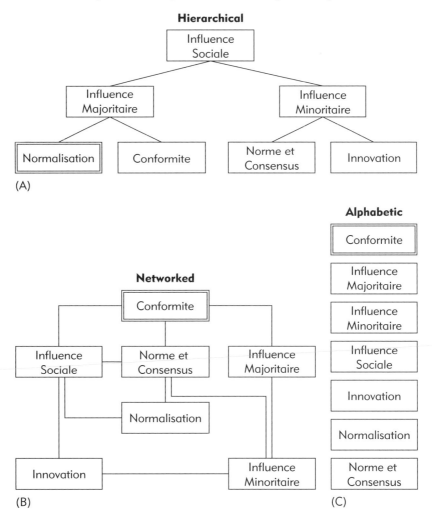

Research has been mixed on the contribution of course maps to learning. Neiderhauser, Reynolds, Salmen, and Skolmoski (2000) included a topic map containing a graphic representation of the hierarchical structure of the hypertext. Learners could access any screen in the hypertext from the topic map. A trace of user paths found that many learners did access the topic map frequently, but rarely used it to navigate. Most would access the map, review the levels, and return to where they were reading. A few participants never accessed the topic map. In correlating map use with learning, the research team found only a slight benefit.

Potelle and Rouet (2003) compared comprehension of a hypertext between novice and content specialists for the three menu layouts shown in Figure 13.7: an alphabetical list, a hierarchical map, and a network map. Low-knowledge participants learned most from the hierarchical map, whereas the type of map made no difference to high-prior-knowledge participants. It may be that course maps are less important for navigational control than for providing learners with an advance orientation to the content structure. Novice learners may benefit most from such an orientation.

Shapiro (2000) compared learning from two versions of site maps for hypertext on a fictitious world of animals. One map version focused on animal categories. For example, a main menu item of reptiles included a submenu of desert shark, fat tail lizard, and so forth. The other map version focused on ecosystems. For example, a main menu item of desert included a submenu of long plume quail, fin lizard, and so forth. Half of the students were given learning goals pertaining to animal categories, whereas the other half were given goals pertaining to ecosystems. The focus of the map had a strong effect on learning, whereas the learning goals did not. Shapiro (2005) suggests that: "The influence of a site map can be powerful enough not only to guide the structure of a learner's internal representations, but also to overshadow the effect of a learning goal during that process" (p. 317).

We recommend the following guidelines regarding course maps:

- Consider using course maps for courses that are lengthy and complex and/or for learners who are novice to the content.

- Use a simple hierarchical structure.

- If your content will apply to learners with different tasks and instructional goals, consider multiple versions of a course map adapted to the instructional goals most appropriate to different learners.

Provide Basic Navigation Options

In asynchronous e-learning, make elements for forward and backward movement, replay of audio and video, course exit, and menu reference easily accessible from every display. In courses that use scrolling pages, navigation should be accessible from both the top and bottom of the page to avoid overloading learners with unnecessary mouse work (having to scroll back to the top of the page to click "next"). Additionally, some sort of a progress indicator such as "Page 1 of 10" is useful to learners so that they know where they are in a topic and how far they have to go to complete it.

What We Don't Know About Learner Control

Although we have seen evidence that learners low in prior knowledge or metacognitive skills benefit from program control, we need to know more about the relationship between prior knowledge, metacognitive skills, and various navigational control options. For example, do high metacognitive skills override low prior knowledge? Do learners with high metacognitive skills benefit from a different type of navigational structure than those with low metacognitive skills?

Although adaptive advisement seems to have advantages compared to program control or learner control, we need more information on the cost benefit of dynamic adaptation. Under what circumstances will the resource investment made in adaptive designs pay off in more efficient learning outcomes?

How should navigational elements such as course maps and lesson menus be displayed? Is there an advantage to having them always visible, as in a left navigation display, or will a drop down course map be as effective?

DESIGN DILEMMA: RESOLVED

Ben and Reshmi's disagreement about the amount and type of learner control to use in the database lesson led to the following options:

A. Ben is correct. The "digital natives" are experienced with high levels of learner control and will be turned off by excessive guidance.

B. Reshmi is correct. Learners do not make good decisions about what to study and what to skip. Program control will result in better learning.

C. Reshmi and Ben can compromise by providing learner control but giving learners guidance about what options they should select.

D. Not sure which options are best.

Based on the research summarized in this chapter, we recommend providing learner control but offering generic guidance by suggesting that learners proceed through the lesson in the prescribed sequence. If budget and time allow, providing personalized adaptive advice based on responses to practice questions might lead to more efficient learning. Adaptive advice is most beneficial when considerable instructional efficiencies can be gained by highly paid workers, when the learners are likely to be heterogeneous regarding their prior knowledge and learning abilities, and when task criticality demands a high standard of performance for all learners.

WHAT TO LOOK FOR IN e-LEARNING

Consider high learner control when:

☐ Your goal is primarily to provide information rather than to build skills

☐ Your content is relatively low in complexity and topics are not logically interdependent

☐ Your audience is likely to have high metacognitive or learning self-regulation skills

☐ Your audience is likely to have prior knowledge of the content

☐ The lessons or courses are later in a series so that learners have built a knowledge base

☐ Designing the pacing options such as moving forward, backward, or exiting the course

☐ You can easily add generic advisement such as "If you are new to these skills, take the lessons in the sequence shown"

☐ You can include important instructional elements such as examples and practice in the default navigational path

☐ Your course includes practice exercises with feedback shown to improve learner calibration

Consider *adaptive* advisement when:

☐ Your audience has a mix of background knowledge and skills related to the content

☐ Saving learning time is a high priority and there are sufficient numbers of highly paid staff to cost justify the resources needed for adaptive advisement

☐ Reaching high levels of skill and knowledge proficiency is a high priority

☐ Resources are available to create the decision logic necessary for advisement

Consider program control when:

☐ Your audience is primarily novice and a high level of proficiency is a priority

ON *THE e-LEARNING AND THE SCIENCE OF INSTRUCTION* CD

In our demonstration lesson on how to create a database, we relied primarily on learner control. On Screen 2 we include generic advice to new learners recommending they take the course in the sequence designed. However, our pull-down menu allows learners to select any of the topics in the lesson. Important instructional elements such as worked examples and practice are displayed as the default navigational options. Pacing control, audio replay, exit options, and progress indicators appear on every screen. Our resources, including time and budget, precluded any type of adaptive control or adaptive advisement.

COMING NEXT

In Chapter 1 we distinguished between instructional goals that are procedural (near transfer) and those that are strategic or require problem solving (far transfer). Many e-learning courses currently in use are designed to teach procedural skills, especially computer skills. What is the potential of e-learning to teach more complex problem-solving skills? In the next chapter we look at this question.

Suggested Readings

DeRouin, R.E., Fritzsche, B.A., & Salas, E. (2004). Optimizing e-learning: Research-based guidelines for learner-controlled training. *Human Resource Management, 43*(2–3), 147–162.

Leung, A.C.K. (2003). Providing navigation aids and online learning helps to support user control: A conceptual model on computer-based learning. *The Journal of Computer Information Systems, 43*(3), 10–17.

National Research Council. (1994). Illusions of comprehension, competence, and remembering. In D. Druckman and R.A. Bjork (Eds.), *Learning, remembering, believing*. Washington, DC: National Academy Press.

Nelson, T.O. (1996). Consciousness and metacognition. *American Psychologist, 51*(2), 102–116.

Rouet, J.F., & Potelle, H (2005). Navigational principles in multimedia learning. In R.E. Mayer (Ed.), *The Cambridge handbook of multimedia learning*. New York: Cambridge University Press.

Shapiro, A.M. (2005). The site map principle in multimedia learning. In R.E. Mayer (Ed.) *The Cambridge handbook of multimedia learning*. New York: Cambridge University Press.

Stone, N.J. (2000). Exploring the relationship between calibration and self-regulated learning. *Educational Psychology Review, 12*(4), 437–475.

e-Learning to Build Thinking Skills

WHETHER IT'S CALLED CRITICAL THINKING or creativity training, the goals are similar: to build more effective problem-solving skills. As digital information from diverse sources grows exponentially, assessment of the quality and relevance of that information is just one example of the expanding need for critical thinking skills. Competitive edge in a knowledge economy depends on a workforce able to quickly adapt to changing conditions and to excel in creative design of products and services (Pink, 2005).

In our first edition we provided evidence and guidelines for building job-specific thinking or problem-solving skills through e-learning. We emphasized the unique ability of e-learning to make mental problem-solving skills explicit. We recommended against using a broad approach to thinking skills training in favor of a job-specific or domain-specific focus. Since the first edition, many articles and several books have addressed how to teach thinking skills. However, valid evidence supporting the implementation and outcomes of thinking skills training programs remains scarce.

In this edition, we summarize new meta-analytic data that point to the potential value of thinking skills training and that specify some of the features associated with effective programs. We also describe new examples of multimedia learning environments designed to foster thinking skills as well as some new research showing the benefits of case-based learning over traditional didactic instruction.

DESIGN DILEMMA: YOU DECIDE

"I wish our employees were better at critical thinking! They are really good at quickly Googling information. But once they get the information, they assume it's good, no matter what the source. Blogs, wikis, websites—they are all treated in the same manner—as valid and reliable. And when it comes to creative new products or processes, we just hear the same tired ideas recycled again and again. Our success relies on innovation. I want everyone to take creative thinking skills training!"

That was the message from upper management to the training department. Your team leader led the kickoff meeting: "Upper management wants training on problem-solving skills and they want it for everyone, including operations, marketing, sales, engineers, and supervisors. We've got two weeks to report back with either a design for the training or with recommendations for off-the-shelf courseware that would do the job."

Back at your desk, you do a Google search on creativity training. You are amazed to receive over sixteen million hits! As you access websites like the one in Figure 14.1, you are surprised to see the number of different classes and books that promise to make people more creative and better problem solvers. After reviewing some of the options, you end up with more questions than you had originally. Does creativity training work? Wouldn't it be better to teach creativity in the classroom than with e-learning? Are there any advantages to building your own course compared to buying one of the many off-the-shelf courses available?

Figure 14.1. A Website Promoting Critical Thinking Skills Training.

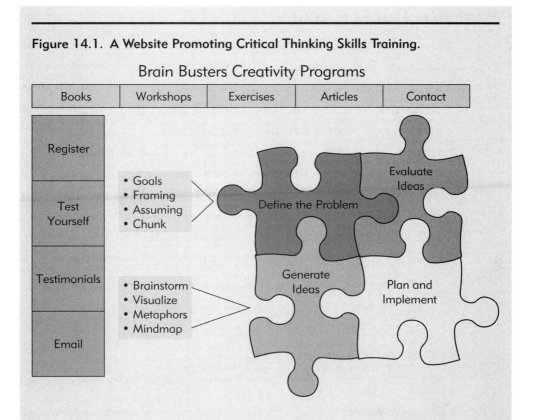

Based on your own experience or intuition, which of the following options would you select:

A. Money can be saved by purchasing an off-the-shelf course that includes techniques like the ones listed in Figure 14.1.

B. Creativity training would be most effective in a face-to-face environment.

C. Creative thinking training should be job specific; no one general creative thinking course will be effective for everyone.

D. There is no way to improve creativity through training; it's like intelligence—you either have it or you don't.

E. Not sure which options are correct.

What Are Thinking Skills?

Creativity training programs are popular. Over 25 percent of organizations with over one hundred employees provide some form of thinking or creativity skills training (Scott, Leritz, & Mumford, 2004). But what is creative thinking? Scott and her colleagues (2004) define creativity as involving "the production of original, potentially workable, solutions to novel, ill-defined problems of relatively high complexity" (p. 362). From designing websites to troubleshooting equipment problems, creative problem solving spans a broad range of workforce activities. In this chapter we use the terms *creative thinking, critical thinking,* and *problem solving* interchangeably to focus on the skills that help workers solve new non-routine problems in effective ways.

Mayer (1998) suggests that success in problem solving rests on:

- Cognitive skills—the facts, concepts, and guidelines unique to a skill field

- Metaskills—the ability to plan, monitor, and assess actions associated with problem solving

- Motivation—an investment of effort to persist and solve the problem

Success in problem solving relies on both cognitive and metacognitive skills. For example, consider the following math problem. *An army bus holds thirty-six soldiers. If 1,128 soldiers are being bused to their training site, how many buses are needed?* In a test containing this item, 70 percent of respondents did the math correctly. But 29 percent selected the answer: *31 remainder 12.* Eighteen percent said *31 buses* needed, while 23 percent gave the correct answer of *32* (Schoenfeld, 1987). Here we see a good example of problem-solvers who knew the mathematical operations—that is, they had the cognitive skills. It was their metacognitive skills that were lacking. They failed to ask themselves: "What is the problem asking? Does my answer make sense?" Consequently, they chose either too few buses or "fractions" of buses.

In Chapter 13, we defined metacognition as the skill that sets goals, plans an approach, monitors progress, and makes adjustments as needed. People with good metacognitive skills focus not only on the outcome of the job, but on the steps and decisions they make to achieve that outcome. When working in a team, the person with high metacognitive skills will be the one to say: "Wait! Let's stop and see if we are making progress. Will our individual efforts come together?" When working on a problem alone, they might say: "This approach might work eventually, but it's really labor-intensive. How could I accomplish this more efficiently?" In other words, they are mindful of their mental work. When they don't see progress toward a goal, they shift gears and try another approach.

Can creative thinking be trained? If so, what training methods are best? In what ways can technology support the learning of critical thinking skills? Can practice with techniques like the ones shown in Figure 14.1 build more creative thinkers? These are some of the issues we consider in this chapter.

Can Creativity Be Trained?

Before considering specific guidelines for building problem-solving skills, it makes sense to first ask whether there is any evidence that creativity can be enhanced through training at all and, if so, what types of training work best. Hundreds of creativity programs have been created and quite a few of these have been evaluated, giving us at least some preliminary answers to our questions. Scott, Leritz, and Mumford (2004) reviewed seventy research studies on creativity programs that measured results with (a) divergent thinking tests, (b) production of original solutions to novel problems, or (c) generation of creative products. When aggregating the outcomes across these different criteria, they found an overall positive effect for creativity training programs of .68, which is moderate. The research team concludes that "Well-designed creativity training programs typically induce gains in performance, with effects generalizing across criteria, settings, and target populations" (p. 361). In fact, the research team found that creativity training is more effective in organizational settings (effect size of 1.41) than in academic settings (effect size of .65).

What Kinds of Thinking-Skills Programs Work Best?

We see that at least some creativity programs can have positive effects on measures of divergent thinking and problem solving. Scott, Leritz, and Mumford (2004), however, found considerable variation across different programs. Some were much more effective than others. We might wonder then what distinguishes an effective from an ineffective program.

In Table 14.1 we summarize three types of creativity training programs, ranging from those that focus on very general non-verbal techniques to those that focus on specific domain or job problem-solving skills. General creativity training uses strategies such as visualization, metaphors, and puzzle problems, such as number sequences or visual insight problems. Programs that fall in the middle range of specificity focus on cognitive skills that can be applied across a range of settings. For example, they teach skills such as problem finding, information gathering, concept search, idea generation, idea evaluation, and implementation planning. The most specific type of problem-solving programs focus on unique domains or jobs, such as scientific thinking, mathematical problem solving, various types of troubleshooting, medical diagnosis and patient treatment, to name a few. Which of these three approaches to thinking skills training is most effective?

Table 14.1. Three Types of Thinking-Skills Training Programs.

Type	Description	Examples
1. Non-Verbal	Emphasizes non-verbal approaches to creativity	Imagery exercises Metaphors Puzzle problems "Right-brain" thinking
2. General Cognitive and Metacognitive Skills	Emphasizes cognitive skills that apply to a broad spectrum of problem solving	Compare and contrast Uncover assumptions Brainstorming techniques Avoid group think Take a different view
3. Specific Cognitive and Metacognitive Skills	Emphasizes problem-solving processes and skills that are unique to a domain or job role	Medical diagnosis Equipment troubleshooting Reading comprehension Scientific reasoning

Focus on Job-Specific Cognitive and Metacognitive Skills

Scott, Leritz, and Mumford (2004) found that programs using cognitive techniques, such as convergent thinking, critical thinking, and metacognitive strategies, resulted in better outcomes than general non-verbal techniques that relied on imagery and metaphors, which were negatively related to learning. In comparing Type 2 and Type 3 programs, they found that domain-specific programs exerted the greatest positive outcomes. They conclude that specific programs are most useful when cognitive skills must be applied in a certain arena: "The most clear-cut finding to emerge in the overall analysis was that the use of domain-based performance exercises was positively related to effect size" (p. 380).

In a review of three problem-solving courses that have been used in schools, Mayer (2008) concludes that effective programs: "a. focus on a set of specific problem-solving skills, b. contextualize the skills within tasks like those the learner is expected to perform, and c. give practice in processes of problem solving" (p. 454). Although problem-solving courses may seem to be addressing a general set of skills, they are actually building task-specific skills that enable learners to better perform similar tasks that benefit from those skills. The future of educational problem-solving instruction rests with subject-matter-specific programs targeted to specific cognitive skills, such as how to collect and analyze scientific information. Mayer predicts that "Every subject matter will incorporate teaching of relevant cognitive and metacognitive skills" (p. x).

Building Critical Thinking Skills in the Workforce: Overview

Based on evidence to date, we recommend the following guidelines for building critical or creative thinking skills that will pay off in better workplace performance:

- Use domain-specific or job-specific cases as a context to teach problem-solving skills;

- Make thinking processes explicit through expert models and activities that require learners to articulate their mental processes; and

- Base the lesson on an analysis of job expert problem-solving processes.

Use Job–Specific Cases

In Chapter 1 we defined three types of instruction for e-learning courses: teaching by show-and-tell (receptive), teaching by show-and-do (directive), and teaching by problem solving (guided discovery). We have evidence from successful thinking-skills programs that a guided discovery approach that relies on case-based learning is the most appropriate instructional technique for building workforce thinking skills. To illustrate this approach, we describe two domain-specific multimedia programs: BioWorld, designed to teach biology students scientific reasoning, and Accelerate Expertise, designed to teach bank agents how to research and analyze a commercial loan application.

BioWorld: A Case-Based Environment for Scientific Reasoning

BioWorld is a multimedia environment designed to teach scientific reasoning processes, including evidence gathering and analysis, through hospital case scenarios (Lajoie & Nakamura, 2005). As shown in Figure 14.2, the learner selects relevant phrases mentioned in the case description in the center frame and drags them into the evidence table located in the left frame. For example, in this case, the learner had already identified poor nutrition and is currently selecting sore throat as relevant case evidence. After identifying relevant evidence, learners select an initial hypothesis from the "Select Hypothesis" pull-down menu located in the upper-left-hand corner. For example, as you can see in Figure 14.3 in this case, the learner selects Infectious Mononucleosis. The learner uses the slider bar under "Belief Meter" to indicate confidence in the diagnosis as he or she progresses through the program. By clicking on the chart icon, various tests can be selected and the results recorded on the chart, as shown in Figure 14.3. Learners can access resources from the online library at any time. The library contains information on biological terms, diagnostic tests, and symptoms. At the conclusion of a case, learners prioritize their evidence in the right "prioritized evidence" window and can compare

Figure 14.2. The Learner Moves Relevant Symptoms into the Evidence Table.

Accessed October 25, 2006, from www.education.mcgill.ca/cognitionlab/bioworld/en/research/narrator.html. Reprinted with permission of Susanne LaJoie.

Figure 14.3. The Learner Orders Diagnostic Tests.

Accessed October 25, 2006, from www.education.mcgill.ca/cognitionlab/bioworld/en/research/narrator.html. Reprinted with permission of Susanne LaJoie.

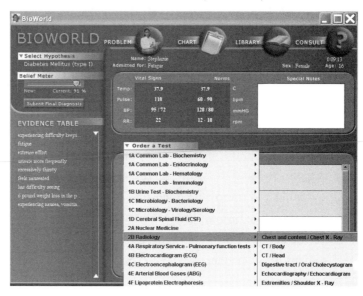

their priorities to those of a doctor listed in the left window, as shown in Figure 14.4.

Figure 14.4. The Learners Compare Their Evidence to an Expert List.
Accessed October 25, 2006, from www.education.mcgill.ca/cognitionlab/bioworld/en/
research/narrator.html. Reprinted with permission of Susanne LaJoie.

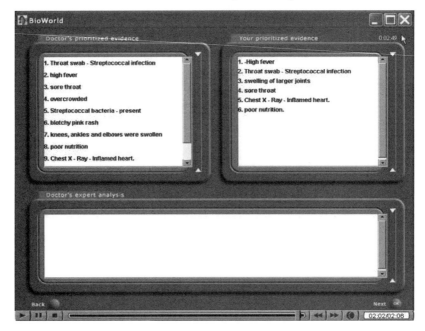

BioWorld includes many elements of an effective critical-thinking-skills program. First, it is domain-specific, focusing on teaching of scientific reasoning in biology. Second, it is case-based. The learning is contextualized within the process of gathering evidence about a patient and forming diagnostic hypotheses. Third, it makes scientific reasoning explicit by requiring participants to select a hypothesis, indicate their confidence in their hypothesis, and build and prioritize evidence to support it. Fourth, it offers instructional support in the form of library resources. Fifth, BioWorld provides feedback on the accuracy of the hypotheses as well as with the table comparing the student list of evidence with an expert's list shown in Figure 14.4.

Accelerate Expertise: A Case-Based Environment for Loan Analysis

In this program, the learner is asked to evaluate a new client applying for a commercial loan. As illustrated in Figure 14.5, learners have a number of resources in their virtual office interface. These include a fax machine for requesting credit checks, a bookshelf with literature on the client's industry, and a telephone for checking references. The office computer includes a program to guide learners through a loan analysis process. When sufficient evidence has been collected, the learner completes the loan transmittal form, making a loan recommendation, along with a justification statement. At any point, the learner can access instructional tutorials by clicking on the agent icon located in the bottom menu. The learner can also review the completed steps to analyze a loan (shown in Figure 14.6) as well as compare the steps with those of an expert.

Figure 14.5. The Learner Can Access Many Resources While Analyzing a Loan Request.

With permission from Moody's Investment Service.

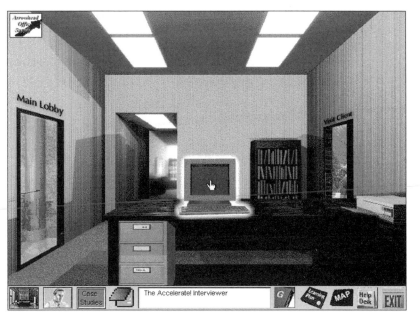

Figure 14.6. The Learner Can Review the Loan Analysis Process.
With permission from Moody's Investment Service.

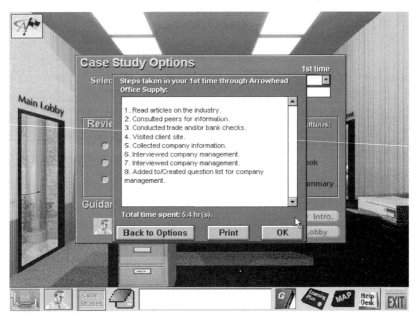

Accelerate Expertise includes many features of an effective thinking-skills program. First, it is job-specific, as it is based on a defined analytic process to collect and analyze data relevant to loan risk. Second, it is case-based. A series of loan applicants offers learners multiple specific cases. Third, it makes thinking processes explicit as follows: (a) it tracks the learners' activities and allows learners to compare their process with that of an expert and (b) it requires learners to recommend acceptance or rejection of the loan based on evidence collected. Fourth, it offers instructional support in the form of guidance from an agent, as well as from online tutorials.

Psychological Reasons for Job-Specific Training

It would be wonderful if Type 2 creativity training on general cognitive skills could build thinking skills that applied to a variety of jobs. If this were the case, we could propose that metacognitive skills that underlie problem-solving are *general,* with applicability to many different career fields. The general thinking skills training approach would be quite efficient, since one training course on a set of generic problems would suffice for all employees in all jobs. The thinking guidelines would be general problem-solving hints such as, "Think outside the box," "Revisit your assumptions," "Use metaphors," and "Avoid group think."

What's wrong with this approach? We know that successful training must transfer back to the job after the learning event, and transfer has proven to be a thorny problem. Our goal in improving worker thinking skills is to enable them to solve non-routine problems, that is, novel problems for which they do not have a standardized response. We know that work-related problems are encountered in a specific job context, such as management, patient care, or commercial bank lending. It is unlikely that the general skills derived from broad thinking-skills training will transfer effectively to these diverse settings. Good thinking-skills courses will need to include the unique skills that underlie effective problem solving in a specific domain. Mayer (1990) summarizes the situation: "An important instructional implication of the focus on metacognition is that problem-solving skills should be learned within the context of realistic problem-solving situations" (p. 53).

Think of metacognitive skills like a hand. A hand is a useful and flexible tool, but without something to grasp, a hand can't accomplish much. Further, the way a hand grasps a baby will differ from how a hand picks up a basket of laundry (Perkins & Salomon, 1989). Similarly, metacognitive skills must be wedded to job-specific knowledge to be useful. And metacognitive skills must be shaped to the type of work involved. In other words, highly generalizable guidelines such as "set your goal," "plan your approach," or "monitor your progress" are fine as far as they go; but how they apply to specific job problems will differ. Unfortunately, there is no one general set of thinking skills that all workers can apply successfully to their skill fields. Each job domain requires its own customized set of metacognitive strategies to be applied to specific and unique job cognitive knowledge. These skills need to be taught in the context of authentic work problems.

Evidence for Job-Specific Problem-Solving Training

Unfortunately, there has not been sufficient empirical research on the effectiveness of case-based learning approaches to make definitive statements about their use. We need to know that, in general, they are effective, which features of case-based learning are most relevant to building thinking skills, and also how case-based learning compares with more traditional approaches using a receptive or directive training design. In this section we review limited evidence that supports the power of case-based guided discovery e-learning.

Evidence from BioWorld

Lajoie, Lavigne, Guerrera, and Munsic (2001) report results of a field trial with BioWorld in which they evaluated how pairs of ninth-graders worked collaboratively to solve BioWorld cases. Groups of students worked as pairs with BioWorld with or without teacher coaching support. The team found that 90 percent of the learners solved the problems in BioWorld. Successful case resolution was related to the amount of evidence collected overall, as well as to the frequency of use of the online library. There were no differences in case solution success between those pairs working on their own and those teams with a human tutor. This study showed that BioWorld can support successful case resolution among teams working on their own. However, the research did not evaluate whether new scientific reasoning skills could be applied outside of the BioWorld context, nor did it compare BioWorld to a more traditional approach to building scientific reasoning skills.

Evidence from Sherlock

One case-based problem-solving training program that has been evaluated extensively is Sherlock, an intelligent multimedia instructional environment designed to train Air Force technicians how to troubleshoot the F-15 test station (Lesgold, Eggan, Katz, & Rao, 1993). Sherlock provides learners with many simulated test station failures to solve, accompanied by computerized tutorial help. Thirty-two airmen with some electronics background experience along with sixteen experts were included in an evaluation study. The thirty-two new technicians were divided into two groups of sixteen. One group completed twenty-five hours of Sherlock training, and the other served as a comparison group. The skills of all thirty-two were evaluated through pre- and post-tests that required them to solve simulated test station diagnosis problems—problems that were different from those in the training.

The sixteen expert technicians also took the post-test. Figure 14.7 shows the average test scores. Note that the average skill level of the trained group was equivalent to that of the advanced technicians. The researchers conclude that "the bottom line is that twenty to twenty-five hours of Sherlock practice time produced average improvements that were, in many respects, equivalent to the effects of four years on the job" (p. 54).

Figure 14.7. Acceleration of Expertise Using Sherlock.
Based on data from Eggan, Kutz, and Rao, 1993.

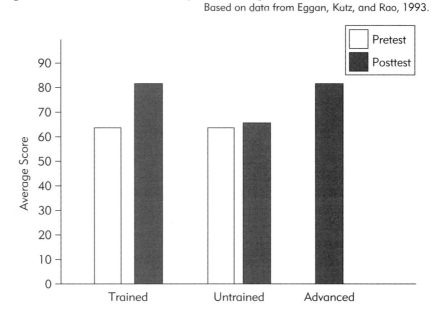

While this acceleration of expertise seems almost too good to be true, it points to the power of technology-delivered case-based learning to compress experience. In essence, the Sherlock learners received the equivalent of four years of on-the-job experience in twenty-five hours. This reflects the acceleration of expertise that can be gained by exposing learners to a systematic series of job-specific problems to solve, along with tutoring to help them solve the problems. The Sherlock results suggest that case-based training delivered via multimedia can effectively use simulation to compress experience and build skills that would take many months to build in the actual work setting.

Internet Cases vs. Face-to Face Instruction

While the results from BioWorld and Sherlock are encouraging, it would be useful to compare learning from case-based programs to learning from traditional approaches. Kumta, Psang, Hung, and Chenge (2003) did just that. The research team compared learning of 163 medical students from a three-week program of case-based online instruction supplemented by regular face-to-face discussions to learning from traditional didactic methods. The research was conducted in the context of a three-week rotation required of all final-year medical students in a department of orthopedics. A series of computer-based clinical case simulations was designed to foster reasoning and logical thinking abilities. The simulations required students to comment on radiographs, interpret clinical and diagnostic test results, select appropriate investigations, and demonstrate logical reasoning for their clinical decisions. During each case, learners started with patient assessment, selected appropriate tests, interpreted test results, and made treatment decisions. The web-based training was augmented by regular face-to-face meetings with faculty moderators. The comparison group participated in the traditional teaching program that included didactic lectures, bedside tutorials, and outpatient clinics.

At the conclusion of the three-week module, all participants completed an assessment that included a computer-based test, an objective structured clinical examination, and a patient-based clinical examination. The test results are shown in Figure 14.8. The differences were significant and reflect an effect size of .9, which is large. The research team observed that the students felt the "simulations complemented and deepened their understanding of patient care as they could relate this information to real cases present in the wards. In fact, the scenarios reinforced the need to obtain the necessary clinical history and to complete a comprehensive physical assessment of patients in order to make clinical decisions" (p. 272). The research team further noted that "students valued the weekly facilitator-led discussions, at which time student answers to the cases were reviewed, discussed, and critiqued. These active student-teacher interactions ensured that the *evaluation of the thinking process,* not just the resources uncovered, provided the value to the information gained through the case scenarios" (p. 272).

Figure 14.8. Better Learning from Case-Based Learning.

Based on data from Kumta, Psang, Hung, and Chenge, 2003.

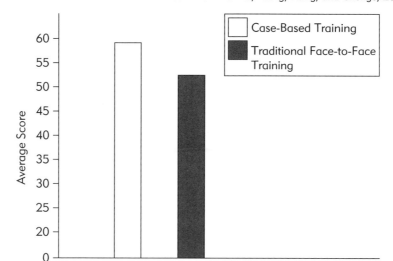

The results from this comparison of case-based to "traditional" didactic methods support the benefits of e-learning designed to be job-specific and case-based. Still, we cannot make a solid case for case-based approaches to thinking skills training until we have many more studies involving different job roles, different learner populations, and diverse outcome measures.

Make Thinking Processes Explicit

In the BioWorld and the Accelerate Expertise programs, we saw that domain-specific or job-specific thinking processes were made salient. For example, in BioWorld, learners are required to identify, post, and prioritize relevant evidence to support their disease hypotheses. At the end of each case, they compare their evidence priorities with those of an expert. Likewise, in Accelerate Expertise, the learner must collect and evaluate evidence regarding the risk of a loan application. The learner can compare his or her evidence-gathering activities with those of an expert.

Effective problem-solving training must focus on the metacognitive thinking skills of the job. Most job training today concentrates on knowledge of job facts, concepts, and procedures. This job knowledge is typically taught using a teaching-by-telling (receptive) or show-and-do (directive) architecture. Whether in the classroom or through multimedia, learners generally listen to lectures or read text, complete short exercises, and follow the steps to practice performing a task. The training emphasis is on direct job knowledge. Rarely are the processes, especially the invisible mental processes involved in solving job problems, explicitly trained.

For example, in many mathematics classes, the focus is on the calculation procedures needed to solve a problem. Rarely has it been on the mental processes—especially the metacognitive processes underlying problem solution. The outcome is learners who can get the right answer, but fail to assess its relevance, as in the army bus problem described previously.

Teach Metacognitive Skills

In the last twenty years, educators have designed programs with the explicit goal of building metacognitive skills in their learners. Alan Schoenfeld, a mathematics professor, has developed one such classroom program (1987). He noted that his graduate students were quite adept at specific mathematical techniques taught in their classes, but they lacked problem-solving skills. In studying the thinking processes of students, he noted that about 60 percent would read a problem, start down a solution path, and continue down that path, whether it was productive or not. Schoenfeld characterizes this as the "read the problem, make a decision to do something, and then pursue it come hell or high water" approach (p. 207). In contrast, experts solving the same problem were more reflective. In Figure 14.9 you can see Schoenfeld's visual representations of problem-solving activities of experts compared to novices. He gathered this data by analyzing the dialog of experts and novices who talked aloud while they solved problems. Unlike the novices who stuck to one approach, the expert problem solvers moved iteratively among planning, implementing, and evaluating problem-solving actions.

Figure 14.9. Different Problem-Solving Activities in Novice and Expert Mathematicians.

From Schoenfeld, 1987.

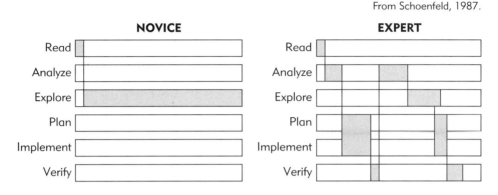

Schoenfeld designed training to make student problem-solving skills more like those of experts. He used worked examples and practice as his main instructional methods. He solved demonstration problems in class, during which he would voice aloud his thoughts—including his monitoring and adjusting thoughts. On occasion he might deliberately go down an unproductive path. After a bit he would stop and say something like, "Wait—is this getting me anywhere? What other alternatives might I consider?" In this way he provided examples not only of problem solutions but *also of the thinking processes* behind them. Second, he assigned problems to small student groups. As they worked together, he would visit the groups and ask "metacognitive questions" such as, *"What are you doing now?" "Why are you trying that approach?" "What other approaches might you consider?"* By first demonstrating and then holding learners responsible for applying these problem-solving process skills, they soon learned to incorporate this kind of thinking in their problem-solving sessions.

Based on these teaching methods, we suggest two guidelines for making problem-solving processes explicit through e-learning:

- Provide examples of expert problem-solving actions and thinking; and

- Promote learners' awareness of and reflection on their problem-solving processes by making learners document their thinking processes and by showing maps of student and expert problem-solving paths.

Provide Examples of Expert Problem-Solving Processes

Similar to the Schoenfeld techniques described in the previous section, e-learning can make expert thinking processes explicit. For example, consider the screen shown in Figure 14.10. This e-learning program focuses on teaching of metacognitive skills associated with reading comprehension of stories. Example skills include defining the theme or focus of a story, identifying the sequence of main events, and considering the feelings and motives of the main characters. In the screen shown in Figure 14.10, a pedagogical agent uses audio to demonstrate his comprehension processes. As he starts his analysis, he makes a mistake about what the story is about. As he reads on, he recognizes his error and crosses out his initial thoughts, replacing them with a more accurate summary.

Figure 14.10. Reading Comprehension Skills Modeled.

With permission from Plato Software.

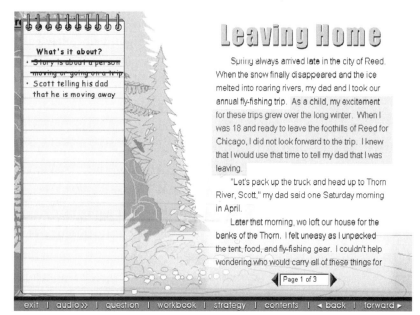

In Chapter 10, we reviewed the power of worked examples. In this example we apply this powerful instructional method to the demonstration of thinking skills rather than task-specific skills. We recommend that you use techniques to encourage learner processing of worked examples. For example, throughout a demonstration, learners can be asked questions about the techniques illustrated. Responding to these questions requires learners to process the example rather than skip it or just give it cursory attention.

Promote Awareness of Problem-Solving Processes

By requiring learners to record the key actions or outcomes of a problem-solving process, e-learning can make thinking processes explicit. For example, in Figure 14.11, the reading comprehension skills demonstrated in Figure 14.10 are practiced by the learner. A new story is presented on the screen and the learner is asked to type in an analysis of the story in the workbook area. When done, an expert response (on the left-hand portion of the screen) allows learners to compare their statements with a model answer. We saw similar functionalities in the BioWorld and Accelerate Expertise examples shown in Figures 14.4 and 14.6.

Figure 14.11. Reading Comprehension Skills Practiced.
With Permission from Plato Software.

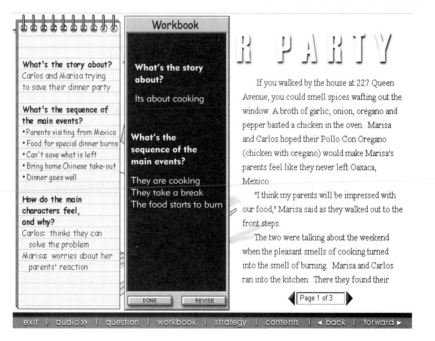

Define Job-Specific Problem-Solving Processes

As you review e-lessons that claim to build problem-solving skills in your workforce, look for case scenarios, research tools, data sources, activities, and thinking processes that expert job performers would use in your organization. If the lessons incorporate these elements, you are more likely to obtain performance improvement than from a program that is more general.

These job-specific elements must be identified during the planning phases of the e-learning program. While some elements such as the tools and observable activities can be readily seen, the most important elements of problem solving, namely the reasoning processes of experts, are invisible. Special techniques to define the case problems to be solved in the training and the processes experts use to solve them must be applied during the design of the training.

For example, the developers of an intensive care nursing problem-solving (SICUN) training documented their planning process in some detail (Lajoie, Azevedo, & Fleiszer, 1998). They started by interviewing three head nurses from the intensive care unit to determine the most difficult aspects of their jobs. These were used to define the job competencies that distinguish expert from beginning practitioners. Interviews with additional nurses ensured that the types of problems built into the training would reflect the most difficult parts of the job a nurse would have to encounter.

Following the interviews, the team worked with expert nurses to identify specific case problems that would incorporate the key competencies identified earlier. Once some cases were developed on paper, the actions that experienced nurses would take to solve them were defined by asking three nurses unfamiliar with the case to talk aloud as they solved the problem. These problem-solving interviews followed a specific sequence. For every action that a nurse would mention, the interviewer would ask the reason for the action. Then the interviewer would state the outcome of the action and the nurse would state his or her interpretation of the outcome. The transcripts collected from these problem-solving sessions were coded into categories, including hypothesis generation, planning of medical interventions, actions performed, results of evidence gathering, and interpretation of results, along with overall solution paths. The goal of this phase was to define the problem-solving processes and actions experts used to provide the basis for the training program.

The activities involved in identifying the actions and thoughts of experts during problem solutions are called a *cognitive task analysis.* The task analysis is a major project in itself that needs to be completed before starting to design the e-lessons. Initial interviews are used to define skills and competencies that distinguish expert practitioners from others. Based on these, specific cases are built that incorporate those competencies. Since expert job practitioners can rarely articulate their thinking processes in a direct way, these must be inferred indirectly through a cognitive task analysis technique such as the one described here. Through a combination of interviews and cognitive task analysis, you define: (1) target case problems, (2) the normal tools and resources available to the worker, and (3) expert solution paths. All three of these problem-solving elements should be incorporated in the design of your e-lesson.

As you plan your analysis project, use care to define who is considered an expert, since it is the expert processes that will serve as the basis for your training. Ideally, you can identify experts based on metrics that objectively point them out as best practitioners. For example, sales records can be used to identify top sales practitioners. In other situations, you will need to use a combination of years of experience, job position, and/or practitioner consensus as indicators of expertise.

Teaching Thinking Skills: The Bottom Line

In this chapter we have seen evidence and examples for the design of job-specific case-based e-learning that builds problem-solving metacognitive skills as much as (or layered on) technical knowledge and skills. We have advocated for a domain-specific or job-specific approach that uses real-world cases as a context for learning the problem-solving techniques unique to a discipline. e-Learning can be used to make invisible thinking processes explicit as well as to prompt practice applying those processes. We look forward to additional research to shape these guidelines.

What We Don't Know About Teaching Thinking Skills

In Table 14.1 we outlined three approaches to teaching thinking skills, ranging from very broad to quite specific. Based on evidence to date, we recommended using the more specific approaches for workforce learning. However, many questions remain:

- Can moderately general thinking skills training (Type 2) be tailored to benefit a variety of job problems through job-specific examples and practice?

- How does case-based thinking skills training compare with a more directive approach that incorporates examples and practice?

- Are case-based learning environments more effective for learners with greater job-relevant experience, rather than for novices?

- How important is collaboration (among learners and between learners and instructors) to optimizing results in case-based problem-solving environments?

- Which techniques can be used to guide learners in a case-based environment in order to ensure efficient and effective learning?

DESIGN DILEMMA: RESOLVED

Your training department was charged with providing courses that would improve workforce critical thinking skills. In reviewing the many courses claiming to improve creative thinking, you wondered which of the following options were correct:

A. Money can be saved by purchasing an off-the-shelf course that includes techniques like the ones listed in Figure 14.1.

B. Creativity training must be conducted in a face-to-face environment, so any effective program must be classroom-based.

C. Creative-thinking training should be job-specific; no one general creative-thinking course will be effective for everyone.

D. There is no way to improve creativity through training; it's like intelligence—you either have it or you don't.

E. Not sure which options are correct.

Based on evidence to date, we believe that Option C offers the greatest promise for performance results from problem-solving training. However, this option requires customized training focusing on job-specific problem-solving skills. Alternatively, the training department might recommend a needs analysis to define which job categories engage in problem solving that most directly links to organizational competitive advantage. Then perhaps, tailored training should focus on leveraging the problem-solving skills of those work groups.

WHAT TO LOOK FOR IN e-LEARNING

☐ Case-based learning that allows learners to observe and apply job-specific problem-solving skills

☐ Lessons that require learners to make their reasoning process and products explicit

☐ Thinking processes modeled and practiced in training based on job-specific analysis of expert strategies

☐ Various forms of instructional guidance provided to ensure successful case resolution and learning of problem-solving skills

☐ Several diverse cases included to foster building of a more robust set of problem-solving skills

---

ON *THE e-LEARNING AND THE SCIENCE OF INSTRUCTION* CD

Our CD lesson uses a directive instructional approach and primarily focuses on cognitive skills (rather than metacognitive skills), including the concepts and guidelines involved in building a database. However, we believe that construction of effective databases is a task that relies on creative problem solving. We recommend that once the basics are learned with lessons such as our example, case-based lessons that emphasize the thinking and planning processes behind database construction could apply the guidelines of this chapter.

COMING NEXT

Games and simulations are one of the hottest topics in e-learning today. But before you jump on the bandwagon, you might wonder what evidence we have for the instructional value of games and simulations. In the next chapter we define the key elements of games and simulations, show some examples, and review what lessons we have learned from these environments so far.

Suggested Readings

Lajoie, S.P., & Nakamura, C (2005). Multimedia learning of cognitive skills. In R.E. Mayer (Ed.), *The Cambridge handbook of multimedia learning*. New York: Cambridge University Press.

Mayer, R.E. (2008) *Learning and instruction* (2nd ed.). Upper Saddle River, NJ: Pearson Merrill Prentice Hall. See Chapter 12: Teaching by Fostering Problem-Solving Strategies.

Richart, R., & Perkins, D.N. (2005). Learning to think: The challenges of teaching thinking. In K.J. Holyoak & R.G. Morrison (Eds.), *The Cambridge handbook of thinking and reasoning*. New York: Cambridge University Press.

Schoenfeld, A.H. (1987). What's all the fuss about metacognition? In A. Schoenfeld (Ed.), *Cognitive science and mathematics education*. Mahwah, NJ: Lawrence Erlbaum.

Scott, G., Leritz, L.E., & Mumford, M.D. (2004). The effectiveness of creativity training: A quantitative review. *Creativity Research Journal, 16*(4), 361–388.

CHAPTER OUTLINE

The Case for Simulations and Games

Popularity of Games

Games and Brains

What Are Simulations and Games?

Do Simulations and Games Teach?

What Research Tells Us About Games and Simulations

Balancing Motivation and Learning

The America's Army Game

Indiana Jones

When Motivation and Learning Clash

Games and Simulations Principle 1: Match Game Types to Learning Goals

Games and Simulations Principle 2: Make Learning Essential to Progress

Features That Lead to Learning

Discovery Learning Receives an F

Games and Simulations Principle 3: Build in Guidance

Evidence for Explanatory Feedback

Games and Simulations Principle 4: Promote Reflection on Correct Answers

Evidence for Reflection of Accurate Responses

Games and Simulations Principle 5: Manage Complexity

Move from Simple to Complex Goals

Minimize Interface Complexity

Provide Training Wheels

Use Faded Worked Examples

Manage Game or Simulation Pace

Provide Instructional Support

What We Don't Know About Games and Simulations

15

Simulations and Games in e-Learning

WILL ONLINE LEARNING GAMES soon replace books and traditional step-by-step e-learning? Are younger generations better served by highly experiential and high-intensity multimedia learning games? Unfortunately, when it comes to learning, there is more we don't know about simulations and games than we do. However, we do have some accumulating evidence about how games and simulations can be designed to promote learning. In this chapter we focus on the evidence we do have to help you define tradeoffs and leverage proven techniques when considering simulations and games to achieve your learning goals.

In Chapter 1 we introduced three e-learning architectures, ranging from low to high in interactivity. Receptive forms of e-learning are low in overt opportunities for interactivity. Learning from these environments relies on psychological engagement, not visible activity. In Chapters 10 and 11 we focused on moderately interactive e-learning. In those chapters we looked at directive learning environments characterized by explanations, examples, and interspersed practice exercises designed to promote active learning. In this chapter we move to the far end of the activity spectrum as we review highly interactive forms of e-learning found in games and simulations.

DESIGN DILEMMA: YOU DECIDE

Scene: The Database Training Project Meeting

Sandy: "Did you know that 55 percent of our staff play either video or computer games in their free time? And it's not just the young new hires either! Some tell me they spend up to twenty hours a week playing these games. The workforce of today—those who have been playing online games for years—have different brains! Their nervous systems are attuned to high engagement multimedia experiences. These digital natives are bored by anything that even looks like traditional training!

Let's leverage the popularity of games with a database adventure theme. We could design a mystery scenario where databases contain clues to reach goals. The more clues that are accumulated, the closer the player is to achieving the mission!"

Matt: "OK. This sounds exciting ... but how long will it take to develop this game? And how will it affect our production budget? And what about learning time? How long do you think it will take to play the game compared to completing an old-fashioned tutorial? If we invest in this game, will they learn how to construct databases as effectively and efficiently as a traditional lesson that just shows them how?"

Sandy is excited about embedding the database content into a highly interactive learning environment. But Matt has some questions. Based on your own experience or intuition, which of the following options would you select:

A. Sandy is correct. Raised on games, the younger workforce will learn more effectively from game-type lessons.

B. More participants will complete a game-type course than a traditional tutorial.

C. Learning by exploration and experience is more effective than learning by explanations and traditional practice exercises.

D. Constructing a gaming environment will be more expensive than developing a traditional course; however, the investment will pay off in higher course completion rates and better databases.

E. Not sure which options are correct.

The Case for Simulations and Games

A rash of conference presentations, books, and articles tout the use of simulations and games for learning. At the 2006 e-Learning Guild conference, over 12 percent of the presentations included the words "game" or "simulation" in their titles. Issenberg, McGaghie, Petrusa, Gordon, and Scalese (2005) report that 385 research studies on the use of high-fidelity medical simulations were published between 2000 and 2003.

Enthusiasts hope to leverage the popularity of entertainment games and simulations to improve learning outcomes. Some argue that the younger generation of "digital natives" raised on games and simulations have different neurological requirements for learning—requirements that demand highly interactive media-intensive learning environments.

In medical education high-fidelity simulations are recommended because (a) managed health care has resulted in shorter patient stays with consequent fewer clinical teaching opportunities than in the past, (b) patient safety is enhanced when procedures can be learned and practiced on simulators, (c) new medical procedures such as sigmoidoscopy, laparoscopy, and robotics involve motor and perceptual skills that can be effectively practiced via simulators, and (d) deliberate practice involving repetitive performances leads to improved skills (Issenberg, McGaghie, Petrusa, Gordon, and Scalese, 2005).

Popularity of Games

According to the 2006 Entertainment Software Association report, games are not just for the young. Sixty-nine percent of American heads of households play computer or video games. The average age of game players is thirty-three, with 25 percent over the age of fifty. Males outplay females almost two to one, making up 62 percent of the gaming population. You can see in Figure 15.1 that action and sports are the most popular video games and strategy and family-children's games are the most popular computer games. Since 1996, there has been a steady increase in the annual dollar sales of computer and video games, which has leveled at the $7 billion range since 2002.

Figure 15.1. Sales of Video and Computer Game Types.

Source: Entertainment Software Association, 2006 Report.

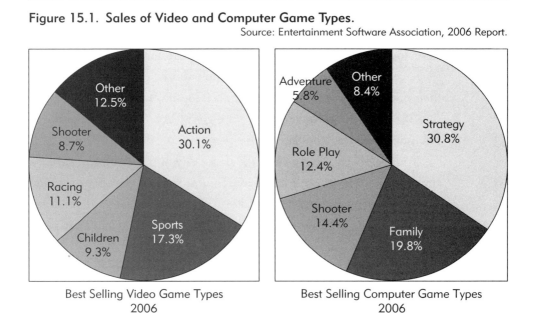

Best Selling Video Game Types
2006

Best Selling Computer Game Types
2006

Games and Brains

Some say that extensive childhood experience with digital games is changing brains. According to Carstens and Beck (2005): "The immense amount of time spent with games during a child's formative years has led them to be literally 'hard wired' in a different way than those who came before" (p. 23). Along similar lines, Prensky (2001) claims that: "Immense changes in technology over the past thirty years, of which video games are a major part, have dramatically and discontinuously changed the way those people raised in this time period think, learn, and process information.... The change has been so enormous that today's younger people have, in their intellectual style and preferences, very different minds from their parents and, in fact, all preceding generations" (p. 17).

To leverage the minds of the gamer generation, Prensky (2001) recommends that educators plan learning environments that:

1. Are fast-paced to take advantage of "twitch speed" information-processing capabilities;

2. Emphasize high learner control and multiple tracks to leverage greater multitasking abilities; and

3. Actively engage participants in highly visual environments that encourage learning by exploration.

What evidence do we have about the instructional effectiveness and efficiency of simulations and games? Will a simulation or game result in higher e-learning completion rates compared to standard tutorials? Will learning be faster? Will learners feel more positive about the instructional experience as well as about the knowledge and skills learned? What is the cost-benefit of simulations and games? What distinguishes an effective game or simulation from an ineffective one? In this chapter we review what evidence we do and do not have regarding these questions.

What Are Simulations and Games?

Suppose you wanted to learn the basics of genetics. You could work through a structured linear interactive tutorial. Alternatively, you could opt for a more experiential environment like the genetics simulation in Figure 15.2. In the simulation, learners can change the genes on the chromosomes and immediately see how the dragon features are altered. In Figure 15.3, the simulation has been converted into a game by giving learners a goal to change the lower-left dragon to match the one in the upper left.

What Are Simulations?   A simulation is a model of a real-world system. Simulated environments respond in dynamic and rule-based ways to user responses. For example, if in the simulation in Figure 15.2 the user changes

Figure 15.2. Simulation of Laws of Genetics.
From Biologica Project: http://biologica.Concord.org

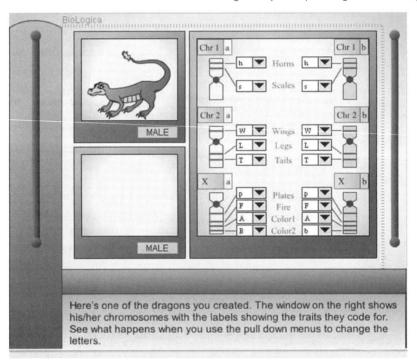

Here's one of the dragons you created. The window on the right shows his/her chromosomes with the labels showing the traits they code for. See what happens when you use the pull down menus to change the letters.

the h on chromosome 1 to a dominant gene H, horns appear on the dragon based on laws of genetics. De Jong and van Joolingen (1998) define a computer simulation as a "program that contains a model of a system (natural or artificial; e.g. equipment) or a process" (p. 180).

There are two basic types of simulations: *operational* and *conceptual*. Operational simulations are designed primarily to teach procedural skills, whereas conceptual simulations focus on learning of domain-specific strategic knowledge and skills. In workforce learning, operational simulations have been used for training of software applications, medical procedures, and safety-related skills such as aircraft piloting and industrial control operations. In contrast, conceptual simulations such as the one shown in Figure 15.2 are primarily designed to build *far-transfer* knowledge of a specific domain as well as associated problem-solving skills. Conceptual simulations in the

Figure 15.3. Game Based on Simulation of Laws of Genetics.

From Biological Project: http://biologica.Concord.org

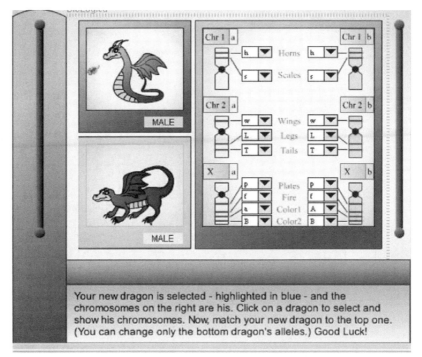

educational arena have focused on principles of physics, genetics, chemistry, botany, and ecology, to name a few. In workforce learning, conceptual simulations have been designed to teach management and communication skills, bank loan analysis, medical diagnostics, and equipment troubleshooting among others. For example, in Figure 15.4 we show a screen from a simulation designed to teach commercial bank loan analysis. The learner is presented with a loan applicant and is free to explore the office interface in order to collect data about the applicant and ultimately make a funding recommendation.

What Are Games?   From Solitaire to Jeopardy to Doom, online games reveal a diverse array of formats and features. The common elements of all games include (1) a competitive activity with a challenge to achieve a goal, (2) a set of rules and constraints, and (3) a specific context. For example, the

Figure 15.4. A Simulation for Commercial Loan Analysis.
With permission from Moody's Investment Service.

genetics game shown in Figure 15.3 has a goal to match the features of the test dragon to the target dragon by changing the genes of the test dragon one at a time. As the genes of the test dragon are changed, the learner receives immediate feedback by seeing a change in dragon features. Gene changes result in feature changes based on the laws of genetics. Additional game rules could be added that, for example, assigned points based on the number of moves required to match the target dragon. Like many adventure, action, or strategy online games, the genetics game involves a simulation. However, not all games incorporate simulations. For example, game-show quiz games such as Jeopardy are not simulation-based.

Do Simulations and Games Teach?

Rieber (2005) tested the effectiveness of the simulation shown in Figure 15.5 for teaching physics principles of velocity and acceleration. The player manipulates the ball's acceleration by clicking on the large arrows. To add a motivational

Figure 15.5. The Flip-Flop Game Interface.

From Reiber, 2005. © Cambridge University Press 2005.
Reprinted with the permission of Cambridge University Press and L. Rieber.

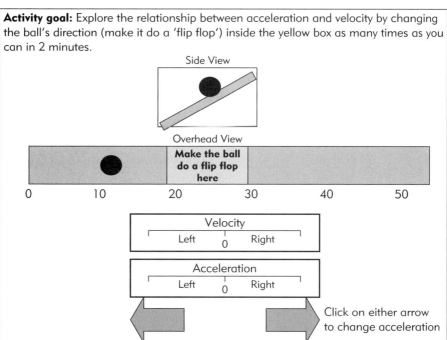

Activity goal: Explore the relationship between acceleration and velocity by changing the ball's direction (make it do a 'flip flop') inside the yellow box as many times as you can in 2 minutes.

element to the simulation, some participants were given a game goal to earn points by making the ball flip-flop as many times as possible inside the small box in the center of the overhead view.

Participants using the game version reported much higher enjoyment than those who worked with the simulation without the game goals. However, when tested on physics principles, the gaming group scored significantly lower than those who explored the simulation without a game goal! The flip-flop game players became obsessive, focusing exclusively on improving their scores, and in the process failed to reflect on the physics principles underlying the model.

In this experiment we see that a gaming environment can be a lot of fun and at the same time depress learning. Why? The game goals led to behaviors that were antagonistic to the instructional goals. The Oregon Trail Game also failed to support learning objectives (Hays, 2005). The Oregon Trail Game was designed to teach school children the problem-solving challenges of managing food, dealing with disease, and crossing rough terrain in a covered wagon. Children converted the game into a target practice and racing game by shooting as many animals as possible and by getting to the end of the trail rapidly. Most of the domain-specific information was ignored.

Those who played the flip-flop and Oregon Trail games learned. They learned to play the games. However, game play did not translate into achievement of the intended objectives. Games must be designed in ways that promote learning. That way we can get the best of both worlds—fun and learning! Later in this chapter we will focus on design guidelines to optimize learning from simulations and games.

What Research Tells Us About Games and Simulations

Several research teams have recently gathered and analyzed a number of individual experiments that tested the effectiveness of simulation-based learning or games. There are no clear conclusions except that we need better-quality research studies. For example, Gosen and Washbush (2004) found that, while at face value many studies support the effectiveness of computer-based simulations, very few of the studies meet high standards for research design. They reported that, of 155 studies reviewed, not one met all of the criteria for sound research. They conclude that: "There is evidence the approaches are effective, but the studies showing these results do not meet the highest of research design and measurement standards. Thus we believe any conclusion about them must be tentative" (pp. 283–284).

Randel, Morris, Wetzel, and Whitehill (1992) reviewed sixty-seven experiments, finding that twenty-two favored simulation games over conventional instruction, three showed advantages for conventional instruction, and thirty-eight showed no difference.

In a review of research on high-fidelity medical simulations Issenberg, McGaghie, Petrusa, Gordon, and Scalese (2005) conclude: "Outcomes research on the use and effectiveness of simulation technology in medical education is scattered, inconsistent, and varies widely in methodological rigor and substantive focus" (p. 10).

Hays (2005) located over 270 documents on games, of which only forty-eight included empirical data. He concludes that "The empirical research on the effectiveness of instructional games is fragmented, filled with ill-defined terms, and plagued with methodological flaws. Some games provide effective instruction for some tasks some of the time, but these results may not be generalizable to other games or instructional programs" (p. 3).

Balancing Motivation and Learning

The goal in game-based learning is to provide an instructional environment that is enjoyable AND achieves the learning objectives. What makes a game or simulation fun? Malone (1981) and Malone and Lepper (1987) identified four features that motivate persistence and enjoyment of games: (1) a challenge: a structure that is neither too simple nor too difficult; (2) control: the players must feel that they can affect the outcomes of the game and that the game maintains an optimal pace; (3) curiosity: for example, when exploratory opportunities lead to unpredictable outcomes; and (4) fantasy: the perception of participation in a made-up environment.

The America's Army Game

The America's Army game is a first-person perspective adventure/shooting game with advanced graphics and sound effects. Figure 15.6 shows a screen shot from the target practice segment. Belanich, Sibley, and Orvis (2004) identified the features of America's Army that players did and did not like, summarized in Figure 15.7. Game realism was one commonly mentioned popular element. The authors suggest that high degrees of realism contribute to the fantasy element of the game by engaging participants in a military environment. Challenge was a positive element for those who perceived a match and a negative element for those who felt the game was too easy or too hard. Control was also a major motivational factor. In America's Army it was rated as a negative due to a perceived lack of control.

Figure 15.6. Target Practice in the America's Army Game.

Accessed from www.americasarmy.com

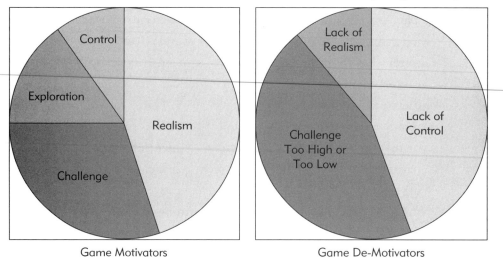

Figure 15.7. Features That Players Did or Did Not Like in America's Army Game.

From Belanich, Sibley, and Orvis, 2004.

Game Motivators | Game De-Motivators

Indiana Jones

Ju and Wagner (1997) asked players of the Indiana Jones game what made it fun, challenging, or unattractive. Players liked the fun factors included in the story—its richness, play, and its narrative speed, as well as the graphical interface. The authors (p. 89) report that "a game became unattractive in the subjects' view when it had a poor ('cheesey') interface, with poor graphics, sound, and input controls." Game tasks that were either too difficult or too repetitive were mentioned as unattractive. Pacing was also identified by some participants reviewing Indiana Jones commenting that the story was a little too slow moving.

When Motivation and Learning Clash

The designer's challenge in a marriage of motivational and instructional features is managing extraneous mental load so that the game challenge, fantasy, and control elements do not subvert learning. A game or simulation runs the risk of overloading or distracting learners in ways that are counterproductive to learning. For example, a game that incorporates "twitch" elements allows little time for reflection. A game or simulation that includes highly detailed and realistic visuals and audio may overload memory. Simulations or games that are highly exploratory can lead to a great deal of activity but little learning. The solution is to shape motivational elements in games in ways that support and do not defeat basic psychological learning processes. In the next section, we summarize evidence-based guidelines for design and development of simulations and games for instructional success.

GAMES AND SIMULATIONS PRINCIPLE 1

Match Game Types to Learning Goals

To be effective, the goals, activities, feedback, and interfaces of simulations and games must align with the desired instructional outcomes. The Oregon Trail and flip-flop games described previously included elements that were antagonistic to the intended learning objectives. Learning took place—just not the intended learning. In the Oregon Trail game, children co-opted game features that appealed to them, such as shooting animals, that did not contribute to the learning goal. The "twitch" feature of the flip-flop game was counterproductive to the deeper reflection needed to learn physics principles.

In Figure 15.1 we summarized the categories of commercial video and computer games. What types of games are best suited for various learning outcomes? Van Eyke (2006) suggests: "Jeopardy-style games, a staple of games in the classroom, are likely to be best for promoting the learning of verbal information (facts, labels, and propositions) and concrete concepts. Arcade-style games … are likely to be best at promoting speed of response, automaticity, and visual processing. Adventure games are likely to be best for promoting hypothesis testing and problem solving. It is critical, therefore, that we understand not just how games work, but how different types of games work and how game taxonomies align with learning taxonomies" (p. 22).

We will look to future research to validate the match between game types and learning outcomes. For any game used for learning purposes, it's critical to embed the key knowledge and skills into the game environment.

Make Learning Essential to Progress

It's important to ensure that game progress and success translate into learning. In other words, learning required to succeed in the game should be the same learning required by your instructional objectives. Belanich, Sibley, and Orvis (2004) evaluated learning of twenty-one individuals who played the America's Army game with questions assessing information presented during the game. Participants completed four sections of the game, including marksmanship training, an obstacle course, weapons familiarization, and an operational training mission. The research team compared learning of information that was relevant to playing the game with information that did not impact progress in the game. For example, a relevant question asks: "During basic rifle marksmanship qualifying, how many rounds are in a magazine?" In contrast, "What is written on the lane posts of the obstacle course?" is irrelevant to game progress. As you can see in Figure 15.8, learning of relevant information was greater, with an effect size of .65, which is moderate.

Figure 15.8. Players Recognized More Game-Relevant Information Than Game-Irrelevant Information.

Based on data from Belanich, Sibley, and Orvis, 2004.

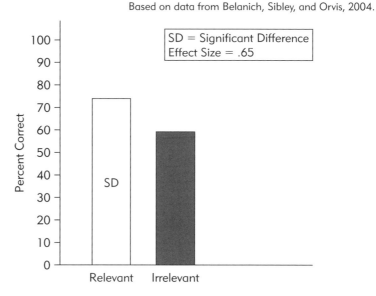

The research team recommends that "instructional objectives should be integrated into the game's story line so that the training material is relevant to the progression of the game" (p. 17).

Features That Lead to Learning

So far we have seen that games can either lead to or defeat learning. Rather than asking whether games or simulations work, we think it's more useful to consider what characteristics of games and simulations lead to learning. Recent research comparing different versions of simulations and games points to the criticality of learning support. Any element included in a simulation or game that leads to the important cognitive processes we summarized in Chapter 2 constitutes learning support. A simulation or game will be successful to the extent that it does not overload working memory and at the same time promotes generative processing aligned with the instructional goal. In the remainder of this chapter, we will review evidence for features of simulations and games that realize these cognitive goals.

Discovery Learning Receives an F

If there is one thing we do know about experiential learning, it's that pure discovery learning, whether by an individual alone or with a group, does not pay off in learning. The popular view that learning must involve active engagement in discussions, hands-on activities, or interactive games, rather than more traditional passive environments such as reading books, attending lectures, or viewing online presentations is one of the defining arguments behind the use of games and simulations. Simulation and game enthusiasts often equate physical activity and mental activity. For example, Prensky (2001) claims that "We now see much less tolerance in the workplace among the Games Generations for passive situations such as lectures, corporate classrooms, and even traditional meetings. Games Generation workers rarely even think of reading a manual. They'll just play with the software, hitting every key if necessary, until they figure it out" (p. 59).

The assumption that mental activity must be predicated on physical activity is a teaching fallacy (Mayer, 2004). The challenge facing instructional professionals is to "promote appropriate processing in learners rather than methods that promote hands-on activity or group discussion as ends in themselves.... Instructional programs evaluated over the past fifty years consistently point to the ineffectiveness of pure discovery. Activity may help promote meaningful learning, but instead of behavioral activity per se, the kind of activity that really promotes meaningful learning is cognitive activity" (p. 17).

Judge the value of any simulation or game not on the activity, but rather on the degree to which the activity promotes appropriate cognitive processing. "Guidance, structure, and focused goals should not be ignored. This is the consistent and clear lesson of decade after decade of research on the effects of discovery methods" (Mayer, 2004, p. 17).

We discourage the creation of games and simulations that are highly exploratory—environments that at best are inefficient for learning and at worst defeat learning completely. One way to mitigate these unintended consequences is to incorporate guidance into simulations and games. The next section offers guidelines and evidence on how to structure simulations and games for learning success.

Build in Guidance

Design simulations and games in ways that offer structure and learning support. Research is just starting to uncover ways to incorporate effective guidance. In the sections to follow, we describe the following techniques for guidance, summarized in Table 15.1.

- Incorporate instructional explanations;
- Encourage reflection on instructional content;
- Manage complexity; and
- Provide instructional support.

Table 15.1. Techniques for Guidance in Games and Simulations.

Technique	Description	Examples
Incorporate Explanations	1. Provide explanatory feedback rather than corrective-only feedback 2. Provide brief instructional explanations between simulation rounds	Remember that you need two recessive genes to see a recessive trait. Try again. To see recessive traits expressed, two recessive genes must be inherited.
Encourage Reflection	After seeing a correct response, provided by a learning agent, for example, ask learners to explain the answer	The dragon changes color from purple to green when I select the two recessive genes for green color. Select the reason for this change:
Manage Complexity	1. Sequence tasks from easier to more complex by constraining variables	In the first game, only a single gene change from recessive to dominant is needed.

(Continued)

Table 15.1. (Continued).

Technique	Description	Examples
Manage Complexity (continued)	2. Make only some elements in the interface functional (training wheels)	Only some chromosomes allow gene changes.
	3. Use faded worked examples	The agent changes some genes and the learner changes the rest.
	4. Manage pacing to minimize extraneous load and promote reflection	There is no goal that involves speed of response.
Optimize Interface Fidelity	1. Avoid highly realistic images and sounds, especially for novice learners	The dragon is a line drawing with a limited number of features.
	2. Minimize realism that is not aligned to the instructional objectives	The dragon does not roar or exhibit features irrelevant to the goal.
Provide Instructional Support	1. Demonstrate how to play the game	Watch me change a gene and see what happens to the dragon.
	2. Provide memory support	Look in the online notes for a list of what you tried and what happened.
	3. Include process guidance	Try changing only one gene at a time and record what happens.
	4. Include visualization support	Look at this diagram showing how genes are passed from parents to offspring.

Evidence for Explanatory Feedback

An instructional explanation is a brief tutorial that states the principles or concepts being illustrated in the simulation or game. We have evidence that learning from games or simulations with explanations is better than from games and simulations without explanations. There are two main ways to integrate explanations. They can be included as feedback to learner responses, as described in Chapter 11. Or explanations can be offered in the form of hints appearing between simulation rounds. When using a simulation or game lacking explanations, learners try to achieve the goals of the game and learn at the same time. These two activities may lead to mental overload and it's usually the game, not the learning, that takes precedence.

Knowledge of results that incorporates guidance is one of the most important instructional elements in any simulation or game. Feedback was the single most commonly mentioned success factor among research studies on the effectiveness of medical simulations (Issenberg, McGaghie, Petrusa, Gordon, & Scalese, 2005). Feedback may be built into a simulator, provided by an instructor, or provided in a video replay reviewed after a simulator session. The source of the feedback is less important than its presence. Evaluations of Design-A-Plant and Hunger in the Stahl games summarized in the following paragraphs support the value of incorporating feedback into games or simulations.

Feedback in Design-A-Plant. Moreno (2004) evaluated learning and efficiency of two versions of a botany game called Design-A-Plant. In Design-A-Plant learners are given a goal to construct a plant with the best combinations of roots, leaves, and stems to survive in planets of different environmental features. The game goal is to design a plant that succeeds in a specific environment. The instructional goal is to learn how plant features are adaptive to various environmental conditions.

In one version of Design-A-Plant, a learning agent provided explanatory feedback to learner responses. A comparison version offered only "correct–incorrect" feedback. In the explanatory feedback version, when the learner makes a correct selection, the agent confirms the choice with a statement such as: "Yes, in a low sunlight environment, a large leaf has more room to make food by photosynthesis." For an incorrect choice, the agent responds with a statement such as: "Hmmmm, your deep roots will not help your plant collect the scarce rain that is on the surface of the soil." This feedback is followed by the correct choice.

As you can see in Figure 15.9, the explanatory feedback version resulted in better learning and was also rated as more helpful than the comparison versions. There were no differences in student ratings of motivation or interest for the two versions. Adding explanations to the feedback improved learning, but did not detract from the enjoyment of the game. Efficiency calculations found that better learning occurred with less mental effort in the explanatory feedback versions.

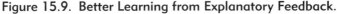

Figure 15.9. Better Learning from Explanatory Feedback.

Based on data from Moreno, 2004.

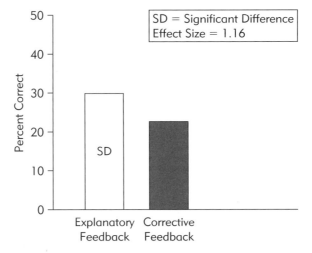

In a follow-up experiment, Moreno and Mayer (2005) confirmed these findings. Learners working with versions that provided explanatory feedback scored twice as much on a transfer post-test, with an effect size of 1.87, which is very high.

Feedback in Hunger in the Sahel. Leutner (1993) evaluated learning ecological principles from a simulation game in which the student plays the role of a farmer and makes decisions regarding how to use ten lots of land with different geophysical features. Decisions made in the game determine the agricultural profit and, in turn, the family's ability to survive. Each game round simulates a year. The simulation model is set so that without a suitable land-use strategy, starvation results within only a few years. Leutner measured game performance as well as ecological knowledge such as what erosion is, ways to manage erosion, and so forth.

Some participants were free to explore the simulation without any support. Others received feedback based on their choices. For example, they were told, "If you dig too many water holes, the ground water level may collapse." Explanatory feedback improved scores on the domain test, but diminished game performance. In contrast, participants who did not receive feedback learned to perform the game more effectively, but scored lower on domain knowledge. It seems that learning to play the game effectively built implicit knowledge that did not translate into verbal knowledge. Leutner concludes: "If the goal of discovery learning is to promote the acquisition of verbal knowledge related to concepts, facts, rules, and principles of the simulated domain of reality, then it is very useful to make pieces of information, which are implicitly available in the system, explicit through appropriate instructional support during system exploration." In other words, success in game play does not necessarily lead to knowledge and skills that can be explicitly articulated. Additional support in the form of explanations can bridge that gap.

Embedded Explanations in a Physics Game.   Rieber, Tzeng, and Tribble (2004) evaluated learning of laws of motion from a game in which learners clicked to kick a ball to position it on a target on the screen. The game score was based on the time needed to reach the goal. The team measured: scores on a multiple choice test that assessed understanding of the physics principles, game scores, and user frustration ratings. Some participants received hints between game rounds such as: "This simulation is based on Newton's laws of motion. Newton's second law says that the speed of an object depends on size of the force acting upon it. Therefore, an object kicked two times to the right would move at a speed twice as fast as a ball kicked only once" (p. 314). Those who received hints had an average pretest-post-test gain of 32 points, compared to 13 points for those who did not receive hints!

Rieber, Tzeng, and Tribble (2004) conclude that "Discovery learning within a simulation can be very inefficient, ineffective, and frustrating to students, but providing students with short explanations at just the right time can offset these limitations" (p. 319). A brief and succinct instructional explanation incorporated into a simulation can improve learning and at the same time not detract from the game experience.

Taken together, these studies point to the benefits of embedding brief instructional explanations into a game or simulation. Explanations may be in the form of feedback to learner responses or placed as hints between simulation rounds. The explanations may come from the program, an instructor, or by way of a post-simulation review of actions. We need additional research to tell us the best timing, format, source, and placement of effective explanations for different learning goals.

Promote Reflection on Correct Answers

Achieving the goal of a game or attempting to master a simulation may preclude reflection—reflection that is needed to abstract lessons learned from the game. Rieber, Tzeng, and Tribble (2004) suggest that: "The experiential nature of an educational simulation is very compelling—users often become very active and engaged in a simulation, similar to the experience of playing a video game. However, the intense and demanding interactivity of many simulations may not provide adequate time for the user to carefully reflect on the principles being modeled by the simulation" (p. 318). The Reflection Principle states that learning from simulations and games will be better when learners have opportunities to actively explain correct responses.

Evidence for Reflection of Accurate Responses

Moreno and Mayer (2005) used versions of the Design-A-Plant game, all of which provided explanatory feedback based on our Principle 3 on providing instructional explanations. In some versions, after seeing the correct answer displayed by a learning agent, learners were asked to give an explanation for the answer. In alternative versions, learners were asked to explain their own solutions. Students asked to reflect on the program's correct solutions scored significantly higher on a transfer test, with an effect size of .80. However, reflection on their own answers (some of which were incorrect) did not yield as good learning. In other words, for reflection to be effective, be sure you ask learners to explain correct, not inaccurate choices. Thus "reflection alone does not foster deeper learning unless it is based on correct information" (p. 127).

Manage Complexity

Throughout this book we have described multimedia design principles designed to avoid mental overload. For example, in Chapter 9 we reviewed evidence showing that segmenting and sequencing instructional content can reduce cognitive load and improve learning. Likewise, there are a number of ways to help learners manage mental load in games. These include managing the complexity of the simulation or game goal, optimizing the complexity of the interface, as well as providing instructional support in the form of memory aids or activity guidance. In this section, we summarize the following approaches to complexity management in simulations and games: (1) goal progression, (2) interface design, (3) training wheels, (4) faded worked examples, (5) pacing, and (6) several forms of instructional support.

Move from Simple to Complex Goals

Begin a game or simulation with a relatively low-challenge task or goal and move gradually to more complex environments. For example, in the genetics simulation shown in Figure 15.3, the challenge of the game can be adjusted by changing the number of genes needed to match the test dragon to the target dragon or by the complexity of the genetic relationships required to achieve a given match. Game complexity can be controlled by asking learners to select a game difficulty level based on their relevant experiences or by dynamically adapting game complexity based on accuracy of responses during the game.

Minimize Interface Complexity

Interface complexity is a function of the type and display of images used in a game or simulation. Lee, Plass, and Homer (2006) created a conceptual simulation of Boyles and Charles Laws that describe the relationships between gas pressure and gas volume (Boyles Law) and gas temperature and gas volume (Charles Law). The research team created four different interfaces based as follows:

1. Combined interface (high complexity) that allowed manipulation of both temperature and pressure on the same screen;

2. Separated interface (low complexity) that allowed manipulation of temperature on one screen and pressure on a separate screen;

3. Abstract interface that used slider bars only to manipulate temperature and pressure; and

4. Concrete interface that used a flame adjuster and weights to represent adjustments in temperature and pressure.

Figure 15.10 shows the combined interface that used concrete symbols. As students adjust the temperature or pressure icons, changes in the volume of the gas are recorded in the right-hand graph.

Figure 15.11 shows the effects of these simulation interfaces on learning. As you can see, the most complex combination, the combined interface with abstract controls, resulted in the least learning, with an effect size close to 1. This type of research that compares learning from different interface elements in games and simulations will help guide our design of these environments in the future.

Highly realistic images and sounds in the interface are primary satisfiers for game play. These features may promote the fantasy elements of a game environment. However, highly realistic interfaces are more expensive to create and may impose extraneous mental load. Van Merrienboer and Kester (2005) suggest that "for novice learners, a high-fidelity task environment often contains irrelevant details that may deteriorate learning" (p. 79). Norman (2005) similarly notes that in medical education the degree of fidelity in the simulation is best matched to the learning goal and to the background experience of the learner. "You are unlikely to benefit much from a explanation of wave

Figure 15.10. Simulation Interface for Ideal Gas Laws That Combines Both Laws (High Complexity) and Uses Concrete Representations of Variables (Weights and Flames).

Adapted from Lee, Plass, and Homer, 2006.

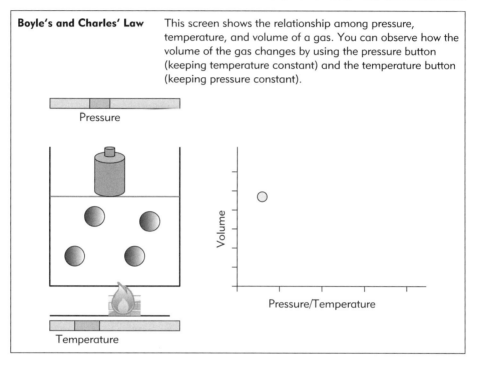

formation to a multimedia animated narrated version, Mayer and Jackson (2005) found better learning from the paper group, probably because learners could interact with the material at their own pace and were less likely to experience cognitive overload.

Games that rely on "twitch" behaviors are likely most beneficial for jobs that require "twitch" responses based on speed and accuracy. If your instructional goals require application of concepts and rules, games that proceed under learner control of pacing and do not reward speed are more likely to succeed. 747 simulation unless you already have a lot of hours on big jets, and the medical student trying to learn physiology in the simulated operating room is a bit like the Piper Cub student pilot in the 747 simulator. . . . Both are little more than tourists in a foreign country" (p. 88).

Figure 15.11. Worst Learning from Complex Simulation Interface That Used Abstract Symbols.

Based on data from Lee, Plass, and Homer, 2006.

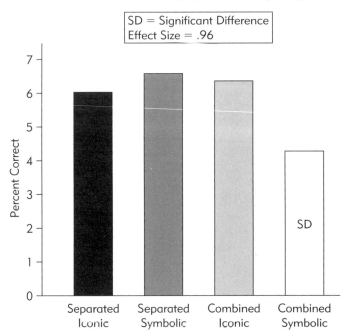

We reviewed evidence in Chapter 7 that interesting visuals and words related to the topic of lightning but not relevant to the instructional goal depressed learning. The potential antagonism between the highly realistic interfaces that lead to motivation and the lower-fidelity interfaces that lead to learning requires additional research for resolution.

Provide Training Wheels

Carroll (2000) described a "training wheels" principle for software simulations. He recommends that learners work with a simulation in which only some of the functionality is enabled. Although the full interface may be visible, only relevant elements of it work. In that way, learners cannot go too far astray during early trials. As more tasks are learned, the functionality constraints are gradually released until the user is working with a highly functional system. For example, when working with a software simulation, only a few commands or icons are functional. As the learner gains experience, greater functionality is added.

Use Faded Worked Examples

In Chapter 10 we saw the benefits of transitioning from worked examples to practice by way of fading. The instruction begins with a complete demonstration of the task. Next learners view a demonstration of the first few steps of the task and finish it on their own. Gradually, the learner assumes more and more task responsibility until she is doing it on her own. A simulation or game can also incorporate a fading strategy. Initially the learner observes a successful game round with explanatory commentary. For example, a pedagogical agent may demonstrate how to play the game or interact with the simulation. In the next round, the agent completes some of the steps, assigning others to the learner. Gradually the learner assumes greater control until she is working on her own. In a game scenario, the beginner may play the role of the apprentice working under the direction of a game agent who serves as the master performer. Over time the agent assigns greater responsibility to the apprentice as her skills build.

Manage Game or Simulation Pace

According to some, the new generation of gamers is not patient. They have learned to multitask and to respond to multiple digital information sources quickly. Slow game pace was one complaint of players of the Indiana Jones adventure game (Ju & Wagner, 1997). While fast-paced games may be more popular, they are also likely to lead to greater overload and to fewer opportunities for reflection. For example, in comparing learning from a paper-based explanation of wave formation to a multimedia animated narrated version, Mayer and Jackson (2005) found better learning from the paper group, probably because learners could interact with the material at their own pace and were less likely to experience cognitive overload.

Games that rely on "twitch" behaviors are likely most beneficial for jobs that require "twitch" responses based on speed and accuracy. If your instructional goals require application of concepts and rules, games that proceed under learner control of pacing and do not reward speed are more likely to succeed.

Provide Instructional Support

We have already discussed the importance of explanations and reflection on correct answers. There are many other potential instructional resources you can consider. These include simulation or game instruction, memory support, and game play aids.

Provide Instruction in Using the Game.   A simulation or game will require cognitive effort to master the mechanics of the environment—cognitive effort that will not be available for learning. You can free mental resources for learning   the instructional goals by explicitly teaching how the simulation or game works. The focus of this suggestion is on the interface mechanics— not the strategic decisions required by the game. An agent can start the game or simulation with a tour or example of how the goals are achieved by manipulation of the various interface elements. For example, the America's Army game provides a working aid that summarizes the keyboard symbols for various actions such as running, loading a rifle, and others.

Provide Memory Support.   Many problem-solving or strategy games and simulations take place over time, during which the participant accumulates data or draws conclusions from experiences. Provide facilities for records of actions taken, facts accumulated, and conclusions reached. In the bank loan simulation shown in Figure 15.4, learners can access data from a number of sources, including interviews, credit reports, and referrals. The file cabinet located under the left side of the desk stores all data automatically as it is gathered throughout the game. At any point, the learner can open the file drawer and refer to the data collected. In the genetics game, a record of gene manipulations and results could be maintained by the game or by the learner on an electronic note pad. Such a record will help learners derive conclusions based on a series of experiments.

Include Process Guidance.   Some games and simulations focus on a defined process or strategy that reflects best practices for goal achievement. For example, commercial loan analysis requires completion of a prescribed sequence of stages, including evaluation of the applicant's credit, economic forecasts for an industry segment, and evaluation of the applicant's prior financial performance. Incorporate process worksheets as well as automated process tracking into these types of games or simulations. The process worksheet directs the learner through specific problem-solving stages. In addition, you may provide action tracking, as we discussed in Chapter 14. As the learner progresses through the game, her actions may be recorded so she can view her breadcrumbs upon completion of a game or a segment of it. Upon request, she can compare her solution path to that of an expert.

Include Visualization Support. Success in some simulations or games may rely on spatial skills. Instructional aids promote learning by providing external spatial representations as guides. For example, Mayer, Mautone, and Prothero (2002) evaluated different types of support for a geology simulation game called the Profile Game. During the game, learners collect data from a planet whose surface is obscured by clouds. Players draw a line and the computer shows a profile line indicating how far above and below sea level the surface is at each point on the line. By drawing many lines, learners can determine whether the section contains a mountain, trough, island, or other feature.

Participants were provided with strategy aids in text, visual aids diagramming the features listed in the previous sentence, or no aids. A sample of a visual aid is shown in Figure 15.12. The visual aids led to best game

Figure 15.12. This Visual Aid Helped Learners Identify Geological Features in a Geology Simulation Game.

From Mayer, Mautone, and Prothero, 2002.

Ridge on Land | Ridge in Ocean

Trench on Land | Trench in Ocean

Basin on Land | Basin in Ocean

Island in Ocean | Seamount in Ocean

performance. The research team concludes that "students need support in how to interact with geology simulations, particularly support in building and using spatial representations" (p. 181).

What We Don't Know About Games and Simulations

There is far more we don't know about games than what we do know. We do know that, for some, games are both motivational and when well-designed can improve learning. We are also confident that well-designed simulations can offer instructional environments for practice and learning that are unavailable or unsafe in the workplace. The research of the next few years should give more guidance about how to design simulation and game features that effectively balance motivational and learning elements. Here is a list of some important questions for which we need empirical data:

1. *Guidance for guidance.* We know that guidance is an essential ingredient for deriving learning from a simulation or game. We presented evidence for guidance in the form of explanations and reflection support. However, we need more information on the most appropriate format, source, timing, and type of guidance to use for different instructional goals at different learning stages.

2. *Simulation and game taxonomies for different learning outcomes.* We know it's important to match the simulation or game goal, actions, feedback, and interface to the instructional goals. However, we have only general guidelines for making an appropriate match, most of which lack empirical verification. Will arcade games with "twitch" features be most effective for visual or motor skills? Will adventure or strategy games be best aligned for learning cause-and-effect relationships? Are memory goals such as learning product knowledge best supported by game-show type formats? An empirically based taxonomy of game formats aligned to learning outcomes should help game and simulation designers make optimal matches.

3. *Cost-benefit of games and simulations.* To design and implement a computer game or simulation of any complexity will require an investment of time and resources. In addition to development costs, participant

time is invested in interacting with the simulation or game. What are the efficiencies of games? How does the time to achieve an instructional goal from a game compare with achieving the same goal from a book or tutorial? When does the motivational appeal of a game offset the investment in development and learning time? For example, will an embedded game result in higher completion of e-learning as well as equal or better learning contrasted to traditional methods? In most commercial settings, there is a cost attached to the development and use of learning environments and we have much to learn about the cost-benefit tradeoffs to games and simulations.

4. *Who prefers games?* Are there some individuals of specified professions, ages, or prior knowledge who will find learning from games more motivational than others? For example, will sales professionals enjoy games more than engineers, men more than women, younger staff more than mature staff, college graduates more than non-grads? Would specific types of games appeal to different populations? Until we have better guidelines, run a game pilot to assess your audience's response.

5. *Effective game interfaces.* We have evidence that how game elements—the interface, the feedback, and the support—are represented affect outcomes. However, we need more data to guide interface design. Commercial games use high-end graphics, animations, and sounds. Rich multimedia interfaces increase motivational appeal. However, might a high-fidelity environment impose a mental burden that impedes learning? Van Merrienboer and Kester (2005) recommend that training should start with low-fidelity environments that only represent the essential aspects necessary to accomplish the task. We need evidence on how the interface of a simulation or game affects motivation and learning.

6. *How much interactivity?* There may be optimal levels of interactivity to promote learning. Excessive interactivity may distract learners from the goal of building a mental model of the system. Novices in particular may be overloaded by very high levels of interactivity. On the other hand, purely observational environments may not sustain attention or promote encoding processes. We need research that

compares varying levels of interactivity for novice and experienced learners in the same simulation or game.

7. *Simulations versus games?* When is a simulation more effective than a game? How will learning be affected by simulations used as structured practice exercises compared to using the same simulation in the form of a game? Will the game features add extraneous mental load? Will the game lead to greater learning and learner satisfaction? In what situations, for example, types of learners and nature of the instructional goal, would a game added to a simulation be most effective?

DESIGN DILEMMA: RESOLVED

We started this chapter with a debate between Sandy and Matt on embedding the database content into an adventure game context. The options included:

A. Sandy is correct. Raised on games, the younger workforce will learn more effectively from game-type lessons.

B. More participants will complete a game-type course than a traditional tutorial.

C. Learning by exploration and experience is more effective than learning by explanations and traditional practice exercises.

D. Constructing a gaming environment will be more expensive than developing a traditional course; however, the investment will pay off in higher course completion rates and better databases.

E. Not sure which options are correct.

While we would like to select Option D, at this time we do not have sufficient evidence to support it. For now, we have to go with Option E. However, we are seeing the gradual accumulation of research that points to features such as explanatory feedback and reflection support as well as management of cognitive load in the interface that promote learning in simulations and games. We look forward to additional research that narrows our "what we don't know" list.

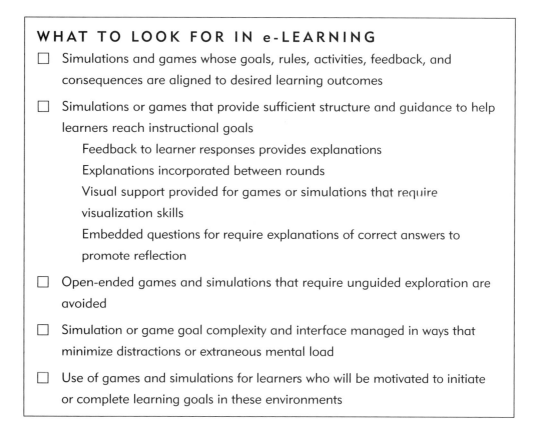

WHAT TO LOOK FOR IN e-LEARNING

☐ Simulations and games whose goals, rules, activities, feedback, and consequences are aligned to desired learning outcomes

☐ Simulations or games that provide sufficient structure and guidance to help learners reach instructional goals

    Feedback to learner responses provides explanations

    Explanations incorporated between rounds

    Visual support provided for games or simulations that require visualization skills

    Embedded questions for require explanations of correct answers to promote reflection

☐ Open-ended games and simulations that require unguided exploration are avoided

☐ Simulation or game goal complexity and interface managed in ways that minimize distractions or extraneous mental load

☐ Use of games and simulations for learners who will be motivated to initiate or complete learning goals in these environments

COMING NEXT

This chapter completes our review of what research tells us about important design and development issues in e-learning. In our final chapter, we integrate all of the guidelines of the previous chapters in two ways. First we offer a checklist of evidence-based features as they apply to receptive, directive, and guided-discovery forms of e-learning. Second, we illustrate the application of the checklist by reflecting on how four e-learning lessons do and do not apply the guidelines effectively. Among the four, we review the two asynchronous database sample lessons on the CD, one synchronous e-learning class on Excel formulas, and one asynchronous guided discovery lesson on bank loan analysis.

Suggested Readings

Hays, R.T. (2005). *The effectiveness of instructional games: A literature review and discussion.* Technical Report 2005–004. Washington, DC: Naval Air Warfare Center Training Systems Division.

Lee, H., Plass, J.L., & Homer, B.C. (2006). Optimizing cognitive load for learning from computer-based science simulations. *Journal of Educational Psychology, 98*(4), 902–913.

Mayer, R.E. (2004). Should there be a three-strikes rule against pure discovery learning: The case for guided methods of instruction. *American Psychologist, 59*(1), 14–19.

Moreno, R., & Mayer, R.E. (in press). Interactive multi-modal learning environments. *Educational Psychology Review.*

Rieber, L.P. (2005). Multimedia learning in games, simulations, and micro-worlds. In R.E. Mayer (Ed.), *The Cambridge handbook of multimedia learning.* New York: The Cambridge University Press.

Van Eck, R. (2006). Digital game-based learning. *Educause Review, 41*(2), 17–30.

CHAPTER OUTLINE

16

Applying the Guidelines

THIS CHAPTER CONSOLIDATES all the guidelines we have discussed by describing how they apply or are violated in four e-learning examples. Here you have the opportunity to consider all of the guidelines in concert as you read how we apply them to some sample e-lessons. In our update to this chapter, we add new guidelines to our checklist, based on the new research we have included. We also put the checklist on the CD. We compare and contrast the application of our guidelines to the asynchronous database example and counter-example lessons included on the book's CD. We also include a new synchronous e-learning example to illustrate how the guidelines apply to the virtual classroom. In our discussion of a bank loan simulation lesson, we can apply new guidelines regarding games and simulations. Finally, we look back at our predictions about the future directions of e-learning for workforce learning.

Applying Our Guidelines to Evaluate e-Courseware

The goal of our book is to help consumers and designers make e-learning decisions based on empirical research and on the psychological processes of learning. In an ideal world, e-courseware effectiveness should be based on measurement of how well and how efficiently learners achieve the learning objectives. This measurement requires a validation process in which learners are formally tested on their skills after completing the training. In our experience, formal course validation is rare. More often, consumers and designers look at the features rather than at the outcomes of an e-learning course to assess its effectiveness. We recommend that, among the features that are assessed, you include the research-based guidelines we have presented. We recognize that decisions about e-learning alternatives will not be based on learning theory alone. A variety of factors, including the desired outcome of the training, the culture of the organization sponsoring the training, the technological constraints of the platforms and networks available to the learners, and pragmatic issues related to politics, time, and budget, will shape e-learning decisions. That is why you will need to adapt our guidelines to your unique training situations.

In Chapter 1 we described three common purposes for e-learning: to inform workers, to teach procedural tasks, and to teach far-transfer or strategic tasks. Your technological constraints will determine whether you can only deliver courseware with low-memory intensive media elements like text and simple graphics or whether you can include media elements that require greater technical resources such as video, audio, and animation. If you are planning an Internet or intranet course, you can use collaborative facilities, including email, chats, and message boards.

Integrating the Guidelines

Taken together, we can make a general statement about the best use of media elements to present content and learning methods in e-learning. In situations that support audio, best learning will result from concise informal narration of relevant graphics. In situations that preclude audio, best learning will result from concise informal textual explanations of relevant graphics in which the text and graphic are integrated on the screen. In all cases, learning of novices is best promoted by dividing content into short segments, allowing learners to control the rate at which they access each segment. In addition, in lessons of any complexity, learning is more efficient when supporting concepts are presented prior to the process or procedure that is the focus of the lesson.

Table 16.1 compares the average effect sizes and number of experimental tests for the multimedia principles described in Chapters 3 through 9. Recall from Chapter 2 that effect sizes tell us the proportion of a standard deviation of test score improvement you will realize when you apply that principle. For example, if you apply the multimedia principle, you can expect overall a test score of one and one half standard deviations greater than a comparable lesson without visuals. As a general guideline effect sizes: less than .2 are small, around .5 are moderate, and .8 or above are quite large. Principles with larger effect sizes based on more experimental tests indicate greater potential practical applicability. As you can see in the table, with the exception of the

Table 16.1. Summary of Research Results from the Eight Multimedia Principles.
From Mayer, 2001, Mayer, 2003b, c, d.

Principle	Effect Size	Number of Tests
Multimedia	1.50	9 of 9
Contiguity	1.11	8 of 8
Coherence	1.32	11 of 12
Modality	.97	21 of 21
Redundancy	.69	10 of 10
Personalization	1.30	10 of 10
Segmenting	.98	3 of 3
Pretraining	1.30	7 of 7

redundancy principles, all effect sizes fall into the large range. Several exceed an effect size of 1! In particular, the multimedia, contiguity, coherence, personalization, and pretraining principles all show large effect sizes based on multiple experiments.

Because the research underlying the multimedia principles was conducted in the same laboratory and used similar instructional materials (Mayer, 2001a; Mayer, 2005b, c, & d), we can make these comparisons among the results. Regarding the principles summarized in Chapters 10 and beyond, however, we do not have data to make a similar comparison.

e-Lesson Reviews

In this chapter we offer three brief examples of how the guidelines might be applied (or violated) in e-learning courses. We do not offer these guidelines as a "rating system." We don't claim to have included all the important variables you should consider when evaluating e-learning alternatives. Furthermore, which guidelines you will apply will depend on the goal of your training and the environmental considerations mentioned previously. Instead of a rating system, we offer these guidelines as a checklist of research-based indicators of some of the psychological factors you should consider in your e-learning design and selection decisions.

We have organized the guidelines in a checklist in Exhibit 16.1 by chapters and according to the technological constraints and training goals for e-learning. Therefore guidelines 1 through 17 apply to all forms of e-learning. Guidelines 18 through 26 apply to e-learning designed to teach specific job tasks. Guidelines 27 through 31 apply to e-learning with facilities that can engage learners in collaborative work. Guidelines 32 through 35 apply to design of navigational elements that apply primarily to asynchronous forms of e learning. Last, guidelines 36 through 43 apply to e-learning designed to build problem-solving skills and to simulations and games. The checklist is also on the CD that accompanies this edition. The commentaries to follow the checklist reference the guidelines by number, so we recommend you print out the copy of Exhibit 16.1 on your CD to reduce split attention as you read the rest of this chapter. We will discuss the following e-lesson samples: Asynchronous directive example and counter-example lessons on How to Design a Database from our CD, a synchronous directive lesson on Constructing Formulas in Excel, and an asynchronous simulation guided discovery course on bank loan funding analysis.

Exhibit 16.1. A Summary of e-Learning Guidelines.

Three Types of e-Learning:

Type	Best Used for Training Goals	Examples
Show-and-Tell—Receptive	Inform	New hire orientation Product updates
Tell-and-Do—Directive	Procedural Tasks	Computer end-user training
Problem Solving— Guided Discovery	Far-Transfer or Problem-Solving Tasks	Bank loan application analysis Sales skills

Chapters 3 through 9. Multimedia Guidelines for All Types of e-Learning

If Using Visual Mode Only:

1. Use relevant graphics and text to communicate content—Multimedia Principle.
2. Integrate the text nearby the graphic on the screen—Contiguity Principle.
3. Avoid covering or separating information that must be integrated for learning—Contiguity Principle.
4. Avoid irrelevant graphics, stories, and lengthy text—Coherence Principle.
5. Write in a conversational style using first and second person—Personalization Principle.
6. Use virtual coaches (agents) to deliver instructional content such as examples and hints—Personalization Principle.
7. Break content down into small topic chunks that can be accessed at the learner's preferred rate—Segmentation Principle.
8. Teach important concepts and facts prior to procedures or processes—Pretraining Principle.

(Continued)

Exhibit 16.1. A Summary of e-Learning Guidelines. (Continued).

If Using Audio and Visual Modes:

9. Use relevant graphics explained by audio narration to communicate content—Multimedia and Modality Principles.
10. Maintain information the learner needs time to process in text on the screen, for example, directions to tasks, new terminology—Exception to Modality Principle.
11. Avoid covering or separating information that must be integrated for learning—Contiguity Principle.
12. Do not present words as both on-screen text and narration when there are graphics on the screen—Redundancy Principle.
13. Avoid irrelevant videos, animations, music, stories, and lengthy narrations—Coherence Principle.
14. Script audio in a conversational style using first and second person—Personalization Principle.
15. Script virtual coaches to present instructional content such as examples and hints via audio—Personalization Principle.
16. Break content down into small topic chunks that can be accessed at the learner's preferred rate—Segmentation Principle.
17. Teach important concepts and facts prior to procedures or processes —Pretraining Principle.

Chapters 10 and 11—Guidelines for e-Learning Designed to Teach Job Tasks
In addition to the above guidelines:

18. Transition from full worked examples to full practice assignments using fading—Worked Example Principle.
19. Insert questions next to worked steps to promote self-explanations—Self-Explanation Principle.
20. Add explanations to worked out steps.
21. Provide a worked example using realistic job tools and situations in the form of demonstrations for procedural skills—Encoding Specificity Principle.
22. Provide several diverse worked examples for far-transfer skills—Varied Context Principle.
23. Provide job-relevant practice questions interspersed throughout the lessons—Practice/Encoding Specificity Principles.
24. For more critical skills and knowledge, include more practice questions—Practice Principle.
25. Provide explanatory feedback for correct and incorrect answers—Feedback Principle.

Exhibit 16.1. (Continued).

26. Design space for feedback to be visible close to practice answers—Contiguity Principle.

Chapter 12—Guidelines for Use of Collaboration in Internet/Intranet e-Learning

27. Assign collaborative projects or problem discussions to heterogeneous small groups or pairs.
28. Use asynchronous communication tools for projects that benefit from reflection and independent research.
29. Use synchronous communication tools for projects that benefit from group synergy and social presence.
30. Make group assignments and assign participant roles that promote deeper processing.
31. Provide structured assignments such as structured argumentation to minimize extraneous cognitive load.

Chapter 13—Guidelines for e-Learning Navigation—Learner-Control Principles

32. Allow learners choices over topics and instructional methods such as practice when:

    They have related prior knowledge and skills and/or good self-regulatory learning skills

    Courses are designed primarily to be informational rather than skill building

    Courses are advanced rather than introductory

    The content topics are not logically interdependent so sequence is not critical

    The default option leads to important instructional methods such as practice

33. Limit learner choices over topics and instructional options when:

    Learners are novice to the content, skill outcomes are important, and learners lack good self-regulatory skills

34. Use adaptive diagnostic testing strategies when:

    Learners lack good self-regulation skills and the instructional outcomes are important

    Learners are heterogeneous regarding background and needs and the cost to produce tests pays off in learner time saved

35. Always give learners options to progress at their own pace, review prior topics/ lessons, and quit the program

(Continued)

Exhibit 16.1. A Summary of e-Learning Guidelines. (Continued).

Chapter 14—Guidelines for e-Learning to Build Thinking Skills

36. Use real job tools and cases to teach job-specific problem-solving processes—Encoding Specificity Principle.
37. Provide worked examples of experts' problem-solving actions and thoughts—Worked Examples Principle.
38. Provide learners with a map of their problem-solving steps to compare with an expert map—Feedback Principle.
39. Base lessons on analysis of actions and thoughts of expert practitioners—Encoding Specificity Principle.

Chapter 15—Guidelines for Simulations and Games

40. Align the goals, rules, activities, feedback, and consequences of the game or simulation to desired learning outcomes.
41. Provide structure and guidance to help learners reach instructional goals.
42. Avoid open-ended games and simulations that require unguided exploration.
43. Manage goal and interface complexity to minimize extraneous cognitive load.

Asynchronous Samples One and Two: Design of Databases

Description of the Samples

Figures 16.2 through 16.10 are screen captures from our example and counter-example lessons included on the book's CD. If you have not viewed these, you may want to look at them in conjunction with this section. The major lesson objectives are:

- To distinguish between records and fields in a database
- To distinguish between parent and child tables in a database
- To use primary and foreign keys to define relations in tables
- To design a relational database from an existing flat file system

We designed these lessons as asynchronous directive e-learning tutorials assuming learners are new to databases. We imagine placing this lesson in a course on how to use database tools such as Access. In Figure 16.1 we show the content

Figure 16.1. Content Outline of Example and Counter-Example Database Lessons.

Example Lesson		Counter-Example Lesson
1. Introduction		1. Introduction
2. Entities and Tables		2. Did you know?
– Fields and records		3. Select Entities
3. Parent and Child Tables	Concepts	– What is an entity?
– Primary keys		4. Determine Characteristics
– Foreign keys		– Fields and records
4. Entity-Relationship Diagram		5. Assign Primary Keys
		– What is a primary key?
5. Full Worked Example with Questions		6. Did you know?
6. Faded Worked Example	Procedure	7. Assign Foreign Keys
7. Full Practice Exercise		– What is a foreign key?
		8. Designate Table Relationships
		9. Did you know?
		10. Practice 1 – Guided
		11. Full Practice Exercise

outlines for the two courses. Note that in the example lesson, we apply Guideline 8 as we sequence the important concepts first, followed by the steps to construct the database. In addition we apply Guideline 18 by starting with a full worked example and fading to a full practice assignment. The counter-example lesson embeds concept topics into procedure steps sections, does not use worked examples, and includes extraneous information in the "Did You Know" topics.

Application of Guidelines

Figures 16.2 and 16.3 illustrate an ineffective and effective application of the multimedia principles on screens presenting the topic of entity relationship diagrams. The counter-example (Figure 16.2) violates Principles 1, 4, and 6. Rather than explaining the concept with a visual and brief text, it uses a large block of text. In addition, there is no learning agent. In contrast, the example screen in Figure 16.3 uses an explanatory visual and applies Principle 9 by describing the visual with audio narration. Note that arrows and circles are used to signal the relationships among the tables and the keys.

Figure 16.2. Screen Explaining One-to-Many Relationships in
                    Counter-Example.

From *e-Learning and the Science of Instruction* CD.

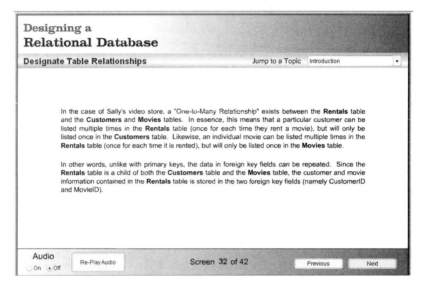

Figure 16.3. Screen Explaining One-to-Many Relationships in
                    the Example.

From *e-Learning and the Science of Instruction* CD.

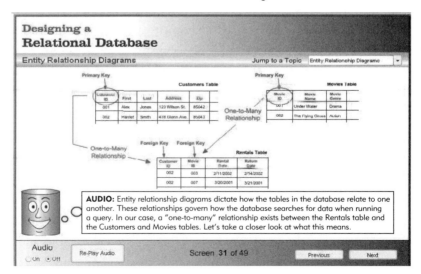

Figure 16.4. Violation of Contiguity in the Counter-Example.
From *e-Learning and the Science of Instruction* CD.

In Figure 16.4 we illustrate a violation of Guideline 3 in the counter-example. Applying the contiguity principle requires an integration of words and visuals on the screen. The example version includes a visual of the spreadsheet and places the text under it. Figure 16.5 illustrates effective practice feedback. When the learner answers incorrectly, the explanatory feedback shown not only tells the learner he is incorrect but gives a brief explanation to lead to a correct answer on a second try. In contrast, the counter-example lesson only tells the learner that he is incorrect. The feedback is presented in on-screen text rather than audio. Feedback in text allows the learner to review the feedback repeatedly in preparation for a second try at the question.

Figures 16.6 and 16.7 illustrate ineffective and effective presentation of examples. Compare the text used to present the step. Note that the text in the example (Figure 16.7) applies Principles 14 and 15 by using the first person pronoun. Figure 16.7 ensures that learners will study the step by including a question in accordance with Guideline 19. In addition, the visual includes an arrow and labels to draw attention to the primary keys in both tables.

Figure 16.5. Feedback Offers an Explanation in the Example.

From e-Learning and the Science of Instruction CD.

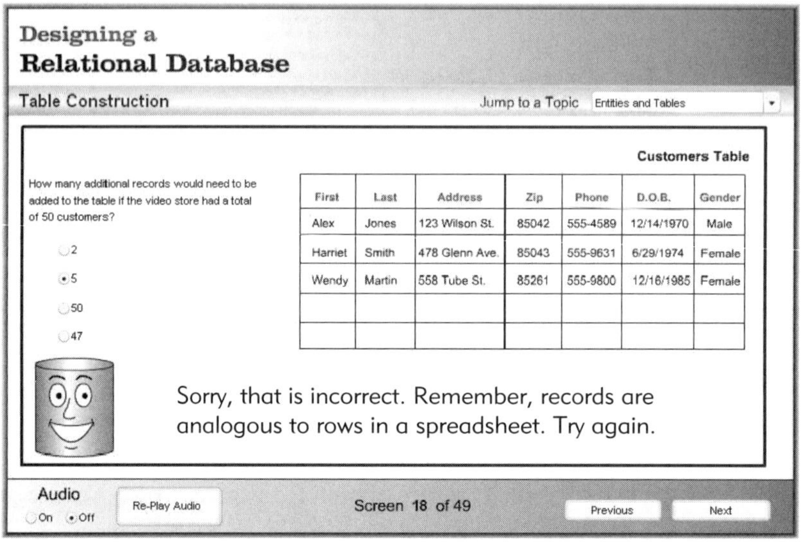

Figure 16.6. An Example from the Counter-Example Lesson.

From e-Learning and the Science of Instruction CD.

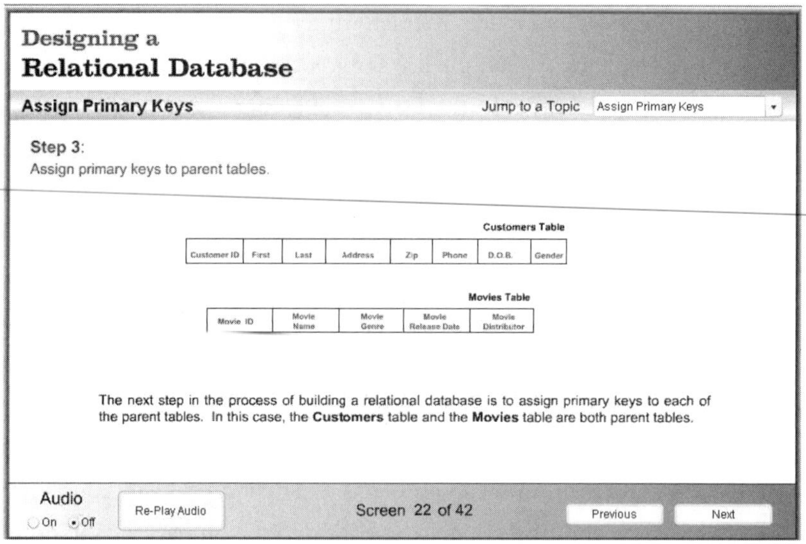

Figure 16.7. An Example from the Example Lesson.
From e-Learning and the Science of Instruction CD.

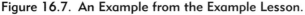

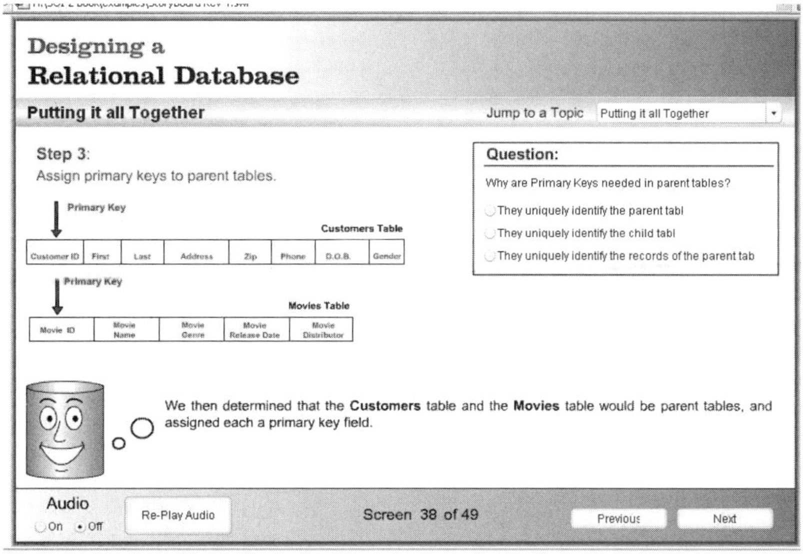

Figure 16.8 is taken from the counter-example lesson and shows one of three brief discussions about the use or abuse of databases. These types of add-ons are intended to sustain interest in the lesson. However, based on Guideline 13 and the coherence principle on which it is based, in many cases, they only serve to depress learning. You will not find these types of additions in the example lesson. Additionally, the counter-example lesson includes background music throughout—yet another violation of coherence.

Synchronous Sample Three: Constructing Formulas in Excel

Description of Sample

Figures 16.10 through 16.12 are taken from a virtual classroom demonstration lesson on How to Use Excel Formulas. Synchronous e-learning has become a major player in e-learning solutions since our first edition, and we wanted to show how to apply our principles to it. If you are new to the virtual classroom, refer to our description of synchronous e-learning features

Figure 16.8. Violation of Coherence in the Counter-Example.
From *e-Learning and the Science of Instruction* CD.

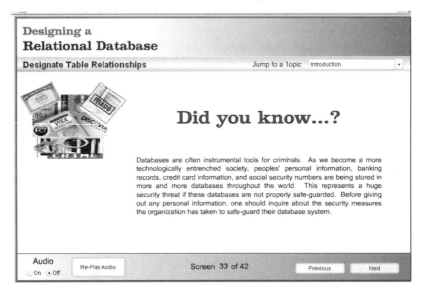

and uses in Chapter 1. The goal of this course is to teach end-user spread-sheet procedures. The lesson objectives are:

- To construct formulas with valid formatting conventions

- To perform basic calculations using formulas in Excel

Figure 16.9 shows a content outline. In applying Guideline 8 based on the pretraining principle, the procedural part of the lesson is preceded by important concepts. Before learning the steps to input a formula in Excel,

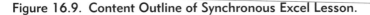

Figure 16.9. Content Outline of Synchronous Excel Lesson.

Example Lesson

1. Introduction
2. What is a formula?   } Concepts
   – Formula formatting
3. How to input a formula?
   – Full worked example
     with questions   } Procedure
   – Faded worked example
   – Full practice exercise

the lesson teaches the concept of a formula, including its formatting conventions. When teaching the procedures, the lesson follows guidelines for worked examples by starting with a full worked example accompanied by questions and fades to a full practice exercise.

Although virtual classroom tools can project a video image of the instructor, in this lesson the instructor used audio alone. Research we reviewed in Chapter 8 showed that it was the voice of a learning agent—not the image—that was most instrumental in promoting learning. Since the main instructional message is contained on the whiteboard slides, we deliberately decided to minimize the potential for split attention caused by a second image. The introductory slide is shown in Figure 16.10. The instructor places her photo on this slide to implement Guideline 6, based on the personalization principle. In addition, the instructor builds social presence by inviting participants to use their audio as they join the session.

Figure 16.10. Introduction to Synchronous Excel Lesson.

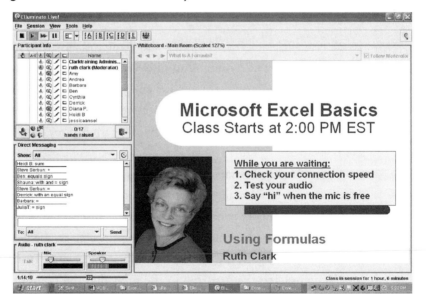

Application of Guidelines

In Chapter 13, we discussed various forms of learner control. Figure 16.11 shows the application of Guideline 34 with a pretest to help learners define

Figure 16.11. Adaptive Control in Synchronous Excel Lesson.

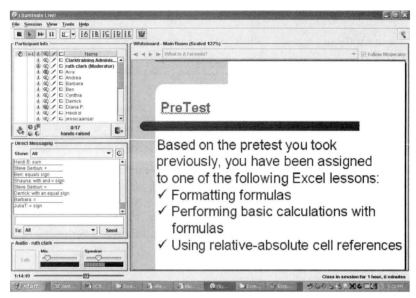

which virtual classroom session they should attend. Asynchronous e-learning can dynamically tailor training to individual needs and progress. However, virtual classrooms are instructor-led and therefore offer few opportunities for dynamic learner control. But a pretest administered prior to the event should help ensure a good match between learner prior knowledge and lesson objectives.

Figure 16.12 illustrates example fading in the virtual classroom. Most virtual classroom tools allow the instructor to share desktop applications for demonstration and practice purposes. The spreadsheet window in the middle of the virtual classroom interface is being projected to the learners through application sharing. In the first example, shown in Figure 16.12, the instructor has completed the first step in the procedure by typing the equal sign into the correct spreadsheet cell. The instructor asks participants to finish the example by typing the rest of the formula in the chat window. Note that in applying Guideline 10, the directions are kept on the screen in text, since participants need to refer to them as they work the exercise. The second example (not shown) is a full practice assignment that requires participants

Figure 16.12. Faded Worked Example.

From Clark and Kwinn, 2007.

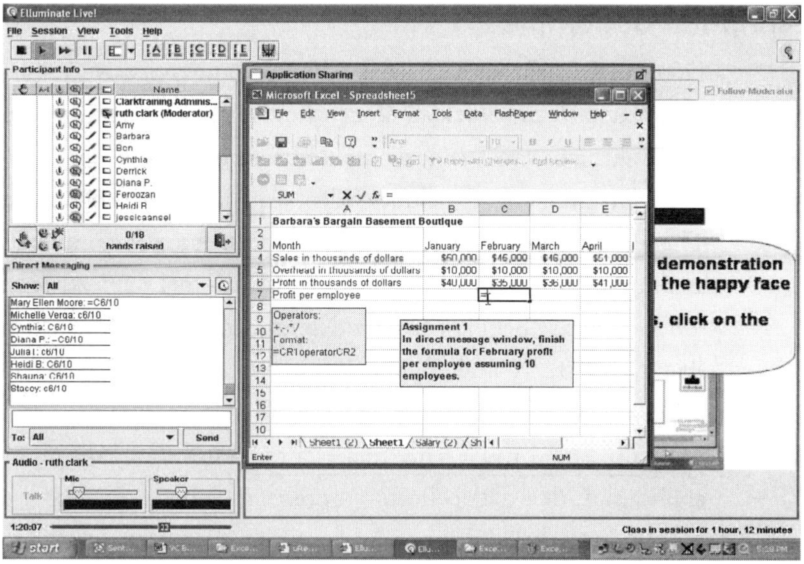

to enter the formula. The fading process gradually assigns more work to the learners, ending with a full practice assignment.

From this brief look at some virtual classroom samples, you can see that just about all of the principles we describe in the book apply. Because the class proceeds under instructor rather than learner control, it is especially critical to apply all guidelines that reduce extraneous mental load. Lesson designers should create effective visuals to project on the whiteboard that will be described verbally by the instructor, applying the multimedia and modality principles. The instructor should use a conversational tone and language and incorporate participant audio to apply personalization. Skill-building classes can apply all of our guidelines for faded worked examples and effective practice exercises. The presence of multiple participants in the virtual sessions lends itself to collaborative projects. Most virtual classroom tools offer breakout rooms in which small teams can carry out assignments. Apply Guidelines 27, 29, and 30 as you plan collaborative activities. As with asynchronous e-learning, instructors should minimize irrelevant visual effects, stories, themes, or audio in accordance with the coherence principle.

Asynchronous Sample Four: Simulation Course for Commercial Bank Loan Analysis

Description of Sample

Figures 16.13 through 16.16 are from a guided discovery simulation course designed to teach bank loan officers how to use a structured process to research and evaluate commercial loan applicants. The course is presented on CD-ROM or via the intranet and includes video, text, and various other graphic elements. The learner starts with a point of view perspective in an office equipped with a computer, telephone, fax machine, file cabinet, and other common office tools. The case begins with a video assignment from the learner's manager (Figure 16.13). Typical of guided-discovery learning environments, the learner is free to use various resources in the office to analyze the loan. For example, in Figure 16.14 the learner makes a request for a credit report on the loan applicant. Other data collection options include interviews of the loan applicant, industry publications, and applicant references. An agent coach is available for advice and offers links to structured lessons related to the loan review

Figure 16.13. Manager Assigns Case to Student Loan Analyst.
Courtesy of Moody's Financial Services.

Figure 16.14. The Simulation Offers Access to Case Data.

Courtesy of Moody's Financial Services.

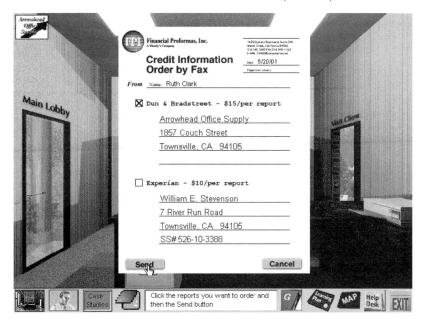

process shown in Figure 16.15. At the end of the research, the learner makes recommendations, along with supporting rationale to the loan committee, and receives feedback from the online agent. The learners can also view the steps they took to solve the case (Figure 16.16) and compare them to expert steps. As the learners progress through the simulation and gather case data, all data is stored in the file cabinet located to the left of the desk in Figure 16.13.

Application of Guidelines

This lesson effectively applies the multimedia Guidelines 7 through 13. It also applies Guidelines 36 through 43 applicable to e-learning to build problem-solving skills and to games and simulations. By situating the learner in a typical office, the designer gives access to the tools and resources needed on the job. The goal, rules, activities, and feedback of the simulation are all aligned to the desired learning outcome, that is, to teach the process associated with commercial loan analysis. Learners can see maps of their steps and compare their maps with an expert approach. Thus the lesson focuses not only on obtaining the correct answer but on how the answer is derived. There are several sources

Figure 16.15. Help from an Agent Offers Advice and Access to Lessons.

Courtesy of Moody's Financial Services.

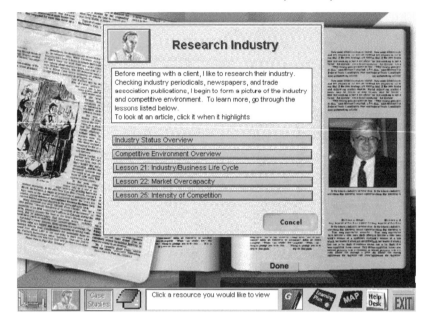

Figure 16.16. Learners Can View Their Steps Taken.

Courtesy of Moody's Financial Services.

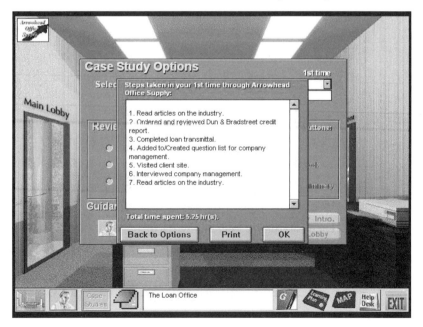

of structure and guidance available congruent with Guideline 41. For example, the agent is always available for advice, and learners can access a series of directive tutorial lessons. The file cabinet reduces mental load by providing memory support. Other than paper documents, there is no on-screen text. Human interactions such as the manager's assignment are presented in video.

Since the structure of the case study is guided discovery, it emphasizes learning during problem solving. Regarding navigation, there was a high level of learner control in the case study segment. However, in the tutorial part of the course (not shown), a pretest is used to give advice regarding which lessons to study. Overall, we feel this course offers a good model for game and simulation environments that are most likely to achieve workforce learning goals.

The Next Generation of e-Learning

What differences will we see in e-learning developed for organizational training in the next few years? In the following section, we first review our predictions from the first edition, followed by our observations four years later.

Prediction One: e-Learning for Job Payoff

Because e-learning developed for workers in organizations is an expensive commitment, we predict more examples of online training that apply guidelines proven to lead to return on investment. Specifically, we believe that there will be:

- Fewer Las Vegas-style courses that depress learning by over-use of glitz and games. Instead, the power of technology will be leveraged more effectively to support acquisition and transfer of job-related skills.

- More problem-centered designs that use job-realistic problems in the start of a lesson or course to establish relevance, in the body of the lesson to drive the selection and organization of related knowledge and skills, and at the end of the lesson to provide practice and assessment opportunities.

- More creative ways to blend computer technology with other delivery media so that the features of a given medium are best used to support ongoing job-relevant skill requirements.

Four Years Later.   As we look back over the past few years, we find this prediction to be valid, although it is perhaps not being realized exactly as we anticipated. We do see a continued and growing focus on e-learning that pays off in job performance. Job-related e-learning has been achieved by an increased integration of e-learning into the work environment and increased blending of media, as predicted in the fourth bulleted point. e-Learning implementations have broadened to include knowledge management resources workers can access during job task completion. For example, if a sales person is writing a first proposal, the company website offers industry-specific information, sample proposal templates, links to mentors, recorded mini lessons on proposal success, and other similar resources.

Prediction Two: e-Learning to Build Problem-Solving Skills

The majority of e-learning currently on the business and industry market is designed to build near-transfer or procedural skills such as end-user software training. However, the increasing economic dependence on knowledge workers, coupled with a shrinking workforce, will drive more courses that focus on building problem-solving skills in specific work domains. Specifically, we believe that:

- e-Learning will increasingly make use of the unique technological features that can support simulations and guided opportunities to learn from them. The current lesson designs that use text, audio, and graphics to describe content will survive. However, these will be supplemented by lessons that encourage the building of mental models and problem-solving skills.

- e-Learning will increasingly be used to make invisible processes and events visible. Learners will be able to see maps of their own problem-solving activities and compare them to expert maps. Additionally, learners will be able to "see" invisible processes, such as how equipment works internally or how to know what a customer is thinking.

- Alternative representations will be used to help to see dynamic relationships in ways that can only be described in other media.

For example, in training of food professionals, a "germ meter" can be used to illustrate the effects of various methods of preparation and handling of food. The relationship between germ density and heat can be illustrated by a dynamic chart that graphs the number of germs as a function of temperature and time of cooking.

- Collaborative e-learning features will be used more extensively and more effectively. Teams of learners will work asynchronously to solve case problems and contribute to ongoing corporate lessons learned about issues relevant to a specific industry or cross-industry profession.

Four Years Later.   We have not seen much evidence that e-learning designed to build problem-solving skills has evolved much beyond our first edition. Trainers remain hard pressed to produce training that teaches the basic tasks of the job and lack time and resources to focus on problem-solving or thinking skills. However, the new interest in games and simulations may offer a window of opportunity for strategic problem-solving e-learning.

Our last point in the second prediction focused on greater use of collaborative e-learning features. The emergence of the Web-2 with social software tools such as blogs and wikis supports this prediction. We hope that the next few years will provide a more cohesive set of research-based guidelines for the application of collaborative tools for learning than we can offer at the present time.

In Conclusion

We have been gratified by the response to the first edition of our book. We believe that workforce learning is moving beyond a crafts approach based on fads and folk wisdom toward a true profession. Professionals base their decisions on many factors, one of which is evidence. We hope the guidelines and supporting evidence in this second edition will support the professional evolution of workforce learning.

REFERENCES

Alexander, P.A., & Winne, P.H. (Eds.) (2006). *Handbook of educational psychology* (2nd ed.). Mahwah, NJ: Lawrence Erlbaum.

Anderson, J.R., Farrell, R., & Sauers, R. (1984). How subject-matter knowledge affects recall and interest. *American Educational Research Journal, 31,* 313–337.

Atkinson, R.K. (2002). Optimizing learning from examples using animated pedagogical agents. *Journal of Educational Psychology, 94,* 416–427.

Atkinson, R.K., & Derry, S.J. (2000). Computer-based examples designed to encourage optimal example processing: A study examining the impact of sequentially presented, subgoal-oriented worked examples. In B. Fishman & S.F. O'Connor-Divelbill (Eds.), *Proceedings of the Fourth International Conference of Learning Sciences* (pp. 132–133). Hillsdale, NJ: Lawrence Erlbaum.

Atkinson, R.K., Derry, S.J., Renkl, A., & Wortham, D. (2000). Learning from examples: Instructional principles from the worked examples research. *Review of Educational Research, 70*(2), 181–214.

Atkinson, R.K., Mayer, R.E., & Merrill, M.M. (2005). Fostering social agency in multimedia learning: Examining the impact of an animated agent's voice. *Contemporary Educational Psychology, 30,* 117–139.

Atkinson, R.K., Renkl, A., & Merrill, M.M. (2003). Transitioning from studying examples to solving problems: Effects of self-explanation prompts and fading worked out steps. *Journal of Educational Psychology, 95*(4), 774–783.

Ayres, P., & Sweller, J. (2005). The split-attention principle in multimedia learning. In R.E. Mayer (Ed.), *The Cambridge handbook of multimedia learning* (pp. 135–146). New York: Cambridge University Press.

Baggett, P. (1984). Role of temporal overlap of visual and auditory material in forming dual media associations. *Journal of Educational Psychology, 76,* 408–417.

Baggett, P., & Ehrenfeucht, A. (1983). Encoding and retaining information in the visuals and verbals of an educational movie. *Educational Communications and Technology Journal, 31,* 23–32.

Bahrick, H.P. (1987). Retention of Spanish vocabulary over eight years. *Journal of Experimental Psychology: Learning, Memory, and Cognition, 13,* 344–349.

Beck, I., McKeown, M.G., Sandora, C., Kucan, L., & Worthy, J. (1996). Questioning the author: A year-long classroom implementation to engage students in text. *Elementary School Journal, 96,* 385–414.

Belanich, J., Sibley, D.E., & Orvis, K.L. (2004). *Instructional characteristics and motivational features of a PC-based game.* Washington, DC: U.S. Army Research Institute for the Behavioral and Social Sciences, Research Report 1822.

Bell, B.S., & Kozlowski, S.W.J. (2002). Adaptive guidance: Enhancing self-regulation, knowledge, and performance in technology-based training. *Personnel Psychology,* 55(2), 267–306.

Bernard, R.M., Abrami, P.C., Lou, Y., Borokhovski, E., Wade, A., Wozney, L., Wallet, P.A., Fixet, M., & Huant, B. (2004). How does distance education compare with classroom instruction? A meta-analysis of the empirical literature. *Review of Educational Research, 74,* 379–439.

Betrancourt, M. (2005). The animation and interactivity principles in multimedia learning. In R.E., Mayer (Ed.), *The Cambridge handbook of multimedia learning* (pp. 287–296). New York: Cambridge University Press.

Brown, P., & Levinson, S.C. (1987). *Politeness: Some universals in language usage.* New York: Cambridge University Press.

Butcher, K.R. (2006). Learning from text and diagrams: Promoting mental model development and inference generation. *Journal of Educational Psychology, 98,* 182–197.

Campbell, J., & Stasser, G. (2006). The influence of time and task demonstrability on decision making in computer-mediated and face-to-face groups. *Small Group Research, 37*(3), 271–294.

Carroll, J.M. (2000). *Making use: Scenario-based design of human-computer interactions.* Cambridge, MA: MIT Press.

Carstens, A., & Beck, J. (2005). Get ready for the gamer generation. *TechTrends, 49*(3), 22–25.

Cassell, J., Bickmore, T., Campbell, L., Vilhjalmsson, H., & Yan, H. (2000). Human conversation as a system framework: Designing embodied conversational agents. In J. Cassell, J. Sullivan, S. Prevost, & E. Churchill (Eds.), *Embodied conversational agents* (pp. 29–63). Cambridge, MA: MIT Press.

Cassell, J., Sullivan, J., Prevost, S., & Churchill, E. (2000). *Embodied conversational agents.* Cambridge, MA: MIT Press.

Catrambone, R. (1998). The subgoal learning model: Creating better examples so that students can solve novel problems. *Journal of Experimental Psychology: General, 127*(4), 355–376.

Chandler, P., & Sweller, J. (1991). Cognitive load theory and the format of instruction. *Cognition and Instruction, 8,* 293–332.

ChanLin, L. (1998). Animation to teach students of different knowledge levels. *Journal of Instructional Psychology, 25,* 166–175.

Clark, R.E. (1994). Media will never influence learning. *Educational Technology Research and Development, 42*(2), 21–30.

Clark, R.C. (2000). Four architectures of learning. *Performance Improvement, 39*(10), 31–37.

Clark, R.C. (2003). *Building expertise: Cognitive methods for training and performance improvement* (2nd ed.). Silver Spring, MD: International Society for Performance Improvement.

Clark, R.C. (2007). *Developing technical training* (3rd ed.). San Francisco, CA: Pfeiffer.

Clark, R.C., & Kwinn, A. (2007). *The new virtual classroom.* San Francisco, CA: Pfeiffer.

Clark, R.C., & Lyons, C. (2004). *Graphics for learning*. San Francisco, CA: Pfeiffer.

Clark, R., Nguyen, F., & Sweller, J. (2006). *Efficiency in learning*. San Francisco, CA: Pfeiffer.

Clark, R., & Nguyen, F. (2007). Behavioral, cognitive, and technological models for performance improvement. In J.M. Spector, M.D. Merrill, J.J.G. van Merrienboer, & M.P. Driscoll (Eds.), *Handbook of research on educational communications and technology* (3rd ed.). Mahwah, NJ: Lawrence Erlbaum.

Cohen, J. (1988). *Statistical power analysis for the behavioral sciences* (2nd ed.). Mahwah, NJ: Lawrence Erlbaum.

Corbalan, G., Kester, L., & Van Merrienboer, J.J.G. (2006). Towards a personalized task selection model with shared instructional control. *Instructional Science, 34,* 399–422.

Craig, S.D., Gholson, B., & Driscoll, D.M. (2002). Animated pedagogical agents in multimedia learning environments: Effects of agent properties, picture features, and redundancy. *Journal of Educational Psychology, 94,* 428–434.

Crossman, E.R.F.W. (1959). A theory of the acquisition of speed skill. *Ergonomics, 2,* 153–166.

Cuban, L. (1986). Teachers and machines: *The classroom use of technology since 1920*. New York: Teachers College Press.

Debowski, S., Wood, R.E., & Bandura, A. (2001). Impact of guided exploration and enactive exploration on self-regulatory mechanisms and information acquisition through electronic search. *Journal of Applied Psychology, 86*(6), 1129–1141.

DeJong, T. (2005). The guided discovery principle in multimedia learning. In R.E. Mayer (Ed.), *The Cambridge handbook of multimedia learning*. New York: The Cambridge University Press.

DeJong, T., & Van Joolingen, W.R. (1998). Scientific discovery learning with computer simulations of conceptual domains. *Review of Educational Research, 68*(2), 179–201.

DeRouin, R.E., Fritzsche, B.A., & Salas, E. (2004). Optimizing e-learning: Research-based guidelines for learner-controlled training. *Human Resource Management, 43*(2–3), 147–162.

De Wever, B., Van Winckle, M., & Valcke, M. (2006). Discussing patient management online: The impact of roles on knowledge construction for students interning at the pediatric ward. *Advances in Health Sciences Education.*

Dewey, J. (1913). *Interest and effort in education.* Cambridge, MA: Houghton Mifflin.

Dillon, A., & Gabbard, R. (1998). Hypermedia as an educational technology: A review of the quantitative research literature on learner comprehension, control, and style. *Educational Psychology, 81,* 240–246.

Dixon, N.M. (1990). The relationship between training responses on participant reaction forms and posttest scores. *Human Resource Development Quarterly, 1*(2), 129–137.

Dolezalek, H. (2005). The 2005 industry report. *Training, 42*(12).

Duncker, K. (1945). On problem solving. *Psychological Monographs, 58,* 270.

Ebbinghaus, N. (1913). *Memory* (N.R., Ruger & C.E., Bussenius, Trans.). New York: Teacher's College. (Original work published 1885.)

Entertainment Software Association. (2006). *Sales, demographic and usage data: Essential facts about the computer and video game industry.* Accessed August 21, 2006, from www.theesa.com/archieves/files/essentail%Facts%202006.pdf

Ericsson, K.A. (2006). The influence of experience and deliberate practice on the development of superior expert performance. In K.A., Ericsson, N., Charness, P.J., Feltovich, & R.R., Hoffman (Eds.), *The Cambridge handbook of expertise and expert performance.* New York: Cambridge University Press.

Eva, K.W., Cunnington, J.P.W., Reiter, H.I., Keane, D.R., & Norman, G.R. (2004). How can I know what I don't Know? Poor self-assessment in a well-defined domain. *Advances in Health Sciences Education, 9,* 211–224.

Fletcher, J.D., & Tobias, S. (2005). The multimedia principle. In R.E. Mayer (Ed.), *The Cambridge handbook of multimedia learning* (pp. 117–134). New York: Cambridge University Press.

Galvin, T. (2001). 2001 industry report. *Training, 38*(10), 40–75.

Garner, R., Gillingham, M., & White, C. (1989). Effects of seductive details on macroprocessing and microprocessing in adults and children. *Cognition and Instruction, 6,* 41–57.

Gay, G. (1996). Interaction of learner control and prior understanding in computer-assisted video instruction. *Journal of Educational Psychology, 78*(3), 225–227.

Gentner, D., Loewenstein, J., & Thompson, L. (2003). Learning and transfer: A general role for analogical encoding. *Journal of Educational Psychology, 95*(2), 393–408.

Gick, M.L., & Holyoak, K.J. (1980). Analogical problem solving. *Cognitive Psychology, 12,* 306–355.

Ginns, P. (2005). Meta-analysis of the modality effect. *Learning and Instruction, 15,* 313–331.

Glenberg, A.M., Sanocki, T., Epstein, W., & Morris, C. (1987). Enhancing calibration of comprehension. *Journal of Experimental Psychology: General, 116*(2), 119–136.

Glenberg, A.M., Wilkinson, A.C., & Epstein, W. (1992). The illusion of knowing: Failure in the self-assessment of comprehension. In T.O. Nelson (Ed.), *Metacognition: Core readings.* Boston, MA: Allyn & Bacon.

Gosen, J., Washbush, J. (2004). A review of scholarship on assessing experiential learning effectiveness. *Simulation and Gaming, 35*(2), 270–293.

Hall, W.E., & Cushing, J.R. (1947). The relative value of three methods of presenting learning material. *Journal of Psychology, 24,* 57–62.

Harp, S.F., & Mayer, R.E. (1997). The role of interest in learning from scientific text and illustrations: On the distinction between emotional interest and cognitive interest. *Journal of Educational Psychology, 89,* 92–102.

Harp, S.F., & Mayer, R.E. (1998). How seductive details do their damage: A theory of cognitive interest in science learning. *Journal of Educational Psychology, 90,* 414–434.

Hays, R.T. (2005). The effectiveness of instructional games: A literature review and discussion. *Technical Report 2005–004.* Washington, DC: Naval Air Warfare Center Training Systems Division.

Hegarty, M., Carpenter, P.A., & Just, M.A. (1996). Diagrams in the comprehension of scientific texts. In R. Barr, M.L. Kamil, P. Mosenthal, & P.D. Pearson (Eds.), *Handbook of reading research* (Vol. II) (pp. 641–668). Mahwah, NJ: Lawrence Erlbaum.

Hegarty, M., Kriz, S., & Cate, C. (2003). The role of mental animations and external animations in understanding mechanical systems. *Cognition and Instruction, 21,* 325–360.

Hegarty, M. (2004). Dynamic visualizations and learning: Getting to the difficult questions. *Learning and Instruction, 14,* 343–351.

Hmelo-Silver, C.E. (2004). Problem-based learning: What and how do students learn? *Educational Psychology Review, 16*(3), 235–266.

Hidi, S., & Renninger, K.A. (2006). The four-phase model of interest development. *Educational Psychologist, 41,* 67–77.

Inglese, T., Mayer, R.E., & Rigotti, F. (2007). Using audiovisual TV interviews to create visible authors that reduce the learning gap between native and non-native speakers. *Learning and Instruction, 16,* 67–77.

Industry Report. (2006). *Training, 38*(12), 20–32. Accessed December 8, 2006, from www.Trainingmag.com.

Issenberg, S.B., McGaghie, W.C., Petrusa, E.R., Gordon, D.L., & Scalese, R.J. (2005). Features and uses of high fidelity medical simulations that lead to effective learning: A BEME systematic review. *Medical Teacher, 27*(1), 10–29.

Johnson, D.W., & Johnson, R.T. (1992). *Creative controversy: Intellectual challenge in the classroom.* Edina, MN.: Interaction Book Company.

Jonassen, D.H. (Ed.). (2004). *Handbook of research on educational communications and technology* (2nd ed.). Mahwah, NJ: Lawrence Erlbaum.

Jonassen, D.H., & Kwon, H.I. (2001). Communication patterns in computer-mediated versus face-to-face group problem solving. *Educational Technology Research and Development 49*(1), 35–51.

Jonassen, D.H., Lee, C.B., Yang, C-C., & Laffey, J. (2005). The collaboration principle in multimedia learning. In R.E. Mayer (Ed.), *The Cambridge handbook of multimedia learning,* New York: Cambridge University Press.

Ju, E., & Wagner, C. (1997). Personal computer adventure games: Their structure, principles, and applicability for training. *The DATA BASE for Advances in Information Systems, 28*(2), 78–92.

Kalyuga, S. (2005). Prior knowledge principle in multimedia learning. In R.E. Mayer (Ed.), *The Cambridge handbook of multimedia learning* (pp. 325–337). New York: Cambridge University Press.

Kalyuga, S., Ayres, P., Chandler, P., & Sweller, J. (2003). Expertise reversal effect. *Educational Psychologist, 38,* 23–31.

Kalyuga, S., Chandler, P., & Sweller, J. (1998). Levels of expertise and instructional design. *Human Factors, 40,* 1–17.

Kalyuga, S., Chandler, P., & Sweller, J. (1999). Managing split attention and redundancy in multimedia instruction. *Applied Cognitive Psychology, 13,* 351–372.

Kalyuga, S., Chandler, P., & Sweller, J. (2000). Incorporating learner experience into the design of multimedia instruction. *Journal of Educational Psychology, 92,* 126–136.

Kalyuga, S., Chandler, P., & Sweller, J. (2004). When redundant on-screen text in multimedia technical instruction can interfere with learning. *Human Factors, 46,* 567–581.

Kalyuga, S., Chandler, P., Tuovinen, J., & Sweller, J. (2001). When problem solving is superior to studying worked examples. *Journal of Educational Psychology, 93,* 579–588.

Kenz, I., & Hugge, S. (2002). Irrelevant speech and indoor lighting: Effects of cognitive performance and self-reported affect. *Applied Cognitive Psychology, 15,* 709–718.

Kiewra, K.A., & Creswell, J.W. (2000). Conversations with three highly productive educational psychologists: Richard Anderson, Richard Mayer, and Michael Pressley. *Educational Psychology Review, 12*(1), 135–159.

Kirschner, P.A. (2005). Technology-based collaborative learning: A European perspective. *Educational Technology, 45,* 5–7.

Kirschner, P., Strijbos, J., Kreijns, K., & Beers, P.J. (2004). Designing electronic collaborative learning environments. *Educational Technology Research and Development, 52*(3), 47–66.

Kumta, S.M., Psang, P.L., Hung, L.K., & Chenge, J.C.Y. (2003). Fostering critical thinking skills through a web-based tutorial program for first-year medical students: A randomized controlled study. *Journal of Educational Multimedia and Hypermedia, 12*(3), 267–273.

Lajoie, S.P., Azevedo, R., & Fleiszer, D.M. (1998). Cognitive tools for assessment and learning in a high information flow environment. *Journal of Educational Computing Research, 18,* 205–235.

Lajoie, S.P., Lavigne, N.C., Guerrera, C., & Munsie, S.D. (2001). Constructing knowledge in the context of BioWorld. *Instructional Science, 29,* 155–186.

Lajoie, S.P., & Nakamura, C. (2005). Multimedia learning of cognitive skills. In R.E. Mayer (Ed), *The Cambridge handbook of multimedia learning.* New York: Cambridge University Press.

Lee, H., Plass, J.L., and Homer, B.C. (2006). Optimizing cognitive load for learning from computer-based science simulations. *Journal of Educational Psychology,* 98 (4), 902–913.

Lee, S., & Lee, Y.H.K. (1991). Effects of learner-control versus program control strategies on computer-aided learning of chemistry problems: For acquisition or review? *Journal of Educational Psychology, 83,* 491–498.

LeFevre, J.A., & Dixon, P. (1986). Do written instructions need examples? *Cognition and Instruction, 3,* 1–30.

Leahy, W., Chandler, P., & Sweller, J. (2003). When auditory presentations should and should not be a component of multimedia instruction. *Applied Cognitive Psychology, 17,* 401–418.

Lesgold, A., Eggan, G., Katz, S., & Rao, G. (1993). Possibilities for assessment using computer-based apprenticeship environments. In M. Rabinowitz (Ed.), *Cognitive science foundations of instruction*. Mahwah, NJ: Lawrence Erlbaum.

Lester, J.C., Towns, S.G., Callaway, C.B., Voerman, J.L., & Fitzgerald, P.J. (2000). Deictic and emotive communication in animated pedagogical agents. In J. Cassell, J. Sullivan, S. Prevost, & E. Churchill (Eds.), *Embodied conversational agents* (pp. 123–154). Cambridge, MA: MIT Press.

Leutner, D. (1993). Guided discovery learning with computer-based simulation games: Effects of adaptive and non-adaptive instructional support. *Learning and Instruction, 3,* 113–132.

Lorch, R.F., Jr., Lorch, E.P., Ritchey, K., McGovern, L., & Coleman, (2001). Effects of headings on text summarization. *Contemporary Educational Psychology, 26,* 171–191.

Lou, Y., Abrami, P.C., & d'Apollonia, S. (2001). Small group and individual learning with technology: A meta-analysis. *Review of Educational Research, 71,* 449–521.

Low, R., & Sweller, J. (2005). The modality effect in multimedia learning. In R.E. Mayer (Ed.), *The Cambridge handbook of multimedia learning* (pp. 147–158). New York: Cambridge University Press.

Leung, A.C.K. (2003). Providing navigation aids and online learning helps to support user control: A conceptual model on computer-based learning. *The Journal of Computer Information Systems, 43*(3), 10–17.

Malone, T.W. (1981). Toward a theory of intrinsically motivating instruction. *Cognitive Science, 4,* 333–369.

Malone, T.W., & Lepper, M.R. (1987). Making learning fun: A taxonomy of intrinsic motivations for learning. In R.E. Snow & M.J. Farr (Eds.), *Aptitude, learning and instruction*. Mahwah, NJ: Lawrence Erlbaum.

Mautone, P.D., & Mayer, R.E. (2001). Signaling as a cognitive guide in multimedia learning. *Journal of Educational Psychology, 81,* 240–246.

Mayer, R.E. (1983). Can you repeat that? Qualitative effects of repetition and advance organizers on learning from visual and verbal summaries of science textbook lessons. *Journal of Educational Psychology, 75,* 40–49.

Mayer, R.E. (1989a). Models for understanding. *Review of Educational Research, 59,* 43–64.

Mayer, R.E. (1989b). Systematic thinking fostered by illustrations in scientific text. *Journal of Educational Psychology, 81,* 240–246.

Mayer, R.E. (1993). Illustrations that instruct. In R. Glaser (Ed.), *Advances in instructional psychology* (Vol. 4, pp. 253–284). Mahway, NJ: Lawrence Erlbaum.

Mayer, R.E. (1998). Cognitive, metacognitive, and motivational aspects of problem solving. *Instructional Science, 26,* 49–63.

Mayer, R.E. (2001a). *Multimedia learning.* New York: Cambridge University Press.

Mayer, R.E. (2001b). Cognitive constraints on multimedia learning: When presenting more material results in less learning. *Journal of Educational Psychology, 93,* 187–198.

Mayer, R.E. (2003). *Learning and instruction.* Upper Saddle River, NJ: Merrill Prentice Hall.

Mayer, R.E. (2004). Should there be a three-strikes rule against pure discovery learning: The case for guided methods of instruction. *American Psychologist, 59*(1), 14–19.

Mayer, R.E. (Ed.). (2005a). *The Cambridge handbook of multimedia learning.* New York: Cambridge University Press.

Mayer, R.E. (2005b). Principles for reducing extraneous processing in multimedia learning: Coherence, signaling, redundancy, spatial contiguity, and temporal contiguity. In R.E. Mayer (Ed.), *The Cambridge handbook of multimedia learning* (pp. 183–200). New York: Cambridge University Press.

Mayer, R.E. (2005c). Principles for managing essential processing in multimedia learning: Segmenting, pretraining, and modality principles. In R.E. Mayer (Ed.), *The Cambridge handbook of multimedia learning* (pp. 147–158). New York: Cambridge University Press.

Mayer, R.E. (2005d). Principles based on social cues: Personalization, voice, and image principles. In R.E. Mayer (Ed.), *The Cambridge handbook of multimedia learning* (pp. 201–212). New York: Cambridge University Press.

Mayer, R.E. (2005e). Introduction to multimedia learning. In R.E. Mayer (Ed.), *The Cambridge handbook of multimedia learning* (pp. 1–18). New York: Cambridge University Press.

Mayer, R.E. (2008) *Learning and instruction* (2nd ed.). Upper Saddle River, NJ: Pearson Merrill Prentice Hall.

Mayer, R.E. (in press). Research-based guidelines for multimedia instruction. In D.A. Boehm-Davis (Ed.), *Annual review of human factors and ergonomics* (Vol. 3). Santa Monica, CA: Human Factors and Ergonomics Society.

Mayer, R.E., & Anderson, R.B. (1991). Animations need narrations: An experimental test of a dual-processing systems in working memory. *Journal of Educational Psychology, 90,* 312–320.

Mayer, R.E., & Anderson, R.B. (1992). The instructive animation: Helping students build connections between words and pictures in multimedia learning. *Journal of Educational Psychology, 84,* 444–452.

Mayer, R.E., Bove, W., Bryman, A., Mars, R., & Tapangco, L. (1996). When less is more: Meaningful learning from visual and verbal summaries of science textbook lessons. *Journal of Educational Psychology, 88,* 64–73.

Mayer, R.E., & Chandler, P. (2001). When learning is just a click away: Does simple user interaction foster deeper understanding of multimedia messages? *Journal of Educational Psychology, 93,* 390–397.

Mayer, R.E., Dow, G., & Mayer, S. (2003). Multimedia learning in an interactive self-explaining environment: What works in the design of agent-based microworlds? *Journal of Educational Psychology, 95,* 806–813.

Mayer, R.E., Fennell, S., Farmer, L., & Campbell, J. (2004). A personalization effect in multimedia learning: Students learn better when words are in conversational style rather than formal style. *Journal of Educational Psychology, 96,* 389–395.

Mayer, R.E., & Gallini, J.K. (1990). When is an illustration worth ten thousand words? *Journal of Educational Psychology, 88,* 64–73.

Mayer, R.E., Hegarty, M., Mayer, S., & Campbell, J. (2005). When static media promote active learning: Annotated illustrations versus narrated animations in multimedia instruction. *Journal of Experimental Psychology: Applied, 11,* 256–265.

Mayer, R.E., Heiser, J., & Lonn, S. (2001). Cognitive constraints on multimedia learning: When presenting more material results in less understanding. *Journal of Educational Psychology, 93,* 187–198.

Mayer, R.E., & Jackson, J. (2005). The case for coherence in scientific explanations: Quantitative details can hurt qualitative understanding. *Journal of Experimental Psychology: Applied, 11,* 13–18.

Mayer, R.E., Johnson, L., Shaw, E., & Sahiba, S. (2006). Constructing computer-based tutors that are socially sensitive: Politeness in educational software. *International Journal of Human Computer Studies, 64,* 36–42.

Mayer, R.E., Mathias, A., & Wetzell, K. (2002). Fostering understanding of multimedia messages through pretraining: Evidence for a two-stage theory of mental model construction. *Journal of Experimental Psychology: Applied, 8,* 147–154.

Mayer, R.E., Mautone, P., & Prothero, W. (2002). Pictorial aids for learning by doing in a multimedia geology simulation game. *Journal of Educational Psychology, 94*(1), 171–185.

Mayer, R.E., & Moreno, R. (1998). A split-attention effect in multimedia learning: Evidence for dual coding hypothesis. *Journal of Educational Psychology, 83,* 484–490.

Mayer, R.E., & Moreno, R. (2003). Nine ways to reduce cognitive load in multimedia learning. *Educational Psychologist, 38,* 43–52.

Mayer, R.E., Moreno, R., Boire, M., & Vagge, S. (1999). Maximizing constructivist learning from multimedia communications by minimizing cognitive load. *Journal of Educational Psychology, 91,* 638–643.

Mayer, R.E., & Sims, V. (1994). For whom is a picture worth a thousand words? Extensions of a dual-coding theory of multimedia learning. *Journal of Educational Psychology, 86,* 389–401.

Mayer, R.E., Sims, V., & Tajika, H. (1995). A comparison of how textbooks teach mathematical problem solving in Japan and the United States. *American Educational Research Journal, 32,* 443–460.

Mayer, R.E., Sobko, K., & Mautone, P.D. (2003). Social cues in multimedia learning: Role of speaker's voice. *Journal of Educational Psychology, 95,* 419–425.

Mayer, R.E., Steinhoff, K., Bower, G., & Mars, R. (1995). A generative theory of textbook design: Using annotated illustrations to foster meaningful learning of science text. *Educational Technology Research and Development, 43,* 31–43.

Mayer, R.E., & Wittrock, M.C. (1996). Problem-solving transfer. In D.C. Berliner & R.C. Calfee (Eds.), *Handbook of educational psychology.* New York: Macmillan.

McDaniel, M.A., & Donnelly, C.M. (1996). Learning with analogy and elaborative interrogation. *Journal of Educational Psychology, 88,* 508–519.

McGill, L., Nicol, D., Littlejohn, A., Gierson, H., Juster, N., & Ion, W.J. (2005). Creating an information-rich learning environment to enhance design student learning: Challenges and Approaches. *British Journal of Educational Technology, 36*(4), 629–642.

Moreno, R. (2004). Decreasing cognitive load for novice students: Effects of explanatory versus corrective feedback in discovery-based multimedia. *Instructional Science, 32,* 99–113.

Moreno, R. (2005). Multimedia learning with animated pedagogical agents. In R.E. Mayer (Ed.), *The Cambridge handbook of multimedia learning* (pp. 507–524). New York: Cambridge University Press.

Moreno, R., & Mayer, R.E. (1999a). Cognitive principles of multimedia learning: The role of modality and contiguity. *Journal of Educational Psychology, 91,* 358–368.

Moreno, R., & Mayer, R.E. (1999b). Multimedia-supported metaphors for meaning making in mathematics. *Cognition and Instruction, 17,* 215–248.

Moreno, R., & Mayer, R.E. (2000a). A coherence effect in multimedia learning: The case for minimizing irrelevant sounds in the design of multimedia instructional messages. *Journal of Educational Psychology, 92,* 117–125.

Moreno, R., & Mayer, R.E. (2000b). Engaging students in active learning: The case for personalized multimedia messages. *Journal of Educational Psychology, 93,* 724–733.

Moreno, R., & Mayer, R.E. (2002a). Verbal redundancy in multimedia learning: When reading helps listening. *Journal of Educational Psychology, 94,* 156–163.

Moreno, R., & Mayer, R.E. (2002b). Learning science in virtual reality multimedia environments: Role of methods and media. *Journal of Educational Psychology, 94,* 598–610.

Moreno, R., & Mayer, R.E. (2004). Personalized messages that promote science learning in virtual environments. *Journal of Educational Psychology, 96,* 165–173.

Moreno, R., & Mayer, R.E. (2005). Role of guidance, reflection, and interactivity in an agent-based multimedia game. *Journal of Educational Psychology, 97,* 117–128.

Moreno, R., & Mayer, R.E. (2005). Role of guidance, reflection, and interactivity in an agent-based multimedia game. *Journal of Educational Psychology, 97*(1), 117–128.

Moreno, R., & Mayer, R.E. (in press). Interactive multimodal learning environments. *Educational Psychology Review.*

Moreno, R., Mayer, R.E., Spires, H., & Lester, J. (2001). The case for social agency in computer-based teaching: Do students learn more deeply when they interact with animated pedagogical agents? *Cognition and Instruction, 19,* 177–214.

Mosteller, F., & Boruch, R. (Eds.). (2002). *Evidence matters: Randomized trials in educational research.* Washington, DC: Brookings Institution Press.

Mousavi, S., Low, R., & Sweller, J. (1995). Reducing cognitive load by mixing auditory and visual presentation modes. *Journal of Educational Psychology, 87,* 319–334.

Nass, C., & Brave, S. (2005). *Wired for speech: How voice activates and advances the human-computer relationship.* Cambridge, MA: MIT Press.

National Research Council. (1994b). Illusions of comprehension, competence, and remembering. In D. Druckman and R.A. Bjork (Eds.), *Learning, remembering, believing.* Washington, DC: National Academy Press.

Nelson, T.O. (1996). Consciousness and metacognition. *American Psychologist, 51*(2), 102–116.

Neiderhauser, D.S., Reynolds, R.E., Salmen, D.J., & Skolmoski, P. (2000). The influence of cognitive load on learning from hypertext. *Journal of Educational Computing Research, 23,* 237–255.

Nolen, S. (1995). Effects of a visible author in statistical texts. *Journal of Educational Psychology, 87,* 47–65.

Norman, D.A. (1993). *Things that make us smart.* Reading, MA: Addison-Wesley.

Norman, G.R. (2005). Inverting the pyramid. *Advances in Health Sciences Education, 10,* 85–88.

Nussbaum, E.M. (2005), The effect of goal instructions and need for cognition on interactive argumentation. *Contemporary Educational Psychology, 30*(3), 286–313.

Nussbaum, E.M., & Kardash, C.M. (2005). The effects of goal instructions and text on the generation of counter-arguments during writing. *Journal of Educational Psychology, 97*(2), 157–169.

Ollerenshaw, A., Aidman, E., & Kidd, G. (1997). Is an illustration always worth ten thousand words? Effects of prior knowledge, learning style, and multimedia illustrations on text comprehension. *International Journal of Instructional Media, 24,* 227–238.

O'Neil, H.F., Mayer, R.E., Herl, H.E., Niemi, C., Olin, K., & Thurman, R.A. (2000). Instructional strategies for virtual aviation training environments. In H.F. O'Neil and D.H. Andrews (Eds.), *Aircrew training and assessment* (pp. 105–130). Mahwah, NJ: Lawrence Erlbaum.

Paas, F.G.W.C., & van Merrienboer, J.J.G. (1994). Instructional control of cognitive load in the training of complex cognitive tasks. *Educational Psychology Review, 6,* 351–371.

Paxton, R. (2002). The influence of author visibility on high school students solving a historical problem. *Cognition and Instruction, 20,* 197–248.

Perkins, D.N., & Salomon, G. (1989). Are cognitive skills context-bound? *Educational Researcher, 18*(1), 16–25.

Phye, G.D., Robinson, D.H., & Levin, J. (Eds.). (2005). *Empirical methods for evaluating educational interventions.* San Diego, CA: Elsevier.

Pink, D.H. (2005). *A whole new mind: Why right-brainers will rule the future.* New York: Penguin Group.

Plant, E.A., Ericsson, K.A., Hill, L., & Asberg, K. (2005). Why study time does not predict grade point average across college students: Implications of deliberate practice for academic performance. *Contemporary Educational Psychology, 30,* 96–116.

Pollock, E., Chandler, P., & Sweller, J. (2002). Assimilating complex information. *Learning and Instruction, 12,* 61–86.

Potelle, H., & Rouet, J.F. (2003). Effects of content representation and readers' prior knowledge on the comprehension of hypertext. *International Journal of Human Computer Studies, 58,* 327–345.

Prensky, M. (2001). *Digital game-based learning.* New York: McGraw-Hill.

Prichard, J.S., Bizo, L.A., & Stratford, R.J. (2006). The educational impact of team-skills training: Preparing students to work in groups. *British Journal of Educational Psychology, 76,* 119–140.

Quilici, J.L., & Mayer, R.E. (1996). Role of examples in how students learn to categorize statistics word problems. *Journal of Educational Psychology, 88*(1), 144–161.

Randel, J.M., Morris, B.A., Wetzel, C.D., & Whitehill, B.V. (1992). The effectiveness of games for educational purposes: A review of recent research. *Simulation and Gaming, 23*(3), 261–276.

Ransdell, S.E., & Gilroy, L. (2001). The effects of background music on word proceeded writing. *Computers in Human Behavior, 17,* 141–148.

Rawson, K.A., & Kintsch, W. (2005). Rereading effects depend on time of test. *Journal of Educational Psychology, 97*(1), 70–80.

Reed, S.K., Dempster, A., & Ettinger, M. (1985). Usefulness of analogous solutions for solving algebra word problems. *Journal of Experimental Psychology: Learning, Memory, and Cognition, 11,* 106–125.

Reeves, B., & Nass, C. (1996). *The media equation: How people treat computers, television, and new media like real people and places.* New York: Cambridge University Press.

Renkl, A. (2005). The worked out examples principles in multimedia learning. In R.E. Mayer (Ed.), *The Cambridge handbook of multimedia learning.* New York: Cambridge University Press.

Renkl, A. (2002). Learning from worked-out examples: Instructional explanations supplement self-explanations. *Learning and Instruction, 12,* 529–556.

Renninger, K.A., Hidi, S., & Krapp. A. (1992). *The role of interest in learning and development.* Mahwah, NJ: Lawrence Erlbaum.

Ricer, R.E., Filak, A.T., & Short, J. (2005). Does a high tech (computerized, animated, PowerPoint) presentation increase retention of material compared to a low tech (black on clear overheads) presentation? *Teaching and Learning in Medicine, 17*(2), 107–111.

Rickel, J., & Johnson, L.W. (2000). Task-oriented collaboration with embodied agents in virtual worlds. In J. Cassell, J. Sullivan, S. Prevost, & E. Churchill (Eds.), *Embodied conversational agents.* Cambridge, MA: MIT Press.

Richart, R., & Perkins, D.N. (2005). Learning to think: The challenges of teaching thinking. In K.J. Holyoak & R.G. Morrison (Eds.), *The Cambridge handbook of thinking and reasoning.* New York: Cambridge University Press.

Rieber, L.P. (2005). Multimedia learning in games, simulations, and microworlds. In R.E. Mayer (Ed.), *The Cambridge handbook of multimedia learning.* New York: Cambridge University Press.

Rieber, L.P., Tzeng, S.C., & Tribble, K. (2004). Discovery learning, representation, and explanation within a computer-based simulation: Finding the right mix. *Learning and Instruction, 14,* 307–323.

Robinson, D.H. (2002). Spatial text adjuncts and learning: An introduction to the special issue. *Educational Psychology Review, 14,* 1–3.

Rosenbaum, D.A., Carlson, R.A., & Gilmore, R.O. (2001). Acquisition of intellectual and perceptual motor skills. *Annual Review of Psychology, 52,* 453–470.

Rouet, J.F., & Potelle, H. (2005). Navigational principles in multimedia learning. In R.E. Mayer (Ed.), *The Cambridge handbook of multimedia learning*. New York: Cambridge University Press.

Sanchez, C.A., & Wiley, J. (2006). An examination of the seductive details effect in terms of working memory capacity. *Memory & Cognition, 34,* 344–355.

Salden, R.J.C.M, Paas, F., Broers, N., & Van Merrienboer, J.G. (2004). Mental effort and performance as determinants for the dynamic selection of learning tasks in air traffic control training. *Instructional Science, 32,* 153–172.

Schmidt, H.E., & Moust, J.H.C. (2000). Factors affecting small-group tutorial learning: A review of research. In D.H. Evensen & C.E. Hmelo (Eds.), *Problem-based learning*. Mahwah, NJ: Lawrence Erlbaum.

Schnackenberg, H.L., Sullivan, H.J., Leader, L.R., & Jones, E.E.K. (1998). Learner preferences and achievement under differing amounts of learner practice. *Educational Technology Research and Development, 46,* 5–15.

Schnackenberg, H.L., & Sullivan, H.J. (2000). Learner control over full and lean computer based instruction under differing ability levels. *Educational Technology Research and Development, 48,* 19–35.

Schoenfeld, A.H. (1987). What's all the fuss about metacognition? In A. Schoenfeld (Ed.), *Cognitive science and mathematics education*. Mahwah, NJ: Lawrence Erlbaum.

Scott, G., Leritz, L.E., & Mumford, M.D. (2004). The effectiveness of creativity training: A quantitative review. *Creativity Research Journal, 16*(4), 361–388.

Seabrook, R., Brown, G.D., & Solity, J.E. (2005). Distributed and massed practice: From laboratory to classroom. *Applied Cognitive Psychology, 19,* 107–122.

Shapiro, A.M. (2000). The effect of interactive overviews on the development of conceptual structure in novices learning from electronic texts. *Journal of Educational Multimedia and Hypermedia, 9*(1), 57–78.

Shapiro, A.M. (2005). The site map principle in multimedia learning. In R.E. Mayer (Ed.), *The Cambridge handbook of multimedia learning*. New York: Cambridge University Press.

Shavelson, R.J., & Towne, L. (Eds.). (2002). *Scientific research in education.* Washington, DC: National Academy Press.

Slavin, R. (1983). Why does cooperative learning increase student achievement? *Psychological Bulletin, 94,* 429–445.

Slavin, R.E., Hurley, E.A., & Chamberlain, A. (2003). Cooperative learning and achievement: Theory and practice. In W.M. Reynolds & G.E. Miller (Eds.), *Handbook of psychology: Volume 7, Educational psychology* (pp. 177–198). New York: John Wiley & Sons.

Slobada, J.A., Davidson, J.W., Howe, M.J.A., & Moore, D.G. (1996). The role of practice in the development of performing musicians. *British Journal of Psychology, 87,* 287–309.

Steinberg, E.R. (1989). Cognition and learner control: A literature review, 1977–1988. *Journal of Computer-Based Instruction, 16*(4), 117–121.

Stone, N.J. (2000). Exploring the relationship between calibration and self-regulated learning. *Educational Psychology Review, 4,* 437–475.

Suomala, J., & Shaughnessy, M.F. (2000). An interview with Richard E. Mayer: About technology. *Educational Psychology Review, 12*(4), 477–483.

Sugrue, B., & Rivera, R.J. (2005). *State of the industry: ASTD's annual review of trends in workplace learning and performance.* Alexandria, VA: American Society for Training and Development.

Suthers, D., Vatrapu, R., Joseph, S., Dwyer, N., & Medina, R. (2005). *Proceedings of the 39th Hawaiian International Conference on the System Sciences.* Institute of Electrical and Electronics Engineers.

Svetcov, D. (2000). The virtual classroom vs. the real one. *Forbes, 166,* 50–54.

Sweller, J. (1999). *Instructional design in technical areas.* Camberwell, Australia: ACER Press.

Sweller, J. (2005). The redundancy principle in multimedia learning. In R.E. Mayer (Ed.), *The Cambridge handbook of multimedia learning* (pp. 159–167). New York: Cambridge University Press.

Sweller, J., & Chandler, P. (1994). Why some material is difficult to learn. *Cognition and Instruction, 12,* 185–233.

Sweller, J., Chandler, P., Tierney, P., & Cooper, M. (1990). Cognitive load and selective attention as factors in the structuring of technical material. *Journal of Experimental Psychology: General, 119,* 176–192.

Sweller, J. & Cooper, G.A. (1985). The use of worked examples as a substitute for problem solving in learning algebra. *Cognition and Instruction, 2,* 59–89.

Sweller, J., van Merrienboer, J.J.G., & Paas, F. (1998). Cognitive architecture and instructional design. *Educational Psychology Review, 10,* 251–296.

Tallent-Runnels, M.K., Thomas, J.A., Lan, W.Y., Cooper, S., Ahern, T.C., Shaw, S.M., & Shaw, L.X. (2006). Teaching courses online: A review of the research. *Review of Educational Research, 76*(1) 93–135.

Tennyson, C.L., Tennyson, R.D., & Rothen, W. (1980). Content structure and instructional control strategies as design variables in computer assisted instruction. *Educational Communication and Technology Journal, 28,* 169–176.

Tversky, B., Morrison, J. B., & Betrancourt, M. (2002). Animation: Can it facilitate? *International Journal of Human-Computer Studies, 57,* 247–262.

Uribe, D., Klein, J.D., & Sullivan, H. (2003). The effect of computer-mediated collaborative learning on solving ill-defined problems. *Educational Technology Research and Development, 51*(1), 5–19.

Van Eck, R. (2006). Digital game-based learning. *Educause Review, 41*(2), 17–30.

Van Merrienboer, J.J.G., & Kester, L. (2005). The four-component instructional design model: Multimedia principles in environments for complex learning. In R.E. Mayer (Ed.), *The Cambridge handbook of multimedia learning.* New York: Cambridge University Press.

Valaitis, R.K., Sword, W., Jones, B., & Hodges, A. (2005). Problem-based learning online: Perceptions of health science students. *Advances in Health Sciences Education, 10,* 231–252.

Walczyk, J.J., & Hall, V.C. (1989). Effects of examples and embedded questions on the accuracy of comprehension self-assessments. *Journal of Educational Psychology, 81,* 435–437.

Wang, N., Johnson, L., Mayer, R.E., Rizzo, P., Shaw, E., & Collins, H. (2006). The politeness effect: Pedagogical agents and learning gains. In

C. Looi, G. McCalla, B. Bredeweg, & J. Breuker (Eds.), *Artificial intelligence in education: Supporting learning through intelligent and socially informed technology* (pp. 868–693). Amsterdam: IOS Press.

Wiley, J., & Voss, J.F. (1999). Constructing arguments from multiple sources: Tasks that promote understanding and not just memory for text. *Journal of Educational Psychology, 91,* 301–311.

Yetter, G., Gutkin, T.B., Saunders, A., Galloway, A.M., Sobansky, R.R., & Song, S.Y. (2006). Unstructured collaboration versus individual practice for complex problem solving: A cautionary tale. *Journal of Experimental Education, 74*(2), 137–159.

Young, J.D. (1996). The effect of self-regulated learning strategies on performance in learner controlled computer-based instruction. *Educational Technology Research and Development, 44,* 17–27.

Active Processing	A psychological principle stating that learning occurs when people engage in appropriate mental processing during learning, such as attending to relevant materials, responding to practice exercises, reflecting on examples.
Adaptive Control	A process in which learners are directed or branched to different instructional materials in a lesson based on the program's evaluation of their responses to lesson exercises.
Advance Organizer	A device placed in the start of a learning event designed to provide an overview or big picture of the lesson content. May take the form of a graphic or table.
Advisement	A form of adaptive control in which learners are given advice as to what actions they should take in a lesson based on the program's evaluation of their responses to lesson exercises or pretests.
Agents	Onscreen characters who help guide the learning process during an e-learning episode. Also called pedagogical agents.
Animation	A graphic that depicts movement, such as a video of a procedure or a moving sequence of line drawings.
Architecture	A course design that reflects a theory of learning. Architectures vary regarding the amount and type of structure and interactivity included in the lesson.
Arousal Theory	The idea that adding entertaining and interesting material to lessons stimulates emotional engagement that promotes learning.
Asynchronous Collaborations	Opportunities for learners and/or instructors to interact with each other via computer at different times such as in a discussion board or email.

Asynchronous e-Learning	Digitized instructional resources intended for self-study. Learners can access training resources any time and any place.
Auditory Channel	Part of the human memory system that processes information that enters through the ears and is mentally represented in the form of sounds.
Automaticity	A stage of learning in which new knowledge or skills can be applied directly from long-term memory without using working memory capacity. Some common examples of automatic tasks are driving a car, typing, and reading. Knowledge becomes automatic only after many practice repetitions.
Blogs	A website on which individuals write commentaries on an ongoing basis. Visitors can comment or link to a blog.
Breakout Rooms	An online conferencing facility that usually supports audio, whiteboard, polling, and chat, used for small groups in conjunction with a virtual classroom event.
Calibration	The accuracy of self-estimates of knowing. If a learner estimates low knowledge and scores low on a test, he or she has good calibration; likewise, if he or she estimates high knowledge and scores high on a test, he or she has good calibration.
Chats	Two or more participants communicating online at the same time via text.
Clinical Trials	Research comparing the learning outcomes and/or processes of people who learn in a test e-learning course versus people who learn in another venue such as a competing e-learning course. Also called controlled field testing.
Cognitive Learning Theory	An explanation of how people learn based on the idea of dual channels (information is processed in visual and auditory channels), limited capacity (only a small amount of information can be processed in each channel

at one time), and active learning (meaningful learning occurs when learners pay attention to relevant information, organize it into a coherent structure, and integrate it with what they already know). Also called *cognitive theory* and *cognitive theory of multimedia learning.*

Cognitive Load	The amount of mental resource in working memory required by a task.
Cognitive Interest	A source of motivation stemming from a learner's ability to make sense of the instructional materials. As a result of understanding the lesson, the learner experiences enjoyment. Contrast with *emotional interest.*
Cognitive Task Analysis	Techniques used to define the thinking processes used during real-world problem solution.
Collaborative Learning	A structured instructional interaction among two or more learners to achieve a learning goal or complete an assignment.
Computer-Supported Collaborative Learning (CSCL)	Any instructional program in which two to five individuals work together on an instructional activity or assignment using digital technology to communicate.
Concept-Lesson Content	Refers to a category that includes multiple instances. For example, web page, spreadsheet, software, e-learning.
Content Analysis	Research to define content and content relationships to be included in an educational course. See also *task analysis.*
Coherence Principle	People learn more deeply from multimedia lessons when distracting stories, graphics, sounds, and extraneous words are eliminated.
Contiguity Principle	People learn more deeply when corresponding printed words and graphics are placed close to one another on the screen or when spoken words and graphics are presented at the same time.
Control	A comparison lesson that does not include the variable being studied in the treatment lesson. For example,

a text-only lesson is a control being compared with a lesson with both text and graphics.

Controlled Studies   Research comparing the learning outcomes and/or processes of two or more groups of learners; the groups are the same except for the variable(s) being studied. Also called *experimental studies.*

Conversational Style   A writing style that uses first- and second-person constructions, active voice, and specch-like phrases.

Corrective Feedback   Instructional responses to answers to a practice exercise that tells the learners whether they answered correctly or incorrectly. Contrast with *explanatory feedback.*

Course Map   A type of menu or concept map that graphically represents the structure of an online course or lesson. Course maps have been shown to influence how learners organize learning content.

Critical Thinking   Production of original solutions to novel, ill-defined problems of relatively high complexity; ability to analyze and base arguments on valid data.

Decorative Graphics   Visuals used for aesthetic purposes or to add humor, such as a picture of a person riding a bicycle in a lesson on how bicycle pumps work.

Deep Structure   The principle that underlies an example. Contrast with *surface features.* See also *varied context.*

Dependent Variable   The outcome measures in an experimental study. In many learning experiments a test score is the dependent variable.

Design   One of the stages in e-learning development in which the content is defined and summarized in the form of outlines, learning objectives, and storyboards.

Development   One of the stages in e-learning development in which the course is created, including graphics, text, programming, etc.

Deliberate Practice   Exercises that fall just outside the learner's level of competence that focus on specific skill gaps and demand focus and reflection. The type of practice that leads to continued performance improvement.

Directive Architecture	Training that primarily asks the learner to make a response or perform a task and then provides feedback. Also called *show-and-do method.* Based on a response-strengthening view of learning.
Discovery Learning	Experiential exploratory instructional interfaces that offer little structure or guidance.
Disruption	A process that interferes with the organization of new content in memory as a result of irrelevant content getting in the way.
Distraction	A process that interferes with the selection process by taking learner focus away from important instructional content or methods.
Distributed Practice	Exercises that are placed throughout a lesson rather than all in one location. Long-term learning is better under conditions of distributed practice. Compare to *massed practice.*
Drag and Drop	A facility that allows the user to move objects from one part of the screen to another. Often used in e-learning practice exercises.
Dual Channels	A psychological principle stating that humans have two separate channels, one for processing visual/pictorial material and a second for processing auditory/verbal material.
Dynamic Adaptive Control	A form of learner control based on a continuous assessment of learner skills during the lesson, followed by branching to needed instructional methods, topics, or lessons. Contrast with *static adaptive control.*
Effect Size	A statistic indicating how many standard deviations difference there is between the mean score of the experimental group and the mean score of the control group. A useful metric to determine the practical significance of

	research results. Effect sizes of less than .2 are considered small, .5 moderate, and .8 or greater large.
e-Learning	A combination of content and instructional methods delivered by media elements such as words and graphics on a computer intended to build job-transferable knowledge and skills linked to individual learning goals or organizational performance. May be designed for self-study or instructor-led training. See *asynchronous* and *synchronous e-learning.*
Emotional Interest	A source of motivation stemming from treatments that induce arousal in learners, such as dramatic visuals or stories. See also *seductive details.* Contrast with *cognitive interest.*
Encoding	Integration of new information entering working memory into long-term memory for permanent storage.
Encoding Specificity	A principle of memory stating that people are better able to retrieve information if the conditions at the time of original learning are similar to the conditions at the time of retrieval. For example, to enable learning of a new computer system, learners should practice with the same system they will use on the job so they encode memories that are identical to the performance environment.
Essential Processing	Mental work during learning directed at representing the content that originates from the inherent complexity of the content. More complex content requires greater amounts of essential processing.
Experimental Studies	See *controlled studies.*
Expertise Reversal Effect	Instructional methods that are helpful to novice learners may have no effect or even depress learning of high-knowledge learners.
Explanatory Feedback	Instructional responses to student answers to practice exercises that tell the learners whether they are correct or

	incorrect and also provide the rationale or a hint guiding the learners to a correct answer.
Explanatory Visual	A graphic that helps learners build relationships among content elements. Includes the organizational, relational, transformational, and interpretive types of visuals.
Exploratory Lessons	Lessons that are high in learner control and rely on the learner to select instructional materials they need.
Extraneous Processing Load	Irrelevant mental work during learning that results from ineffective instructional design of the lesson.
Fact	Lesson content that includes unique and specific information or data. For example, the codes to log into a system or a specific application screen.
Fading	An instructional technique in which learners move from fully worked examples to full practice exercises through a series of worked examples in which the learner gradually completes more of the steps.
Far Transfer Tasks	Tasks that require learners to use what they have learned in a novel situation, such as adjusting a general principle for a new problem. For example, how to troubleshoot an unusual system failure or how to write a sales proposal. See also *strategic knowledge*.
Feedback	Information concerning the correctness of one's performance on a learning task or question. May also include explanations to guide learners to a correct response.
Formative Evaluation	The evaluation of courseware based on learner responses (test results or feedback) during the development and initial trials of the courseware.
Game	An online environment that involves a competitive activity with a challenge to achieve a goal, a set of rules and constraints, and a specific context. Game features vary dramatically and include games of chance, games based on motor skills (also called *twitch games*), and games of strategy.

Generative Processing	Relevant mental work during learning directed at deeper understanding of the content that stems from the motivation of the learner to make sense of the material.
Graphic	Any iconic representation, including illustrations, drawings, charts, maps, photos, organizational visuals, animation, and video. Also called *picture.*
Guided Discovery	An instructional architecture in which the learner is assigned an authentic job task or case study, along with guidance from the instructor about how to process the incoming information. Based on a knowledge construction view of learning.
Heterogeneous Groups	Learners who differ regarding prior knowledge, job background, culture, or other significant features. Contrast with *homogeneous.*
Homogeneous Groups	Learners who are similar regarding prior knowledge, job background, culture, or other significant features. Contrast with *heterogeneous.*
Independent Variable	The feature that is studied in an experiment. For example, in a lesson that uses visuals that is compared to a lesson that uses text alone, visuals are the independent variable.
Inform Programs	Lessons designed primarily to communicate information rather than build skills.
Informal Studies	Research in which conclusions are based on observing people as they learn or asking them about their learning. Also called *observational studies.*
Information Acquisition	A metaphor of learning that assumes that learners absorb information that is provided to them by the instructor. This metaphor is the basis for receptive architectures of learning.
Information Delivery	An explanation of how people learn based on the idea that learners directly absorb new information presented in the instructional environment. Also called the *transmission*

	view or the *information acquisition view.* See also *information acquisition.*
Ill-Defined Tasks	Problems for which there is no one correct answer or approach. For example, designing a website or developing a patient treatment plan.
Instructional Method	A technique in a lesson intended to facilitate cognitive processing that underlies learning. For example, a demonstration, a practice exercise, or feedback to practice responses.
Interdependence	A condition in collaborative group work in which the rewards of each individual member depend to some degree on the outcomes of all group members. Has been shown to be an important condition for successful collaborative learning.
Integration Process	A cognitive process in which visual information and auditory information are connected with each other and with relevant memories from long-term memory.
Interpretive Graphics	Visuals used to depict invisible or intangible relationships such as an animation of a bicycle pump that uses small dots to represent the flow of air.
Interaction	See *practice.*
Job Analysis	See *task analysis.*
Knowledge Construction	A metaphor of learning that holds that learners are active participants in the building of new knowledge by integrating new content into existing knowledge structures. Cognitive approaches to learning are based on this metaphor.
Learner Control	A condition in which the learner can select or manage elements of the lesson, such as the pacing, topics, sequencing, and instructional methods. Asynchronous e-learning can provide various types of learner control. Contrast with *program control.*
Learning Styles	The idea that individuals process information in different ways based on some specific mental differences. For

	example, some learners may have an auditory style and learn better from narration, while others have a visual style and learn better from graphics. There has not been good evidence to support learning styles.
Limited Capacity	A psychological principle stating that humans have a small capacity in working memory, allowing them to actively process only a few pieces of information in each channel at one time. See also *cognitive load*.
Link	An object on a screen (text or graphic) that when double clicked leads to additional information on the same or on different web pages.
Long-Term Memory	Part of the cognitive system that stores memories in a permanent form.
Massed Practice	Practice exercises that are placed all in one location in a lesson. Compare to *distributed practice*.
Media Element	Text, graphics, or sounds used to convey lesson content.
Message Boards	A communication facility in which a number of participants type comments at different times that remain on the board for others to read and respond to.
Metacognition	Awareness and control of one's learning or thinking processing, including setting goals, monitoring progress, and adjusting strategies as needed. Also called *metacognitive skill* and *metaskill*.
Modality Principle	People learn more deeply from multimedia lessons when graphics are explained by audio narration rather than onscreen text. Exceptions include situations in which learners are familiar with the content, are not native speakers of the narration language, or when only printed words appear on the screen.
Mouse-Over	A technique in which new information appears on the screen when the user places his or her mouse over a designed screen area. Also called *rollover*.

Multimedia Presentation	Any presentation containing words (such as narration or onscreen text) and graphics (such as illustrations, photos, animation, or video).
Multimedia Principle	People learn more deeply from words and graphics than from words alone.
Near Transfer Tasks	Tasks that require the learner to apply a well-known procedure in the same way as it was learned. For example, how to access your email, how to complete a routine customer order. See also *procedures*.
Operational Goals	Bottom-line indicators of organizational success such as increased sales, decreased product errors, or increased customer satisfaction.
Organizational Graphics	Visuals used to show qualitative relationships among lesson topics or concepts. For example, a tree diagram.
Pedagogical Agent	See *agents*.
Performance Analysis	Research to determine that training will support organizational goals and that e-learning is the best delivery solution.
Perform Programs	Lessons designed primarily to build job-specific skills.
Personalization Principle	People learn more deeply from multimedia lessons when learners experience heightened social presence, as when a conversational script or learning agents are included.
Polite Speech	Narration that includes courteous phrases.
Power Law of Practice	Learners become more proficient at a task the more they practice, although the improvement occurs at a logarithmic rate. Greatest improvements occur during initial practice, with diminishing improvements over time.
Practice	Structured opportunities for the learner to engage with the content by responding to a question or taking an action to solve a problem. Also called *interaction*.

Pretraining Principle	People learn more deeply when lessons present key concepts prior to presenting the processes or procedures related to those concepts.
Principle-Based Lessons	Lessons based on guidelines that must be adapted to various job situations. These lessons teach strategic knowledge. For example, how to close a sale, how to design a web page. See also *strategic knowledge* or *far transfer*.
Procedural Lessons	Lessons designed to teach step-by-step skills that are performed the same way each time. See also *near transfer*.
Process	Lesson content that refers to a flow of events such as in a business or scientific process. For example, how new staff are hired, how lightning is formed.
Probability	A statistic indicating the chances that differences between the mean scores of the experimental and control groups occurred by chance alone, in other words are not real differences.
Problem-Based Learning (PBL)	A type of collaborative process in which groups define and research learning issues based on their discussion of a case problem.
Program Control	A condition under which the topics, sequencing, instructional methods, and pacing are managed by the instructional environment and not the learner. Instructor-led sessions generally are presented under program control. Also called *instructional control*. Contrast with *learner control*.
Receptive Instruction	An instructional architecture that primarily presents information without explicit guidance to the learner for how to process it. Also called the *show-and-tell method*. See also *inform programs*.
Redundant Onscreen Text	Onscreen text that contains the same words as corresponding audio narration.

Redundancy Principle	People learn more deeply from a multimedia lesson when graphics are explained by audio narration alone, rather than audio narration and onscreen text. Some exceptions to the redundancy principle involve screens with no visuals or when learners are not native speakers of the course language.
Regurgitative Interactions	Practice questions that require learners to repeat content provided in the lesson. Will not generally lead to deep understanding.
Rehearsal	Active processing of information in working memory, including mentally organizing the material. Effective rehearsal results in integration of new content with existing knowledge structures.
Relational Graphics	Visuals used to summarize quantitative relationships such as bar charts and pie graphs.
Representational Graphics	Visuals used to show what an objective looks like, such as a computer screen or a piece of equipment.
Retrieval	Transferring information stored in long-term memory to working memory after the learning event. Also called *retrieving process.*
Response Strengthening	A learning metaphor that focuses on strengthening or weakening of associations based on rewards or punishments provided during the learning event. Is the basis of directive instructional architectures.
Rollover	A technique in which new content appears on the screen when the learner's mouse contacts on-screen objects. For example, when you place the mouse cursor over an on-screen icon, the name or function of the icon appear in a small text box. Also called a *mouse-over.*
Seductive Details	Text or graphics added to a lesson in order to increase the learner's interest, but which is not essential to the learning objective.

Segmenting Principle	People learn more deeply when content is broken into small chunks and learners can control the rate at which they access the chunks. A good strategy for managing complex content that imposes considerable essential processing.
Selecting Process	A cognitive process in which the learner pays attention to relevant material in the lesson.
Self-Explanation Questions	An instructional technique designed to promote processing of worked examples in which the learner responds to questions asking about worked-out steps in a worked example.
Sensory Memory	Part of the cognitive system that briefly stores visual information received by the eyes and auditory information received by the ears.
Shared Control	A form of adaptive control in which the program recommends several tasks based on learner performance and the learners select which tasks they prefer.
Signaling	An instructional technique used to draw attention to critical elements of the instruction. Common techniques include use of arrows, circles, bolding of text, or emphasis in narration.
Simulation	An interactive artificial environment in which features in the environment behave similarly to real-world events. Simulations may be conceptual, such as a simulation of genetic inheritance, or operational, such as a flight simulator.
Social Presence	The extent to which a delivery medium can communicate face-to-face human interactions, including speech, body language, emotions, etc.
Social Software	Computer facilities that allow individuals to correspond or collaborate with others. Some examples include wikis, blogs, discussion boards, and online conferencing.
Static Adaptive Control	A form of learner control based on a one-time assessment of learner skills followed by branching to needed topics

	or lessons, such as in a pretest. Contrast with *dynamic adaptive control.*
Statistical Significance	A measure of the probability that the differences in the outcome results between the test and control groups are real and are not a chance difference.
Storyboard	A layout that outlines the content and instructional methods of a lesson, typically used for preview purposes before programming.
Strategic Knowledge	Guidelines that help in problem solving or completion of tasks that require judgment and reflection. For example, developing a sales proposal or writing an analytic report. See also *far transfer.*
Structure-Emphasizing Examples	Worked examples that vary their cover stories to help learners acquire the principles or deep structure of the content. Useful for far transfer learning.
Structured Controversy	A structured collaborative learning structure involving argumentation and synthesis of perspectives.
Summative Evaluation	Evaluation of the impact of the courseware conducted at the end of the project; may include cost-benefit analysis.
Surface Emphasizing Examples	Worked examples that use similar cover stories to illustrate a task. Useful for near but not far transfer learning. Contrast with *structure-emphasizing examples.*
Surface Features	The cover story of an example. A series of examples on calculation of correlations that all use data about rain and crop growth all have similar surface features. See also *varied context examples.*
Synchronous Collaboration	Opportunities for learners and/or instructors to interact with each other via computer at the same time.
Synchronous e-Learning	Electronic delivery of instructor-led training available to geographically dispersed learners at the same time. Delivered through specialized software such as Webex, Elluminate, and Adobe Acrobat Professional Connect

	(Breeze). Synchronous sessions can be recorded and accessed for asynchronous review after the event. Also called *virtual classrooms*.
Task Analysis	Research to define the knowledge and skills to be included in training, based on observations of performance and interviews of performers.
Technophile	An individual or group that is enamored with technological features and may overload training with more sensory stimuli than learners can process.
Technostic	An individual or group that fails to exploit the potential of a new learning technology by transferring familiar instructional techniques from older media to new technology with little or no adaptation. For example, books transferred to screens.
Transfer	Application of previously learned knowledge and skills to new situations encountered after the learning event. Relies on retrieval of new knowledge and skills from long-term memory during performance.
Training Wheels	A technique introduced by John Carroll in which learners work with software simulations that are initially of limited functionality and progress to higher-fidelity simulations as they master lower-level skills.
Transfer Appropriate Interactions	Activities that require the learners to perform during training as they would on the job. For example, when learning a new computer system, learners practice with case examples and software interfaces that are identical or very similar to the job. See *encoding specificity*.
Transformational Graphics	Visuals used to show changes in time or space, such as a weather cycle diagram or an animated illustration of a computer procedure.
Treatment	A variable or factor incorporated in an experimental lesson to determine its impact on learners.

Twitch Games	Online games that rely on fast and accurate motor responses on a game device such as a joy stick for success. Various arcade games are typical examples.
Varied Context Examples	A series of examples with different surface features but that illustrate the same principles. A series of examples illustrating correlations use rainfall and crop growth, age and weight, and practice time and speed. See also *deep structure*.
Virtual Classroom	See *synchronous e-learning*.
Visible Author	A personal style of writing in which the authors reveal information about themselves or about personal perspectives regarding the content.
Visual Channel	Part of the human memory system that processes information received through the eyes and mentally represented in pictorial form.
Wikis	Websites that allow visitors to edit the contents. Can be controlled for editing/viewing by a small group or by all.
Worked Example	Step-by-step demonstration of how to solve a problem or accomplish a task.
Working Memory	Part of the cognitive system in which the learner actively (consciously) processes incoming information from the environment and retrieves information from long-term memory. Working memory has two channels (visual and auditory) and is limited in capacity.

Chapter 6

Chapter 7

Chapter 10

Chapter 11

Chapter 12

NAME INDEX

SUBJECT INDEX

Note: Page numbers followed by *fig* indicates figure; *t,* table; *e,* exhibit.

RUTH COLVIN CLARK, ED.D., has focused her professional efforts on bridging the gap between academic research on instructional methods and application of that research by training and performance support professionals in corporate and government organizations. Dr. Clark has developed a number of seminars and has written six books, including *The New Virtual Classroom, Building Expertise,* and *Efficiency in Learning,* that translate important research programs into practitioner guidelines.

A science undergraduate, she completed her doctorate in instructional psychology/educational technology in 1988 at the University of Southern California. Dr. Clark is a past president of the International Society of Performance Improvement and a member of the American Educational Research Association. She was honored with the 2006 Thomas F. Gilbert Distinguished Professional Achievement Award by the International Society for Performance Improvement and is an invited *Training Legend* Speaker at the ASTD 2007 International Conference. Dr. Clark is currently a dual resident of Southwest Colorado and Phoenix, Arizona, and divides her professional time among speaking, teaching, and writing. For more information, consult her website at www.clarktraining.com.

RICHARD E. MAYER is professor of psychology at the University of California, Santa Barbara (UCSB), where he has served since 1975. His research interests are in educational and cognitive psychology, with a current focus on multimedia learning and computer-supported learning. He is past-president of the Division of Educational Psychology of the American Psychological Association, former editor of the *Educational Psychologist,* and former co-editor of *Instructional Science,* former chair of the UCSB Department of Psychology, vice president of the American Educational Research Association, and the year 2000 recipient of the E. L. Thorndike Award for career achievement in educational psychology. He was ranked number one as the most productive educational psychologist for the latest ten-year period in *Contemporary Educational Psychology.* He is the author of eighteen books and more than 250 articles and chapters, including *Multimedia Learning* (2001), *The Cambridge Handbook of Multimedia Learning* (editor, 2005), and *Learning and Instruction* (2nd ed.) (2008).

System Requirements

PC with Microsoft Windows 98SE or later

Mac with Apple OS version 8.6 or later

Using the CD with Windows

To view the items located on the CD, follow these steps:

1. Insert the CD into your computer's CD-ROM drive.

2. A window appears with the following options:
   Contents: Allows you to view the files included on the CD-ROM.
   Software: Allows you to install useful software from the CD-ROM.
   Links: Displays a hyperlinked page of websites.
   Author: Displays a page with information about the Author(s).
   Contact Us: Displays a page with information on contacting the publisher or author.
   Help: Displays a page with information on using the CD.
   Exit: Closes the interface window.

If you do not have autorun enabled, or if the autorun window does not appear, follow these steps to access the CD:

1. Click Start → Run.

2. In the dialog box that appears, type d:<\\>start.exe, where d is the letter of your CD-ROM drive. This brings up the autorun window described in the preceding set of steps.

3. Choose the desired option from the menu. (See Step 2 in the preceding list for a description of these options.)

In Case of Trouble

If you experience difficulty using the CD-ROM, please follow these steps:

1. Make sure your hardware and systems configurations conform to the systems requirements noted under "System Requirements" above.

2. Review the installation procedure for your type of hardware and operating system.

It is possible to reinstall the software if necessary.

To speak with someone in Product Technical Support, call 800–762–2974 or 317–572–3994 M–F 8:30 a.m. – 5:00 p.m. EST. You can also get support and contact Product Technical Support through our website at www.wiley.com/techsupport.

Before calling or writing, please have the following information available:

- Type of computer and operating system
- Any error messages displayed
- Complete description of the problem.

It is best if you are sitting at your computer when making the call.

Pfeiffer Publications Guide

This guide is designed to familiarize you with the various types of Pfeiffer publications. The formats section describes the various types of products that we publish; the methodologies section describes the many different ways that content might be provided within a product. We also provide a list of the topic areas in which we publish.

FORMATS

In addition to its extensive book-publishing program, Pfeiffer offers content in an array of formats, from fieldbooks for the practitioner to complete, ready-to-use training packages that support group learning.

FIELDBOOK Designed to provide information and guidance to practitioners in the midst of action. Most fieldbooks are companions to another, sometimes earlier, work, from which its ideas are derived; the fieldbook makes practical what was theoretical in the original text. Fieldbooks can certainly be read from cover to cover. More likely, though, you'll find yourself bouncing around following a particular theme, or dipping in as the mood, and the situation, dictate.

HANDBOOK A contributed volume of work on a single topic, comprising an eclectic mix of ideas, case studies, and best practices sourced by practitioners and experts in the field.

An editor or team of editors usually is appointed to seek out contributors and to evaluate content for relevance to the topic. Think of a handbook not as a ready-to-eat meal, but as a cookbook of ingredients that enables you to create the most fitting experience for the occasion.

RESOURCE Materials designed to support group learning. They come in many forms: a complete, ready-to-use exercise (such as a game); a comprehensive resource on one topic (such as conflict management) containing a variety of methods and approaches; or a collection of like-minded activities (such as icebreakers) on multiple subjects and situations.

TRAINING PACKAGE An entire, ready-to-use learning program that focuses on a particular topic or skill. All packages comprise a guide for the facilitator/trainer and a workbook for the participants. Some packages are supported with additional media—such as video—or learning aids, instruments, or other devices to help participants understand concepts or practice and develop skills.

- *Facilitator/trainer's guide* Contains an introduction to the program, advice on how to organize and facilitate the learning event, and step-by-step instructor notes. The guide also contains copies of presentation materials—handouts, presentations, and overhead designs, for example—used in the program.

- *Participant's workbook* Contains exercises and reading materials that support the learning goal and serves as a valuable reference and support guide for participants in the weeks and months that follow the learning event. Typically, each participant will require his or her own workbook.

ELECTRONIC CD-ROMs and web-based products transform static Pfeiffer content into dynamic, interactive experiences. Designed to take advantage of the searchability, automation, and ease-of-use that technology provides, our e-products bring convenience and immediate accessibility to your workspace.

METHODOLOGIES

CASE STUDY A presentation, in narrative form, of an actual event that has occurred inside an organization. Case studies are not prescriptive, nor are they used to prove a point; they are designed to develop critical analysis and decision-making skills. A case study has a specific time frame, specifies a sequence of events, is narrative in structure, and contains a plot structure—an issue (what should be/have been done?). Use case studies when the goal is to enable participants to apply previously learned theories to the circumstances in the case, decide what is pertinent, identify the real issues, decide what should have been done, and develop a plan of action.

ENERGIZER A short activity that develops readiness for the next session or learning event. Energizers are most commonly used after a break or lunch to stimulate or refocus the group. Many involve some form of physical activity, so they are a useful way to counter post-lunch lethargy. Other uses include transitioning from one topic to another, where "mental" distancing is important.

EXPERIENTIAL LEARNING ACTIVITY (ELA) A facilitator-led intervention that moves participants through the learning cycle from experience to application (also known as a Structured Experience). ELAs are carefully thought-out designs in which there is a definite learning purpose and intended outcome. Each step—everything that participants do during the activity—facilitates the accomplishment of the stated goal. Each ELA includes complete instructions for facilitating the intervention and a clear statement of goals, suggested group size and timing, materials required, an explanation of the process, and, where appropriate, possible variations to the activity. (For more detail on Experiential Learning Activities, see the Introduction to the *Reference Guide to Handbooks and Annuals*, 1999 edition, Pfeiffer, San Francisco.)

GAME A group activity that has the purpose of fostering team spirit and togetherness in addition to the achievement of a pre-stated goal. Usually contrived—undertaking a desert expedition, for example—this type of learning method offers an engaging means for participants to demonstrate and practice business and interpersonal skills. Games are effective for team building and personal development mainly because the goal is subordinate to the process—the means through which participants reach decisions, collaborate, communicate, and generate trust and understanding. Games often engage teams in "friendly" competition.

ICEBREAKER A (usually) short activity designed to help participants overcome initial anxiety in a training session and/or to acquaint the participants with one another. An icebreaker can be a fun activity or can be tied to specific topics or training goals. While a useful tool in itself, the icebreaker comes into its own in situations where tension or resistance exists within a group.

INSTRUMENT A device used to assess, appraise, evaluate, describe, classify, and summarize various aspects of human behavior. The term used to describe an instrument depends primarily on its format and purpose. These terms include survey, questionnaire, inventory, diagnostic, survey, and poll. Some uses of instruments include providing instrumental feedback to group members, studying here-and-now processes or functioning within a group, manipulating group composition, and evaluating outcomes of training and other interventions.

Instruments are popular in the training and HR field because, in general, more growth can occur if an individual is provided with a method for focusing specifically on his or her own behavior. Instruments also are used to obtain information that will serve as a basis for change and to assist in workforce planning efforts.

Paper-and-pencil tests still dominate the instrument landscape with a typical package comprising a facilitator's guide, which offers advice on administering the instrument and interpreting the collected data, and an initial set of instruments. Additional instruments are available separately. Pfeiffer, though, is investing heavily in e-instruments. Electronic instrumentation provides effortless distribution and, for larger groups particularly, offers advantages over paper-and-pencil tests in the time it takes to analyze data and provide feedback.

LECTURETTE A short talk that provides an explanation of a principle, model, or process that is pertinent to the participants' current learning needs. A lecturette is intended to establish a common language bond between the trainer and the participants by providing a mutual frame of reference. Use a lecturette as an introduction to a group activity or event, as an interjection during an event, or as a handout.

MODEL A graphic depiction of a system or process and the relationship among its elements. Models provide a frame of reference and something more tangible, and more easily remembered, than a verbal explanation. They also give participants something to "go on," enabling them to track their own progress as they experience the dynamics, processes, and relationships being depicted in the model.

ROLE PLAY A technique in which people assume a role in a situation/scenario: a customer service rep in an angry-customer exchange, for example. The way in which the role is approached is then discussed and feedback is offered. The role play is often repeated using a different approach and/or incorporating changes made based on feedback received. In other words, role playing is a spontaneous interaction involving realistic behavior under artificial (and safe) conditions.

SIMULATION A methodology for understanding the interrelationships among components of a system or process. Simulations differ from games in that they test or use a model that depicts or mirrors some aspect of reality in form, if not necessarily in content. Learning occurs by studying the effects of change on one or more factors of the model. Simulations are commonly used to test hypotheses about what happens in a system—often referred to as "what if?" analysis—or to examine best-case/worst-case scenarios.

THEORY A presentation of an idea from a conjectural perspective. Theories are useful because they encourage us to examine behavior and phenomena through a different lens.

TOPICS

The twin goals of providing effective and practical solutions for workforce training and organization development and meeting the educational needs of training and human resource professionals shape Pfeiffer's publishing program. Core topics include the following:

Leadership & Management

Communication & Presentation

Coaching & Mentoring

Training & Development

e-Learning

Teams & Collaboration

OD & Strategic Planning

Human Resources

Consulting